BLACK'S NEW TESTAMENT COMMENTARIES

General Editor: Henry Chadwick, DD, FBA

THE EPISTLE TO THE PHILIPPIANS

Black's New Testament Commentaries

Companion volume

A COMMENTARY ON

THE EPISTLE TO THE PHILIPPIANS

MARKUS BOCKMUEHL

LECTURER IN DIVINITY, UNIVERSITY OF CAMBRIDGE

A & C BLACK
LONDON

First published 1997
A & C Black (Publishers) Limited
35 Bedford Row, London WC1R 4JH
ISBN 0–7136–4010–3

A CIP catalogue record of this book
is available from the British Library.

Typeset in Great Britain by Fakenham Photosetting
Limited, Fakenham, Norfolk

Printed in Great Britain by Biddles Ltd, Guildford,
Surrey

CONTENTS

PREFACE

After a brief dip in the tide of new ideas and studies about St Paul's letter to the Philippians, the 1990s have witnessed the publication of several fine critical commentaries and over a dozen monographs. Some of these have at long last begun to advance our understanding of the historical setting of Philippi and of Paul's letter beyond the pioneering work of Philippe Collart and Paul Lemerle, published well over half a century ago. Others have offered new insights into the likely implications of Paul's captivity, the nature of his relationship with the Philippian church, and the social and rhetorical conventions implicit in his letter.

Students reading in English are now well served by the full-scale commentaries of Peter T. O'Brien (1991) and Gordon D. Fee (1995), whose strengths complement each other; the best of the current crop of commentaries in German is probably that of Ulrich B. Müller (1993). Of the most recent historical monographs on Philippi, we must highlight the path-breaking and complementary studies by Lukas Bormann (1995) and Peter Pilhofer (1995). Along similar lines, the Oxford dissertation of Peter Oakes (1996) appears to offer a significant contribution, although it was unfortunately unavailable to me at the Bodleian during several months in the summer of 1996. Dozens of other publications on the literary, social, rhetorical and discourse analysis of Philippians have appeared in the last five years, not all of which can here be cited and discussed. My debt to a number of these and other studies will, I trust, be evident, even if in some respects I differ substantially.

In view of such a wealth of existing monograph and commentary literature I am not here in a position to 'reinvent the wheel', or to justify every exegetical decision against the whole gamut of previous critical opinion. The recent full-scale commentaries admirably rehearse much of the earlier discussion; it is also worth consulting the useful surveys by E.A.C. Pretorius (1989, 1995). Those who seek exhaustive coverage on this front will in any case resort to a different commentary series (note also the remarks of Best 1996: 358). The needs of students and expositors have here been kept in mind, so that references to secondary literature are offered for further reading rather than primarily for detailed debate with fellow scholars.

Secondary literature is given in the text by name, year of publication, and page reference; full details are in the main bibliography at the back. There is a separate bibliography for commentaries on Philippians, which in the text appear under the author's name only; page numbers are offered mainly in case of ambiguity. (A commentator's other relevant writings may of course be cited in the regular fashion, and listed in the main bibliography.) Wherever possible, ancient texts have been taken from the most readily accessible editions and translations: Philo, Josephus, Eusebius, Apostolic Fathers and Graeco-Roman authors from the Loeb Classical Library where available; rabbinic literature from the Soncino or other bilingual editions (see also the list of abbreviations below); Dead Sea Scrolls from García Martínez 1996 with consultation of the DJD series; and so on. Other patristic literature has usually been cited from the widely available *ANF* and *NPNF* translations, but these have been compared with the Greek and Latin originals (MPG, MPL, SC or GCS). I have attempted to indicate wherever unusual editions or sources were employed.

Acknowledgements

It is true not only of the biblical authors but equally of their modern interpreters that what they write is best understood within their context of experiences and relationships. My own work, such as it is, could certainly not have been written without the help and encouragement of a great many people, even if some of them will be unaware of it.

My thanks must go first to Henry Chadwick, the long-standing editor of Black's series, for entrusting this volume to an untried and initially reluctant commentator, as well as for his unfailingly shrewd and incisive comments on the first draft. I am grateful, too, to Anne Watts at A & C Black and her copy editor, Margaret Baker, for their expert help in seeing the revised work to publication.

Students and colleagues helped in various ways to shape the final product. Even before the initial invitation to contribute to this series, in 1990–92 some of my Cambridge students graciously put up with two rather unpolished and experimental lecture series on Philippians, while raising stimulating questions for my further work. Several patient congregations in Cambridge churches and college chapels heard sermons on parts of the letter and offered valuable feedback. Gordon Fee kindly sent me an advance copy of his 1995 commentary on disk, well before it appeared in print. Francis Watson and members of the Hermeneutics seminar at the 1994 British New Testament conference offered constructive criticism of an early paper on the 'effective history' of

Philippians, subsequently published (Bockmuehl 1995). In the summer of 1995, Steve Pfann in Jerusalem kindly facilitated a computer search of the Dead Sea Scrolls concordance, while Marc Bregman and Michael Fishbane gave invaluable assistance with several rabbinic queries. Later, Morna Hooker critically and patiently engaged with successive pre-publication drafts of a somewhat unconventional paper on 'the form of God' in Phil. 2.6 (Bockmuehl 1997); she and the members of her Cambridge New Testament seminar also afforded me repeated opportunities to 'try out' and rethink this and various other expositions in the Michaelmas and Lent Terms 1995–6. My colleagues James Carleton Paget and Bruce Longenecker generously read and commented on an early draft of the commentary. In August 1996, a week's lectures and questions on Philippians at the Vacation Term in Biblical Studies at St Anne's College, Oxford, also provided a valuable opportunity to present and refine parts of my rough draft.

Grants from the Bethune-Baker Fund and the University Travel Fund at Cambridge made it possible to undertake visits for research and writing to Philippi and Macedonia (1993), Tübingen (1994, 1996) and Jerusalem (1995). The final period of revision during my 1996–7 sabbatical at Tübingen was supported by an Alexander von Humboldt fellowship.

During these and other periods of study away from Cambridge, quiet and undisturbed hospitality in several places provided much-needed space in which to read and think, pray and write. Among these was a week at the Albrecht-Bengel-Haus in Tübingen (September 1994). During another week at Hope Cove, South Devon, in January 1996, it was invigorating to engage in the 'ecclesial' task of interpreting Philippians at the same table, and on bracing cliff-top walks, with Steve James who was preparing a sermon series for his parish in Liverpool. I am especially grateful to Bodil and Jens Arne Skjøtt in Jerusalem and to their neighbours, the Masvie family, for arranging the use of their flat on French Hill during five weeks in Jerusalem in the summer of 1995. To exegete Scripture day after day while looking out over the barren splendour and deafening stillness of the Judaean desert was at once unforgettably humbling and quickening.

Perhaps the most remarkable experience of working on Philippians came during an intense final phase of writing at Tübingen in July 1996. The sheer ardour and joy of this letter from captivity were powerfully brought to a point when at the Stuttgart Staatsgalerie I came across Rembrandt's arresting picture of Paul in prison (1627) – a copy of which, together with Boccherini's resplendent cello concertos, became my constant companion while drawing together, and subsequently revising, the disparate strands of this exposition.

M. Bockmuehl
Trinity 1997

A Note on Internet Resources

Readers may gain access to a rapidly increasing amount of historical, archaeological, geographic and literary information about Philippi at a number of Internet sites. In addition to relevant ancient texts, the available resources include maps and numerous excellent colour photographs of the site excavations and the general area. The best and most useful access to this information is available by submitting a search for 'Philippi' on the home pages of the Perseus project at Tufts University in the USA (http://www.perseus.tufts.edu) and of the Democritus University of Thrace, in Greece (http://www.duth.gr). An illustrated tourist's guide to the Prefecture of Kaválla (including Thasos and Philippi) is at http://www.pref-kavala.gr/english.

A full, searchable English translation of most of the patristic sources cited, including St Chrysostom's homilies on Philippians, can be found in the Christian Classics Ethereal Library (http://ccel.wheaton.edu). The Mishnah, Talmuds and other rabbinic resources (in the original) are available through the Snunit project of the Hebrew University in Jerusalem (http://www1.snunit.k12.il).

ABBREVIATIONS

General Abbreviations

ABD	*Anchor Bible Dictionary*
ad loc.	*ad locum*, on the passage in question
AGJU	Arbeiten zur Geschichte des antiken Judentums und des Urchristentums
AnBib	Analecta Biblica
ANF	*The Ante-Nicene Fathers*, ed. A. Roberts & J. Donaldson, 10 vols. (Grand Rapids: Eerdmans; Edinburgh: T&T Clark, n.d. frequent reprints).
ANRW	*Aufstieg und Niedergang der römischen Welt*
Aram.	Aramaic
ASP	American Studies in Papyrology
ATANT	Abhandlungen zur Theologie des Alten und Neuen Testaments
AUSS	*Andrews University Seminary Studies*
BA	*Biblical Archaeologist*
BAGD	W. Bauer, W.F. Arndt, F.W. Gingrich & F.W. Danker, *Greek–English Lexicon of the New Testament and Other Early Christian Literature*, 2nd edn. (Chicago: University of Chicago, 1979)
bar.	*baraita*, a Tannaitic (early rabbinic) tradition preserved in the Talmud
BAR	*Biblical Archaeology Review*
BDF	F. Blass, A. Debrunner & R.W. Funk, *A Greek Grammar of the New Testament* (Chicago: University of Chicago, 1961)
BET	Beiträge zur Evangelischen Theologie
BHT	Beiträge zur Historischen Theologie
BibInt	*Biblical Interpretation*
BJRL	*Bulletin of the John Rylands Library*
BTB	*Biblical Theology Bulletin*
BU	Biblische Untersuchungen
BWANT	Beiträge zur Wissenschaft des Alten und Neuen Testaments
BZAW	Beihefte zur Zeitschrift für die alttestamentliche Wissenschaft

BZNW	Beihefte zur Zeitschrift für die neutestamentliche Wissenschaft
c.	*circa,* approximately
CBET	Contributions to Biblical Exegesis and Theology
CBNT	Coniectanea Biblica, New Testament Series
CBQ	*Catholic Biblical Quarterly*
CCC	*Catechism of the Catholic Church* (London: Chapman, 1994)
CIJ	*Corpus Inscriptionum Iudaicarum,* ed. Jean-Baptiste Frey, 2 vols. (Rome: Pontifical Institute of Christian Archaeology, 1936–52)
CIL	*Corpus Inscriptionum Latinarum,* 55 vols. (Berlin: Reimer, 1869–1900)
CRBS	*Currents in Research: Biblical Studies*
CRINT	Compendia Rerum Iudaicarum ad Novum Testamentum
DBSup	*Supplément au Dictionnaire de la Bible*
DJD	Discoveries in the Judaean Desert (Oxford: Clarendon, 1955–)
DPL	*Dictionary of Paul and His Letters,* ed. G.F. Hawthorne & R.P. Martin (Downers Grove/ Leicester: InterVarsity Press, 1993)
DSS	Dead Sea Scrolls
EB	Études Bibliques
EDNT	*Exegetical Dictionary of the New Testament,* ed. H. Balz & G. Schneider, 3 vols. (Grand Rapids: Eerdmans, 1990–3).
ET	English Translation
ETL	*Ephemerides Theologicae Lovanienses*
ETR	*Études Théologiques et Religieuses*
ExpT	*Expository Times*
FAT	Forschungen zum Alten Testament
FJS	Frankfurter Judaistische Studien
FNT	*Filología Neotestamentaria*
FRLANT	Forschungen zur Religion und Literatur des Alten und Neuen Testaments
GCS	*Die griechischen christlichen Schriftsteller*
Gk.	Greek
Göttingen LXX	*Septuaginta: Vetus Testamentum Graecum Auctoritate Academiae Scientiarum Gottingensis editum* (Göttingen: Vandenhoeck & Ruprecht, 1931–)
GTA	Göttinger Theologische Arbeiten
HBT	*Horizons in Biblical Theology*

HCNT	*Hellenistic Commentary to the New Testament*, ed. M.E. Boring, K. Berger & C. Colpe (Nashville: Abingdon, 1996)
Hebr.	Hebrew
HFT	Helps for Translators
HNT	Handbuch zum Neuen Testament
HTKNT	Herders Theologischer Kommentar zum Neuen Testament
HTKNTSup	HTKNT Supplement volumes
HTR	*Harvard Theological Review*
ICC	International Critical Commentary
Int	*Interpretation*
ISBE	*International Standard Bible Encyclopedia*
ital.	italics
JBL	*Journal of Biblical Literature*
JFSR	*Journal of Feminist Studies in Religion*
JGWR	*Journal of Gender in World Religions*
JIWE II	David Noy, *Jewish Inscriptions of Western Europe*. Vol II: *The City of Rome* (Cambridge: University Press, 1995)
JSNT	*Journal for the Study of the New Testament*
JSNTSup	JSNT Supplement Series
JSOT	*Journal for the Study of the Old Testament*
JSOTSup	JSOT Supplement Series
JTC	*Journal of Theology and the Church*
JTS	*Journal of Theological Studies*
KD	*Kerygma und Dogma*
KEKNT	Kritisch-Exegetischer Kommentar zum Neuen Testament
KJV	King James (= Authorised) Version of the Bible
lit.	literally
LSJ	H.G. Liddell & R. Scott, *A Greek–English Lexicon*, ed. H.S. Jones with a supplement by E.A. Barber, 9th edn. with supplement (Oxford: University Press, 1968)
LXX	Septuagint (Greek Old Testament)
mid.	(Greek) middle voice
MPG	*Patrologia Graeca*, ed. J.P. Migne
MPL	*Patrologia Latina*, ed. J.P. Migne
MS(S)	manuscript(s)
MTS	Marburger Theologische Studien
n(n).	note(s)

NA²⁷	*Novum Testamentum Graece*, ed. E. Nestle, B. & K. Aland *et al.*, 27th edition (Stuttgart: Deutsche Bibelgesellschaft, 1993)
NASB	New American Standard Bible
n.d.	no date
Neot	*Neotestamentica*
NIBC	New International Biblical Commentary
NICNT	New International Commentary on the New Testament
NIGTC	New International Greek Testament Commentary
NIV	New International Version
NovT	*Novum Testamentum*
NovTSup	Novum Testamentum, Supplement Series
NPNF	*A Select Library of the Nicene and Post-Nicene Fathers of the Christian Church*, ed. P. Schaff, Series I & II, 13 & 14 vols. (Grand Rapids: Eerdmans; Edinburgh: T&T Clark, n.d. [frequent reprints])
NRSV	New Revised Standard Version
N.S.	New Series
NT	New Testament
NTAbh	Neutestamentliche Abhandlungen
NTS	*New Testament Studies*
NTTS	New Testament Tools and Studies
NW	*Neuer Wettstein: Texte zum Neuen Testament aus Griechentum und Hellenismus*, ed. G. Strecker & U. Schnelle, vol. 2.1 (Berlin/New York: de Gruyter, 1996). [References are assumed to be *ad loc.*, citing only the relevant entry, e.g. '*NW* §6'.]
ODCC	*Oxford Dictionary of the Christian Church*, ed. F.L. Cross & E.A. Livingstone, 2nd edn. (Oxford: Oxford University Press, 1974)
OT	Old Testament
par(r).	and parallel(s)
pass.	passive voice
pl.	plural
pop.	population
RAC	*Realenzyklopädie für Antike und Christentum*
REB	Revised English Bible
REJ	*Revue des Études Juives*
repr.	reprinted
rev.	revised (by)
RevB	*Revue Biblique*

RHPR	*Revue d'Histoire et de Philosophie Religieuses*
RevSR	*Revue des Sciences Religieuses*
RivBib	*Rivista Biblica*
RSV	Revised Standard Version
SANT	Studien zum Alten und Neuen Testament
SBLDS	Society of Biblical Literature Dissertation Series
SBS	Stuttgarter Bibelstudien
SC	Sources Chrétiennes
sg.	singular
SIJD	Schriften des Institutum Judaicum Delitzschianum
SNTSMS	Society for New Testament Studies Monograph Series
SNTW	Studies of the New Testament and its World
STDJ	Studies on the Texts of the Desert of Judah
Str-B	Hermann L. Strack & Paul Billerbeck, *Kommentar zum Neuen Testament aus Talmud und Midrasch,* 7 vols. (Munich: Beck, 1922–61)
TDNT	*Theological Dictionary of the New Testament,* ed. G. Kittel & G. Friedrich, trans. G. Bromiley, 10 vols. (Grand Rapids: Eerdmans, 1964–76)
THKNT	Theologischer Handkommentar zum Neuen Testament
TNTC	Tyndale New Testament Commentaries
TPINTC	TPI New Testament Commentaries
TQ	*Theologische Quartalschrift*
trans.	translator, translated by
TRE	*Theologische Realenzyklopädie*
TSAJ	Texte und Studien zum antiken Judentum
TynB	*Tyndale Bulletin*
TZ	*Theologische Zeitschrift*
v.l.	*varia lectio* (textual variant)
WMANT	Wissenschaftliche Monographien zum Alten und Neuen Testament
WUNT	Wissenschaftliche Untersuchungen zum Neuen Testament
ZBKNT	Zürcher Bibelkommentar, NT Series
ZNW	*Zeitschrift für die neutestamentliche Wissenschaft*
ZTK	Zeitschrift für Theologie und Kirche

Books of the Bible (with LXX/Deuterocanonical books)

Books of the Hebrew Old Testament

Gen.	Genesis
Exod.	Exodus
Lev.	Leviticus
Num.	Numbers
Deut.	Deuteronomy
Josh.	Joshua
Judg.	Judges
Ruth	
1–2 Sam.	1–2 Samuel
1–2 Kgs.	1–2 Kings
1–2 Chr.	1–2 Chronicles
Ezra	
Neh.	Nehemiah
Esth.	Esther
Job	
Ps.	Psalms
Prov.	Proverbs
Eccl.	Ecclesiastes
Cant.	Song of Songs
Isa.	Isaiah
Jer.	Jeremiah
Lam.	Lamentations
Ezek.	Ezekiel
Dan.	Daniel
Hos.	Hosea
Joel	
Amos	
Obad.	Obadiah
Jon.	Jonah
Mic.	Micah
Nah.	Nahum
Hab.	Habakkuk
Zeph.	Zephaniah
Hag.	Haggai
Zech.	Zechariah
Mal.	Malachi

Additional LXX books cited

Bar.	Baruch
1–4 Macc.	1–4 Maccabees
Pr. Man.	Prayer of Manasseh
Sir.	Sirach (=Ecclesiasticus)

Tob.	Tobit
Wisd.	Wisdom of Solomon

Books of the New Testament

Matt.	Matthew
Mark	
Luke	
John	
Acts	
Rom.	Romans
1–2 Cor.	1–2 Corinthians
Gal.	Galatians
Eph.	Ephesians
Phil.	Philippians
Col.	Colossians
1–2 Thess.	1–2 Thessalonians
1–2 Tim.	1–2 Timothy
Tit.	Titus
Phlm.	Philemon
Heb.	Hebrews
Jas.	James
1–2 Pet.	1–2 Peter
1–3 John	
Jude	
Rev.	Revelation

Old Testament Pseudepigrapha

Apoc.Abr.	Apocalypse of Abraham
Asc.Isa.	Ascension of Isaiah
2 Bar.	2 Baruch
1–3 Enoch	Ethopic, Slavonic, Hebrew Enoch
Ep.Arist.	Epistle of Aristeas
4 Ezra	4 Ezra (= 2 Esdras)
Od.Sol.	Odes of Solomon
Ps.Sol.	Psalm(s) of Solomon
Sib.Or.	Sibylline Oracles
T. 12 Patr.	Testaments of the 12 Patriarchs
–T. Dan	Testament of Dan
–T. Levi	Testament of Levi
–T. Naph.	Testament of Naphtali
–T. Reub.	Testament of Reuben
–T. Zeb.	Testament of Zebulon
T. Sol.	Testament of Solomon

Other Jewish writings

Dead Sea Scrolls

Abbreviations for the Dead Sea Scrolls are given in the standard format indicating the number of the cave at Qumran where the documents were found, followed by a number or alphabetic siglum for the title (e.g. 1QS, 4Q246). The most complete English translation at present is García Martínez 1996, where a listing of the scrolls and places of publication can be found on pp. 465–519.

1Q19	1QNoah
1Q34	1QPrFêtes, Festival Prayers
1QH	*Hodayot*, Thanksgiving Prayers
1QM	*Serekh ha-Milhamah*, War Scroll
1QpHab	Habakkuk Pesher
1QS	*Serekh ha-Yahad*, Community Rule
4Q169	4QpNah, Nahum Pesher
4Q171	4QpPs[a], Psalms Pesher
4Q174	4QFlor, Florilegium
4Q177	4QCatena[a]
4Q403	4QShirShabb[d], Songs of the Sabbath Sacrifice
4Q405	4QShirShabb[f]; Songs of the Sabbath Sacrifice
4Q509	4QPrFêtes, Festival Prayers
4Q510	4QShir[a], Songs of the Sage
4Q511	4QShir[b], Songs of the Sage
4Q521	4QMessianic Apocalypse
4Q544	4Q[c]Amram[b]ar, Visions of Amram[b]
4QMMT	*Miqṣat Ma'aśê ha-Torah*, Halakhic Letter from Qumran
11Q17	11QShirShabb, Songs of the Sabbath Sacrifice
11Q19	11QTemple, Temple Scroll

Philo

Abr.	*De Abrahamo*, On Abraham
Cher.	*De Cherubim*, On the Cherubim
Conf.	*De Confusione Linguarum*, On the Confusion of Tongues
Congr.	*De Congressu Eruditionis Gratia*, On the Preliminary Studies
Decal.	*De Decalogo*, On the Decalogue
Det.Pot.Ins.	*Quot Deterius Potiori Insidiari Soleat*, The Worse Attacks the Better
Gig.	*De Gigantibus*, On Giants
Leg.Gai.	*Legatio ad Gaium*, Embassy to Gaius

Mos.	*De Vita Mosis,* The Life of Moses
Plant.	*De Plantatione,* On Planting
Rer.Div.Her.	*Quis Rerum Divinarum Heres sit,* Who is the Heir of Divine Things
Sacr.	*De Sacrificiis Abelis et Caini,* On the Sacrifices of Abel and Cain
Virt.	*De Virtutibus,* On the Virtues

Josephus

Ant.	*Antiquitates Judaicae,* Jewish Antiquities
B.J.	*De Bello Judaico,* On the Jewish War
C.Ap.	*Contra Apionem,* Against Apion
Vita	*Vita Iosephi,* Life of Josephus

Rabbinic writings

Mishnah and Talmud

The Mishnah (*m.*) and Tosefta (*t.*) are quoted according to chapter and halakhah (e.g. *m.Suk.* 2.3, *t.Suk.*. 2.3), the Babylonian Talmud (*b.*) according to folio, side a or b (e.g. *b.Suk.* 17b). In quotations from the Palestinian Talmud (i.e. Yerushalmi, '*y.*'), the first two digits represent the chapter and halakhah as in the Mishnah, the third gives the folio, column (a–d) and line number (e.g. *y.Suk.* 2.3, 17c23). The presence of a *baraita* [*bar.*], i.e. an early tradition preserved in the Talmud, is indicated where it was thought appropriate. The tractates are consistently abbreviated as follows:

Abot	
Bek.	*Bekhorot*
Ber.	*Berakhot*
Ket.	*Ketubbot*
M.Sh.	*Ma'aser Sheni*
Meg.	*Megillah*
Ned.	*Nedarim*
Pes.	*Pesaḥim*
Sanh.	*Sanhedrin*
Shab.	*Shabbat*
Sot.	*Sotah*
Suk.	*Sukkah*
Taan.	*Ta'anit*

Other Rabbinic writings

A.R.N.	*Aboth de-Rabbi Nathan* [S. = ed. S. Schechter (Vienna: Lippe, 1887)]
Exod.R.	*Exodus Rabbah* [*Midrash Rabbah* (Romm: Wilna, 1887); ed. & trans. H. Freedman & M. Simon, 10 vols. (London: Soncino, 1939)]

Lev.R.	*Leviticus Rabbah [Midrash Rabbah* (Romm: Wilna, 1887); ed. & trans. H. Freedman & M. Simon, 10 vols. (London: Soncino, 1939)]
Mek.	*Mekhilta de-Rabbi Ishmael* [L. = ed. J. Z. Lauterbach, 3 vols. Philadelphia: Jewish Publication Society of America, 1933–5]
Midr. Pss.	*Midrash Tehillim (Shocher Tob)*, Midrash on Psalms [ed. S. Buber (Wilna: Romm, 1891); ed. & trans. W.G. Braude, 2 vols. (New Haven: Yale University Press, 1959]
Pes.R.	*Pesikta Rabbati* [trans. W.G. Braude (New Haven: Yale University Press, 1968)]
P.R.E.	*Pirke de-Rabbi Eliezer* [trans. G. Friedlander (4th edn. New York: Sepher-Hermon, 1981)]
Sifre Deut.	*Sifre on Deuteronomy* [ed. L. Finkelstein (New York: Jewish Theological Seminary of America, 1939); trans. R. Hammer (New Haven/London: Yale University Press, 1986)]
Sifre Num.	*Sifre on Numbers* [ed. H.S. Horovitz, 2nd edn. Jerusalem: Wahrmann, 1966; trans. J. Neusner & W.S. Green, 3 vols. (Atlanta: Scholars, 1986–)]
Tanh.	*Midrash Tanḥhuma* [edn. Warsaw, n.d.; trans. S.A. Berman (Hoboken: Ktav, 1996)]
Targ. Jon.	*Targum Jonathan on the Prophets*
Targ. Neof.	*Targum Neofiti I on the Torah*
Targ. Ps.-J.	*Targum Pseudo-Jonathan on the Torah*

Cairo Genizah

Gen. Wisd.	Cairo Genizah Wisdom Text [ed. K. Berger, *Die Weisheitsschrift aus der Kairoer Geniza* (Tübingen: Francke, 1989.]

Early Christian writings

Apostolic Fathers

Ignatius

Ign. *Rom.*	*Letter to the Romans*
Ign. *Phld.*	*Letter to the Philadelphians*

Polycarp

[Pol.] *Phil.*	*Epistle to the Philippians*

Shepherd of Hermas
   Mand.   *Mandate*
   Sim.   *Similitude*
   Vis.   *Vision*

Other
   1 Clem.   *1 Clement*
   2 Clem.   *2 Clement*
   Barn.   *Epistle of Barnabas*
   Did.   *Didache*

Other Patristic writings
Ps.-Clem.Hom.   *Pseudo-Clementine Homilies*

Clement of Alexandria
   Protr.   *Protrepticus,* Exhortation to the Greeks
   Strom.   *Stromata,* Miscellanies

Eusebius
   Hist. Eccl.   *Historia Ecclesiastica,* Ecclesiastical History

Irenaeus
   Haer.   *Adversus Haereses,* Against Heresies

Justin
   1 Apol.   *First Apology*
   2 Apol.   *Second Apology*
   Dial.   *Dialogue with Trypho*

Other ancient writings

Aristotle
   Eudem. Eth.   *Eudemian Ethics*
   Nic. Eth.   *Nicomachean Ethics*
   Rhet.   *Rhetoric*

Pliny
   Nat. Hist.   *Naturalis Historia,* Natural History

Tacitus
   Hist.   *Historiae,* Histories

Dio Chrysostom
   Or.   *Orations*

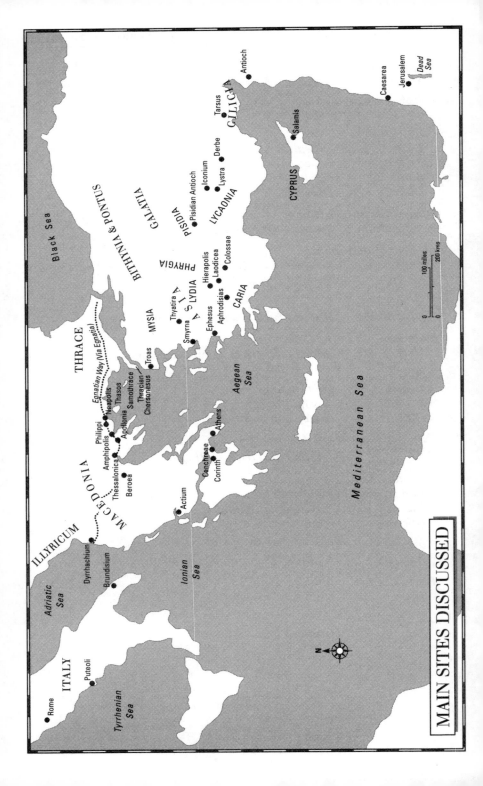

MAIN SITES DISCUSSED

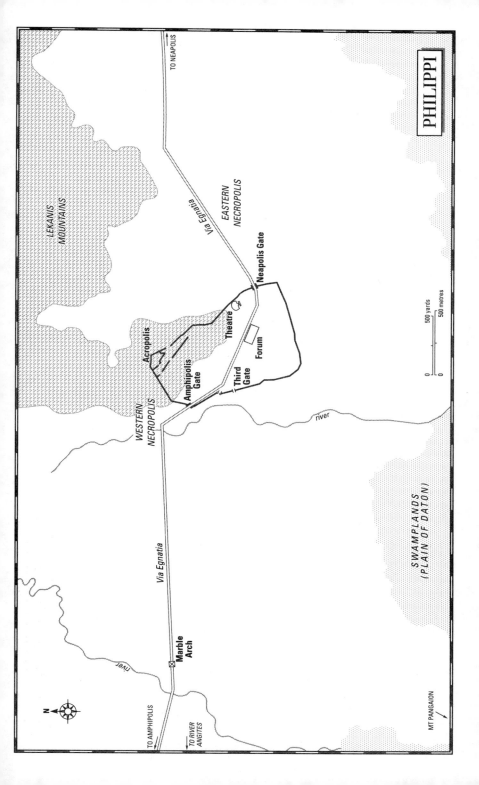

PHILIPPI

N

TO AMPHIPOLIS
TO RIVER ANGITES

river

Via Egnatia

Marble Arch

MT PANGAION

SWAMPLANDS
(PLAIN OF DATON)

river

WESTERN NECROPOLIS

LEKANIS MOUNTAINS

Acropolis

Amphipolis Gate

Theatre

Forum

Third Gate

Neapolis Gate

Via Egnatia

EASTERN NECROPOLIS

TO NEAPOLIS

500 yards
500 metres

INTRODUCTION

St Paul's letter to Philippi sparkles with joy – the sort of life-giving, heart-refreshing joy that is tangibly transforming in its effect on the mundane realities of everyday existence. Philippians is, at the same time, an epistle of joy tested and refined, written in Roman captivity while Paul awaits trial on a capital charge and is prevented from carrying out the remainder of his life's work. It shows us Paul at his most mature, having weathered the storms of his earlier ministry: disputes with religious conservatives and ritualists in Antioch and Galatia, with moral relativists and extremists in Corinth, and with various unworldly forms of spirituality in places like Corinth and Thessalonica. Near the end of his hard and adventurous road, we find a man whose faith in Christ has not merely survived but aged with grace and wisdom, refined and true as gold.

Aside from his short personal note to Philemon, Philippians is St Paul's only undisputed letter from captivity. As such, it sheds important light on his self-understanding as a prisoner; indeed it offers invaluable testimony on how the apostle and his churches responded in the face of what seemed a serious setback. If Paul was meant to carry on the vital eschatological ministry of proclaiming the gospel to the Gentiles, then how could God imperil this work by permitting the apostle's ministry to be jeopardized in a lengthy imprisonment and possible execution? The fact that this question is the first to surface in the body of the letter (1.12–26) shows the extent to which it occupies the minds of author and readers alike.

Philippians offers distinctive testimony not only to the life and thought of its apostolic author, but also to the situation of the intended readership. The church at Philippi was the first Pauline church, and the first Gentile church, in Europe; only the Jewish-Christian community at Rome predates it. Philippi also represents Paul's first move from cities with sizeable Jewish populations in Asia Minor to a much more clearly Gentile and pagan environment in Greece – which may explain why in Phil. 4.15 he can look back to his Macedonian days as 'the beginning of the gospel', i.e. his gospel specifically 'for the Gentiles' (Gal. 2.7, 9). The importance of this pioneering mission, following Paul's apparent loss of Antioch as his main sending base (cf. e.g. Hübner 1996: 138; Müller 3 on Gal. 2.11–14), is dramatically represented in Luke's account in Acts 16 of Paul's night-time call vision and subsequent

1

adventures at Philippi. Luke vividly captures the encounter with local Macedonian and Philippian culture: the importance of pioneering women believers (Acts 16.13ff.; cf. Phil. 4.2f.); Paul's powerfully symbolic exorcism of a demon-possessed servant girl (cf. similarly Jesus in pagan Decapolis, Mark 5.1–20 par.) and proclamation of the true 'Most High God' instead of Jupiter and Caesar; the night-time worship of the shackled Paul and Silas which frees the prisoners (Acts 16.25f.); and Paul's first appeal to his Roman citizenship (Acts 16.37) in the face of a charge of un-Roman activities (16.21). From now on, Paul's mission in Acts concentrates primarily on Roman cities rather than on the Jewish diaspora (Becker 1989: 132–3; Müller 3). These same themes of Christ-like lifestyle, integrity and 'citizenship' in a Roman world find repeated expression in Philippians.

The church at Philippi is also, arguably, a community with which Paul enjoys exceptionally warm and friendly relations. He is clearly writing to a group of Christians who exercise a uniquely active, 'stake-holding' partnership with Paul in the gospel ministry, both materially and spiritually. In this respect Philippians differs from Paul's correspondence with rather more fraught and problematic churches in places like Corinth, Galatia or even, perhaps, Thessalonica. Here, then, is a letter of joy, and vivid testimony to a Christian relationship that 'works'.

Before turning to our exposition of this text, it will be useful to acquaint ourselves briefly with first-century Philippi and its church, with Paul's situation and the main features of his letter, and with a number of other factors affecting the interpretation of Philippians and its significance in history.

Philippi

GEOGRAPHY AND HISTORICAL SETTING

Philippi is located in the north-eastern corner of Macedonia, about 16 km by road from its harbour town at Neapolis (modern Kaválla) on the Aegean Sea, and 180 km north of Thessalonica. The first-century city was not large: a conservative estimate based on the size of the theatre would suggest fewer than 10,000 inhabitants (cf. Pilhofer 1995: 74–6). By contrast, the modern village called Filíppoi has a population of only a few hundred people and is easily dwarfed by bustling Kaválla (pop. c. 60,000), which today is the second largest city in Greek Macedonia and the diocesan seat of the Greek Orthodox archbishop of Philippi, Neapolis and Thasos. (Cf. Barber 1990: 623–8, 634–9 *passim.*)

The ancient Acropolis of Philippi looks across the fertile plain of Daton to Mt Pangaion in the south (NB *not* in the north, *pace* Fee 25; Hendrix 1992: 314). The city itself is situated below on a relatively narrow shoulder between the Lekanis mountains to the north and swamplands to the south, guarding the ancient Via Egnatia, the main overland route from Rome to the Eastern Empire. In addition to several tributaries to the river Angites (sometimes spelled Gangites to reflect an initial *digamma*), the area benefits from a multitude of natural springs (the first ancient Thracian village on the site was called *Krenides*, 'Fountains'). Its location made the city ideally placed for trade links and especially for agriculture, including grain and the wine for which the area around Philippi had long been famous (excavations of the fourth- or fifth-century Bishop's House have brought to light two very large wine presses, presumably for his own and diocesan use ...). Nearby gold and silver mines at Mt Pangaion across the plain, which had once been an important source of wealth for Philip of Macedon, were in Roman times long since exhausted. Cf. Pilhofer 1995: 78–81.

Apparently founded by Greek colonists from the island of Thasos in the early fourth century BC, Philippi was then fortified by Philip of Macedon; royal coins issued after 356 BC first call the city 'Philippou'. Two centuries later (168 BC), the Romans defeated Perseus, the last king of Macedon, at Pydna, just south of Thessalonica. From then on, Philippi was incorporated into the first of four Macedonian regions (*merides*: cf. Acts 16.12 and Hemer 1989: 113; Pilhofer 1995: 159–65) and became a way-station along the Via Egnatia. (At Neapolis, travellers on this route could speed up their journey by taking a boat directly to Troas in Asia Minor – or vice versa, as Paul does in Acts 16.11.)

In 42 BC, Philippi was the site of the decisive battle in which Mark Antony and Octavian (the later emperor Augustus) defeated Brutus and Cassius, the assassins of Julius Caesar. After Augustus in turn defeated Mark Antony at the battle of Actium in 31 BC, he refounded Philippi as a Roman colony in honour of the Julian family (*Colonia Iulia Augusta Philippensis*: NB not named 'after his daughter', *pace* Hendrix 1992: 314, Fee 25 n.70) and under his personal patronage, boosting its native population with army veterans and landed Italian farmers whom he had displaced as former supporters of Mark Antony (Dio Cassius, *Roman History* 51.4.6; cf. Elliger 1978: 43; Pilhofer 1995: 78; for the social composition of Philippi see also Peterlin 1995: 135–70 and L.M. White 1995; and note Oakes 1996).

With this change in status just over a hundred years prior to Paul's letter, Philippi now enjoyed the considerable privilege of

Italian legal status (*ius italicum*): its colonists had not only citizenship but extensive property and legal rights, and they were exempt from poll taxes and land taxation. In return, the colony carefully maintained and groomed its image as a city loyal to the emperor's authority in both government and religion. Paul's first visit to Philippi will have impressed on him the city's emphatically *Roman* appearance and public culture, evidenced not least in the fact that the public inscriptions in the forum, on the streets and buildings of this Hellenistic-Roman town were exclusively in Latin. Not only citizenship and political loyalties were Roman, but even the form of local government was patterned on that of Rome itself, with two chief magistrates (*duumviri iure dicundo*) at the head. Citizens of Philippi were at the same time citizens of the city of Rome, assigned to the ancient family line of the *tribus Voltinia,* which appears in half of all first- and second-century public inscriptions found at Philippi. See further Pilhofer 1995: 121f.

The aristocracy, then, were emphatically Roman and Latin speaking. Nevertheless, Thracians, Greeks and other nationalities of the region were also present in the area, perhaps predominantly as agricultural workers or skilled tradesmen, retainers or slaves, and foreign merchants. They constituted the majority of the region's population, and the city's Latin culture and language began to give way to the resurgent influence of Greek from the third century onward.

The native Thracian population was concentrated in some of the surrounding agricultural villages and in the region of Mt Pangaion; Thracian names are absent from first- and second-century public and funerary inscriptions in Philippi itself. It is, of course, true that the arrival of politically privileged Roman *coloni* or settlers usually also engendered an underclass made up largely of a region's previous inhabitants, the *incolae,* many of whom would not have enjoyed the benefits of Roman citizenship (cf. e.g. Müller 2). Nevertheless, some Thracians did achieve considerable economic prosperity, and Thracian veterans acquired Roman citizenship.

A similar situation will have obtained in the case of Greeks, who of course had been culturally and linguistically dominant prior to Philippi's refounding as a Roman colony. Greek speakers included the skilled labourers who worked as construction workers and as stonemasons in the local marble quarries (cf. Pilhofer 1995: 82 and n.18f., citing Lazarides). One Greek-speaking group of tradesmen is of particular interest for New Testament studies: inscriptional evidence (cf. e.g. Hemer 1989: 115) shows that Philippi, like many ancient Hellenistic cities, had its purple dyers and traders in purple goods. Purple was a highly prized dye most properly derived from certain marine molluscs native to the Eastern Mediterranean (*Murex brandaris*); cheaper mineral and vegetable imitations were also produced, for instance from the juice of the madder root (Danker 1992; Irvin 1986; Gross 1979; Hemer 1989: 114; note also Richter Reimer 1992: 127–31 and see the detailed account in Pliny, *Nat. Hist.* 9.125–41).

Lydia, the leader of Paul's first group of women converts, was one such merchant (Acts 16.14), having moved from Thyatira in the region of Lydia. She may not in fact have been the only native of that city in the area, since purple dealers from Thyatira are well attested in inscriptions from Thessalonica (cf. Hemer 1989: 115; Pilhofer 1995: 176f.) and, perhaps, in Philippi itself (see Pilhofer's judicious remarks, 1995: 177–82, on an inscription first published by Mertzides).

Contrary to the assumption of some commentators, the uncertain origin of her purple product means that Lydia need not have been wealthy. Indeed she was clearly someone who had to work for a living, at least as a merchant – if not necessarily as a less respectable manual dyer of purple. (She is described as a *porphuropôlis*, not a *porphurobaphos*; *pace* Richter Reimer 1992: 133–7 and Schottroff 1993, who fail to distinguish sufficiently. On the cultured contempt for dyers and their unsavoury workshops see e.g. Plutarch, *Pericles* 1.4; cf. Pliny, *Nat. Hist.* 9.133–5, 138.) At any rate, Lydia's trade appears to have given her at least a modest social and economic independence, which is also confirmed in the hospitality she was able to offer to the church (see below). This in turn may bear witness to the relatively prominent status of women in Macedonia and in Thyatira, where some are attested as carrying responsibility in municipal government and in athletic contests (Trebilco 1991: 120–22; see also pp. 8, 18 below). Lydia may have become a 'god-fearer' (Acts 16.14) by acquaintance with the Jewish community in her home town (cf. Schürer/ Vermes 1987: 3.19; it is also worth noting Jewish membership of the guild of purple-dyers at Hierapolis (see ibid., p. 27). The existence of Gentile 'god-fearers' sympathetic to Judaism used to be widely contested, but appears now to have been unambiguously confirmed by an inscription discovered at Aphrodisias in Caria, now south-western Turkey (see Reynolds & Tannenbaum 1987, esp. pp. 48–66; Levinskaya 1990b; Trebilco 1991: 145–66). 'God-fearing' women are later also attested at Rome (e.g. *JIWE* II, Nos. 207, 364; and cf. Josephus, *Ant.* 20.195 on Poppaea Sabina).

Greek culture and language did go on to regain predominance in Philippi in the third century, as we noted; these later developments suggest that in some ways Latin never became much more than an official, culturally fashionable veneer (so also Pilhofer

1995: 90; Murphy-O'Connor 1996: 213). In the meantime, however, it remains significant that when Paul wrote Philippians, the citizenship, language, culture and religion of Rome had been the city's dominant public frame of reference for over a century. The importance of this fact in the account of Acts 16 is powerfully evident (beginning with Luke's unique identification of the city with the Latin loan word *kolónia* rather than the less specific Greek equivalent *apoikia*: cf. Tajra 1989: 5–8; also Mason 1974: 109). This same context surfaces repeatedly in Paul's letter – though of course it is significant for the church's social setting that he writes in Greek and not in Latin.

THE RELIGION OF PHILIPPI

From the start, Paul's mission to Gentiles had of necessity to address a situation where both pagan and Jewish religious claims vied for his converts' attention. This bipolar conflict usually takes its most acute form in relation to the advocates of Jewish-Christian beliefs and practices (e.g. Romans, 2 Corinthians, Galatians), whose opposition to Paul's vision of the church also surfaces at least briefly in Philippians 3.2ff. Elsewhere in this letter, however, we also obtain an unusually acute glimpse of the gospel's costly encounter with *paganism*. This is true not only in the general context of Paul's experiences in the Roman penal system (1.12–13) or in the persecution of Philippian Christians at the hands of their compatriots (1.28–30), but also in the implied opposition between Christ and Caesar as supreme Lord and Saviour (2.9–11), as well as in the call for Christians to shine as stars in a crooked and perverse generation (2.15).

This is, of course, just as we would expect: Paul is writing to a Roman colony in which the Jewish presence, if any, is negligibly small; and as we shall see below on 3.2ff., there is little reason to think that the conflict with Judaizing opponents is in fact an acute problem in Philippi itself. As a result, the religious context of the Philippian church immediately becomes a subject of some interest. It is worth commenting briefly on both the pagan and the Jewish dimensions.

PAGAN RELIGION

On the pagan side, commentators rightly point out the importance of traditional Roman religion, including a particular Philippian penchant for the Emperor Cult with all its official temples and sacrifices, festal calendar and related cultural trappings, and personnel such as flamens, priestesses of Livia, and *seviri Augus-*

tales. At the same time, commentators have frequently assumed that first-century Philippi presented a considerable religious syncretism, incorporating numerous aspects of local Thracian, Greek and oriental cults (cf. e.g. Beare 7–9, O'Brien 4–5). Much of the evidence from Philippi, however, both for the imperial cult and for religious syncretism, has too often been compiled in an anachronistic and cumulative fashion, with little care being taken to demonstrate the specific circumstances of the first century. Lukas Bormann (1995: 61–7 and *passim*) has recently documented the fact that the traditional Graeco-Roman character of Philippian religion in all likelihood remained dominant throughout the first century, and that the large-scale popularity of the cults of Isis and Silvanus in particular cannot be substantiated prior to the mid-second century, even if we have earlier evidence of their existence. While Bormann may overrate the importance of the Emperor Cult in the first century (Pilhofer 1995: 93 notes the relative dearth of attested priests in the relevant period), he provides a much needed corrective to the usual assumption that first-century Philippi already manifested religious syncretism 'in one of its most ample expressions' (so Beare 7; cf. recently L.M. White 1995: 250–51). It is worth bearing in mind the fact that the inscriptions of Philippi at this time are almost exclusively in Latin and concerned with *Roman* interests (cf. Hemer 1989: 231 n.33).

At the same time, Bormann's potentially misleading picture of first-century Philippi as homogeneously Roman in population and religion must be balanced with Peter Pilhofer's important treatment (1995). The latter unfortunately ignores the official Roman cult. Nevertheless, he offers three useful illustrations of other influences on the popular religion of Romans, Greeks and Thracians at Philippi: (i) the unofficial 'folk religion' (Dorcey 1992) of the distinctively Roman deity Silvanus, almost exclusively a cult for lower-class Roman men and attested nowhere else in Greece or Macedonia (Pilhofer 1995: 108–13); (ii) the local cult of Dionysus (= Bacchus, also known in Roman times as Liber Pater) was long established in the region of Philippi and on Mt Pangaion, promising the god's devotees a life of eternal bliss after death (Pilhofer 1995: 100–107); (iii) the well-attested cult of the leading indigenous deity known as the Thracian Rider or 'Aulonite Hero' (typically depicted as a knight on horseback). Without accepting earlier commentators' largely anachronistic picture of massive religious syncretism at Philippi, we may allow that widely popular religious cults such as these would have been known and practised alongside (but not in serious competition with) the official religion. (It is particularly interesting in this connection that a Philippian coin showing the Thracian Rider on one side and the 'divine' Emperor Augustus (inscribed *Divo Augusto*) on the other was found in Thasos in the 1980s (cf. Pilhofer 1995: 97). Note also that Paul's missionary companion Silvanus/Silas (Acts 15.40; 16.19ff.; cf. 1 Thess. 1.1) was evidently named after that popular Roman deity (cf. also Melick 25).)

Given the exclusively male domain of the cult of Silvanus, it is worth mentioning one other line of evidence which strongly and prominently links pagan religion with *women*. The importance of women in the social and religious life of Macedonia has long been the subject of scholarly attention (e.g. Thomas 1971, Gillman 1990 and others cited in Fee 391 n.31; cf. Kron 1996 on religion in the lives of Greek women generally). More specifically, the works of Portefaix and Abrahamsen have noted the prominence of women in the Philippian cults of Diana, Dionysus and Isis. In particular, the second- and third-century rock reliefs at the acropolis provide evidence both of women's importance in the cult generally, and of their identification with the divine huntress Diana in the hope of participating in her transcendent life (Portefaix 1988: 75–128; cf. also Abrahamsen 1987, 1988, 1995: 69–127, but note the serious critique of the latter's epigraphical work in Pilhofer 1995: 38–41). While one must take care not to extrapolate unduly from these studies of somewhat later evidence (cf. also the caution of L.M. White 1995: 257 n.70), Abrahamsen and Portefaix have usefully drawn attention to the public attestation of women's religious experiences and responsibilities in Roman Philippi. This is a point to which we shall have occasion to return below.

A less common expression of the Graeco-Roman cult is of interest in relation to Philippi: Macedonian inscriptions occasionally refer to Zeus Hypsistos or Jupiter Optimus Maximus, 'the most high god'. The Philippian slave girl's labelling of Paul and Silas as 'servants of the most high god' (Acts 16.17), however, reflects a deliberate *double entendre* commonly encountered in Jewish writings from Asia Minor and elsewhere: Jews and Christians knew the true *theos hypsistos* to be the God of Israel. Cf. Hemer 1989: 231; Trebilco 1989, 1991: 127–44.

JUDAISM

There is no written or archaeological evidence of a resident Jewish community at Philippi, and no indication of a synagogue or even of Jewish homes. Among Philippi's nearly 1,400 attested inscriptions, the only exception appears to be the word *sunagōgē* on an unpublished funerary stele discovered in 1987 and dating from the Byzantine period: see Pilhofer 1995: 232 and n.3; this is apparently the same as that mentioned in L.M. White 1995: 247–8 and n.38. Jews did settle in Macedonia, as we know from Philo (*Leg. Gai.* 281), but we have no documentary evidence to substantiate this in the case of Philippi.

As we shall see in the commentary below, Paul's letter to Philippi confirms the impression that the local Jewish presence was either non-existent or negligible in importance. The readership's lack of familiarity with the Jewish Scriptures may account for the complete absence of quotations from the Old Testament (but see on 1.19; 2.10–11, 15; and note that by the time of Polycarp, half a century later, the Philippians had become 'well trained' in Scripture, *Phil.* 12.1). What is more, Paul's polemical words about Judaizing adversaries in Phil. 3.2 concern a threat which, although familiar to his readers, is at present potential rather than real, and which is focused on individuals arriving from elsewhere – either directly from Palestine or via Jewish communities in places like Thessalonica (see on 1.28 and 3.2; and note Acts 17.5–7 and Horbury 1982 with reference to 1 Thess. 2.3, 16).

The account of Acts 16 is sometimes assumed to provide evidence of a Jewish community (e.g. Schürer/Vermes 1987: 3.65), but in fact it offers very little. Paul and his team apparently found only a small group of God-fearing Gentile women gathered in an admittedly identifiable Jewish place of prayer outside the city walls (a *proseuché*, Acts 16.13, 16). Significantly, Luke mentions 'synagogues of the Jews' at Salamis (13.5), Pisidian Antioch (13.14), and Iconium (14.1), Thessalonica (Acts 17.1), Beroea (17.10), Athens (17.17) and Corinth (18.4, 7) – but at Philippi, as indeed at Lystra and Derbe (14.8–21), he never speaks either of Jews or of a synagogue. The word *proseuché* did of course commonly denote a building used for prayer to the God of the Jews, generally in the diaspora (cf. Hengel 1971, Hüttenmeister 1993, Levinskaya 1990a). Everywhere else in Luke's own writings, however, *proseuché* means an *act* rather than a *place* of prayer. His usage in Acts 16, therefore, may well suggest that he does not consider the Philippian site to be a 'synagogue of the Jews' properly speaking, and perhaps that he nevertheless accepts the local Philippian designation used by his source (so Hengel 1971: 175). The Philippian *proseuché* for him was certainly a place that one 'entered' (Acts 16.16), although perhaps not necessarily a formal building. Either way, Luke's sustained interest in Paul's contact with synagogues makes it significant that he fails to mention either 'Jews' or 'synagogue' in his account of the important Pauline mission to Philippi, about which he seems in other respects to be remarkably well informed. Luke's picture in this regard agrees with that in Polycarp's letter to Philippi, which remains silent about Jews or Jewish Christians there.

Given the evidence thus far available, it would appear that there was at best only a minimal Jewish presence in first-century Philippi. This is not in fact particularly surprising. Philippi was a relatively small and primarily agricultural colony rather than a major commercial or military centre; and thus there is no obvious reason why significant numbers of Jews should have been attracted to settle there. Those who met in the *proseuché* were apparently a group of women, only one of whom is even explicitly described as a 'god-fearer' (*sebomené ton theon*, 16.14). No Jews are mentioned, and no men (though there may of course have been some), so that we cannot even be sure of what at least in Palestine would later be considered a full Jewish congregation or *minyan*, i.e. with a quorum of at least ten men (cf. *m.Meg.* 4.3; *m.Abot* 3.7).

Without concluding too much from silence, these observations do lend a heightened significance to the unusual presence of an exclusively or at any rate predominantly female Sabbath congregation. This phenomenon may well correspond to the common numerical predominance of women among proselytes and god-fearers, due partly to the absence of circumcision as a deterrent and partly to the relatively more respected status of women within Judaism. (See Feldman 1993: 328; an awareness of this particular appeal to women may underlie the Jewish Hellenistic text *Joseph and Asenath*, and on the Christian side John Chrysostom's invective in *Against the Jews* 2.3 (MPG 48.860), perhaps along with that of 2 Tim. 3.6–8.) The attraction of women, and thus presumably in many cases children, to diaspora Judaism might add an argument of 'transgenerational proselytism' in support of the case that the very large increase in the number of Jews in the Second Temple period is best explained by the existence of a widespread, but usually informal, Jewish missionary consciousness. See the nuanced argument of Carleton Paget 1996, mediating between recent maximalist (e.g. Feldman 1993) and minimalist (McKnight 1991, Goodman 1994) positions; cf. also Rokéah 1996. (For the general point about the female congregation in Acts 16 compare further the intriguing feminist account of Richter Reimer 1992: 91–114 and *passim*.)

The church at Philippi

HISTORICAL ORIGIN

Paul's letter to the Philippians repeatedly alludes to the time when the Christian message first came to Philippi and was received there. These allusions, however, are so unspecific as to be of little help in reconstructing the events surrounding the first Pauline mission: all we learn is that Paul's early mission was accompanied by conflict and suffering (1.29f.; cf. 1 Thess. 2.2) and that the Philippian church entered into a unique partnership with Paul to support his mission in financial and other ways (1.5, 4.15–16).

PROBLEMS OF METHOD

To understand the origin of the church at Philippi, therefore, we must look primarily to Luke's account of Paul's mission in Acts 16. Unfortunately, this raises a number of methodological difficulties about Luke's reliability as a historian, the nature of his sources, and the overall purpose of his composition. Scholarly opinion on this question has been highly divided, ranging from the blithely uncritical to those who combine a radical scepticism about Acts with an unshakeable faith in their own methods and judgements. Some would regard much of the account in Acts 16 as wholly fabricated on the basis of Philippians and other Pauline passages like 1 Thess. 2.2. Thus for Schenk 339–40, Paul's Philippian imprisonment is spun out of Phil. 1.30, while the repentant Philippian jailer is somehow discovered in the name Clement in Phil. 4.3. (Carls 1995 similarly opts for an implausibly allegorical reading of the names in Phil. 4.2–3.) In other treatments, by contrast, the problem of Luke's historical reliability and vested theological interests can be virtually ignored: thus, even a major critical commentator like Fee can brush the matter aside in a single brief sentence and footnote (p. 27 and n.73). This approach side-steps important problems such as Luke's failure to mention a single one of Paul's epistles or his conflicts in Galatia and Corinth, and his puzzlingly different perspective on the method and chronology of Paul's mission.

We cannot do justice to these complex issues within the scope of the present commentary. At the same time, readers of Philippians may wish to note that a growing movement within international Acts scholarship has since the 1980s begun to turn away from the determinedly sceptical stance that dominated an earlier generation. Writings like Hengel 1979 and 1991, Hemer 1989, Thornton 1991 and the six-volume series of *The Book of Acts in Its First Century Setting* (incl. e.g. Rapske 1994, Bauckham 1995) have made available a wealth of new archaeological data and research on ancient Hellenistic historiography, pointing to a rather more positive and more nuanced assessment of the value of Acts as a historical source. (A significant contrasting voice remains that of Boismard & Lamouille 1990 as complemented by Taylor 1994.) It is this new, cautiously sympathetic reading of

Luke's work which will characterize our approach here. As well as the critical assessment of Acts as a whole, recent research on Philippi in particular shows Luke's account in Acts 16 (the beginning of the so-called 'We' narrative) to be unusually rich in local knowledge and information (e.g. Pilhofer 1995: 153–9, 252–4; Hemer 1989: 346f. and *passim*). As we shall see presently, this reassessment of the Philippian pericope in Acts has led to a revival of the theory, first advanced by William Ramsay (1905: 201–5), that Luke himself was a Macedonian, perhaps even from Philippi.

With these caveats in mind, we now turn briefly to an examination of Luke's narrative in Acts 16.

THE ACCOUNT IN ACTS 16

Having received the Apostolic Decree in Jerusalem and returned to Antioch, Paul takes Silas and sets out on his second 'missionary journey', most probably in the year 49 or 50. After visiting existing Pauline congregations in Syria and Asia Minor, ostensibly for encouragement and to pass on the Apostolic Decree (Acts 15.36; 16.4), the two missionaries continue their travels towards the west coast of Asia Minor. Along the way, Luke speaks of repeated experiences of divine guidance: the Holy Spirit prevents the apostles from carrying out their intended mission in the western provinces of Asia and Bithynia (16.6–8).

As Paul approaches the coast at Troas, the narrative of Acts reaches a turning point which is highly significant in several respects. On the literary level, Luke's description suddenly switches from the third person to the first person plural: the departure from Troas marks the first of the characteristic 'We' sections of Acts, in which the author appears to present his story as an eye-witness account. There has been much discussion about whether this narrative feature suggests (i) that Luke himself was an eyewitness of these events, (ii) that he is using another first-hand account, or (iii) that it constitutes a literary fiction designed to make for a more vivid story. This is not of course the place to synthesize several decades of scholarly debate. For present purposes, however, it may suffice to note that several recent studies seem inclined to revert from the sceptical assumptions of a generation ago to a position resembling that once held by William Ramsay. The 'We' sections, on this account, are best understood as incorporating material which arises from the author's own first-hand acquaintance with the Pauline mission (so e.g. Hemer 1989, Thornton 1991).

More particularly, some have taken the first appearance of the

'We' section in connection with the unusually detailed report of the mission to Philippi to suggest that Luke himself may have been from Philippi, indeed that he was the 'Macedonian man' (Acts 16.9) who appeared to Paul in his vision (so Ramsay 1905: 201–5, followed by Pilhofer 1995: 153–9; cf. Bruce 138; Fee 394). The details of Luke's narrative in Acts 16 do indeed make his own (or at any rate his source's) close personal association with Philippi and this part of Macedonia a very strong possibility, as even Taylor 1994: 245 affirms. At the same time, the specific identification of Luke's first appearance with the man in Paul's vision must of course remain a matter of speculation (so rightly Haenchen 1968: 429; Hemer 1989: 346 and n.77).

Commentators have at times over-dramatized the significance of Paul's move from Asia into Europe (cf. recently Gnilka 1996: 78–9). In antiquity, however, the crossing of the Aegean Sea was of far less cultural or political significance than is assumed from a modern Western perspective. In terms of culture and language, both sides of the Aegean were in the Greek sphere of influence, and had been so for centuries of Greek settlement and colonization (cf. Pilhofer 1995: 154f.). Paul's further westward movement from Troas, therefore, would be understood as no more or less significant than Luke in fact describes it: it is the move from Asia Minor into Macedonia (Acts 16.9–10).

Having reached Neapolis via Samothrace, Paul and his team proceed immediately along the Via Egnatia to Philippi, on the first of what seem to be at least three visits to that city (16.11–40; cf. 20.1–6; 2 Cor. 7.5). In all the best MSS Philippi is described somewhat awkwardly and ambiguously as, literally, 'the first city of the district (*prôté tés meridos ... polis*) of Macedonia, a colony' (Acts 16.12). The Greek phrase and its several textual variants have been the subject of much debate, and are of considerable interest for Luke's view of Philippi. Part of the problem is that Philippi was by no means the most important city of Macedonia. Nor is it possible to translate '*the* leading city of that district of Macedonia' (so Fee 25, erroneously citing Wikgren 1981; my italics), since Amphipolis was in fact the 'leading city' of the administrative district to which Philippi belonged. On balance, it is probably best to follow the long-standing textual emendation adopted by NA[27] and a good many recent writers on the basis of ancient versions: 'a city of the first district (*prôtés tés meridos ... polis*) of Macedonia, a colony'. (See e.g. Bruce 1 n.1; Elliger 1978: 51–3; Hemer 1989: 113–14 n.31; Lüdemann 1989b: 179; Müller 2; Pilhofer 1995: 159–65 and n. 17; Wikgren 1981; contrast Metzger 444–6.) Macedonia's division into four administrative districts by the Romans has long been known, but the use of the Greek term *meris* to designate these districts has only recently been attested in an as yet unpublished inscription (Pilhofer 1995: 162).

On a related note, inscriptional evidence also sheds interesting light on Luke's oddly placed apposition *kolônia* ('a colony'): as in the case of the German city that came to be known as Köln or Cologne (*Colonia*), it would appear that first-century Greek speakers in the first district of Macedonia referred to Philippi simply as 'the colony' (cf. inscription 711/G736 discussed in Pilhofer 1995: 160). Among other things, this provides local confirmation of Philippi's self-consciously colonial status.

We are told that, on the following Sabbath after arriving at Philippi, the Pauline team went to look first for a Jewish place of worship, repeating a pattern consistently attested in Acts (9.20; 13.5, 14–48; 14.1; cf. 17.1, 10, 17; 18.4, 19.8). Luke does not mention a synagogue, as we saw earlier; indeed the fact that the missionaries go '*outside* the gate by the river' (16.13) confirms that there can have been no Jewish building, and no *mikveh* (ritual bath), inside the city walls.

There were three city gates. Through the eastern gate led the Via Egnatia towards Neapolis, which crossed the city's necropolis (cemetery) and did not lead to a river; for both these reasons it is not a likely option for the local Jewish *proseuché* which the apostles found (Acts 16.13, 16). Passing through the city and along the north side of the Forum in a straight line (as the city's *Decumanus*), the Via Egnatia then exits through the western gate, continuing in an initially westbound direction towards Amphipolis *c.* 50 km away, and thence to Thessalonica and across Macedonia to the Adriatic Sea. (Some scholars call the western gate the 'Crenides Gate' in recognition of the numerous springs (*krénides*) in this area; but this is best avoided to prevent confusion with the nearby village of Krenides to the *east.*) Most commentators have tended to suggest a 'prayer house' somewhere beyond this western gate. In particular, since Collart 1937: 458–60 (cf. recently Gnilka 1996: 79) it has been thought that an arch about 2 km outside the city gate marked the formal religious boundary of the city (called the *pomerium*), inside which no foreign cultic practices were permitted. On this account, Luke would be referring to the 'river' a few hundred metres beyond that arch. However, this would imply an implausibly extended regular Sabbath walk of 2.5 km each way from the western gate (the traditional limit is 2,000 cubits, i.e. *c.* 1 km); and the discovery of tombs along the Via Egnatia *inside* the proposed boundary of the *pomerium* must raise serious difficulties for this location from the perspective of Jewish purity halakhah (cf. Pilhofer 1995: 67–73, 167–9). As it happens, the Roman law prohibiting foreign cults inside the *pomerium* was probably in any case no longer enforced at this time (cf. Taylor 1994: 248–50).

Numerous variations on this theory of a *proseuché* beyond the western gate have been proposed. On balance, however, it may be that both Roman and Jewish religious concerns are most readily accommodated by Peter Pilhofer's recent proposal to identify the lesser known third gate as the one intended by Luke. This smaller southern gate merely leads out to the nearest river, which at this point flows barely 50 m from the city wall; no tombs have been discovered here. What is more, Luke's wording could in fact be read so as to strengthen this proposal, i.e. as identifying specifically 'the gate by the river' (*tés pulés para potamon*); and the proximity of this location makes good sense of Paul's apparently frequent (cf. Acts 16.16, 18) walk to the place of prayer. See Pilhofer 1995: 171–3.

It was most likely here, then, just outside the south-western wall of the city by the small local river (sometimes erroneously identified as the Angites, of which it is a tributary), that Paul and Silas first made contact with the Gentile worshippers of the God of Israel who were to become Philippi's first Christian believers, including Lydia of Thyatira (Acts 16.14–15), who invites the apostles to stay in her house. Richter Reimer 1992: 147–56 offers the interesting argument that Lydia's 'urging' (*parebiasato*, 16.15) the visitors to stay with her is not only her first outpouring of Christian hospitality, but also an expression of her desire to offer Paul and Silas protection from the official or mob violence that is likely to come their way.

Luke's further account reports of the exorcism of a lucratively clairvoyant slave-girl (Acts 16.16–18; cf. O'Toole 1992b; Richter Reimer 1992: 162–201). This results in a public commotion during which her incensed owners bring Paul and Silas before the magistrates and formally accuse them of disturbing the city with the proselytizing propagation (*katangelousin*, 'they proclaim') of repugnant, un-Roman behaviour (*ethé*, cf. Latin *mores*), which by common prejudice they seem to associate with the Jewish cultic site outside the walls (16.20). (Tacitus, by no means unusually polemical on this matter (cf. Rokéah 1995), deemed Jewish practice (*mos*) 'absurd and sordid' (*Hist.* 5.5.5), since Jews 'consider profane everything that we hold sacred' and vice versa (*Hist.* 5.4.1).) The specific charge, then, is not so much that Paul and Silas follow a Jewish way of life, but rather that they are commending their *mores* to people who are Roman citizens (so rightly van Unnik 1973; Pilhofer 1995: 192; cf. Rapske 1994: 116–19). It is at least possible that in Roman Philippi such a charge might have carried additional odium at a time when the

Emperor Claudius had only recently expelled rioting Jews from Rome (cf. Sherwin-White 1963: 81).

We are told that Paul and Silas were beaten and then briefly imprisoned (Acts 16.22–4, 35; cf. Rapske 1994: 123–7). Hagiographical embellishments have often been suspected in the subsequent story of an earthquake freeing all the prisoners during the apostles' midnight worship, followed by the sudden conversion of the frightened jailer and his family. As a result, some scholars doubt that Paul was ever imprisoned in Philippi at all. (Haenchen 1968: 440 manifests the self-assured scepticism of the earlier Acts scholarship in calling this episode 'such a nest of improbabilities that it must be struck out as unhistorical'.)

A 'neutral' historical reconstruction of this part of Luke's account may indeed be neither possible nor appropriate. Nevertheless, the fact of Paul's early mistreatment, imprisonment and release at Philippi is plausibly enough attested in his own letters (Phil. 1.30; 1 Thess. 2.2; also 2 Cor. 11.25), and it remains entirely possible that Luke's account reflects an authentic local tradition about the Philippian jailer as one of that city's first Christian converts (cf. also O'Toole 1992a; Pilhofer 1995: 198, 240 n.1).

Throughout this episode of confrontation with the authorities, Luke identifies the relevant officials with unusually precise terminology. After the generic term for magistrates (*archontes*, Acts 16.19), Luke employs the specific term used of a colony's chief public officers, the *duumviri iure dicundo* (*stratégoi*, 16.20: cf. Mason 1974: 87; also Pilhofer's (1995: 196) correction of a much cited essay by W.M. Ramsay). The police officers who carry out the orders of the *duumviri* are lictors (*rhabdouchoi*, 16.35, 38), who generally walked before the former while bearing the distinctive bundle of rods (*virgae*) that signified their authority to use physical coercion or corporal punishment (though not capital punishment, as in the case of *fasces* with an axe: see Haenchen 1968: 435; Rapske 1994: 124 and n.24). As expected, the jailer is called a *desmophulax* (16.23).

Finally, it is significant that Luke highlights Paul's appeal to his Roman citizenship in the Philippian context. When the news of their release is received from the lictors the next morning, Paul and Silas insist that as Roman citizens they should never have been beaten and imprisoned without a trial, and demand to be seen by the *duumviri* themselves (Acts 16.35–8). Alarmed at the possible consequences of their miscarriage of justice, these officials duly appear in person to apologize for their error, but also ask the missionaries to leave the city – no doubt in the interest of public order (vv. 38–9). Having encouraged the church in Lydia's house, Paul and Silas set out for Thessalonica along the west-

bound Via Egnatia via Amphipolis and Apollonia (17.1), a journey
of several days. Interestingly, we hear of no stopover in Amphipolis, the capital of the first district of Macedonia, perhaps because
Paul remained unsuccessful in his customary search for a Jewish
place of prayer as a point of contact (cf. Acts 16.13 and see
above).

THE PAULINE CHRISTIANS AT PHILIPPI

Philippi, then, is the place where Paul's gospel of God's Jewish
Messiah and Saviour of the world first reached Macedonia and
took root in an entirely Gentile, Roman setting. The local Jewish
community, if it existed, was small and not a major threat; indeed
we shall discover in the commentary below that acute local
dangers to the gospel's progress at Philippi arose primarily from
internal strife (2.1–5) and pagan opposition (see on 1.28 and 3.2;
and note Polycarp's mention of apparent Philippian martyrs in
Phil. 9.1).

The church at Philippi was made up of Gentiles; but unfortunately we know very little else about the first Christians, either
from Philippians or from Acts. It would seem safe to assume from
Acts that Lydia and the family of the Philippian jailer were among
these early believers – although we do not even know the latter's
name. Even 'Lydia' has frequently been assumed to be an ethnic
or geographical epithet ('Lydian woman') rather than a personal
name. Nevertheless, the Latin personal name Lydia, although
rare, has been discovered on inscriptions from Ephesus and from
Sardis, not far from Thyatira, the home of the Philippian Lydia
(Hemer 1989: 114 and n.32, 231; Gill 1994a: 114). Similarly, it may
be of interest for the Roman context of Philippi that Horace (*Odes*
1.8.1; 1.13.1; 1.25.8; 3.9.6–7) and Martial (*Epigrams* 11.21) also
envision the use of Lydia as a proper name. The idea that the
Lydia of Acts may have been known by another name, perhaps as
the Euodia or Syntyche of Phil. 4.2 (so e.g. W.M. Ramsay, cited in
Fee 390 n.28; cf. Beare 144), is of course theoretically possible; but
it remains entirely unsubstantiated.

None of the three leading characters in the Acts account –
Lydia, the jailer and the slave-girl (whose conversion Luke of
course does not assert, *pace* Lightfoot 55–8) – is identified in
Philippians. There could be many plausible reasons for this,
including the simple fact that there was no need to single out
individual old friends (note the absence of a list of personal
greetings; cf. Gnilka 1996: 79). Lydia, as both an immigrant and a
merchant of luxury goods, might in any case have had occasion

either to travel on business or indeed to move on to another town.

Philippians does, however, provide the names, if little else, of several other local Christians. A certain Clement is asked to help make peace between two feuding women, Euodia and Syntyche, both of whom also occupy sensitive positions of leadership within the church (4.2–3). Undoubtedly the most significant Philippian figure for the purposes of Paul's letter is Epaphroditus, who risked his life while travelling to Rome with the church's financial gift for the apostle, and who is now concerned about his imminent return to Philippi (see below on 2.25–30). Some of these leading figures may well be among the 'bishops and deacons' whom Paul so enigmatically greets in 1.1 (see below).

The list of names culled from Philippians and Acts permits few conclusions about the social make-up of this church. It certainly confirms the exclusively or largely Gentile-Christian constituency at Philippi (but note e.g. *JIWE* II, No. 110 for a third-century Jewish Euodia). More specifically, there are several Greek names and at least one Roman one (Clement, possibly Lydia), but none that are of Thracian origin; in fact, Pilhofer 1995: 240–43 shows that there are no Thracian names among the 64 Philippian Christians of the first six centuries who are known to us by name from literary and inscriptional evidence. This in turn suggests that the Philippian congregation continued to be drawn exclusively or at least predominantly from the town itself, since the native Thracian population was overwhelmingly rural (cf. p. 4 above).

On another note, the list of New Testament Christians clearly suggests Paul's acceptance of the socially prominent positions often enjoyed by Macedonian women (see pp. 5, 8 above). Along with Lydia in Acts, Euodia and Syntyche in particular seem to enjoy sufficiently independent social stature within the church to be addressed as public agents in their own right (cf. Meeks 1983: 57 and see p. 5 above on Lydia). While not all three of these women need have been affluent (*pace* Meeks, their widely attested Greek names suggest little about socio-economic status), the Philippian church clearly did contain women and men who had the means to own or rent homes in which the church could meet (Acts 16. 15, 40), and to make repeated financial contributions to the apostle's mission (see on Phil. 4.15–18). Epaphroditus, too, was evidently able to travel freely and independently to Rome and to maintain himself there.

Finally, it is worth noting briefly that the Philippian Christians to whom Paul writes are clearly no strangers to conflict. Scholarly discussion about the opposition to Pauline Christianity in Philippi has been long and involved; excessive 'mirror-reading' (on which see Barclay 1987) has produced a multitude of options, amply documented in the full-scale commentaries (cf. also Klein 1989; Kähler 1994). Judaizing adversaries are, to be sure, a threat that is constantly on Paul's mind; but their interference specifically in Philippi may well be potential and general rather than acute and present (see on 1.28 and especially 3.2 below; also p. 9 above). As had been the case since the gospel's arrival at Philippi (Acts 16.20–21), the main external threat continued to arise from Gentile opposition (see on 1.28–30; 2.15; 3.18–19). It found its likely focus in Christianity's supposedly un-Roman commitments and practices which would necessarily clash with the loyalty to the imperial constitution and religion that were foundational to Philippi as a Roman colony (cf. Bormann 1995: 217–24 and see below p. 100). Even for the pagan opposition, however, there is in fact no point in attempting a very specific reconstruction, since the available data are insufficient. It is in any case by no means obvious that a single, well-defined Gentile group must lie behind both the persecutors of 1.28–30 and the ethical libertines of 3.18–19, as we shall see in our discussion of those passages. The problem of *internal* disunity in the church is less serious by comparison (*pace* Peterlin 1995); it will be addressed below on 2.2–4 and especially 4.2–3.

Beyond these basic observations, our only significant information about the New Testament church at Philippi concerns its relationship with the apostle Paul. For reasons that will become apparent, however, this subject is best discussed in connection with the genre and purpose of his letter (see below, 'Purpose and nature of the letter', p. 32). In the second century, Philippi continued to be a city of some importance for the Christian church. Ignatius of Antioch visited it on his way to martyrdom in Rome (*c.* AD 110; see Pol. *Phil.* 9.1; 13.1f.). Not long afterwards Polycarp, the bishop of Smyrna, wrote an important letter to Philippi – though many have argued for two: one (*Phil.* 13–14) shortly after Ignatius's death and another (*Phil.* 1–12) around twenty years later (so Harrison 1936 and most continental scholarship, e.g. recently Bauer 1995: 18–19; Pilhofer 1995: 206–12; contrast Paulsen 1985: 112). Popular Christian awareness of the city's importance in the apostolic period was also maintained by the largely legendary *Acts of Andrew*, which locate several stories about that apostle at Philippi (chapters 11–12, 15, 20). Flavianus, a prelate from Philippi, took part in the Council of Ephesus in AD 431 (cf. Lightfoot 65 n.3). Significant Christian archaeological remains from the fourth century onward include the Basilica of St Paul and numerous inscriptions (cf. Pilhofer 1995: 16–28, 241–2).

Paul's letter to Philippi

A third cluster of introductory questions deals more specifically with the nature of Paul's letter, including its literary structure and integrity, the date and place of its composition, and the occasion and purpose of Paul's writing.

LITERARY STRUCTURE AND INTEGRITY

Philippians and Philemon are Paul's only letters from prison whose authenticity is not seriously disputed. The only partial exception is the debate on the origin of 2.6–11, to which we shall return in the commentary below (but note also Doughty 1995, who somewhat implausibly questions Pauline authorship of 3.2–21; Carls 1995: 141 allows for the possibility of its pseudonymity). This relative consensus on the letter's authenticity is itself remarkable, not least in the light of certain peculiarities of language and vocabulary: in contrast to the rest of Paul's letters there is, for instance, no use of his verbs for salvation, and remarkably little on faith, grace, and justification (cf. Fee 18–21).

More problematical are the letter's literary structure and integrity, which have generated a large amount of ongoing scholarly debate. Only an outline of the arguments can be given here, and a working hypothesis sketched. More detailed recent treatments include the major commentaries as well as Alexander 1989, Bormann 1995: 87–126, Garland 1985, Koperski 1992 (with the reply by Schenk 1994), Schoon-Janssen 1991: 119–45; D.F. Watson 1988 and Wick 1994.

Two basic difficulties have given rise to persistent doubts about the present literary structure of the epistle.

First, the overall argument does not follow that of other Pauline epistles (e.g. thanksgiving, doctrine, exhortation, personal news). By itself, this need not mean much; indeed it is an observation which applies equally to other letters such as 1 and 2 Corinthians. It does, however, raise the possibility that the structural problems may be due either to the letter's composite nature (as has also been widely argued for 2 Cor.) or to an unusual purpose or genre (as in 1 Cor., which answers questions arising from a letter Paul had received from Corinth). There seems in fact to be little obvious logic in the overall organization of the argument: it is very difficult to discern a convincing outline of Philippians, and many conflicting proposals have been made. The very difficulty of recognizing a clear purpose and argument continues to raise the question of whether this is indeed written as one letter.

Second, Philippians in its present shape has a number of rough transitions, which have long suggested to scholars the possibility of seams between two or, more commonly, three different letter fragments (for the early history of the debate see Koperski 1993a). The three resulting letters, in proposed chronological order, are A (4.10–20), B (1.1–3.1 + usually 4.4–9 + 4.21–3), and C (3.2–4.3, possibly sent after Paul's release).

The most severe break clearly occurs at 3.1, where Paul seems, after his customary concluding travel news and personal commendations (2.19–30), to be preparing to end the letter: 'Finally, my brothers and sisters, rejoice in the Lord.' After this, we expect a concluding benediction of the kind offered in 4.21–3. Instead, the confrontational material about Judaizing (3.2(or 3.1b)–11) and libertine (3.18–19) adversaries is introduced very abruptly and without a clear transition from the warm and eirenic flavour of chapters 1–2, in which the only opposition seemed to be pagan. Thus, not only the style and logic but even the subject matter of chapter 3 ('Letter C') presents a rough break: there had been no previous hint of a problem with Judaizing opponents. Having had no room for words of praise in this interlude, Paul returns to his sweeter and more placid tone only after chapter 3. At the same time, 3.2–4.3 is the only major section in the present epistle which makes no mention of Paul's imprisonment – not even at 3.10–11, where one might expect it; Pesch 1985: 25–58 and other advocates of partition therefore propose that it must have been written after his release, while Bruce 1981: 281 regards it as pre-dating Paul's detention.

In addition, a considerable number of scholars have argued that 4.10–20 constitutes a third, separate letter of thanks (Letter A) for the Philippian donation. This letter would have been written first, immediately upon receipt of the gift, followed by 1.1–3.1. The reasons for this are a little more subtle, but they include (i) the unlikelihood that Paul should make only fleeting mention of the Philippian gift (1.5; 2.25) but fail to express his thanks until the very end of the letter; (ii) the presence of further 'concluding phrases' in 4.7–9, and then again in 4.19–20; and (iii) the fact that ancient conventions of letter writing make 4.10–20 almost complete by itself, while its removal does not adversely affect the flow of the remaining material. Some (e.g. Murphy-O'Connor 1996: 216f.) regard this brief 'Letter A' as also not written from prison.

It is of course true that the striking break at 3.1 in particular cries out for explanation, and that the excision of 3.2–4.3 would somewhat alleviate the structural difficulty. Advocates of the various partition theories sometimes point for external evidence to Polycarp's letter to Philippi, which appears to mention several 'letters' of Paul to that church (*Phil.* 3.2; contrast 11.3, though this is textually uncertain). In reply to this particular suggestion, however, it is worth returning to Lightfoot's still serviceable argument that this is by no means the only plausible reading of Polycarp: instead, it could either be a generalizing usage, or else a reference to a Pauline letter or letters no longer extant (see Lightfoot 138–42). Polycarp's phrase certainly cannot be used as evidence that well into the second century he knew the proposed fragments of Philippians as discrete letters – a suggestion which is in any case made unlikely by the lack of any textual support. (See also below, p. 40; Weiss 1 n.1 and others, including recently Bauer 1995: 46 and Schnelle 1996: 167 n.386, suggest that Polycarp's doubtful plural might itself be simply an inference from Paul's ambiguous talk of writing 'again', in 3.1.)

A more interesting argument has been advanced by Sellew 1994 (cf. Bockmuehl 1995: 70 and n.36), who points out that the compiler of the apocryphal *Epistle to the Laodiceans* appears to have used material drawn sequentially from Philippians – but leaving out chapter 3 as well as 4.10–20. While this observation does seem intriguing at first sight, by itself it can of course serve only as a somewhat tenuous argument from silence. On similar grounds one could argue for separate fragments containing the so-called 'hymn' of 2.6–11 and the personal news of 2.19–30, both of which are also omitted by the apocryphal author. Nevertheless the evidence of *Laodiceans* might indeed serve as corroborating evidence if the case for partition could be established on other grounds.

On balance, however, this commentary opts for the unity of Philippians. More detailed exegetical arguments supporting this choice will be offered in discussion of 3.1ff. and 4.10ff. below; here we may confine ourselves to a few general observations.

First, and most importantly, it must be said that many of the arguments on both sides have been singularly inconclusive. Partition theories for Philippians have been legion, and to a surprising degree mutually contradictory. Such incompatibility applies especially to the extent of letter C (i.e. 3.2–4.3; see e.g. the lists and tables in Bormann 1995: 110, 115, Schoon-Janssen 1991: 119–22 and Wick 1994: 20). An extraordinary circularity becomes apparent where one dismisses as special pleading the usual defence of unity at 3.1–2 on the basis of new information or changed circumstances, while appealing for one's own partition scenario to precisely such additional developments (e.g. Bormann 1995: 118–26; Becker 1989: 322–32). What is more, in highlighting the tensions between chapter 3 and the rest of the epistle, advocates of partition very largely ignore the important verbal parallels and themes which the supposed fragments hold in common: note, for example, the consistent emphasis on right thinking, *phronein*, as well as recurring links with the opening *exordium* of 1.3–11 and especially between 3.7–11, 20–21 and 2.5–11 (cf. Fee 22–3, 285–7; Silva 15). Similarly, the excision of chapter 3 *tout court* downplays a number of real or potential tensions *within* that supposedly coherent letter (e.g. between Judaizing and libertine opponents, or between the eschatological conceptions in 3.14 and 3.20–21; cf. Niebuhr 1992: 82). One way for partitionists to face up to such problems is to resort to ever more complex redistributions of the canonical text between the three hypothetical letters, as Collange and others demonstrate. Treating the letter as a whole has the prima facie advantage of allowing one to acknowledge all apparent connections and disparities in the argument as they present themselves.

The case for the unity of Philippians, however, has often been no less arbitrary and unpersuasive. Some of the most sustained efforts of recent years have relied heavily on arguments drawn either (i) from the structure required by epistolary and rhetorical convention (e.g. Alexander 1989, Bloomquist 1993: 97–118, Garland 1985, Luter & Lee 1995, Reed 1996, Rolland 1990, Schoon-Janssen 1991: 126–9, D.F. Watson 1988: 80–88, Wick 1994 and Witherington 1994 *passim*) and/or (ii) from modern discourse analysis and 'text-linguistic' theory (e.g. D.A. Black 1995, Guthrie 1995, Koperski 1992, Reed 1997; cf. also Combrink 1989; Aspan 1992 as cited in Pretorius 1995: 279–84). However, what strikes one about many of these efforts, *mutatis mutandis*, is a remarkably similar sort of paradigmatic rigorism and excessive confidence in frequently idiosyncratic methods and constructs (so e.g. Wick 1994: 53, 160 n.418; or Bloomquist 1993: 117, who speaks of the 'scientifically ascertained foundation' of his own rhetorical argument for unity). Rhetorical, epistolographic and text-linguistic arguments for unity (as indeed for disunity: e.g. Schenk 277–80 and 1994, Reumann 1991: 137) too often remain methodologically arbitrary, inappropriately prescriptive in their use of ancient parallels and patterns, or indeed mutually contradictory. They frequently require one to conform Philippians to rigid rhetorical schemes and conventions – or to interpret it solely through the myopically 'synchronic' spectacles of a strictly internal linguistic analysis, analysing the text in splendid isolation from the historical flesh-and-blood complexities affecting the author and his readers. For all their apparent methodological sophistication, such proposals tend to tax credulity and in the end prove very little indeed. (Cf. usefully Bormann 1995: 96–105, 108; Müller 13f.; Silva 1995; see also Reed 1997.)

What, then, is to be done? Given the problems with existing explanations, two fairly straightforward and common-sense considerations about the text and the composition of Philippians suggest that for the time being we may indeed reasonably continue to interpret the letter in its received form.

First, the manuscript transmission of Philippians *as a whole* is consistent without exception. This remains a weighty and significant factor which lends a considerable credence to the prima facie appearance of the received text, especially given the well-documented tenacity of textual variants (cf. K. Aland & B. Aland 1989: 291–7).

More seriously, perhaps, the various proposed partition theories beg numerous questions about what exactly the supposed editor might have had in mind. A modest case might be made, for example, that 2 Corinthians consists of two letters, chapters 1–9 and 10–13, which an editor simply appended back to back (but note Barnett 1997 for a recent defence of unity); a similar compilation has been thought to underlie Polycarp's letter to Philippi (chapters 1–12, 13–14; cf. p. 19 above). No obvious parallel comes to mind, however, for the sort of complex splicing operation apparently required for Philippians. The editor's treatment of the fragments and torn pages in his hypothetical 'bottom drawer' must in that case have been unusually sophisticated, producing a complex new document by variously copying extensive blocks of material from three different manuscripts. (This would be a very different process from the selective but straightforwardly *sequential* copying of Philippians in the *Epistle to the Laodiceans*, discussed above; cf. Sellew 1994: 22.) Given such sophistication, however, it seems hard to see why some of the obvious breaks should not have been improved by someone trying to produce a new work. Why, for example, should one not leave out 3.1a or move it to its 'proper' place at 4.4? Why insert 3.2ff. at quite such an obtrusive location? Why not introduce 4.10–20 immediately after the opening paragraph, at 1.12? (Bornkamm 1971: 203 imaginatively suggested that the Philippian editors placed 4.10–20 near the end to maximize its effect as highlighting their local church's crowning achievement. But this would seem to substitute a wholly undocumented provincial jingoism in place of the early Christian compilers' evident respect for the received apostolic corpus (note Pol. *Phil.* 3.2) – and at the end of the day it still does not account for the structural problems which the partition theory was meant to explain in the first place.)

The combination of such editorial cleverness with such clumsiness is not easy to account for (and is hardly explained by fanciful appeals to the redactor's supposed literary aesthetic or his desire to create a manual for anti-heretical polemics, as Schenk 1987: 3285f. proposes). If even the finished product still has no clear overall argument, it becomes particularly difficult to ascribe a convincing literary or theological motive to the supposed editor.

On balance, therefore, it seems fair to conclude that partition theories have turned out to raise more questions than they answer. The best course of action will be to acknowledge the structural problems of Philippians as it stands, and to try as far as possible to account for each in turn as we come to it – admitting if necessary what Müller 12 n.33 calls a 'temporal' rather than a literary partition at 3.1. That, at any rate, is the conclusion drawn by all the major recent commentaries in English; Meeks 1991: 331 n.6 even suggests, perhaps prematurely, that the scholarly consensus has shifted in favour of the letter's integrity. In any case, the argument for unity continues to enjoy steady support even in some continental scholarship on Philippians (e.g. Balz 1996; Carls 1995, Conzelmann/Lindemann 1995: 247–8, Kümmel 1975: 332–5, Mengel 1982, Müller, Schnelle 1996: 164–7; Schoon-Janssen 1991, Wick 1994; Pilhofer 1995: 114 remains open).

DATE AND PLACE OF COMPOSITION

We will assume, then, that Paul wrote this letter in its entirety to the church at Philippi. But when and where did he write it? Once again, debate on this matter has been complex, and we can only give the briefest of outlines.

The data in the letter are as follows: Paul writes with Timothy (1.1) and from prison (1.12–30), where he has dealings with an 'imperial guard' (Greek *praitôrion*, 1.13). There appear to be fears for his life (1.20ff.), although he himself is hopeful of being released and returning to visit the Philippians (1.25f.; 2.24). Timothy will be sent soon (2.19–23), but in the meantime Epaphroditus, an envoy from the Philippian church, has been with Paul for some time and will now apparently take the letter back with him. All in all, Paul is supported by very few trusted friends (2.20). At the conclusion, we are not told where Paul is or who else is with him, except that there appears to be a distinct Christian congregation including members of 'Caesar's household' (*hoi ek tés Kaisaros oikias*, 4.22).

The three main options for the place of composition are Ephesus, Caesarea, and Rome, in that chronological order; these in turn determine the likely date of Philippians.

EPHESUS

A majority especially of continental scholarship has for some time favoured Ephesus (see the recent surveys in Riesner 1994: 189f.; Bormann 1995: 121; but also Carson/Moo/Morris 1992: 319–21, Murphy-O'Connor 1996: 220, 222; Wright 1991b: 183). We know from Acts (e.g. 19.10, 22) and 1 Corinthians that Paul spent considerable time there (probably AD 52–5) and encountered some public resistance, including an episode of 'fighting with wild beasts' (1 Cor. 15.32). Especially if this latter assertion is meant literally rather than as an allusion to troubles like those of Acts 19.23–20.1, it is plausible that Paul was at least briefly imprisoned at Ephesus (a literal interpretation is assumed in the apocryphal *Acts of Paul*, ed. Schneemelcher 1992: 251f.; but contrast Malherbe 1968, Fitzgerald 1992: 323, Riesner 1994: 190). In 2 Cor. 11.23, written around AD 55, Paul claims at any rate to have been jailed on numerous occasions, while forty years later *1 Clement* 5.5 affirms seven imprisonments. Another interesting hint about this period in Ephesus concerns Prisca and Aquila, who had joined Paul on his first visit to the city and stayed on (Acts 18.19, 26): they turn up in Rome shortly after Paul's final departure from Ephesus (along with Epaenetus, the earliest Christian convert of the province of Asia), having 'risked their necks' for his life (Rom. 16.3–5). Quite possibly, then, Paul had indeed experienced a narrow escape from death in Ephesus (cf. 2 Cor. 1.8–10), giving him good reasons to avoid Ephesus and Asia on his way to Jerusalem (Acts 20.16).

These potential links with Ephesus may be further strengthened by the fact that while Acts (16.12; 20.1, 3, 6) and 2 Corinthians (1.16; 2.13; 7.5; 13.1) suggest that Paul has visited Philippi at least three times, his letter to the church there seems to give no indication that he has seen them since 'the early days of the gospel' (4.22). As a result, it is argued, Philippians must date from a period of Ephesian imprisonment prior to the writing of 2 Corinthians (*c*. AD 55).

Perhaps the weightiest argument in favour of Ephesus is its relative proximity to Macedonia, which would facilitate the otherwise long and arduous travels of Epaphroditus and Timothy

(2.19–30); this shorter distance is also particularly convenient for advocates of a partition theory, as it would allow two or three letters to be sent in relatively rapid succession. Circumstantial support for this location is derived from the fact that Timothy was with Paul in Ephesus (Acts 19.22; cf. Phil. 1.1), from where he (1 Cor. 16.10; cf. Phil. 2.19–24) and eventually Paul himself (Acts 20.1; 2 Cor. 1.8; 2.13; cf. Phil. 2.24) travelled to Macedonia and Greece. Furthermore, Paul's own and other people's evangelistic activity around his place of imprisonment (1.12–14) is similarly compatible with Acts 19.10, 25–6.

Nevertheless, there are overwhelming difficulties with an Ephesian origin of this letter. The most serious of these concerns Paul's imprisonment in that city, which on balance remains an improbable hypothesis. To be sure, the main problem is not so much the *fact* that Paul may have been in jail at Ephesus (though even this is a somewhat tenuous inference from 2 Cor. 1.8–10; 6.5; 11.23) but rather the *nature* of that imprisonment. Firstly, Philippians requires him to have been detained on a capital charge for a considerable length of time, unsure whether he would live or die (1.13–14, 20; 2.17; cf. 2.19–30). Acts and the Epistles, by contrast, are not only silent about an Ephesian imprisonment but give the impression that alongside a certain amount of opposition Ephesus afforded him plenty of open doors for travel, teaching and evangelism – so much so that he deliberately changed plans and extended his stay (Acts 19.8–10, 20–22; 1 Cor. 16.6–9). If in the end he may have had a 'narrow escape' from a threat to his life in that city, that could just as plausibly be due to events surrounding the episode in Acts 19.23–20.1 (cf. 19.30 with Rom. 16.4?).

Paul's failure to mention his later visits to Philippi is admittedly a significant observation, but even so it remains of course no more than an argument from silence. It must be countered by the similarly ponderous silence of Philippians on the subject of the Collection for Jerusalem, even though Paul is clearly happy enough to talk to the Philippians about money (4.10–20): this makes better sense in Rome, where the Collection has been completed, than in Ephesus, where Paul is busy organizing it (1 Cor. 16.1–4; 2 Cor. 8–9; cf. Schnelle 1996: 160). What is more, although no account of subsequent visits is given in Philippians, several passages are at least compatible with a scenario of growing acquaintance and repeated personal contact over several years (1.5, 27; 2.12; 3.17f.; cf. 2.22; 4.9). Along with this, one must accommodate what seems to be Paul's increasingly distant memory of his founding visit, which can happily lump together all of his extensive early ministry in the province as 'setting out from

Macedonia' (4.15). All in all, the evidence may in fact be reconciled more easily with a time frame spanning as many as twelve to fifteen years (Rome), rather than in what could be as little as two or three (Ephesus).

Third, we hear that the capital charge against Paul is specifically related to his preaching of the gospel (1.7, 12–13, 16), while his detention is in the *praetorium*, i.e. on the Emperor's authority (1.13). For Paul *as a Roman citizen*, however, the scenario of lengthy imprisonment on these grounds seems far less probable at Ephesus (cf. already Acts 16.37–9) than it becomes after he provocatively rests his case on an appeal to Caesar (Acts 25.11–12, 25–7; 26.32; see further Tajra 1994: 36; Hemer 1989: 272; cf. also Rapske 1994: 316–23 on extended incarceration). As the capital of the *senatorial* province of Asia (i.e. governed by a proconsul) Ephesus is in any case highly unlikely to have had a *praetorium*, which tended to designate the governor's headquarters in *imperial* provinces like Judaea (Jerusalem in Mark 15.16 par.; John 18.28, 33; 19.9; Caesarea in Acts 23.35), and in Rome denoted the Praetorian Guard (see p. 75 below). Arguments for Ephesus as Paul's place of writing have frequently appealed to three inscriptions referring to a *praetorianus* (member of the Praetorian Guard) near Ephesus, but Bruce 12 points out that this refers to a *former* member of the Guard who later served on police duty in the province of Asia. (This corrects the otherwise helpful excursus in Dibelius 64f.)

Finally, and on a somewhat different note, it seems clear that Paul's rhetorical point in regard to both the *praetorium* in 1.13 and the 'household of Caesar' (i.e. the imperial civil service) in 4.22 is geared specifically to the effect which his mention of certain people in positions of authority would have on his readers in the self-consciously Roman colony of Philippi. Otherwise it seems unlikely that he would place quite such an emphasis on using the official Roman terminology. Paul's point is precisely that at a time of persecution for both him and the Philippians, the gospel is none the less advancing even into the very centres of Roman power (see further on 1.13 and 4.22 below). Such an argument, however, would carry rather more weight if he was writing from the imperial capital rather than from the provincial metropolis of Ephesus. (Indeed we shall see that the syntax of 1.13 seems to demand a reference to *people*, i.e. the Praetorian Guard at Rome, rather than to a governor's building in the provinces.)

An early Ephesian imprisonment (*c.* AD 52–4), then, remains a possible and widely supported location for Paul's composition of Philippians. On balance, however, it is not the most satisfactory option.

CAESAREA

Leading advocates of Caesarea as the place of composition include Lohmeyer, Hawthorne, Robinson 1976: 57–61 and Thornton 1991: 203–16; Kümmel 1975: 329, Riesner 1994: 190 and Silva 8 also allow for it. Caesarea has the advantage that we know Paul to have been imprisoned there for two years before being transferred to Rome (c. AD 57–9), and that the governor's headquarters there were indeed named after its architect as 'Herod's *praetorium*' (Acts 23.35). Here, Paul is kept in closer confinement than seems to be the case in Acts 28.16, 30f. (cf. 'in chains', Phil. 1.7, 13, 14, 17). His friends need to provide for his material sustenance (24.23; cf. Phil. 2.25, 30), as is typical for ancient Roman prisons (cf. Rapske 1994: 209–16; on Roman prisons generally see Krause 1996). The length of his imprisonment would accommodate the required communication and travels to and from Philippi. What is more, the implied setting of a trial involving a 'defence' (*apologia*, Phil. 1.7, 16) is easily compatible with what we learn in Acts 24.10; 25.8, 16; 26.1–2, 24. Paul's disappointment about selfish Christian leaders (1.15, 17; 2.20–21; cf. Col. 4.11; 2 Tim. 3.12) and his sudden outburst against the Judaizers in 3.2ff. could be explained either by reflection on the recent lack of support from the Jerusalem church (Acts 21–3), or by news of other Jewish–Christian activities which had reached him through his friends. Even the hope of visiting Philippi upon his release (1.26; 2.24) agrees with Paul's stated desire to reach Spain via Rome (Rom. 15.28), and does not require the change of plans which a Roman origin of Philippians (and indeed of Philemon and Colossians) would necessitate.

However, a number of considerations make the Caesarean option seem doubtful. The first applies equally to Rome: the journey to Philippi is long and involved, and one must wonder about the apparent frequency of communication. This is admittedly not a decisive matter: merchants and people on official duties could and did quite often travel long distances even from Palestine to Rome; indeed the Empire's remarkably successful administration of its vast territories *depended* on efficient communication and the infrastructure for a rapid deployment of troops and personnel. Thus, at the time of Paul's letter, the threat of piracy had been much reduced by Pompey's campaigns a century earlier, and both roads and shipping lanes were in fact better and safer than ever before (see also below). Nevertheless, it does of course remain the case that travel over such long distances was by modern standards dangerous, arduous and time-consuming, and would not be lightly undertaken.

Another problem is that from the Roman perspective Caesarea was a provincial backwater. In that context, Paul's claims about his gospel contacts in the *praetorium* and among at best a few dispersed members of the 'household of Caesar' would have sounded decidedly hollow and pretentious in Philippian ears – in fact one cannot help but think that he was rhetorically and culturally astute enough not to have made them.

Most seriously, perhaps, a Caesarean location is very difficult to square with a number of circumstances affecting Paul's imprisonment. In particular, Acts gives the distinct impression that Paul was never seriously in danger of execution at Caesarea, indeed that Felix was prepared to let him buy his freedom (24.26) and that even Festus could detect no capital charges against him (25.27). Paul, meanwhile, confident by divine revelation that he would travel to Rome, exercised his Roman citizen's right to have his case transferred to the imperial court; this also served to foil Festus's plan to have Paul tried in Jerusalem as a favour to his Jewish opponents (25.7–11). If Philippians is written from Caesarea, it is distinctly odd that none of these reassuring factors are mentioned; instead, Paul shows himself quietly prepared to face either death or release (1.20; 2.17). Clearly in the Caesarean context the danger to his life would be Jewish, and one would expect comment on the fact that he is experiencing Jewish persecution *in Judaea* (cf. 1 Thess. 2.14–16; Rom. 15.31). Instead, however, Philippians seems to be most compatible with a situation in which he faces the consequences of a *Roman* trial.

ROME

For all these and other reasons, the traditional view since antiquity has been that Philippians was composed in Rome. The second-century Marcionite Prologue mentions Rome as the place of composition, as do the postscripts of a number of MSS (incl. B^1, 075 and the Majority Text). This most easily accounts for the references to Roman authorities and to a sizeable local Christian community, well connected with the civil service, which nevertheless had few direct loyalties to Paul. (Some, less plausibly, appeal to Acts 18.24ff. and 1 Cor. 16.9 in asserting a similar situation for Ephesus as well; see e.g. Müller 15.)

Another significant argument in favour of Rome is Paul's reference to the 'family of Caesar' in 4.22. It is true that these imperial slaves and freedmen who constituted the clerical and senior administrative levels of the civil service could be found throughout the empire, including provincial branch offices such as at Ephesus (Weaver 1972: 7). The vast majority, however, were in the first century based in the West: one study suggests that out of 660 individuals identified in inscriptions as *Caesaris*, i.e. 'belonging to Caesar', about 70 per cent lived in Rome and 96 per cent were either in Rome, Italy or North Africa. (See Weaver 1972: 78f. He notes that mention of the slaves and freedmen 'of *Augustus*' is often later and in any case more common in other provinces; this would account e.g. for the examples mentioned by Dibelius 97 for Ephesus; cf. also Bormann 1995: 198f. for Philippi.) If, therefore, the Christian presence within the civil service at Paul's place of imprisonment was significant enough to warrant a separate mention, Rome will be the most plausible place of composition; this general probability may be further strengthened by the mention in Rom. 16.10f. of Christians with possible civil service connections. See further the commentary on 4.22 below.

A further consideration, as we saw earlier, is that Paul's silence about the Collection makes better sense in Rome than in Ephesus. The Roman scenario of awaiting a capital trial before Caesar may also best explain why Paul still enjoys certain freedoms to receive friends and advance the gospel, and yet why precisely on account of the gospel he is facing a situation of whose outcome he is very uncertain. Rome is still supported by the vast majority of commentators in English; cf. also Wick 1994: 182–5; Schnelle 1996: 160. Lüdemann 1984: 262f. and *passim* seems not to rule out unitary composition in Rome, although in 1989a he lists Philippians before Romans.)

At the same time, several difficulties with the Roman hypothesis have inclined many scholars to prefer Ephesus. Perhaps the most important of these is the capital city's distance from Philippi (*c.* 1,300 km) and the time and effort involved in repeated travels between them. On the basis of 2.26, it is sometimes argued (e.g. Collange; cf. Balz 1996: 508) that five or more trips must have been required; that number could be further increased if one accepts that Philippians is in fact made up of two or three letters.

However, the amount of communication implied is almost certainly less than this (see below, p. 172), and in any case we know that a great many people did travel and communicate across long distances, especially to and from Rome. Hemer 1989: 273f. and n.59 also points out that members of the imperial household (cf. Phil. 4.22) sometimes served as couriers, covering 80 km a day in horse-drawn chariots during most seasons; daily distances of 30 km would be more likely if travelling on foot (on the courier system see further Llewelyn 1995: 339–49).

What is more, Greece and Macedonia also enjoyed excellent connections by sea. In exceptionally good weather the port of Dicaearchia (= Puteoli, modern Pozzuoli near Naples, cf. Acts

28.13) could be reached from Corinth within five days (e.g. Philostratus, *Life of Apollonius* 7.10), though even in summer one would normally allow a few days longer. From Philippi the Via Egnatia crossed to Macedonia's major Adriatic port of Dyrrhachium (=modern Durrës in Albania), from where one could easily travel on to neighbouring Illyricum, as Paul may have done (Rom. 15.19; cf. Gill 1994b: 399; Hemer 1989: 260 n.34), or take one of the frequent crossings to Brundisium (= Brindisi) in Italy; Livy's repeated references to this naval passage imply that favourable winds allowed it to be done in as little as a day (e.g. 45.41; cf. Pliny, *Nat. Hist.* 4.42 and see further Riesner 1994: 262–3, 273–82; Elliger 1978: 45–7.) Conversely, the hardship of Epaphroditus' journey (2.30), and his concerns about communication with his home church (2.26), are of course well accounted for by the distance from Rome: the argument cuts both ways. Nevertheless, in the face of good evidence about the availability of efficient travel, it is surely right to agree with Silva 5–8 that the arguments from geography should finally be laid to rest. See further Thompson 1997.

Other problems include the silence of Acts about Timothy's presence in Rome (Phil. 1.1; 2.19; cf. Ephesus: Acts 19.22) and Paul's implied change of travel plans since the writing of Romans 15.23–8 (but see on 1.26 and 2.24 below; note also Phlm. 22). Similarly, as we saw earlier, a number of passages could be taken to suggest that Paul has not been in Philippi since his founding visit (1.26, 30; 2.12; 4.15; contrast Acts 20.1–6) – but those same passages are in fact readily compatible with a scenario in which Paul had not visited the church for some considerable time (viz., since *c.* AD 56).

By way of conclusion, we may say that although weighty arguments have been advanced for all three locations, in the absence of definitive evidence the case for Rome remains the least problematic. If, then, Paul is most likely writing from the imperial capital, Philippians must have been written some time after AD 60 – and probably after 62, since Luke's picture of the first two years in Rome (Acts 28.16, 30–31) seems to envision a somewhat less severe and perilous situation than Paul faces at the time of writing. (Cf. Müller 50f., who incorrectly suggests that this difference between Philippians and Acts 28 rules out a Roman origin.)

PURPOSE AND NATURE OF THE LETTER

Having discovered a little about the congregation to whom Paul sent Philippians from Rome, it is appropriate to comment briefly on the occasion that led Paul to write it, as well as on the nature of the letter and what it reveals about his relationship with the church at Philippi.

OCCASION

The occasion of Philippians has, not surprisingly, evoked considerable scholarly discussion. This debate has often been linked with the question of opponents at Philippi, about which we commented earlier (p. 19 above; cf. p. 100). Here, therefore, we shall confine ourselves to observations arising more or less directly from the text. Paul, as we saw, enjoys an unusually warm and friendly relationship with the Philippians; this is described as an active 'partnership' (*koinōnia*, 1.5) in the course of which the Philippians have repeatedly contributed financial support to his ministry (4.15–16). One such gift, the first after a long time (4.10), has recently reached Paul through Epaphroditus, a member of the Philippian church who had been dispatched to carry their contribution and to be of service to Paul's general needs (2.25–30). Paul's letter, then, firstly acknowledges the Philippian gift (but see below on why he does not do so earlier or more profusely) and commends Epaphroditus who is now returning home, apparently as the bearer of the letter. The commendation of Epaphroditus is clearly a second purpose of Philippians: it would appear that he is concerned, perhaps not without reason, about his reputation at home after falling ill on his important assignment (and perhaps returning before time: see below on 2.25–30).

Indeed the return of Epaphroditus is probably the primary reason for writing at this particular time: no other pressing problem or subject stands out as requiring precisely this letter. Paul commends Epaphroditus, acknowledges the Philippian gift – and of course takes this welcome opportunity to bring his friends up to date on his own situation and to give them Christian encouragement in theirs. This letter, in other words, is indeed 'more of a progress-oriented than a problem-solving letter' (Witherington 1994: 41). It is in this vein that he discusses issues such as his own suffering and theirs (1.29f.); their need for unity and the mind of Christ (2.1–5), not least in the dispute between Euodia and Syntyche (4.2–3); the danger of Judaizing opponents (3.2–11); and the self-serving 'enemies of the cross' (3.18–19). The problems addressed are not the main occasion for writing the letter, which roots instead in the nature of his relationship with his friends at Philippi. And throughout all of this, the christological argument of 2.6–11 provides the spiritual focus, assurance and incentive for the letter's various instructions.

A NOTE ON SOCIAL CONVENTION AND RHETORICAL ANALYSIS

At the same time, additional light may be shed on the nature of this epistle by an analysis of Paul's relationship with the recipients; indeed the questions of genre and historical occasion are in this case closely linked (cf. Fee 1, though he may overstate the case). Recent studies of Philippians have increasingly drawn attention to the importance of the rhetorical and social conventions used within it, for a better understanding of the nature and purpose of the letter as a whole. Four basic paradigms of Paul's implied relationship with the Philippians have recently been in vogue:

(1) A Graeco-Roman model of Philippians as (in whole or in part) a letter of *friendship* has been suggested by Schenk, P. Marshall 1987: 158–63, Stowers (1986, 1991), L.M. White (e.g. 1990) and others, and continues to find advocates among recent commentators (e.g. Müller 25f., Fee 2–7; also Berry 1996, Schoon-Janssen 1991: 136, Wick 1994: 149–57, Witherington 1994 *passim*; cf. the studies in Fitzgerald 1996 and note Alexander 1989 on the related category of 'family letters'). This suggestion certainly does justice to the warmth of Paul's relationship with Philippi, to his consistent emphasis on the readers' own direct relationship with Christ (Fee 13f. rightly suggests a 'three-way bond') and to the recurrent affirmation (1.5, 7; 4.14f.) of their long-standing active partnership (*koinônia*) in the gospel. That language of partnership comes to expression throughout the letter, beginning (some have argued) with Paul's unusual omission in 1.1 of his title as 'apostle'. Both the terminology of friendship and certain structural elements of such letters seem to be present in Philippians (cf. Alexander 1989; Fee). What better way, then, to describe the unusual warmth and trust between Paul and his readers than in terms of a friendship?

Critics rightly point out, however, that while several of the terms and polite phrases of a classical *philia* relationship are indeed used in Philippians (e.g. 2.2–4; 4.10–20), it is no accident that Paul never actually employs the words *philia* and *philos* in this or any other letter. (Indeed there is little evidence that the NT writers and the Apostolic Fathers regarded Graeco-Roman *philia* in positive terms (note Jas. 4.4, the NT's only use of the noun; Hermas, *Mand.* 10.1.4). The first tentatively positive estimations are in Justin and Irenaeus; Clement of Alexandria is the first to engage with the classical tradition on the subject (*Strom.* 2.19, GCS 2: 168f.), which was only subsequently reshaped in Christian terms (see Treu 1972: 426f.; cf. C. White 1992).) Significantly, too, the social equality which was thought on the whole to be desirable in such a relationship – typically between two individual males of equal standing – is lacking here. Paul's seniority in the relationship is implicit throughout: in the priority of his apostolic example, in the authority of his moral appeals to humility or to unity, in the forcefulness of his warnings against 'dogs' and 'enemies of the cross'. The Greek patristic commentators, moreover, while acknowledging the general theme of friendship in this text (e.g. Chrysostom on 1.5–9; 2.20), give no indication that they regard Philippians as a 'letter of friendship' (cf. Reumann 1996: 100–104). Together with the subtle, but arguably deliberate avoidance of any notion of mutual reciprocity, such factors illustrate the problems of using 'friendship' as the dominant social paradigm, at least in any formal and culturally documented sense. Philippians certainly manifests many informal aspects of a warm human friendship (and one should resist misguided attempts to bypass this unmistakably Christ-centred relational dynamic in the interest of historically uncontrolled, impressionistic categories of psychoanalysis – e.g. Paul as 'ego-centric' and self-absorbed: so Fortna 1990; Murphy-O'Connor 1996: 224f.). That recognition alone, however, does not suffice to confirm the requisite social and epistolary conventions of Graeco-Roman *philia*. See further Bormann 1995: 164–70; Reumann 1996. Konstan 1995 and 1997: 122–48 notes the abiding importance of freedom and reciprocity: even in the later Empire, when scruples about social status could indeed be thought to be transcended among friends, friendship between unequals always remained vulnerable.

(2) The Graeco-Roman conventions of mutual *benefaction* are also adduced by P. Marshall 1987 and L.M White 1990 to elucidate Paul's relationship with Philippi. This somewhat more promising avenue frequently appeals to the classic description in Seneca's *De beneficiis*, which carefully defines the proper handling and interpretation of such matters. Despite certain similarities, however, it is worth noting that Paul's remarkable ambivalence in acknowledging the Philippian gift (4.11–13) would in Seneca's view have constituted a reprehensible breach of etiquette (compare *Benef.* 2.24.2–3). Benefactions needed to be freely given, received with exuberant gratitude, and generously reciprocated – although both Seneca (*Benef.* 4.11.3) and Paul (4.19) allow for reciprocation to be entrusted to the deity whenever the recipient himself is prevented by absence or misfortune from offering it himself. It is, however, in Paul's decidedly muted and guarded (if not exactly 'thankless': cf. Gnilka; Mengel 1982: 283; Peterman 1991) thanks that he places himself outside the formal conventions governing benefactions. See Bormann 1995: 171–81; and the discussion of 4.10–20 below, p. 256.

(3) A somewhat different approach has been promoted by

J.P. Sampley (1980), who argues for the consensual association (*societas*) as the basic paradigm for the relationship. This more flexible model does have significant merits, especially in addressing the arguably quasi-contractual aspects of the stake-holding 'partnership' into which the Philippians entered with Paul before he left Macedonia (1.5, 4.15). Critics, however (e.g. Peterman 1997: 124–7, Witherington 1994: 118f., Bormann 1995: 182–4), have pointed out that there is no demonstrable equivalence between the Latin term *societas* and Paul's Greek word *koinônia* ('fellowship, partnership'). More seriously, perhaps, this Roman institution of *societas* usually bears upon contractual relationships in the public and commercial sphere (a point pursued to somewhat implausible lengths by Capper 1993), rather than to broader social relations including a personal and religious dimension (cf. Bormann 1995: 184–7). And as we shall see below on 1.5 and 4.15, it is in any case less than plausible to construe Paul's unique 'partnership in the gospel' with the Philippians in predominantly material terms (see also Hainz 1994). The true meaning of this relationship should not be narrowly assessed by the extent to which the financial aspect of the Philippian support may admittedly have been of significant help to Paul.

(4) A number of writers have proposed that the primary paradigm is that of a *patron–client relationship* (so recently Bormann 1995: 187–217). In the wide and complex variety of such relationships, the most useful parallels may exist with clienteles formed on the basis of shared social and political concerns. Specifically in the Philippian situation, two well-known and important aspects of public life would have been the exclusive (and religiously coloured) imperial patronage extended to the colony in accordance with the law known as the *Lex Coloniae Genetivae*, as well as the presence of a significant imperial clientele of freed slaves (cf. also Phil. 4.22). While one common manifestation of patronage concerned domestic arrangements within the extended household, it is important to note that the paradigm could in fact cover a much broader range of quasi-familial partnerships of asymmetric dependency, contracted for mutual benefit and extending even to a complex web of political loyalties secured by imperial favours. (See Saller 1982: 7–39 in general, 41–78 on imperial *beneficia*; Bormann 1995: 197–9 and *passim*; P. Marshall 1987: 143–7; L.M. White 1995: 260–61). In allowing both for the element of Philippian loyalty and obligation and for Paul's seniority in the relationship, the patronage model offers certain advantages; its definition was quite flexible and could even accommodate the language of friendship (Saller 1982; Konstan 1995, 1997: 135–7).

At the same time, it remains significant that Paul does not employ the typical language of patron–client relationships. What is more, the Philippians clearly take their own initiatives in this mutual partnership; their free and responsible agency is evidenced not least in their dispatching of Epaphroditus to Rome. The inadequate explanatory power of this model is suggested in the fact that even Bormann 1995: 217 as one of its advocates finds himself resorting to the notion of an 'emancipated' clientele – thus threatening to burst that very category.

At the end of the day, each of these proposed Graeco-Roman relational conventions sheds useful light on the likely social context within which the Philippian church read Paul's letter and understood their relationship with him. In particular, the widespread influence of paradigms (3) and (4) suggests the likelihood that the Philippians would have accepted the need for dependable, quasi-contractual commitments in this 'partnership for the gospel'. Similarly, these latter two Graeco-Roman conventions allow us to compare Paul's dealings with his church at Philippi with other contemporary relational frameworks of unequal mutuality contracted for a common purpose. At the same time, the sincere warmth and loyalty of the relationship clearly conveys several significant characteristics of a friendship.

An important additional perspective in all this is the specifically local, Philippian context of this 'relationship of giving and receiving' (*logos doseôs kai lémpseôs*), which Peter Pilhofer has recently documented. Local inscriptions show Philippi to have been a city with a particularly developed interest in such matters as the close reciprocity of public benefactions and public office, the corporate investment of financial resources on behalf of certain political and religious interest groups, and mutual aid organizations such as burial societies (Pilhofer 1995: 147–51). For the Philippian Christians, their supreme political and religious loyalties had been transferred from Rome to their 'heavenly commonwealth' (3.20; cf. 1.27); as a result, they now felt encouraged and committed to engage with Paul in the public-spirited support of advancing the gospel. (Cf. also Peterman 1997: 51–89).

At the same time, one should beware of the temptation to use such comparative material schematically and prescriptively. Where it affords a genuine advance in understanding, well and good. It is telling, however, that several of the more astute exegetes find themselves having to qualify the standard paradigms, implying that they do not really apply in any straightforward sense (e.g. Bormann 1995: 217 '*emancipated* clientele'; Fee 12–13 '*Christian hortatory* letter of friendship', expanding on Stowers 1991: 107f.;

cf. Wick's oscillation between 'friendship' and 'family letter', 1994: 153–7). Such descriptions merely go to show that no one Graeco-Roman social convention adequately captures what is undeniably a new and distinctive social phenomenon: a Jewish Apostle teaching Gentiles about faith in a Jewish Messiah, with the vision of a church composed equally of Jews and Gentiles. And without wishing to assert an overly defined view of apostolic authority, it remains the case that some sort of implied seniority and divine commission is the basic subtext of all of Paul's letters. This is true regardless of whether his relationship with the particular recipients is one that is further characterized by personal warmth and friendship (Phil.), by an element of parental correction and rebuke (2 Cor., Gal.; cf. 1 Cor. 4.14f.), or by politeness in encouraging a church he has never met (Rom., Col.).

Moreover, while such Graeco-Roman social paradigms may to a greater or lesser extent have coloured the thinking of a Philippian church that was entirely Gentile (or at any rate nearly so), Paul's own view of the relationship will also have brought to bear the interpretative assumptions of his *Jewish* socio-cultural and religious background – a background that in significant ways had remained surprisingly impervious to Hellenistic culture and ideas (cf. recently Barclay 1996: 381–95; Niebuhr 1992: 181–4 and *passim*). Influential Jewish typologies for his relationship with the Philippians could have included those of a rabbi (or even a prophet: Bockmuehl 1990: 143 and nn.69–70) and his pupils, an official emissary visiting diaspora congregations, the leadership of structured polities such as that in the sectarian *Community Rule* (1QS) or the apostolically overseen Jewish-Christian communities of Palestine. Given these other likely influences on Paul's thought, therefore, we will be well advised to remain cautious about attempts to construe the personal dynamics of his relationship with the Philippians straightforwardly along the classic lines of Graeco-Roman social convention.

A similar assessment, *mutatis mutandis*, must be offered for attempts to interpret Philippians in ancient rhetorical terms, an approach closely related to many of the issues raised in this section. As we saw earlier in discussing matters of literary integrity, various rhetorical and epistolographical analyses of Philippians have in recent years been advanced to account for the argument of Philippians – usually in the context of trying to establish the letter's literary integrity. The approach to the Pauline letters from ancient rhetoric and epistolography, which was raised to prominence by writers like H.D. Betz 1979, Kennedy

1984, J. L. White 1986 and Stowers 1986, has recently been the subject of a frenzy of scholarly activity (see the surveys of Anderson 1996, C.C. Black 1989 and D.F. Watson 1995; cf. further Classen 1991, Jegher-Bucher 1991, Probst 1991, Schnider & Stenger 1987, Porter & Olbricht 1993). The application of these methods to Philippians has also kept pace with the wider discussion (e.g. Schenk; rather differently Bloomquist 1993, Geoffrion 1993, several essays in Porter & Olbricht 1993, Schoon-Janssen 1991, D.F. Watson 1988, Witherington 1994).

It would of course be foolhardy to deny the significant and valuable stimuli which have arisen for the study of the New Testament in the wake of this activity. To understand Paul's letter it is clearly helpful to know something of how other ancient letters were composed and read; similarly, we are well advised to ask about the extent to which the conventions of his Jewish or Hellenistic background and environment bear upon his mode of persuasion and on the structure of his argument.

At the same time there are those, including a few cooler, wiser heads, who would plead for a cautious and light-handed application of these approaches. As with all methodological advances, there is a danger of elevating the useful ancillary function of rhetorical criticism to a kind of exegetical 'pan-rhetoricism' (similarly in the case of social convention, text-linguistics, etc.). Despite claims to the contrary, highly precise models of rhetoric or social convention are proving less than helpful as tools for the analysis of Philippians – not least because few of them tend to agree. What is more, the complexity of Paul's background and the *ad hoc* nature of his correspondence suggests that his letters are not conceived in terms of formal 'deliberative Graeco-Roman rhetoric' (thus Witherington 1994: 11; cf. D.F. Watson 1988: 59–60, Bloomquist 1993: 84–96, J.W. Marshall 1993: 363; Kennedy 1984: 77 and Basevi & Chapa 1993: 349 suggest 'epideictic'), even if his style of argument does manifest the influence of a number of basic rhetorical conventions (cf. Murphy-O'Connor 1995: 73). In addition to the importance of Paul's Jewish background, the complex and unusual genre of these writings relates to the fact that while as personal *letters* they are neither deliberative treatises nor public speeches committed to writing, their intended designation for oral delivery before a whole congregation immediately renders less cogent the application of standard principles of ancient *epistolography* – e.g. as manifested in the correspondence of Seneca or of Cicero. (See further Classen 1993, Hengel and Schwemer 1997: 3f, and n. 14, Porter 1993b and Reed 1993: 314–22 and *passim*. On the oral dimension of Paul's letters note the important remarks by Fee 16–17; also Achtemeier 1990; Vielhauer 1975: 59–63.)

This commentary, therefore, will adopt a somewhat eclectic and pragmatic perspective on these methods. Certain recent specialist accounts of Philippians are in danger of losing sight of the fact that Paul's *own* account of his relationship with his addressees is emphatically theological and christological from beginning to end: it is that perspective which is the driving force behind the social conventions and exchanges that may or may not be formally classifiable by the modern exegete. In light of the powerfully christological thrust of the whole letter, including 4.10–20, one marvels at the methodological tunnel vision involved in treating the financial transactions behind Phil. 4.10–20 as the key to Philippians. To regard Paul's 'partnership in the gospel' as governed principally by social convention rather than theological conviction seems indeed to put the cart before the horse; by the same token, 'friendship and finances' can hardly be said to capture the essence of why or what Paul writes in this letter. For our present purposes, it remains of vital importance that every new methodological insight should be deployed as no more and no less than what it is: a welcome ancillary tool for the exegete's foundational task of hearing the text as it is intended to be heard. (See further below, 'The interpretation of Philippians', pp. 42–5.

THE TEXT OF PHILIPPIANS

Happily, the study of Philippians is free from major text-critical uncertainties; the judgement of Vincent xxxvii a century ago still holds: 'The epistle presents no textual questions of importance.' Among commentators, Silva 21–7 offers one of the fullest discussions (see also Metzger). In all, he cites 112 variant readings given in the Nestle-Aland text, complete with statistical information and tables (NA^{26} in his case, but there are no significant differences in NA^{27}). The vast majority of these instances are standard scribal omissions or alterations which for our purposes require no detailed attention. Where there is serious doubt about the text, we will deal with each case in the course of our exposition. The most interesting variants will be found at 1.1, 11; 2.4; 3.3, 12; 4.7, 23.

One other small observation pertains to our earliest extant (but selective) collection of Paul's works, a papyrus of the highly regarded 'Alexandrian' text type known as p^{46} and usually dated around AD 200, though it may possibly be earlier (cf. Y.K. Kim 1988). Intriguingly, it is precisely in Philippians that p^{46} supports several of the more interesting departures from the standard critical text and leaves us with difficult text-critical decisions in one or two cases. (At the same time it is worth noting that the manuscript does not in any case preserve a complete text, and in Philippians lacks 1.2–4, 16, 29; 2.13, 28; 3.9; 4.1, 13.)

A NOTE ON THE 'THEOLOGY' OF THE LETTER

It is sometimes thought desirable that commentators on Paul should give an account of the theology of the epistle at hand. Some, indeed, have published whole treatises on this subject (see I.H. Marshall 1993; Perkins, Scroggs, Stowers and Wright in Bassler 1991). Such an undertaking, however, raises considerable methodological qualms in the mind of the present writer. This is not because, like some contemporary New Testament scholars, he regards theology as alien to his undertaking; on the contrary, it is because he considers the theological import of this letter to be more serious than could be meaningfully addressed in a so-called 'theology of Philippians'. What matters, surely, inasmuch as it is accessible to us at all, is the theology of St Paul and of Holy Scripture, not 'the theology' of a short, *ad hoc* and highly situation-specific piece of correspondence viewed in isolation. We are poorly enough placed to try and understand something of the working of Paul's mind from the whole body of his letters, let alone from a single one of them. (One might argue that the parallel (and, like I.H. Marshall 1993, idiosyncratically structured) 'partial syntheses' in the edited volume of Bassler 1991 are themselves an indication that such a project cannot succeed – even if N.T. Wright's careful prolegomena allow his contribution to do better than the others. See further the acknowledgement of a methodological dead end in Kraftchick 1993b: 34 on Bassler 1991, and cf. Bassler 1993.)

Philippians is indeed eloquent testimony to a great apostolic mind, and many of its themes loom large in Pauline and in biblical theology as well as in Christian doctrine: the sure and unhalting advance of the gospel; the knowledge and joy of Christ as the supreme good; the example of his humility and the promise of fellowship with him even after death; his future coming and a resurrection like his; confident prayer and Christian contentment in every situation; the pursuit of virtue, and so forth. Above all, perhaps, the sovereign power and generosity of God the Father (cf. Schlosser 1995a) and the all-encompassing centrality of Christ himself (no other noun occurs more frequently: cf. Reumann 1991: 134). As the commentary will show, these and other theological themes do indeed pervade every page of Paul's short letter to Philippi; and the christology of 2.6–11 could be said to underwrite the argument of every other part of this document (cf.

e.g. Fee 50, 226–8; Meeks 1991; Minear 1990; Wick 1994: 178–80).

Nevertheless, it seems to me entirely unclear what genuine insight might be gained either for Pauline interpretation or indeed for Christian theology by rushing in to paint a contrived 'freeze-frame' of these themes on the arbitrarily restricted canvas of just one letter. Such an enterprise may well obscure rather than clarify Paul's theology: it cannot fail to exaggerate situational aspects, to over-interpret silences, and to distend supposed theological differences which to the writer may hardly have merited a second thought. The commentator's task, at any rate, is to present the text, to narrate and expound it in its particularity, to display its different facets of meaning, but also to show up the connection of the parts with the whole: with all of Paul's letters, with Scripture, with Christian faith and experience. It is that task to which we must attend.

The interpretation of Philippians

APPROACH AND METHOD

The approach of this commentary deliberately holds together a classic 'historical' exegesis with an attempt to give due recognition to the theological force of Paul's argument. This is in part a considered departure from the current fashion to reduce the exegetical task either to a case study in linguistic or social theory, or indeed to any number of reader-generated interpretations or 'readings' in which the text becomes little more than a tool in the service of an unabashedly extraneous vested interest. My desire is not, of course, to deny the valuable results of several new interpretative approaches, a number of which have been discussed above and found their way into the exposition offered below. It is merely to insist, usually alongside the claims of other methods, that the text itself begs to be read and understood both historically and, perhaps first and foremost, *theologically*. (Cf. in this regard the incisive remarks of C.S. Lewis 1950: 23–5, at the very dawn of the literary critical approaches to Scripture.)

In a commentary of this (or any other) kind, some methodological lacunae and 'ways not taken' will always be due to the author's limited space, patience and talent; and I for one must acknowledge all three limitations in ascending order of magnitude. At the same time, my lack of interaction with several of these newer approaches is not because I advocate the supposed factual neutrality of an 'objective' or 'scientific' exegesis in the older, modernist sense. Historical criticism in that sort of splendid isolation is indeed rapidly approaching its demise.

Instead, this commentary will doubtless betray to all but the most casual reader the vested viewpoint of a Christian author who regards this letter as part of Holy Scripture. The text from this perspective bears apostolic witness to the Word of God in first-century words; and the Christian exegete's work both instructs and learns from the larger interpreting community that is the Church, as together it hears and heeds that Word.

But secondly, and in conjunction with that ecclesial stance of faith, this commentary also proceeds from the considered critical judgement that it is in any case only a historically grounded theological exegesis which can come close to uncovering the agenda implicit in the texts themselves, i.e. the central convictions they were written to communicate (cf. also N. Watson 1987). Those convictions, of course, may in principle be the subject of honest inquiry and debate for readers of any persuasion – even if it is true that in the interpretation of writings claimed (and claiming) to be Holy Scripture there can really be no such thing as a 'neutral perspective' (cf. rightly F. Watson 1996b: 12). Regardless of one's confessional stance, however, any serious engagement with the biblical text will call for a conscious departure from the professional sophistries of interpreters more occupied with taking their turn on the merry-go-round of each other's opinions than with understanding (and in that sense 'standing under') the biblical authors' own concerns. The text itself has something to say and invites the reader to hear it and engage with it: the task of accountable biblical interpretation does not end there, but it certainly begins there. It is for such a beginning that I hope this commentary may serve as a catalyst.

HISTORICAL INTERPRETATION: A NEGLECTED DIMENSION

In order to make observations which have any meaningful bearing on history, it is of course true that a commentator must be aware not just of the place and setting of the ancient text, but also of his or her own culturally conditioned context. The very attempt to gain such awareness, however, quickly shows the elusiveness of an Archimedean vantage point for viewing either one's own or the ancient context. The best we can do on both fronts is to approximate: to ask why the ancient writer said this or that, and how it related to the world and to his readers; and to ask why *we ourselves* ask this or that question, or find this or that observation noteworthy.

The slippery nature of this enterprise, however, does not mean that it is either pointless or fruitless, as if even serious readers could undertake no more than to jumble and disperse the author's words into a multitude of playful or cynical deconstructions, a thousand self-indulgent or ideological 'readings', each one as valid as any other, and calling into question the very need for exposition or comment (cf. Best 1996: 360). This problem may well be the Cinderella of today's much heralded 'ethics of biblical interpretation': an approach to the text that resembles a pianist defending the value of using his Steinway for firewood. It is too early to risk forgetting that many of this past century's gravest injustices have been the consequence of callously ahistorical and unhistorical misappropriations of texts for ideological purposes.

Instead, the secret of knowing both the interpreter and the text in their respectively situated historical context is precisely to view them not as isolated singularities (the Protestant caricature of the individual's immediate encounter through *sola Scriptura* of the word of God *pro me*), but rather as inextricably related and indebted to the texts and the interpreters that have gone before. By asking how the text has been understood and 'lived' by its readers, from its first recipients all the way to those who taught us to read it, we can gain something of the historical perspective which may enable us to approximate the question of what the text was written to say in its context – and perhaps how (and whether) that message is to be heard in ours.

Even for the non-Christian reader, this sort of questioning will broaden and ground the judgements involved in the task of interpretation. For the Christian reader, it will be a welcome reminder of the fact that the interpretation of Scripture is a fundamentally corporate and indeed ecclesial task, to be carried out in common loyalty to the Christian author (cf. Berger 1995) and in dialogue with the living tradition of the whole communion of saints, from faith to faith. For any and all readers, an awareness – however vague – of the chain of previous engagement that links us with our text and its author will enrich our understanding and serve to confirm the practical value of what G.K. Chesterton once powerfully called 'the democracy of the dead' (*Orthodoxy*, ch. 4):

> Tradition refuses to submit to the small and arrogant oligarchy of those who merely happen to be walking about. All democrats object to men being disqualified by the accident of birth; tradition objects to their being disqualified by the accident of death. Democracy tells us not to neglect a good man's opinion, even if he is our

groom; tradition asks us not to neglect a good man's opinion, even if he is our father.

It goes without saying that to do justice to this task here would take us outside the parameters of the present commentary series in terms of both length and subject matter; it would also lie outside the author's expertise. In this volume, therefore, we can offer only occasional signposts to this tradition; beyond that, a certain division of labour is inevitable. This nevertheless is the place at which to signal the need for a companion volume on Philippians which would provide much needed resources for the letter's history of interpretation and, equally, for the history of its effects upon those who heard and interpreted it (i.e. *Wirkungsgeschichte*). Preliminary collections of material for such a volume are more readily available with respect to the history of interpretation: they include Schenk 339f., Silva 28–35, Vincent xxxix–xlii and Weiss (*passim*) among commentators; for the earliest period see also e.g. Souter 1927, Staab 1933, M.F. Wiles 1967, Lindemann 1979 and Noormann 1994. Prolegomena for the method and substance of an 'effective history' of Philippians have been collated in Bockmuehl 1995; the scope especially of recent volumes in the *Evangelisch-Katholischer Kommentar* series (e.g. U. Luz on Matt., W. Schrage on 1 Cor.) suggests that its forthcoming contribution on Philippians may also have a good deal of valuable material to offer.

This commentary, then, can be intended only as a gateway, an overture to the interpretation of Philippians – and perhaps as a pointer beyond itself to the larger historical and theological tasks that remain to be addressed.

For helpful further exploration of these and related hermeneutical themes see e.g. Childs 1995, Stuhlmacher 1995, F. Watson 1994: 223–64 and 1996a and b; and note the Pontifical Biblical Commission's 1993 document 'The Interpretation of the Bible in the Church' (e.g. in Fitzmyer 1995, esp. pp. 155–7).

Outline of Philippians

COMMENTARY

I INTRODUCTION (1.1–11)

(1) Paul and Timothy, slaves of Christ Jesus, to all the saints in Christ Jesus who are in Philippi, along with the 'bishops' and 'deacons': (2) grace to you and peace from God our Father and the Lord Jesus Christ.

(3) I thank my God every time I remember you, (4) constantly and in all my prayers for you all. I pray with joy (5) because of your partnership in the gospel from the first day until now. (6) In this I am convinced that he who began a good work among you will bring it to completion by the day of Christ Jesus.

(7) It is right that I should think this about you all, since I have you all in my heart as my partners in grace, both in my captivity and in the defence and confirmation of the gospel. (8) God knows how I long for you all with the affectionate love of Christ Jesus. (9) And this I pray, that your love may continue to abound more and more in full knowledge and all discernment, (10) so that you may determine what really matters and so be sincere and blameless until the day of Christ – (11) filled with the fruit of righteousness that comes through Jesus Christ for the glory and praise of God.

A ADDRESS AND SALUTATION (1.1–2)

Paul opens his letter to the Philippian church in his usual fashion, by adapting the standard Hellenistic letter format in a distinctively Christian way. Where modern letters would address the recipient at the beginning ('Dear Jane') and name the sender only at the end ('Yours, John'), ancient letters normally began by naming first the sender and then the recipient, and then adding a greeting. A good example of this is Acts 23.26: 'Claudius Lysias to his Excellency the governor Felix, greetings [Gk. *chairein*].' We have many other examples of this in the Bible (Ezra 7.12; Dan. 4.1) and elsewhere (note 2 Macc. 1.10; *2 Bar.* 78.2 and see J.L. White 1986 and Stowers 1986). (Letters then might often end, as does Acts 23.30 in variants, with 'Good health/farewell' (*errōsthai*).)

Paul and other apostolic writers altered this form in a variety of ways, thereby considerably lengthening the letter prescript. Paul typically modifies both the sender and the addressee and offers a distinctively effusive greeting. Instead of being a mere formality, the letter opening became charged with theological force, being enrolled to communicate from the start something of the essence of the gospel. Such documents are still unmistakably letters, but they are immediately set apart as communications in the presence and for the sake of God in Christ.

And it was not just formal communication which followed this pattern; even more personal correspondence like the letter to Philemon adopts this Christian format (cf. also 2 John). With this distinctive letter opening, the apostolic writers inaugurated a whole new genre of Christian letter writing, inspiring Clement of Rome, Ignatius of Antioch and countless subsequent Christian correspondents.

1 The letter claims to be written by Paul and Timothy, and no one has thought of a good reason to dispute this. **Paul** (*Paulos*, from Latin lit. 'small') is the name which the apostle consistently used in Greek- and Latin-speaking circles, in place of his Hebrew name *Sha'ul* (Saul). In addition to their Hebrew names, Jews in Greek-speaking areas would commonly choose a Greek name that either sounded like or approximately translated their Hebrew name (e.g. Jason for Joshua/Jesus, Silvanus for Silas, Theodotus for Jonathan/Nathanael, etc.). According to the narrative in Acts, Paul began to use his Roman name consistently when he set out on his first missionary journey to Greek-speaking Cyprus and Asia Minor (Acts 13.9; cf. 26.14).

Paul and Timothy are both mentioned in the letterhead. **Timothy** was Paul's most valued team-mate in the apostolic ministry. According to Acts, he grew up at Lystra in Lycaonia, near Iconium (modern Konya, South Central Turkey), as the son of a Greek father and a Jewish-Christian mother (Acts 16.1). Timothy was apparently already a Christian when Paul met him, but the apostle asked the young man to join his team after he had separated from Barnabas and loosened his ties with Antioch (Acts 15.37–40). Acts suggests, and Romans permits, a view of Paul's missionary strategy as continuing to win even Gentile converts initially within the context of Jewish synagogues: indeed there would appear to be little evidence for Paul's conversion of completely uninitiated pagans. Because Timothy was legally considered Jewish, Luke suggests it was expedient for Paul to have him circumcised (Acts 16.3). (Some scholars consider this historically implausible; but while there is no confirmation of it in

Paul's letters, one might see it as consistent with his principle in 1 Cor. 7.17f.) Be that as it may: it would not be inappropriate to regard Timothy as exercising a degree of *joint responsibility* for Paul's Gentile mission. He was charged with sensitive assignments in Thessalonica (1 Thess. 3.2, 6; cf. Acts 17.14; 19.22) and in Corinth (1 Cor. 4.17; 16.10). Paul's warmest and most affectionate commendation, however, is given in Philippians (2.19–24): Timothy is presented to the Philippians as a Christ-like example, who is sure to represent the Pauline gospel faithfully. This warm relationship is further reflected in the Pastoral Epistles, where Timothy is portrayed as being (temporarily? 2 Tim. 4.21) in charge of the church in Ephesus; Eusebius later describes him as that city's first bishop (*Hist. Eccl.* 3.4). Hebrews 13.23 suggests that he was also imprisoned for a period; according to the fourth-century *Acts of Timothy*, he was martyred under Domitian in AD 97 (see *ODCC*, p. 1378).

Timothy is also named as a co-sender of 2 Corinthians, Colossians and Philemon, while in 1–2 Thessalonians he is named along with Silvanus. To be sure, this prominent appearance need not mean co-authorship in any significant sense. Here in Philippians, Paul immediately continues his letter in the first person (1.3ff.) and later refers to Timothy in the third person (2.19ff.). The precise role of the co-senders in Paul's letters is debated, but will not have been merely ornamental. Timothy's appearance in the prescript is in the first place intended to raise his status as a fully approved emissary of Paul, perhaps especially in view of his apparent timidity (1 Cor. 16.10–11; cf. 1 Tim. 4.12). Whether he also took Paul's dictation or helped to draft various aspects of his letters is impossible to determine. See further Byrskog 1996, Ellis 1993, Murphy-O'Connor 1995: 6–34; Richards 1991 *passim.*

Commentators frequently point out Paul's omission of his status as an *apostle* from the prescript of Philippians. Aside from the early correspondence with his other Macedonian congregation in Thessalonica, Paul's only epistle without this 'official' self-designation is his personal note sent to Philemon. Whether or not Philippians is rightly regarded as a letter of friendship (see pp. 34ff. above), we have here eloquent testimony to the apostle's warm relationship with the Macedonian churches – and, conversely, to the significance of Paul's appeal to his apostolic authority in cases where it does appear.

Paul and Timothy, then, appear not as apostles but as **slaves** (*douloi*). Although Paul's self-designation as a 'servant' or 'slave' of Jesus Christ is not rare (e.g. 1 Cor. 3.5; Gal. 1.10; cf. Col. 1.23, 25), the only other letter prescript which uses it is Romans 1.1, where Paul is both 'apostle' *and* 'servant' (perhaps as a mark of respect to win the goodwill of that non-Pauline church). At least three factors could account for its use here. (i) It may well have to do with the special significance of Timothy's role in this letter: in 2 Cor. 1.1 and Col. 1.1, Timothy's appearance in a letter prescript follows Paul's self-identification as an apostle ('Paul the apostle ... and Timothy'). In writing to his friends at Philippi, to whom he is about to send Timothy as his representative (2.19), it may be more important for Paul to include him as his equal. (ii) It could be that Paul's warm relationship with the Macedonian churches does not require his conventional assertion of authority. In Philippians the Greek word *apostolos* ('apostle, messenger') is used only in an apparently non-technical sense of Epaphroditus (2.25), while in the Thessalonian correspondence Paul also uses it only once, in a somewhat apologetic self-description (1 Thess. 2.7). (iii) Whether or not one should read into the word 'slave' a desire to 'set the tone' for the letter as a whole, it is nevertheless significant that the term's only other use is in relation to the paradigm of Christ, who took on 'the form of a slave' (2.7). Paul's own example as one who adopts the mind of Christ is repeatedly highlighted throughout Philippians (see e.g. on 3.15–17 below). Timothy, too, has served Paul in exemplary fashion (2.22). See also Minear 1990: 205–6.

'Servant' is a traditional Old Testament and Septuagintal term for the righteous believer's relationship to God (note e.g. Num. 12.7–8 for Moses; Ps. 89.20 (LXX 88.21) for David; Jer. 25.4 generally for the prophets), but in a Gentile Hellenistic context the same Greek term would carry the potentially more objectionable meaning of a 'slave'. The institution of slavery was widespread in the ancient world (cf. Bradley 1994, Garnsey 1996; also Volkmann 1990), and included people in a remarkably wide range of social standing – from the poorest of the poor all the way up to the higher echelons of the imperial civil service (cf. p. 30 above), where it was not uncommon for slaves to have slaves of their own. At the same time, the connotations of subservience were every bit as repugnant to the fashionable bourgeoisie of the first century as they are to that of today.

Despite these unpalatable overtones of the language of 'slavery', and in full awareness of its theological limitations (note Rom. 6.19a; Gal. 4.7), Paul nevertheless specifically adopted it as expressing an essential aspect of the life of faith. While even Stoics might encourage masters to consider their slaves to be their equals, and wise slaves to think themselves truly free, Paul jarringly considers that the only freedom is in being a slave to God. Human beings become slaves either of Christ or of the evil one (cf. Rom. 6.16–19); Paul has become the former (cf. Col. 1.23), and so have the Gentile Christians who 'turned from idols to

serve (*douleuein*) a living and true God' (1 Thess. 1.9). The Book
of Common Prayer, following Augustine, later famously captured
this Pauline perspective in its Collect for Peace, addressing God as
the one 'whose service is perfect freedom' (Second Collect, Morning Prayer). Here in Philippians, as we saw, the term takes on a
special pregnancy, since its only other use pertains to Christ
himself in 2.7. From the very first verse, therefore, Paul deliberately writes as one who views himself in accordance with the
'mind' of Christ (cf. 2.5), the slave of the one who became a slave
for his sake (2.7–8). On the social and theological encounter of
Christianity and slavery see further D.B. Martin 1990; Bartchy
1992; Laub 1982).

Paul and Timothy serve **Christ Jesus**, who appears twice in
this verse and 37 times in this letter – not to mention around 400
times in the Pauline corpus. He is clearly the most important
subject of all, and there can be no adequate understanding of Paul
or his writings that fails to come to terms with this basic fact.
Students of the New Testament can easily lose sight of this reality
amidst a multitude of exciting interpretative 'backgrounds',
'methods' and 'approaches'. The irreducible message of the text –
Philippians or any other in the New Testament – is that this above
all is what made its author tick, and this above all is what he
wanted to communicate. It is not the only point of reference, but it
is the most important. It has profound historical, literary, religious, psychological, social and political implications, which are
well worth uncovering. But Paul's first and last concern is
theological, concerning God in his relationship with every creature through Jesus Christ. (See the Introduction; cf. Lemcio 1991.)
Philippians 1.1 indicates that this transcendent sphere of reference is the shared assumption of both the author and his readers;
no account of their faith and self-understanding can be complete
without this recognition.

Christ Jesus juxtaposes two terms which together constitute a
fundamental Christian confession: Jesus is the Messiah, the
promised 'anointed one'. The order of the two terms appears to be
reversible without change of meaning (cf. e.g. 1.1, 2, 6, 8, 11).
However, there has been much discussion as to whether Paul's
frequently almost formulaic use of 'Christ' reduces its meaning to
that of a familiar epithet (as in 'Judas Maccabaeus'), which may
function like a surname whose original sense is not necessarily
present every time it is used.

This is not the place for a full discussion of this question.
Nevertheless, Paul does use 'Christ' repeatedly in explicitly Messianic contexts, and this suggests that he himself at any rate
retained something of its distinctive significance – even if the

terms 'Jesus' and 'Christ' now mutually interpret each other (see e.g. Rom. 1.3f.; 9.5; and repeatedly with Messianic prophecies). Whether his Gentile readers shared this awareness in every case is of course another matter: to them, the name *Christos* could conceivably look like a somewhat perfunctory proper name without any obvious Jewish Messianic implications. (See further Hengel 1983: 65–77; contrast Chester 1991: 65–78 with responses pp. 79–80, and Zeller 1993; cf. more generally Karrer 1991; Wenham 1995.)

Our letter is sent, again in fairly typical Pauline fashion, **to all the saints in Christ Jesus who are in Philippi**. Paul addresses himself not to a church hierarchy or particular associates, but to *all* the holy ones in Christ Jesus: this is a reflection of the universality and all-inclusiveness which is characteristic especially of the later Pauline writings. The same motif figures prominently in the opening remarks of 1.3–11 (cf. vv. 3–4, 7–9), and has sometimes been seen as part of the exhortation to unity which Paul stresses in this letter (cf. e.g. Lightfoot; Peterlin 1995: 19–30). *Holiness* in the OT designates all those (people and things) that are specifically set apart and designated for God's service. As such, the **saints** or holy ones are especially the people of Israel: in their relationship with God, they *are* holy and are called to live as such (Exod. 31.13; Lev. 11.45; 19.2; Dan. 7.18, 27). Thus, what makes people 'saints' is that they belong to the holy people. In the New Testament, this term continues to be used of God's chosen people, the believers from both Jews and Gentiles. Their holiness is thus given to individuals by virtue of belonging to Christ and his people (as here; cf. 1 Cor. 1.30); at the same time such membership includes the moral aspect of a Christ-like purity and integrity which is both granted and aspired to (e.g. 2 Cor. 7.1; 1 Thess. 4.3–7; cf. Phil. 2.12f., 15). This dimension of an exemplary sanctity is rightly enshrined in the Church's later use of the term 'saints', although in the course of time the apostolic emphasis on the fundamentally equal holiness of *all* Christians was too often neglected. Just as today one often encounters a fascination with a return to 'first-century Christianity' as somehow inherently superior, so this usage has tended to regard the saints of the past as necessarily 'saintlier' than those of the present.

Here, however, all Philippian Christians are described as holy – not in themselves, of course, but only **in Christ Jesus**. There has been a great deal of debate about the meaning of this phrase 'in Christ' throughout the twentieth century, but an emerging consensus appears to allow for a spectrum of interpretations in primarily corporate, modal and instrumental terms: to be in

Christ means to be incorporated into his body, to live in relation to him and through him. (See Wedderburn 1985; Dunn 1992; cf. Seifrid 1993.) In Philippians, the phrase recurs in this sense a number of times (1.13, 26, 29; 2.1, 5; 3.3, 9, 14; 4.7, 19, 21). It has long been noted that the 'in Christ' formula is more frequent in the letters from captivity (e.g. Reumann 1991: 135, citing A. Deissmann). Here in Philippians, the phrase 'in Christ Jesus' has particular significance not just because of its repeated use but in view of the centrality of the example of Christ (esp. 2.5 with 2.6–11), who reconstitutes the newness of both Christian being and doing.

Paul addresses the saints **in Philippi**. We introduced the city earlier (see Introduction); here it will suffice to note that the prescript makes no special allowance for the privileged position and self-image of this Roman colony – as indeed, unlike various secular writers to Hellenistic cities, Paul had seen no reason in his earlier letters to sing the praises of Corinth or Rome. Secular fame and political status are entirely ignored in favour of the Christians' identity as *Christ's people* in Philippi. Later in Philippians, Paul goes so far as to hijack the language of citizenship to show where Christians belong first of all: not to Rome, but to the Kingdom of God (see on 1.27; 3.20; 4.15; note, however, the concession to Latin usage in the form *Philippésioi* used in 4.15).

The difficult phrase **with the 'bishops' and 'deacons'** has exercised the minds of exegetes for many generations. Depending on their churchmanship, readers have either found delight in this early mention of hierarchies or taken comfort in the fact that at least these officials are mentioned *after* the church at large (e.g. Calvin). Some have even wanted to excise the phrase altogether, since the notion of episcopal oversight is thought to be necessarily late and un-Pauline (e.g. Schenk 78–82, 334). It is true that a number of secondary variants read 'fellow bishops', *sunepiskopois*; but both external attestation and internal considerations suggest the text as given in NA^{27} is authentic (cf. Metzger; more cautiously Skeat 1995).

While 'deacons' are found more commonly and in a variety of meanings (e.g. Rom. 16.1; 1 Cor. 3.5; 2 Cor. 3.6; 11.23; Col. 1.7), it is true that Paul does not elsewhere use the word 'bishop' (*episkopos*) in the undisputed letters. In the wider context of Pauline Christianity, however, we find such overseers as early as the Pastoral epistles (1 Tim. 3.2.; Tit. 1.7) and in the speech attributed to Paul in Acts 20.28; it is also interesting to note the task of oversight (*episkopé*) assigned to the replacement apostle Matthias in Acts 1.20, quoting LXX Ps. 108(= 109).8. This same task is in effect entrusted by Paul himself to certain leaders as early as 1 Thess. 5.12ff. (cf. 1 Cor. 16.16). Moreover, 'oversight' is clearly assumed in Paul's assignments to Timothy or Epaphroditus, and it is explicitly included among the spiritual gifts (Rom. 12.8). (It is worth noting that Clement of Rome *c.* AD 96 quotes Isa. 60.17 in support of an apostolically instituted structure of bishops and deacons (*1 Clem.* 42.4–5): his variant reading includes both *episkopoi* and *diakonoi.*) Some have thought to find interesting connections with the communal organization at Qumran (e.g. Jeremias 1969: 260ff.; cf. Hawthorne 8; O'Brien 47), but the links are especially tenuous in view of the plurality of 'bishops' here (cf. Caird). See further Josephus, *Ant.* 10.53 on OT *episkopoi.*

On yet another note, it has been suggested that these were roles or offices *invented* by the Philippian church in keeping with a Macedonian penchant for officialdom (see Reumann 1993a: 449f., 1993b: 88–90; Pilhofer 1995: 140–47; Bormann 1995: 210f. and cf. p. 16 above). Although possible, this remains in the end a somewhat speculative argument from silence. No other evidence suggests that *episkopoi* and *diakonoi* were a peculiarly Philippian invention; indeed Polycarp's letter to Philippi mentions no bishop. Elsewhere, on the other hand, widespread Christian use within half a century of Paul's letter is well attested. In secular texts, the term *episkopos* occurs in a non-technical sense as early as Homer and Sophocles, while Aristotle uses it of a public inspector (see H.W. Beyer in *TDNT* 2: 604–10).

Paul is not, of course, speaking of bishops and deacons in the sense of well-defined church offices as found in Ignatius of Antioch and later church history; indeed we would at this stage be hard put to differentiate clearly between the offices of bishops and deacons. It is interesting, moreover, that Polycarp's letter to the Philippians mentions only *presbyters* and deacons (*Phil.* 5.2–6.1), while Clement of Rome seems to suggest that it is the presbyters who exercise oversight (*episkopé*, 44.4–5). In any case, the plural use of 'bishops' here in Phil. 1.1 indicates that it is not a monepiscopate which is in view.

Nevertheless, one might argue that Paul's language here and elsewhere suggests a nascent concern for church government which then continued to grow and develop. While the apostle's practical ecclesiology and view of Christian ministry provided for considerable local freedom and variation, this was always understood to be under the umbrella of apostolic oversight: the primacy of the apostolate (1 Cor. 12.28) emerges in a variety of contexts and is invested with a considerable authority, though this may (1 Cor. 5.3ff.; 7.12; 2 Cor. 10.6–11; 1 Thess. 4.8) or may not (1 Thess. 2.7; 1 Cor. 9.1ff.; 2 Cor. 13.10) be exercised. Although it is of course true that Timothy and others appear to have served as Paul's authorized representatives, it is clear from the later letters of doubtful Pauline authorship that the apostle endorsed, or was perceived by his churches to have endorsed, a view of his own ministry as vested with a distinctive significance and authority relating both to the origin of the Christian revelation and to church polity (e.g. Eph. 2.20; cf. Ign. *Rom.* 4.3). At the same time, however, it is entirely plausible that Paul's extended absence due to imprisonment prepared the way for an increasing role of local church leadership even during his own lifetime (cf. Holmberg 1978: 116 and *passim* pp. 96–123; Roloff 1996: 146 argues that Phil. 1.1 continues the same pragmatic trend which is already manifest in 1 Cor. 16.15f.).

Why, then, does Paul employ this unusual phrase at the beginning of his letter? One could plausibly speculate that perhaps the overseers had organized the gift for Paul, and so are politely recognized (4.10–19; cf. Acts 15.23; Lightfoot 82; Witherington 1994: 31, Mengel 1982: 224). A growing number of commentators (e.g. Collange 41; Hawthorne 10; Fee *ad loc.*) also see Paul as wanting to reinforce the *unity* of the church and therefore of its leadership, perhaps especially in view of the apparent squabbling among prominent members in 4.2–3. In this vein it has sometimes been supposed that these leaders are mentioned in order to strengthen their hand, perhaps in the face of challenges from the congregation (the 'murmuring and arguing' of 2.14?); but the rest of the letter does not bear this out.

Paul's address here, then, appears at the very least to recognize and respect a group of people who in his own absence exercise a ministry of supervision and care for the Christian polity at Philippi, possibly according to its several 'households' (Acts 16.15, 31–4; but NB the church is together in one person's house in 16.40). However, although these 'bishops and deacons' are here specially mentioned, they are subsequently never singled out as such or assigned special roles. Neither function is clearly defined in Paul's letters, and although distinct roles are almost certainly envisioned (cf. O'Brien 48), attempts to specify their respective responsibilities are highly tenuous. Even the leaders, of course, are implicitly challenged to a view of authority that rests not in titles or offices: this much is implied in the 'counter-office' of servanthood which Paul and Timothy claim for themselves.

2   The salutation continues with Paul characteristically wishing the congregation **grace** and **peace** – a phrase used in every Pauline letter prescript. Used to refer to God's free favour in the Old Testament, **grace** for Paul represents God's free redemptive initiative in Jesus Christ (Rom. 3.24; 5.2, 15), and the gifts which

flow from it (Rom. 6.14; 12.6; 2 Cor. 4.15). **Peace** for the Old
Testament is not just the absence of conflict, but a profound
relationship of moral harmony and security with God and human
beings; typically, this harmony is achieved when grace and
faithfulness, righteousness and peace 'shall kiss each other' (Ps.
85.10). Both grace and peace can only be the gift of God (Isa.
54.10; cf. Sir. 50.23f.); K. Barth 12 memorably speaks of this gift as
God's merciful 'nevertheless!' by which in Christ he reaches out
to a corrupt humanity. The two terms, however, are not synonymous: peace is the condition of wholeness which *results* from
God's freely extended grace, mercy and favour in Christ.
Together, as Aquinas suggests, they comprise every good gift.

Despite the frequency of this phrase in Paul's letters, however,
its purpose should not be seen as perfunctory. Here in Philippians, for instance, both **grace** and **peace** feature prominently
in important theological contexts later in the letter (note 1.7; 4.23;
and 4.7, 9), and the affirmation of peace may well bear upon the
danger of discord within the church (e.g. 2.1–4; 4.2–3 and *passim*).

Commentators often make the point that *charis* ('grace') may
be a deliberate allusion to the typical Greek epistolary greeting
chairein ('greeting', lit. 'rejoice'), while 'peace' reflects the Jewish
greeting *shalom*. While this particular derivation is difficult to
verify absolutely, it is clear that Paul has indeed developed his
own theologically charged Christian letter opening; what was a
mere formality has been transformed into a divine blessing (cf.
Hawthorne 10–11).

These gifts are received **from God our Father and the Lord
Jesus Christ**. This is a phrase which Paul uses very frequently in
his letters (compare Rom. 1.7; Gal. 1.3; 2 Cor. 1.2; 2 Thess. 1.2;
Phlm. 3; cf. Eph. 1.2, etc.). The view of God as **Father** is of course
widespread in Paul and early Christianity, and has good precedent both in the Old Testament (e.g. Ps. 103.13; Isa. 63.16; 64.8) and
in contemporary Judaism. Above all, it seems that the importance
of God's Fatherhood in early Christianity is related to the influence of Jesus, for whose spirituality a close relationship to God as
his heavenly Father was definitive (see Mark 14.36; Rom. 8.15;
Gal. 4.6 and cf. e.g. Dunn 1976: 26–37). In view of certain
contemporary misunderstandings it may be useful to note that,
with a few OT exceptions, this image does not function as a
human analogy. It is not that God is *like* an idealized human
father, but rather that God *is* the one from whom human parenthood receives its very definition, as regards both its success and
its failure (note esp. Ps. 27.10; 68.5; Isa. 49.15; 63.16; 64.8; Matt.
7.11 par.; Eph. 3.14f.). The analogy runs the other way round.

While it should not be over-interpreted, the close correlation in Paul's phrase of Jesus and the Father reinforces the idea of their common purpose and agency, and thus of the 'high' christology which this letter most clearly develops in 2.9–11. (Indeed the only other reference to the Fatherhood of God in Philippians is in 2.11, where Christ's incarnation, death and exaltation are said to occur 'to the glory of God the Father'.) The gift of the **Lord** Jesus is at once the gift of God the Father: that is the acorn from which could sprout a wealth of subsequent christology. Cf. pp. 142–8 below.

In his customary Christian greeting, then, Paul tersely encapsulates all that he is about. For those who have ears that can set aside the familiar drone of its liturgical declamation, Paul's letter begins with a bang, an unassuming device that detonates with the full force of the gospel: the grace and peace of God in Christ, for Philippi and its inhabitants.

B INTRODUCTORY THANKSGIVING   (1.3–8)

As in all Pauline letters, the address is now followed by an introductory section intended to set the tone and to highlight some of the essential themes of the letter. (It corresponds perhaps most closely to the proem or *exordium* in classical rhetoric; see e.g. Witherington 1994: 18, 35–41 and D.F. Watson 1988: 61–5, though he extends the section to v. 26. Note also p. 39 above.)

Typically, Paul accomplishes this exposé with a specific statement of his thanksgiving and prayer for the readers, which has the double effect of securing their goodwill (*captatio benevolentiae*) and allowing him to sound the notes that will dominate in the body of the letter, such as joy, sharing, the progress of the gospel, etc. Such thanksgivings are found at the beginning of virtually all of Paul's letters, while a more doxological formula is used in 2 Corinthians (and Ephesians): 'Praise be to the God and Father of our Lord Jesus Christ'. Fee shows that while some contemporary secular letters share religious proems, Paul's introductory thanksgiving is distinctively Christian (although patterned in part on Jewish forms of benediction). It has become such an established part of Paul's letter format that even its absence is rhetorically significant, as in Galatians. (Cf. O'Brien 1977.)

3 The reference to **'my' God** is found elsewhere in Paul (cf. 4.19; Rom. 1.8; 1 Cor. 1.4; Phlm. 4) and indicates not the uniqueness but rather the confidence and the personal nature of his relationship with the God of Jesus Christ. The expression is frequent in OT prayers and occurs about sixty times in the Psalms alone.

The apostle offers his thanks **'every time I remember you'**. Syntactically, two predicates ('I give thanks' and 'making my prayers') each carry a dependent (*epi-*) clause specifying either the cause or the circumstances.

The meaning of this remembrance clause continues to be seriously contested (cf. the similar ambiguity in v. 7). Some commentators see here a subjective genitive (*mneia humōn*) indicating not the time but the reason for Paul's thanksgiving; they would translate 'for all your remembrance of me' (e.g. R.P. Martin, O'Brien; Witherington 1994: 38). Given Paul's gratitude for the financial gift sent through Epaphroditus (4.10–20), this certainly seems rhetorically plausible; it is grammatically possible, too, if somewhat unusual (for the arguments see more fully O'Brien 58–61).

Two arguments, however, make this option unlikely, one linguistic and the other relating to Paul's own style. Regarding the first, a personal pronoun in the genitive with verbs of remembering denotes the *person* remembered. And secondly, every other use of 'remembrance' in Paul's introductory thanksgivings (Romans, 1 Thessalonians, Philemon; cf. 2 Timothy) unmistakably has his readers as the object. The Vulgate, early commentators and most English translations rightly render these words in this way: Paul calls to mind the Philippians. The reason is given in verse 5.

4   The length of Paul's continuing sentence creates a number of syntactical ambiguities in this verse, chiefly concerned with whether to take the various adverbial phrases ('constantly', 'with joy', 'in every one of my prayers', etc.) with what precedes or what follows. Despite the grammatical uncertainties, however, the overall meaning is hardly affected. First, the studied repetition of **all** (*pas*) and 'always' (*pantote*, **constantly**) captures something of Paul's deliberate universality and inclusiveness, and of his special emphasis throughout the letter on church unity – even in the face of strife (cf. 1.27; 2.1–4; 4.2–9; see Lightfoot 83 and subsequent commentators). The double reference to **prayer** indicates the indispensable importance which ongoing and specific prayer had for Paul's work and for every aspect of the Christian life (cf. esp. 4.6; 1 Thess. 3.10; 5.17). Christian intercession is fundamentally a participation in Christ's mission and care for the church and the world (cf. *CCC*, §2632).

This verse also begins to sound the characteristic note of **joy** which recurs throughout this letter (1.18, 25; 2.2, 17, 18, 28, 29;

3.1; 4.1, 4, 10). The importance of this theme in Philippians is not accidental: 2 Cor. 8.2 shows joy in the midst of affliction to be a hallmark of Paul's churches in Macedonia, as indeed 1 Thess. 1.6–7 recalls how the gospel was received there with great 'joy in the Holy Spirit' (cf. 1 Thess. 5.16–18; Acts 16.34). Its significance in Philippi apparently continued for some time (cf. Pol. *Phil.* 1.3). Joy for the biblical writers is not primarily a mood or an emotion; it is not dependent on success or well-being or outward circumstances (note **I pray with joy**; cf. 2.17; 2 Cor. 6.10; Col. 1.24; Jas. 1.2; 1 Pet. 4.13; see also G. Barth). After all, Paul writes while languishing under Roman detention, unsure if he will live or die, reduced to watching his competitors and adversaries advance in Rome and Philippi! Instead, joy is a basic and constant orientation of the Christian life, the fruit and evidence of a relationship with the Lord (Gal. 5.22; cf. Rom. 14.17). As Philippians shows (note 4.4–7; cf. Ps. 40.16–17; 63.7; 126.5–6), joy arises from the quiet hope and confidence that the Lord of life will turn affliction into deliverance. Joy in the Lord is not a feeling but an attitude, and as such it can be positively commanded (3.1; 4.4; cf. 2.18; Rom. 12.12, 15; 1 Thess. 5.16), as it is already in the Old Testament (e.g. Lev. 23.40; Deut. 12.7, 12; 16.11, 14; Zeph. 3.14; Joel 2.23; Zech. 9.9).

Its prominence in OT restoration prophecies indicates that joy is especially characteristic of the age of redemption (note esp. Isa. 12.3, 6; 25.9; 26.19; 29.19; 35.1–10; 41.16; 49.13; 51.3, 11; 52.8; 55.12; 61.7, etc.). This eschatological dimension is confirmed in many post-biblical Jewish texts, including the Dead Sea Scrolls, where 'God's joy' is written on banners of the victorious army of God (1QM 4.14; cf. further 1.9; 12.13; 13.12f.; 14.4; 4Q171[pPs^a] 4.11f.; 4Q177[Catena^a] 4.15; 1QS 4.7). Similarly, joy is viewed as a reward in Matt. 25.21, 23. Philo, too, relates joy to the future inheritance of virtue and wisdom (*Det. Pot. Ins.* 120; *Rer. Div. Her.* 315), just as he makes very clear that it is a quality resident not in oneself but in God alone (e.g. *Abr.* 202; *Cher.* 86).

It is God, then, who makes his people rejoice (e.g. 1Q34[PrFêtes] 1–2.4 [= 4Q509 1.23]), while believers may participate in the joy of the heavenly worship (4Q403[ShirShabb^d] 36). Early rabbinic literature, too, affirms that Israel's joy in the Lord corresponds to the joy that is in heaven (e.g. *Mek. Amalek* 2 on Exod. 17.15 [L. 2:160]; *Mek. Kaspa* 4 on Exod. 23.15 [L. 3:183–4]; and note Luke 15.7, 10). Joy is described as the receptacle of the Holy Spirit, who lives with a person only due to joy in God's commandments (e.g. *b.Pes.* 117a [*bar.*]; *b.Shab.* 30b; *y.Suk.* 5.1, 55a68–70).

Christian joy, too, finds its object outside itself, transforming the sadness of circumstance into delight in the Lord who is near

(4.4–5). As such, it is an eschatological quality and not a preliminary or passing 'happiness'. The fact that it is 'in the Lord' (2.29;
3.1; 4.4, 10) indicates that it arises from belonging to him who is
both its source and its object. (There may also be a hint of sharing
in Christ's own joy, and of the theme of imitation developed in
2.5–11: Christ's joy, like Paul's, is seen as exemplary in 1 Thess.
1.6; cf. Luke 10.21; 15.5f.; John 15.11; 17.13; also Heb. 12.2.) The
theme recurs and builds up throughout Philippians to its climax
in chapter 4. See further our comments below on 2.17f., 3.1 and
4.4; cf. e.g. Michel 1972, Morrice 1985 and H. Conzelmann in
TDNT 9: 359–76 on the development of this theme in early
Christianity.

5   The joyfulness of Paul's thanks and prayers is due to the
Philippians' participation in the work of the gospel **from the first
day**, ever since Paul came to preach the gospel there (cf. 4.15).
The Philippians – most plausibly including the people mentioned
in 4.2–3 – have regarded the missionary effort as a matter of
teamwork and have therefore taken an active part in it since the
very beginning. Their **partnership** (*koinōnia*) in the gospel is
certainly spiritual in nature (note 1.7 'my partners in God's grace',
2.1 'fellowship in the Spirit'; cf. 3.10; 1 Cor. 9.23). But this spiritual
reality has found its concrete expression both in the Philippians'
participation in the task of proclamation (1.7) and in their
repeated financial contributions to Paul's mission (4.15); indeed
the same idea of evangelical sharing can have clearly financial
implications elsewhere (cf. Rom. 15.26; 2 Cor. 9.13). Peterman
1997: 91f. stresses the significant verbal and thematic parallels
between 1.3–11 and Paul's thanks for the Philippians' recent gift
in 4.10–20; note especially the reference to 'sharing' in 4.14f. The
reference must not be read as merely financial or merely theological; rather, 'participation' carries distinctly financial and practical implications precisely *because* it is grounded in theology. On
both fronts, the Christians at Philippi are affirmed as active
partners with Paul, and 'stake-holders' in the gospel. See also
Hainz 1982: 89–95, 1994.

In every sense, then, Paul and the Philippians share a vested
interest **in** (*eis*: cf. 2 Cor. 9.13; Phlm. 6) **the gospel**. This term
(*euangelion*) designates both the *message* of redemption in Christ
(1 Cor. 15.1–4; cf. 2 Cor. 5.19) and God's power at work in the
proclamation of that message (Rom. 1.16), in which Paul is
continually engaged (1.12–18). (See Fitzmyer 1981; Beker 1982; S.
Kim 1981; Stuhlmacher 1991.) The gospel is the gospel of Christ
(1.27) – so much so that 'proclaiming Christ' and 'proclaiming the
gospel' can almost be used interchangeably (e.g. 1 Cor. 1.17, 23; 2

Cor. 11.4, 7; Gal. 1.11, 16; Col. 1.23, 28). At the same time, by the time Paul writes Philippians the gospel of Christ has become such a fundamentally shared assumption in his friendship with the Philippians that he can use the term freely and frequently, without further modification ('the gospel': 1.5, 7, 12, 16, 27; 2.22; 4.3, 15). To live as Christians at Philippi means to share both in its message and in the ministry of its proclamation – and by extension, presumably, in its 'advance' (v. 12) and its 'defence and confirmation' (vv. 7, 16).

The words **until now** are a further indication that despite certain concerns about unity and about potential Jewish-Christian interference, Paul's relationship with Philippi continues to be essentially harmonious and unwrinkled. This 'now' finds its immediate reference and counterpart in the 'now' of 4.10: just recently, the Philippian partnership in the gospel has once again been demonstrated in the gift they sent to Paul (cf. Bruce 31). At the same time, however, the present reference in this phrase 'until now' (*achri nun*) is eschatologically complemented in the parallel phrase 'until the day of Jesus Christ' (*achri hēmeras Iésou Christou*) in v. 6.

The next three verses go on to offer additional reasons for Paul's gratitude. They form a bridge between the thanksgiving of vv. 3–5 and the intercession of vv. 9–11.

6 Paul's confident gratitude about the Philippians' partnership in the gospel in fact derives not just from their track record past and present ('from the first day until now'). Just as importantly, that engagement is itself part of God's **good work** of redemption which, having once begun, God is sure to bring to completion. (Oblique references to God are also found elsewhere in Paul: e.g. Rom. 8.11, 32; 2 Cor. 1.10; 9.10; cf. Gal. 2.8.) Paul is **convinced** of this divine completion: the verb here expresses present certainty, or, as in the Psalms (e.g. 25.2 = LXX 24.1–2), confident trust in God. The same word recurs with the theme of confidence in God's work and the ministry of the gospel in 1.14, 25; 2.24; 3.3–4. This Christian confidence is rooted not in some assessment of intrinsic likelihood, but in the character of God who unfailingly accomplishes what he sets out to do. Fee rightly stresses that 'this confidence has very little to do with them and everything to do with God', the author and perfecter of the good work of redemption at Philippi.

Nevertheless, from everything Paul has said it is also clear that this **good work** is at the same time being carried on and advanced by the Philippians themselves. I.H. Marshall 12 rightly points out the recurrent theme in Philippians of Christian growth being ascribed simultaneously to God's activity and to enrolling the believer's own efforts (note especially 2.12–13). Most importantly, however, God has 'begun the good work' in them, and he is sure to complete it (see below on 2.13 and cf. similarly 1 Thess. 5.24; *Ep. Arist.* 195, 239; also 1 Cor. 1.8–9). God's good work in these Christians, then, is to make them active participants in the gospel and its benefits. This participation includes, but goes far beyond, their material contribution to Paul's ministry. The idea of God as the author of 'good works' (sg. or pl.) also occurs in 2 Thess. 2.17 and Eph. 2.10.

Thus, at the parousia, the coming **day of Christ Jesus** as Judge and Lord with power (cf. 1.10; 2.16; 3.20f.; 1 Cor. 1.8; 3.13; 5.5; 1 Thess. 5.2–9), God himself will complete his good work, which has begun in the Philippians' reception of and participation in the gospel. This eschatological dimension is highly significant, from the very earliest Pauline letters to the very latest. For Paul and early Christianity, faith in Christ's victory was of necessity bound up with the conviction that God's work of redemption, which must include the righting of all wrongs, will indeed be completed without fail (cf. 1 Cor. 1.8–9). Belief in this coming day of Jesus Christ, patterned in part on the Old Testament expectation of the 'day of the Lord', is not optional: if God's good work is left unfinished, it cannot finally be a good work at all. Its completion will be the day of the King's return to take possession of his kingdom. (With K. Barth 16 we should resist Christian views that attempt to replace the idea of Christ's final coming into the world with that of the believer's personal exit from it – even though in the history of the church, paradoxically, passages like Phil. 1.21 have often been read to suggest precisely that.)

In all this, Paul's confidence is not in the Christianity of the Christians but in the God-ness of God, who is supremely trustworthy, able, and committed to finish the work he has begun. The 'good work', at the end of the day, is not Paul's, nor that of the Philippians, but God's; as such, participation in it frees one from both self-assurance and despondency.

7 Paul's typically unwieldy opening sentence continues without any obvious finite verb. Here, he suggests why it is **right** (*dikaion*, 'just, righteous') for him to **think this** about the Philippians. This word **think** (*phronein*) indicates a considered disposition: with I.H. Marshall and O'Brien we may see in its recurrence in 2.2a–b, 5; 3.15a–b, 19; 4.2, 10a–b (cf. 4.8) an indication of Paul's sustained concern for a Christ-like and united 'Christian mind' (cf. also 1 Cor. 2.6–16). The phrase 'to think this' (*touto phronein*) here denotes Paul's forward-looking conviction that God's good work among the Philippians will come to completion. The same phrase in 2.5 calls the readers to adopt the mindset of Christ, and in 3.15 to adopt the Christ-centred mind-set of Paul.

Similar to the grammatical problem relating to 'remembrance' in verse 3, the explanatory clause that follows here could mean either 'because I hold you in my heart' (so the majority of commentators), or 'because you hold me in your heart' (NRSV, NEB, Hawthorne 22–3; Witherington 1994: 38). Three considerations tilt the balance in the former direction: (i) in Greek syntax the first accusative following the infinitive normally represents the subject and the second the object (cf. 2 Cor. 2.13, 8.6; Fee, Porter 1993a: 197); (ii) the 'for' (*gar*) of v. 8a virtually requires such a reading (Lightfoot 84); and (iii) John Chrysostom and Theodore of Mopsuestia, as native Greek speakers, see no ambiguity but invariably understand Paul to be describing his affection for the Philippians (cf. also Silva 56–7). The term **heart**, here as elsewhere in Jewish and Christian writing, denotes the seat of moral will and emotional consciousness.

Paul is conscious of the Philippians' sharing in (lit.) '*the grace*' which he himself has received – the definite article indicating that it is the **grace** of God in Christ. Various commentators, including recently Silva and I.H. Marshall, take the Greek to read 'my grace' rather than **my partners** (cf. similarly REB; the Vulgate reads *charis* for *chara* and translates 'my joy'). The syntax is indeed ambivalent, and an anterior placement of the possessive pronoun *mou* is grammatically possible (cf. 2.2; Lohmeyer appealed to the similar phrase in 4.14). On balance, however, **my partners** is somewhat more likely both on syntactical grounds (cf. O'Brien; Fee 91 n. 88) and in the oral context of a public reading: in case of ambiguity, the more common Greek usage would prevail in associating *mou* with the preceding noun (as also in v. 8 'God is my witness'). A native Greek speaker like John Chrysostom shows no doubt that this is the right reading.

In any case the divine grace in view is that which Paul received first and which the Philippians have come to share. Strikingly, it pertains both to his situation in captivity (about which he will have more to say in 1.12ff.) and to his continuing labour for the gospel. Contrary to the assertions of a 'health and wealth' gospel, Paul's understanding of grace does not depend on life, liberty and the successful pursuit of happiness. It is worth noting v. 29, where the cognate verb *charizomai* ('to give as a gift') is used of God's gift of suffering for the gospel.

This passage, then, is the first of several to afford us a glimpse of Paul's reflection on his own suffering and possible death. Bloomquist 1993 lists four main functions of references to suffering in Philippians: (i) a *captatio benevolentiae* in 1.5, 7 (p. 146); (ii) the stress on shared suffering as reinforcing Paul's partnership with the Philippians; an appeal to the example both (iii) of Christ's suffering (p. 193f.) and (iv) of his vindication (p. 196). In general, it is still worth heeding Walter's warning (1978) that over-familiarity has too often blunted interpreters' perception of the extraordinary impact which Paul's Christian views of his own and the Philippians' suffering must have had among Graeco-Roman readers wholly unfamiliar with notions of redemptive or eschatological suffering.

Since Paul explicitly relates the Philippian partnership in grace to his **captivity** (lit. 'bonds'), Lohmeyer saw here one of numerous indications of persecution and impending martyrdom. But quite apart from Lohmeyer's widely criticized overemphasis on the theme of martyrdom in Philippians, one should not assume excessively severe conditions for Paul's detention: he was clearly still permitted to receive and use financial gifts, and to despatch and consort with a considerable number of friends. (Cf. Fee on v. 7; also Witherington 1994: 31f., though the latter's reference to 'house arrest' may owe a little too much to Acts 28.16, 30f.) The Philippian Christians continue their partnership in support of Paul's ministry, even where his detention prevents him from exercising it freely: they have thus accepted a co-responsibility for his mission (cf. Schlosser 1995b). The work of the gospel advances even 'in chains', as Paul shall explain presently (v. 12ff.).

The idea of a **defence** (Gk. *apologia*) and **confirmation** (*bebaiôsis*) of the gospel is often passed over. Taken literally, both of these are forensic terms which may allude to the imminent proceedings against Paul in a Roman court (O'Brien 69). Paul realizes that it is not only he who is on trial, but his ministry and the gospel for which he stands and whose servant he is. His legal pun in this respect suggests that the gospel's defence and vindication matters rather more to him than the outcome of the trial. What is more, that larger task is clearly one in which the Philippians are his **partners**; at issue are the public advocacy and corroboration of the gospel's truth and credibility. For Paul as for his churches, Christian life and ministry in any context involve both the apologetic 'process of removing obstacles and prejudices' (Lightfoot 85; cf. v. 16) and the more positive vindication and **confirmation** of the gospel. To be persuasive, such defence and confirmation must take place not just intellectually and rhetorically, but practically and perceptibly. While Christians are called to participate in this task, Paul suggests elsewhere that it is

of course God himself who underwrites and confirms his own
Word (1 Cor. 1.6–8; cf. Heb. 2.4).

8   In a somewhat emotional moment, Paul invokes **God** as witness of his love for the Philippians. Such emphatic oaths are not
altogether unusual for Paul (cf. 1 Thess. 2.5,10; Rom. 1.9; 2 Cor.
1.23; Gal. 1.20); this one seems particularly apposite in view of the
legal language of 'defence' and 'advocacy' in v. 7. Paul's passionate
longing for the Philippians, not otherwise explained, is presumably to see and commune with them (cf. Rom. 1.11; 1 Thess. 3.6; 2
Tim. 1.4) – though the letter gives only a tentative indication that
he expects a reunion to become possible (1.27; 2.24). The Philippian Christians are not just 'out of sight, out of mind', as both
ancient and modern readers might suppose. Instead, Paul wants to
assure them of his warm and affectionate longing for **all** of them,
and not just for certain favourite individuals or groups. Since only
God can know the sincerity of the heart, Paul appeals to God as the
one who really knows how he feels about this church.

Paul claims boldly that he regards the Philippians with the
affectionate love (lit.: 'bowels') **of Christ Jesus**. Originally a
reference to the inward parts (e.g. heart, liver, lungs), the word
splangchna (almost always plural) comes to be used for the
innermost seat of human emotions. In the New Testament and the
intertestamental period, this word group is occasionally used of
God's heartfelt compassion in bringing redemption: examples
include Luke 1.78; James 5.11, and certain possibly Christian
sections of the *Testaments of the Twelve Patriarchs* (e.g. *T. Zeb.* 8.2
'in the last days the Lord sends his compassion on the earth, and
wherever he finds a merciful heart, he makes his dwelling there';
similarly *T. Naph.* 4.5; *T. Levi* 4.4; cf. Pr. Man. 7; *Ep. Arist.* 211; *1
Clem.* 29.1).

Here, the word serves to reiterate Paul's passionate longing for
his friends (cf. 4.1). His assertion of the affection **of Christ** is not
so much a claim to embody the exalted Lord and his emotions (so
e.g. Bengel, in alleged parallel with Gal. 2.20), but rather that he
loves them **with** and through (*en*) the same love which Christ has
for them. That is to say, the source and occasion of Paul's affection
are neither in himself nor in the Philippians: John Chrysostom
shrewdly suspects that this phrase dispels any thought that Paul
loves the Philippians only for their partnership with him. Instead,
the source is the passionate and compassionate love of Christ, a
love which is reaffirmed in 2.1 and arguably illustrated in 2.6–11.
Paul's deeply emotional expression of Christian affection in this
verse is not primarily the sign of a gushing temperament, but of a
gushing christology!

C PRAYER REPORT (1.9–11)

This expression of love for the Philippians at long last leads Paul to disclose the *content* of his prayer for them, which he briefly anticipated in verse 4. Having kept his readers waiting for this disclosure, the rhetorical effect of these verses is to end the introduction on a distinct climax. This in turn casts an appropriate rhetorical spotlight on these verses, which anticipate several of the key moral and spiritual themes to be addressed in the remainder of the letter. Fee (n. 4) suggests that the substance of these three verses could almost serve as a compendium of Pauline ethics: here is a prayer for love with discernment, for an ability to identify and choose what is best, and for the kind of Christ-empowered life whose fruit will endure in the presence of the Lord.

9 First, Paul prays for an abundance of Christian **love** (*agapē*), the most essential and Christ-like of all Christian virtues, without which all other human achievements are worth nothing (1 Cor. 13) and in which all other moral requirements culminate (Rom. 13.8–10). Love is the general theme to which Paul returns in 1.27–2.18, and it is explicitly highlighted in 2.1–2. There, Paul urges the Philippians to love one another; but no object is mentioned here, and it would seem appropriate to read it comprehensively, as applying broadly to love for God and love for each other. As love in the Old Testament is part of the character of God (Exod. 15.13; Num. 14.19; Deut. 7.7; Ps. 136), so love for Paul is supremely exemplified in Christ ('he who loved us', Rom. 8.37). It can take as its object either God (e.g. Rom. 8.28; 1 Cor. 2.9; 8.3) or, more commonly, one's fellow human beings; quite likely both are intended here. The collective phrase 'your love' also highlights the corporate dimension of Christian love, which is not merely a matter of relationships between individuals but also finds expression in communal life and common ventures (note 1.4–7; cf. Helewa 1994: 371).

Paul prays for love in 1 Thess. 3.12, too; but some commentators point out Paul's lack of *introductory thanksgiving* for the Philippians' love, unlike in 1 Thess. 1.3; and e.g. Col. 1.4f.; 2 Thess. 1.3; Phlm. 5; cf. Eph. 1.15. On this reading, Paul thus may anticipate several later indications (4.2, etc.) that harmony and charity at Philippi leave something to be desired. There is, however, no positive evidence here that the Philippians as a whole are manifestly deficient in this area; on the contrary, Paul is concerned that their love should *continue* to **abound more and more**. Paul's prayer is for persistent, steady Christian growth and refinement in love, marked at every stage by the abundance and exuberance that is in keeping with the measure of God's grace in Christ. (At the same time, it is of course true that discerning and understanding love will in turn foster the desired unity of the church.) Paul returns to this emphasis on abundance in 1.26, 4.12, 18.

Such refined and mature Christian love is shaped and informed by **full knowledge and all discernment** (cf. Col. 1.9–11). 'Full knowledge' (*epignôsis*) is a term usually reserved in Paul for the true knowledge of God and his revelation in Christ; R. Bultmann suggested that it denotes that 'decisive' knowledge of God which is expressed in Christian conversion (*TDNT* 1: 707; cf. Bultmann 1952: 71). As in the OT, Christian 'knowledge' is in any case profoundly existential, relational and responsive. Nevertheless, in English we would not normally link love with clarity of understanding and practical judgement: love, indeed, is proverbially thought to be blind! But Christ, it seems, has no place for love that is selfish, indulgent, and lacking in discrimination – nor indeed for knowledge that does not express itself in love. Merely impulsive, undiscerning love cannot stand the test of time (cf. Chrysostom, Aquinas). So also Shakespeare's Othello discovers to his bitter chagrin that he has 'loved not wisely, but too well' (*Othello*, 5.2.343). Knowledge and love are not merely compatible, but mutually necessary: the measure of one is the measure of the other; genuine growth in love goes hand in hand with genuine growth in understanding and the knowledge of God (cf. 2 Pet. 1.7–8; Irenaeus, *Haer.* 2.28.1; 4.20.1). Only love's knowledge is 'full knowledge'; but knowledge without love is 'nothing' (1 Cor. 13.2). Spicq 1958–9: 2.234 suggests that verses 9–11 are probably the NT's most compact and precise statement of the influence of Christian love on intellectual and moral perception. Such perception here depends on growing love (v. 9), an acute desire to discern what really matters before God (v. 10), and moral integrity gained from an eschatological orientation toward the day of Christ (v. 11). (So Therrien 1973: 186–96; cf. Helewa 1994, whose analysis of this passage suggests important links with the papal encyclical *Veritatis Splendor* (1993); Söding 1995: 166–86; also Spicq 1958–59: 2.234–65; and more generally Furnish 1972; Klassen 1992; Morris 1981; Nygren 1932.)

10 Love's understanding and practical discernment leads to the ability to **determine what really matters** (*dokimazein ta diapheronta*). The verb here has the sense of both testing and approving, e.g. of precious metals and money. It is used in a variety of other texts, notably Romans 2.18; 12.2; and Hebrews 5.14 which talks about people who 'through practice are able to distinguish between good and evil'. A comparable notion appears to be present here: discerning, mature Christian love equips the believer to assess and adopt what is truly essential and excellent in the eyes of God, rather than what is not; to distinguish, not merely right from wrong, but also the best from what is merely second best (so Bengel; cf. Lightfoot, Helewa 1994: 385). For Christian love, warm feelings are not enough (cf. Beare 55); nor is Paul extolling the post-modern preoccupation with individual moral or aesthetic preference. Instead, this passage concerns the criteria of what God truly desires, the Spirit-bred ability 'to discern that which God has already marked off as essential or "superlative" regarding life in Christ' (Fee 101 n. 21). Paul himself goes on in 3.7–14 to illustrate this deliberate choice of what really matters: leaving all else behind, to press on toward the goal for which Christ Jesus has called him (cf. 2.5–11; 4.8). See further Therrien 1973: 166–86, who suggests that this notion of 'discerning what really matters' is the key to New Testament ethics.

For the second time since verse 6 (cf. 2.16), once again there is here a reference to the coming **day of Christ**. Even in this late captivity epistle, when he well knows that his own days may be numbered (1.20ff.), Paul's Christian outlook remains emphatically and vibrantly eschatological. Christian growth to maturity is not an end in itself, but is profoundly goal-oriented and forward-looking, as the passage just mentioned (3.7–14) will go on to make clear. Preparation for the day of the Lord was for Paul neither a pious platitude nor a millenarian obsession, but a way of life concretely attuned to the conviction that 'redemption is nearer to us now than when we first believed' (Rom. 13.11), and that his own ministry might hasten its consummation (Rom. 11.13ff.; cf. 2 Pet. 3.12).

Paul's prayer is not for religious perfection in this world, but for the sort of purity and uprightness which will count in the presence of the returning exalted Lord (cf. Col. 1.28; Jude 24f.). The word **sincere** (*eilikrinés*) means 'unmixed, distinct'; it denotes here the singleness and transparency of the heart which is marked by pure and unmixed desires (cf. its application to the moral image of unleavened dough in 1 Cor. 5.8; also 2 Cor. 1.12; 2.17). Verses 15–17 show that Paul has painful reasons to pray for pure motives. The meaning of **blameless** (*aproskopos*), which is also rarely used by Paul, can be either intransitive, 'without stumbling' (Acts 24.16), or transitive, 'without causing others to stumble' (1 Cor. 10.32). Commentators are divided on the preferred meaning, but both here and in similar eschatological passages (cf. 2.15; 1 Thess. 5.23) Paul's central concern is not primarily the readers' relationship to outsiders but the wider issue of how they will appear in the presence of the coming Lord (cf. Lightfoot 87).

11 Nevertheless, the sincerity and blamelessness envisioned in Paul's prayer are not abstract and detached but profoundly earthed – indeed one wonders yet again if he is not already casting a glance forward to the issues of unity, harmony and Christ-like humility which will arise in 2.2f. and elsewhere in the letter. The point of Paul's prayer, in any case, is that the Philippians will be **filled** (*peplérōmenoi*) with the fruit of righteousness. The use of the ('divine') passive denotes the extent to which this fruit comes from God **through Jesus Christ** in answer to Paul's prayer, while the perfect tense reflects the process by which the believers' maturity is brought to completion on the day of Christ. While it is true that the choice of verb seems a little strained in conjunction with Paul's fruit metaphor, a divine 'filling' of the Christian with spiritual benefits is similarly envisioned in Rom. 15.13 ('may the God of hope fill you with all joy and peace in believing'; cf. 15.14; Col. 1.9; Eph. 3.19; 2 Tim. 1.4). The Letter of James speaks of divine wisdom as 'full of mercy and good fruits', while 'the fruit of righteousness is sown in peace for those who make peace' (3.17–18).

Commentators differ over whether the phrase **fruit of righteousness** is a genitive (i) of apposition (righteousness is itself the fruit, as e.g. in Amos 6.12; Heb. 12.11; Jas. 3.18), (ii) of attribute (i.e. 'righteous fruit'), or (iii) of origin (moral fruit as the result of righteousness: e.g. Prov. 13.2LXX; cf. Prov. 11.30; 12.12; Isa. 3.10). The latter option most fully accommodates the OT and Jewish roots of the expression: it means godly behaviour that in turn grows from the tree of a righteous character. The **fruit of righteousness**, then, is understood in moral terms. Here as in Romans (e.g. Rom. 1.17), however, true **righteousness** (*dikaiosunē*) has its proper source and definition in the character of God; and here as in Romans (e.g. Rom. 3.22), humans participate in it **through Jesus Christ**. This is clear from Paul's further clarification and illustration of the term in 3.9. What is distinctive in Philippians is that true *dikaiosunē* (1.11; 3.9(2x); contrast 3.6) is here orientated towards the future consummation, to judgement and resurrection (cf. Scroggs 1991: 218, 220).

Paul's idea here is related to that of 'the fruit of the Spirit' (Gal. 5.22f.): Christian newness of being manifests itself in newness of doing; the one is invalid (and thus indeed un-Christian!) without the other. A Christianity that does not result in tangible change **for the glory and praise of God** cannot come from God. Or in other words, to be 'filled' with the fruit of righteousness (v. 11) means of necessity to 'abound' and 'overflow' with love (v. 9). It is worth noting that 4.17–18 bears witness to the extent to which the Philippians have already borne 'fruit' for God; Polycarp attests to the fact that two generations later they continued to do so (*Phil.* 1.2; cf. 12.3).

The genitive construction 'glory and praise of God' is clearly an objective genitive (i.e. God is praised) and is seen so by virtually all interpreters, although Schenk 123–8 rather implausibly reads a subjective genitive of origin, 'for the glory and praise which come from God'.

Although the text as it stands will hardly allow for this, an interesting interpretation along similar lines arises from a curious textual variant on this concluding doxology. Among a number of textual confusions, the probably second-century Pauline papyrus collection p[46] offers the interesting phrase 'for the glory of God and *my* praise', while the Western MSS F and G as well as Ambrosiaster similarly read 'to *my* glory and praise'. The appearance of this variant in such early and diverse manuscripts does give one pause, as Hawthorne is right to acknowledge (cf. Metzger); some indeed have argued that the reading of p[46] is original (so Collange and Silva). It is certainly true that Paul does on occasion seem to take eschatological credit for the spiritual success and growth of his congregations (Phil. 2.16; 2 Cor. 1.14; 1 Thess. 2.19). Fee 96 n. 3 suggests that scribes may have independently conformed the text to the usual Pauline application of the word 'praise' (*epainos*) to human beings rather than to God. That, however, would require of our hypothetical scribe an extraordinary statistical awareness of Paul's usage; what is more, there are in any case exceptions to this usage in the Pauline tradition (Eph. 1.6, 12, 14). The hypothesis of a correction in the opposite direction seems theologically just as plausible, i.e. to protect the apostle from the possibly blasphemous claim that he shares in the praise due to God. Either way, the textual evidence clearly suggests considerable confusion early in the tradition.

On balance, the sheer strength and breadth of external attestation supporting Nestle-Aland[27] and the Majority Text probably override other considerations, as Metzger 611 also argues. How then do we explain the origin of the variant? It is not difficult to conceive how in a worn or carelessly executed manuscript the common abbreviation $\overline{\Theta OY}$ (*thou,* i.e. *theou,* 'of God') might have been hastily read as MOY (*mou,* 'of me') and even – perhaps as a supposed idiomatic improvement – as MOI (*moi,* 'to me'). The reading of p[46] then represents a subsequent conflation. (The variant *Christou* ('of Christ') in the original hand of Codex D may in its own way add indirect support for an original *theou,* 'of

God'.) Rhetorically, it would certainly be anticlimactic and counterproductive to end the passage in praise of Paul rather than of God. From the perspective of effective history, finally, it is worth noting that the variants of p[46] and the Western text have been of exceedingly limited importance, despite the considerable general influence of Ambrosiaster as a commentator.

This doxology in praise of God, then, fittingly concludes Paul's prayer and the entire introductory section of the letter. (The same theme of the 'praise and glory of God' as the aim and purpose of all Christian existence is highlighted in the introduction to Ephesians, where it occurs three times: Eph. 1.6, 12, 14.)

II PAUL'S OWN SITUATION   (Philippians 1.12–26)

After the complex introduction with thanksgiving and prayer report, we now come to a formally separate section on personal news and reflections, introduced by the typical disclosure phrase **I want you to know**. Advocates of rhetorical analysis tend to refer to this section as the *narratio*, a narration of facts that may help to remove any obstacles to the author's purpose of persuading his audience. Much as modern readers might wish it, however, Paul in fact does *not* offer here a historical narrative of his relationship with the Philippians or even of the events leading up to his letter (cf. Fee 15–16 n.42). What is more, this rhetorical classification does little to account for an important departure from Paul's own usual format: whereas in Romans and other letters this personal material tends to occur as part of an extended section of news nearer the end of the letter, here in Philippians the current circumstances appear at the beginning and the so-called 'travelogue' at the end of chapter 2 (also 2 Cor. 1.8–11; see also below, p. 163).

Paul's departure from his normal letter structure may be understood in light of the gravity of his present circumstances. His lengthy imprisonment on a capital charge, presumably first at Caesarea and then at Rome, must have seemed a serious setback to his apostolic mission. While Paul had been previously imprisoned and in mortal danger (cf. 2 Cor. 6.4–5, 11.23–7; possibly Rom. 16.7), shortly before his arrest in Jerusalem he clearly still had significant long-term plans for a mission to the western part of the Empire (see Rom. 1.10–15, 15.23–8). Here in Philippians, we find no reference to any of this: instead, Paul reflects on his likely fate with the detachment of one who has come to terms with what may lie ahead. His stated vision as a pioneer missionary to all the Gentile world has had to be put on ice, so to speak. If there is any hint of release, it is phrased in terms of a desire to see his Macedonian friends again (1.25f.; 2.24), rather than of new missionary ventures in the west.

For his friends in the Gentile Churches, on the other hand, his long detention will also have come as a blow. Whereas previously there was always the likelihood of a visit from the indefatigable apostle, disputes over church discipline and doctrine must now be sorted out locally or with the help of one of Paul's assistants (2.19ff.). Verses 15–18 suggest that some of his opponents in particular may have regarded Paul's imprisonment as invalidating his ministry, or at least as rendering him *passé*.

On all counts, therefore, it makes eminent sense that Paul should turn immediately to the subject of his present situation in writing this letter to his friends at Philippi. They had long showed themselves particularly concerned for Paul's welfare and sustenance (1.5; 4.11, 15), and may well have felt the threatened demise of his ministry quite acutely. Perhaps they needed a degree of reassurance that his situation was not desperate (cf. Bloomquist 1993: 148; Witherington 1994: 32; less likely is the suggestion of Capper 1993 that his captivity had led them to withhold support because it meant a breach of contract). But in any case this discussion of his own circumstances serves Paul well when in the next section (1.27–2.18) he encourages the Philippians to persevere in theirs (note 1.30).

The section divides naturally into two halves. The first describes Paul's present situation and its positive effects on those around him (vv. 12–14), while acknowledging that two sorts of people seem to be encouraged by his predicament (vv. 15–18a). The second half then offers something of his outlook toward the future, which in any case will mean life with Christ (vv. 18b-26).

(12) I want you to know, my brothers and sisters, that my own situation has actually turned out to advance the gospel, (13) so that among the whole palace guard and all the others it has become clear that I am imprisoned in Christ. (14) As a result, most of the believers have gained confidence in the Lord from my imprisonment and now dare to speak the Word with increasing boldness and courage.

(15) It is of course true that some proclaim Christ for the sake of envy and contention and others for the sake of God's will. (16) The latter do so out of love, because they know that I am put here for the defence of the gospel. (17) The former, on the other hand, preach Christ out of selfish ambition – not sin-

cerely, but imagining that they will cause me distress in my imprisonment. (18) And so what? What really matters is that Christ is preached in every way, whether from pure motives or false. And in this I rejoice.

Indeed, I will continue to rejoice, (19) since I know that through your prayers and the supply of the Spirit of Jesus Christ this situation will turn out for my deliverance. (20) This is in accordance with my eager expectation and hope that I will in no way suffer disgrace, but rather that through all public boldness, now as always, Christ will be exalted in my person, whether by life or by death.

(21) For me, living is Christ and dying is gain. (22) But if am to continue living in the flesh, that would mean fruitful labour. And which I shall choose I cannot say. (23) In fact I am torn in two directions: I have a longing to depart and be with Christ, since that is better by far; (24) to remain in the flesh, on the other hand, is more necessary for your sakes. (25) And since I am fully convinced of this, I know that I shall remain and continue with you all, for your progress and joy in the faith, (26) so that your jubilation in Christ Jesus may abound when I come to you again.

A   THE EFFECT OF PAUL'S CAPTIVITY   (1.12–14)

The first subsection of three verses discusses Paul's confinement and its effect on the gospel ministry. A similar section offering the reader opening comments about personal circumstances is found in other ancient letters (see O'Brien 86; Fee 106 n. 2 offers several examples). Paul, too, employs this opening convention repeatedly (also in 2 Cor. 1.8; Gal. 1.11; arguably Rom. 1.13). This personal section is by far the most extensive of all his letters (vv. 12–26); he takes pains to relate his circumstances to the ministry of the gospel, formulating his own case as paradigmatic for the exhortation that follows in 1.27ff.

12   The apostle is concerned to stress that his work has not been hindered but instead has in some ways actually been *advanced* by his present circumstances. Paul addresses the Philippians as **my brothers and sisters** (*adelphoi*, lit. 'brothers'), a collective familial address referring in the first instance to siblings of both sexes (compare 4.1 with 4.2!). This term was commonly used between fellow Jews of equal standing, and is also employed among members of pagan Hellenistic cults. In Christian documents, however, it comes to refer distinctively to those who are jointly adopted as children of their heavenly Father through Christ who is himself the first-born Son (Rom. 8.29; Gal. 4.4–6; cf. Col. 4.7; Phlm. 6; Heb. 2.11). In the gospel tradition, Jesus specifically identifies the disciples both as his own (Mark 3.35 parr.) and as one another's (Matt. 23.8) brothers and sisters. Here in Philippians, Paul repeatedly uses the term both as a direct address (cf. 3.1, 13, 17; 4.1, 8) and in third-person reference to fellow Christians (1.14; 2.25; 4.21).

The point being introduced here is that although his captivity might have seemed to be a setback, it has in fact turned out not to hinder but to promote the gospel. And as K. Barth rightly stresses, the very nature of Paul's task demands that he should quickly change the focus of interest from his own circumstances (**my own situation**) to the state of the ministry of **the gospel**: 'To the question how it is with *him* an apostle *must* react with information as to how it is with the *Gospel.*' This consideration overrides other thoughts of private preference and choice, and its effect would be especially striking for the ancient reader led by the opening phrase to expect a brief *personal* communication. Paul views his self-understanding as a Christian and as an Apostle intimately bound up with the gospel: both theologically and personally he is convinced that the gospel's welfare affects his own, and wants his churches to think the same (1.27, 29f.). His notion of the 'progress' or **advance** of the gospel serves to underscore its 'defence and confirmation' in v. 7; the same word recurs in v. 25, perhaps as a deliberate echo, in reference to the Philippians' own progress in faith. One leads to the other. (Note also Rosenblatt 1995: 94–7 and *passim* on the sustained interplay of the motifs of 'Paul the accused' and 'Paul the witness' in Acts.)

The terse allusion to Paul's confinement in this verse may presuppose that the Philippians already know what has happened. Alternatively, Paul may have good reasons to be deliberately vague: to disclose discouraging details might cause undue worry to his friends and comfort to his enemies. In any case, Epaphroditus or Timothy will surely bring the Philippians up to date (cf. Col. 4.7f.).

13 Verses 13–14 go on to show *why* Paul's captivity serves the gospel. The reason for his detention has become plainly obvious to all around him. Here, then, Paul first affirms more straightforwardly that even the palace guard has come to know that he is **imprisoned** for his faith in Christ. Presumably Paul does not ascribe to his Roman jailers (and **all the others**, perhaps other members of the military or legal establishment?) a perspective of

faith, but simply the recognition that it was his convictions about
Christ which have landed him in his present predicament. This
statement, at any rate, clearly aims to encourage his readers in
the Roman colony of Philippi: even at a time of hardship for him
and persecution for them (1.29–30), the gospel's progress continues into the very seat of imperial power.

The term **palace guard** (*praitôrion*) merits a brief word of
explanation. Lightfoot 99–104 showed that in Rome at this time
the Latin term *praetorium* always designated the (*c.* 9,000) soldiers of the Praetorian Guard rather than a building; and even
Paul's grammatical construction itself (**and all the others**, *kai
tois loipois pasin*) calls for a reading of the *praetorium* in terms of
a group of people. As we saw above (Introduction, pp. 28ff.), this
is of significance for the question of where Paul wrote Philippians.

Secondly, Paul also alludes in somewhat awkward syntax to
the fact that he is indeed **imprisoned in Christ** (lit. 'my chains
are manifest *in* Christ'). Some commentators relate this phrase
mainly to a general sense of the apostle's participation in Christ's
suffering (e.g. Fee, Silva, Bruce 41; cf. 3.10); but it is not clear how
this could be 'evident' to anyone other than himself. What seems
more likely is an ironic reference to the fact that Paul is indeed 'in
Christ' (on this phrase see 1.1 above), not just as his slave (1.1)
but – plain to see – also as his prisoner. A similar thought is found
elsewhere, e.g. in Phlm. 1, 9, 13; also Eph. 3.1; 4.1; 6.20; cf. Acts
28.20. In other words, Paul conceives of his imprisonment as
dramatizing a symbolic meaning, perhaps rather like Jeremiah in
the pit (Jer. 38.6ff., 22) or the actions of Hosea (1.2–9; 3.1–5),
Isaiah (20.1–6) and other OT prophets. In fact, Paul is 'Christ's
apostle in chains' in more ways than one: in a much deeper sense
he is also under divine coercion, *bound* to speak the gospel (cf.
further Bockmuehl 1988). It is interesting (and either ominous or
ironic?) that he seems to have thought of himself in terms of a
prophetic compulsion even before he was arrested: see 1 Cor.
9:16; Acts 20:22; and implicitly in the descriptions of his sufferings. 2 Tim. 2.9, similarly, draws the conclusion that despite the
apostle's incarceration, 'the word of God is not chained'. Such a
theological *double entendre* on his present imprisonment will
have been lost on the prison guard, many of whom would
presumably have known only that he was imprisoned for his
religious activity. Nevertheless, his fellow Christians are encouraged by the fact that his imprisonment is 'in (and for) Christ'; his
present circumstances serve to advance the gospel by carrying it
into the very heart of secular political power. This is why, in verse
18, he shows himself rejoicing.

14 What is more, Paul's captivity is not just a sign to pagans but also an inspiration to his fellow Christians in Rome. Christian trust and courage in suffering can be a gift of confidence and conviction to other believers (and return joy to the giver, v. 18). **Most** of the Christians at Rome have been inspired by Paul's chains and become confident **in the Lord** (cf. 2.24; 3.3f.) – not just privately but publicly, as they now **dare to speak the Word with increasing boldness and courage**. Such fearlessness and courage would be increasingly necessary in the deteriorating political climate and growing hostility to Christians in Rome during the early 60s under Nero. Paul's example, which Acts 28.31 also alludes to, was clearly infectious – and yet it remains true that it would have been a socially risky and costly business to identify publicly with a prisoner (cf. Rapske 1994: 293–4).

Some translations (e.g. KJV, NIV, Luther) and commentators take **in the Lord** to modify not the Christian confidence but the **brothers and sisters**. Although grammatically possible, this reading goes counter to Paul's predominantly theological usage of the verb 'to be confident' (perfect of *peithô* + *en*: see 2.24; 3.3f.; Rom. 14.14; Gal. 5.10; 2 Thess. 3.4; 2 Cor. 1.9). As Fee and O'Brien point out, the ground of Christian confidence here is in the Lord, while **from my imprisonment** indicates the instrument God has used.

The Word must be the word of God, the gospel; Paul's absolute use of it in this sense is uncommon, but not without parallel (see 1 Thess. 1.6; Gal. 6.6; Col. 4.3; cf. 2 Tim. 4.2). Most of the best early manuscripts in fact add 'of God'; but on the balance of Pauline usage its later insertion by a scribe is more likely than its omission.

Far from being a frustration of God's gospel purpose, therefore, Paul's captivity turns out to be an instrument of its advance.

B DIFFERENT MOTIVATIONS FOR PREACHING (1.15–18)

The following paragraph is a somewhat unexpected excursus. Paul's joy, we discover, is tempered with a measure of disappointment at the fact that some people's evangelistic boldness appears to be driven by mixed motives, including envy and resentment. The nature and purpose of Paul's confinement have genuinely strengthened many believers in the task of evangelism, the majority being motivated by love and good will. Others, however, smell an opportunity for self-advancement, even at the expense of causing the captive Paul distress (v. 17). The divisions in the Roman house churches are already evident in Paul's letter to Rome several years earlier (e.g. Rom. 14.1–15.6), and competing interests are clearly still at work. What is even more striking, however, is the remarkable spirit of generosity in which Paul reacts to both groups (v. 18).

15 One group is characterized by motivations of **envy** (*phthonos*) **and contention** (*eritheia*), strong terms which, as several commentators point out, elsewhere occur in Paul's lists of vices (e.g. Gal. 5.20f.; Rom. 1.29). In other words, such qualities designate those who are 'of the flesh' (1 Cor. 3.3) and 'who will not inherit the kingdom of God' (Gal. 5.21) – though they also appear to be endemic in the church at Corinth (2 Cor. 12.20); in 1 Tim. 6.4 they are characteristic of false teachers. In Roman public life, similar motivations of **envy and contention** are attested in situations where in the context of court trials public adversaries engage in public manoeuvring to make life difficult for each other. The first-century orator Dio Chrysostom saw envy against one's enemies expressed in plotting against them and gloating at their misfortune (*Or.* 77/78.29, 43 and *passim.* Cf. Winter 1994: 93–5, who suspects that Paul's opponents are intending to cause him as much trouble as possible in his pre-trial detention, mobilizing ill-will and enmity against him and attempting if possible to prejudice the outcome of his trial.).

But who are these opponents? The fact that they **proclaim Christ** (v. 15) implies that they are fellow Christians of some sort, even though their proclamation is for all the wrong motives and thus presumably self-serving rather than in the service of Christ (note 2.21; 3.18f.; cf. Rom. 16.18). Some scholars have argued for a Gnosticizing orientation (as in the case of some at Corinth), others for a Judaizing one (as in Galatia). The vehemence of 3.2ff. might incline one against seeing Judaizing opponents in the more moderate description which Paul offers here (*pace* Lightfoot 88f.; cf. Fee). Nor, however, does Paul's vitriolic reaction to Galatian Judaizers a decade earlier rule out the possibility of a more measured, but still critical view of Roman ones. (Rom. 9–11 and 14–15 begin to suggest, and Eph. 2 later confirms, that even Pauline Christianity could in any case conceive the whole Jew–Gentile problem in a much less polarized fashion. Cf. further Silva; Niebuhr 1992: 136–84 *passim.*) The animosity of these adversaries could arise equally well from Paul's late arrival on an originally conservative Jewish-Christian scene at Rome, as from a Gentile, 'Corinthian' impatience at his supposed lack of enlightened radicalism in either theology or praxis (cf. 1 Cor. 5.1ff.; 6.12ff.; 10.1ff.). It takes little imagination to construct either or both groups from the positions addressed in Rom. 14.1–15.6. If the opponents are Jewish Christians, as may on balance be more likely, Paul's sentiment here could reflect a hardening of the polarity between the so-called 'strong' and the 'weak' since he sent his letter to Rome about five years earlier. In any case these adversaries clearly do 'preach Christ': Fee proposes somewhat speculatively that while Galatians addresses 'sheep stealers' who wish to circumcise Christians, Phil. 1.17 deals with those who evangelize *non-Christians*. It is merely the motivation and conduct of that evangelism which cause Paul hurt and anguish (vv. 15, 17).

At the end of the day, therefore, the primary driving motive of the Roman competitors may well be simply what Paul says it is: not so much the particular content of their preaching but their selfish ambition along with the desire to rub salt in his wounds (so Bruce 44; O'Brien 105, at the end of an extended discussion). It is with distinct sadness and disappointment that Paul refers to the same or a related group of evangelists again in 2.21: the very people who should have been his partners pursue their ministry not for Christ's interests but for their own. Clement of Rome, writing to Corinth in AD 96, writes that it was envy and contention from opponents which caused the apostles to be persecuted (*1 Clem.* 5.2–5). Calculating self-aggrandizement and petty-mindedness have long been endemic in human societies, and the Church has never been exempt. (Note the astute instructions in 1 Pet. 5.2–3 to pastors concerned about money and power.) By his own tolerance here, Paul may also wish to set an example to his readers at Philippi of how to handle personal animosity within their own church (see 4.2–3; cf. Beare, Melick, Fee).

This attitude of serving God with mixed motives can be helpfully illustrated from early rabbinic thought. The rabbis believed that the work of God (which for them meant the study and practice of God's revelation in Scripture) ought to be done not for selfish reasons but *lishmah*, 'for its own sake' (e.g. *m.Abot* 6.1). 'Do not say, I will work in the Torah with the purpose of being called Sage or Rabbi, or to acquire fortune, or even to be rewarded for it in the world to come. But do it for the sake of your love for God, though the glory will come in the end' (*Sifre Deut.* 41 on Deut. 11.13; cf. *b.Ned.* 62a; similarly *Midr. Pss.* 119.46, commenting on Ps. 119.113, 'I hate the double-minded, but I love your Torah'). It is interesting to compare the Pauline motive of 'love' in verse 16, as well as 'God's will' in verse 15.

The second group of evangelists pursue their work **for the sake of God's will** (*di'eudokian*). Most interpreters translate this phrase 'out of goodwill', indicating the human attitude which these people have towards Paul, in parallel with the envy and rivalry of the others. However, it is worth considering that the only other use of the word in Philippians clearly designates the *divine* will and good pleasure (2.13). What is more, almost every other use of the word in the New Testament refers to *God's* will or pleasure; and the only exceptions (Rom. 10.1; possibly 2 Thess. 1.11) clearly denote a person's resolve or desire, rather than a feeling of 'goodwill'. Outside the New Testament, the word is used primarily in Jewish and Christian literature; in the LXX (esp. Sirach) it predominantly denotes God's pleasure or will, rarely human desire, but not 'goodwill' in the sense of a positive and constructive human attitude to others. This in turn corresponds to the use of *ratzón* in the Dead Sea Scrolls, for instance in the phrase 'children of his favour', 1QH 4.32–33; 11.9. (This phrase is now widely recognized as equivalent to 'the people of his favour' in Luke 2.14, where *eudokia* occurs without article or modifier, as here in Phil. 1.15.) The Talmud frequently speaks of 'the will' in this sense, while numerous synagogal prayers begin with the words, 'May it be [the] will before you'. (Cf. also Matt. 11.26 par.; *m.Abot* 2.4, 'do his will as your will'; and see further G. Schrenk, *TDNT* 2: 742–5.)

Contemporary usage, therefore, suggests that for Paul the phrase almost certainly does *not* mean in the first instance a feeling of goodwill towards himself, contrary to the claim of some dictionaries (e.g. BAGD) and many commentators. Instead, the sincere evangelists are primarily motivated by the will of God and the love which according to 2.1 is in Christ (cf. similarly O'Brien). Grammatically, it is in any case worth noting that the Greek construction both here and in the first half of the verse (*dia* + accusative, rather than genitive) suggests not instrumentality ('out of their goodwill') but purpose ('because of' or **'for the sake of'** the divine will). See BDF §222; Moule 1959: 54f.

(Many late MSS, including those following the Majority Text, have displaced verse 17 before verse 16; this is reflected in English notably in the KJV. But there is really no substantive case for originality or even for a wide enough canonical recognition of that order.)

16   Each of these two groups is now described in a further verse, beginning in chiastic sequence with the apostle's friends. They are genuinely motivated by **love**. This presumably includes love for Paul, since it is shaped by their recognition of the real significance of his confinement. It is intriguing that in Paul's prayer for the Philippians love is also explained in terms of an ability to perceive 'what really matters' (1.9–10). The same perceptive love here applies also to Paul's captivity: he is **put**

there, divinely appointed and destined (cf. e.g. O'Brien 101 and n. 16) for the **defence** not of himself but **of the gospel**, as was already indicated in verse 7. These people unselfishly stand in the breach left by Paul. At the same time, it is important to bear in mind that within the context of Philippians (and of Pauline theology) as a whole, Christian love always arises from being 'in Christ': cf. 1.8; 2.1.

17 Certain others, however, are driven by the poisonous fantasies of jealousy and **selfish ambition**: in contrast to verse 16, their actions arise not from what they 'know' but what they (wrongly) *imagine*. They also proclaim Christ, but theirs is a petty, territorial vision; their aim is naked self-advancement. The robe of 'Christian ministry' cloaks many a shameless idolatry. Selfish ambition is apparently a problem in Philippi, too (2.3; cf. 4.2?); here as elsewhere, too many 'look out for their own interests', 2.21. Since Paul's concern is the defence not of himself but of the gospel, the adversaries' desire to cause him **distress** (or 'affliction') can leave him relatively calm and unflustered.

18 The only thing that really matters is **that Christ is preached in every way. Pure motives or false** – this sets out rather starkly a fundamental choice of human disposition: literally, 'pretext or truth'. 'Pretext' (*prophasis*) is a term used in the gospels to describe the actions of hypocritical scholars of religion (Mark 12.40 par.); elsewhere Paul himself uses similar terminology to stress the need for a ministry of transparent truthfulness instead of pretext (2 Cor. 4.2; 1 Thess. 2.5).

'Post-modern' sensibilities tend to balk at this polarity. The twentieth century's experience and philosophy have painfully taught us that few people's motives are entirely unmixed: we can understand Pilate's shoulder-shrugging agnosticism about 'truth', seeing it at best as a subjective intellectual or political expedient (cf. John 18.38). Still, in every century those who resist regimes of falsehood and oppression have staked their lives on the belief in a difference between truth and untruth; and even in happier times the escape from truth makes people champions not of freedom but of fashion.

Be that as it may: most of us still instinctively acknowledge the common-sense distinction between sincerity and duplicity of behaviour; and that is partly what Paul has in mind. Some, that is, pursue evangelism for its own sake, others as a cover for their own or their party's 'success' in numbers, prestige and influence within the Roman church. Beyond that, however, it is worth noting that the biblical understanding of sincerity is in fact never solely subjective. Its point of reference is never finally in a framework of personal or even social plausibility, but in the truth of God: 'refusing to practise cunning or to handle God's word deceitfully, we present ourselves to every human conscience before God in a visible demonstration of the truth' (2 Cor. 4.2; cf. Prov. 21.2; Mark 12.14).

Paul does not of course condone or justify such dubious motives on the part of his competitors; his language is clearly too critical for that. Nevertheless, his tone does seem to have mellowed considerably since writing Galatians (contrast Gal. 1.9) or even 2 Corinthians 11. Suffering and weakness in the meantime (cf. 2 Cor. 1.8–9; 12.7–10) may well have taught him patience and humility; as in 1.6 and Rom. 8, there are also signs of a deeper, steadier trust in God's promise and power to bring the good work of the gospel to certain completion – with or without Paul. Where Christ is insulted or the gospel perverted he can still fiercely object, as 3.2ff. shows. Here, however, the point is more the motivation of the preachers than the content of their message. He has only one criterion: so long as *Christ* is preached, he will rejoice. What really matters is the preaching of Christ; being for or against Paul, albeit sometimes personally painful, is a minor issue. In the wider canonical context this new attitude also evokes, as it may have done even for Paul himself, echoes of Jesus' saying about 'those who are not against you' (Luke 9.49f. par.).

In this I rejoice: for the pervasive theme of joy see our discussion of 1.4 above and 4.4–5 below. The apostle rejoices because the preaching of the gospel in Rome is itself the 'advance' of the gospel which he spoke about in v. 12.

In expressing this single-minded joy in the advance of the gospel rather than in self-advancement, Paul once again demonstrates the kind of practical example which in 3.17 and 4.9 he urges the Philippians to imitate. Not that he does not feel personal injury, or that he has relinquished all ambition: but in Christ his ambition and desire have found a true and satisfying goal – a goal by which all pain and gain are redefined (cf. 3.7–14). Things have turned out well for the gospel (v.12): that is cause for joy.

C   CHRISTIAN CONFIDENCE IN LIFE AND DEATH   (1.18b–26)

Most commentators and translations sensibly take the last part of verse 18 (**Indeed, I will continue to rejoice**) with the following section: offset by a contrastive 'indeed' (*alla kai*, lit. 'but also'), it picks up the same theme of joy in the future rather than the present tense, and finds its elaboration in verse 19f. (note the *gar*, **since**). Others, however (e.g. Beare, Silva), consider all of verse 18 to belong here, so that verses 18–26 form a kind of extended discourse on the apostle's reaction to his captivity and his opponents. Either way, verse 18 clearly functions as a bridge, linking Paul's description of the more particular concerns and conditions of his detention with the more general statement of his overall spiritual attitude and disposition. Paul **will continue to rejoice:** with this change of tense comes a change of key. While his joy in the previous verse is based on the present advance of the gospel, here it arises from his confidence in the future.

19 Verse 19 explains the reason for Paul's joy about the future. In Greek, the sentence begins quite emphatically, 'I will rejoice, since **I know that … this … will turn out for my deliverance**'! Everything else simply modifies this opening assertion.

How can Paul 'know'? And what does he mean by 'deliverance'? Such confident assurance is indeed remarkable, not least in view of the fact that Paul evidently does *not* know whether his trial will bring life or death (v. 20b). A couple of observations, however, can help to make sense of his astonishing claim. First, Paul's assertion is in fact laced with an unmarked but highly evocative Old Testament quotation: in analogous circumstances of innocent affliction the righteous Job, too, says, 'Even this will turn out for my deliverance' (Job 13.16 LXX; similarly the Targum; cf. Schaller 1980; Fee 130f.). Scholars nowadays like to use the fashionable term 'intertextuality' to describe this literary phenomenon of evocative allusions to earlier texts; it is, however, a phenomenon which has long been second nature in Scripture-based communities of faith (see esp. Hays 1989: 23–6 and *passim*). Paul weaves into his discourse the words of a biblical man of faith which, although self-explanatory, nevertheless would evoke in a biblically literate readership both the tense drama and the reassurance of a familiar text (similar examples in Philippians include 2.10, 15f.; 4.5). When friends let him down, Job, too, refuses to give up faith that he will be vindicated. Like Job, Paul confidently expects deliverance before God, the only judge who finally matters (cf. Job 13.18 LXX 'I know that I will appear vindicated [sc. in the judgement]'). Elsewhere, Paul's conviction is that 'all things work together for good for those who love God' (Rom. 8.28). Given the absence of OT quotations from Philippians and the likely background of Paul's original audience, it is not clear to what extent the apostle could have expected his readers to understand such specific allusions (incl. e.g. 2.10 or 4.5). Nevertheless, the use of this phrase would have been particularly resonant for anyone familiar with the Greek Old Testament; and in any case the fact of Paul's own intimate knowledge of the Septuagint makes such 'intertextual' echoes of Scripture an important clue to the structures and formation of his own thought.

(A few decades later, a similar attitude was famously displayed by another 'Jewish Job', Rabbi Akiba's teacher Nahum of Gimzo. Despite constant personal affliction, he became legendary for responding to each new predicament with the confidence, 'This too will turn out for good', *gam zo le-tobah*: *b.Ber* 60a [*bar.*]; *b.Taan* 21a. Other, similar passages suggest that the perspective of Rom. 8.28 may have been widely affirmed: Eccl. 8.12; Sir. 39.25; *b.Ber.* 60b [*bar.*]. Cf. further Plato, *Republic* 10.12 (613a) and *Apology* 41d.)

Secondly, the argument of the letter as a whole is suffused by Paul's conviction that his relationship with Christ and suffering on his behalf will result in victory and vindication (cf. 1.19f.; 3.10–14). In general, this is of course true in other letters as well. But in Philippians such confidence must be understood in specific relation to the great christological passage of 2.6–11, where both Christ's self-humbling and God's resulting exaltation of him serve a paradigmatic purpose for Christians. (See below, pp. 126ff.)

This situation must mean Paul's present circumstances, described since verse 12; but it is also part of the quotation. The word **deliverance** in this context is certainly more than merely physical release from detention. Although its meaning is potentially broader, Paul's use of the term is normally eschatological: it describes people being restored to a full relationship with God, most often in relation to the final judgement (cf. W. Foerster, *TDNT* 7: 993). This is the primary reference here: Paul looks forward to his vindication before God. It is worth comparing 2 Tim. 4.18, where the cognate verb clearly refers to final salvation: 'the Lord will rescue me from every evil work and bring me safely to his heavenly kingdom.' Nevertheless, as we shall also see in 1.20, Paul expects this deliverance to occur not *despite* his trial but in and through it.

Paul's deliverance, moreover, is here said to be worked out **through** the **prayers** of the Philippians and God's concomitant gift of the Spirit. These two factors relate to each other as human 'petition' and divine 'supply' (*epichorégia*). Remarkably, *both* serve as contributing, not to say instrumental, factors in Paul's 'salvation'. There is no warrant here for hypothetical speculation about whether God could not save if the Philippians had not been there to pray; the point is simply that since they have in fact heeded the call to faith and prayer, their prayers play an integral and instrumental part in how God accomplishes that salvation. Clearly this is another vivid example of the Philippians' stake-holding 'partnership' in the gospel (1.5)!

Scholars continue to debate the phrase **the supply of the Spirit**: is the Spirit supplier or supplied (i.e., is this a subjective or an objective genitive)? Those who support the former under-standing generally resort to the translation 'help' for the word which we have rendered in its more common meaning of 'supply' (*epichorégia*). That translation, however, is difficult to support in the literary sources. On balance, the idea of God 'supplying' the Spirit is more plausible and in any case supported by a Pauline parallel in Gal. 3.5.

The Spirit is identified as being **of Jesus Christ**, a phrase which in this form occurs nowhere else in the New Testament. It must mean that the Spirit is *sent* by Jesus Christ (cf. John 15.26), but beyond that it is also clear from other passages (e.g. Rom. 8.9f.; Gal. 4.6; cf. Acts 16.7; 1 Pet. 1.11) that Paul believed the Spirit to be in a distinctive sense the spirit *of* Christ, the powerful presence of the risen and exalted Messiah. In a profound sense the Spirit *is* the Lord (2 Cor. 3.17). The links with subsequent Trinitarian doctrine are unmistakable. Cf. Fee 1994: 740–43.

20 Verse 20 offers the second part of the reason for Paul's confidence for the future. **Eager expectation** is a term which is also intimately linked with **hope** in its only other Pauline occur-rence, Romans 8.19 (cf. 8.20, 24). Here, the two words appear to form a *hendiadys*, i.e. they together express the same idea of fully expectant hope. These terms, too, have for Paul a distinctly eschatological reference point, as Romans 8 shows: they cannot be reduced to a mere improvement in personal circumstances – though of course they may well include it.

It is worth reiterating a basic commonplace on this subject. In contemporary English usage and to some extent in classical Greek, 'hope' expresses an uncertain desire, based at best on plausible outcome (e.g., 'Let's hope it won't rain on our picnic'). Hope in the Bible, by contrast, is based on the fact that God is God and has underwritten the future. In keeping with this under-standing of hope (and contrary to certain alternative interpreta-tions), Paul's 'eager expectation' is therefore a confident rather than an anxious disposition.

Paul's hope in the present context is formulated first negatively and then positively (in the form 'not ... but ...'). On the negative side, he expects and hopes that he will **in no way suffer disgrace**, literally 'not be put to shame'. This has to do not primarily with concerns about his own safety or even about his image, but rather with his desire that the progress of the gospel and the Lord whose servant he is should not be thwarted (and only in *that* sense that Paul should not be made to look and feel the fool). Being put to shame has to do with the outcome not just of Paul's trial before Caesar, but even more of his eschatological standing before God (cf. K. Barth): in that sense, Paul's statement may well be deliberately ambiguous. As several commentators point out, the language is again related to that of the righteous sufferer in the OT, especially in the Psalms of lament, where 'being put to shame' typically means to be abandoned or disqualified by God (e.g. Ps. 6.10; 22.5; 25.2f., 20; 31.1, 17; 53.5).

On the positive side, Paul expectantly hopes instead that Christ will be **exalted**, (lit. 'magnified'). This word, too, has rich Old Testament roots: it is frequently used for the praise and worship of God. More specifically, however, the exaltation of God or of his oppressed servant occurs in several Psalms as the immediate corollary of not being put to shame (e.g. Ps. 34.3–5; 35.26f.; 40.15f.; 70.2f; cf. 1QH 4.23f.; 5.25, 35; *Od. Sol.* 29.1, 11; and see Fee, O'Brien, Gnilka). Citing Sirach 43.35 (=31) ('who will magnify him as he is?'), Aquinas comments that Christ of course cannot be either magnified or diminished in himself but only in us – a sentiment well captured in George Herbert's phrase 'in my heart, though not in heaven, I can raise thee' ('King of Glory', v. 3).

Paul hopes that Christ will be magnified **through all public boldness**. The noun *parrhēsia* can range in meaning from 'free and open speech' to 'boldness', and may here combine both elements (cf. Marrow 1982 and recently Fredrickson 1996, though he may overstate the links with the philosophical and rhetorical traditions). **All** outspokenness contrasts with 'in no way' being put to shame; similarly, boldness for the gospel is clearly the opposite of being ashamed of it (see Rom. 1.16; cf. Bruce). Paul sees no reason why this confidence in the gospel, which has characterized his ministry from the first (and has encouraged the Christians at Rome, v. 14), should be any less relevant in prison and on trial. Indeed it is precisely **through** this confident outspokenness that Christ will be exalted in his **person** ('lit. in my body', including his whole physical being, as in Rom. 12.1 and Hebrew/Aramaic usage; cf. O'Brien 115 n. 46 *pace* Fee n. 47). A similar desire for bold evangelism in captivity is also expressed in Col. 4.3f. and Eph. 6.19f. And while a positive estimation of apostolic suffering is fairly common in Paul and in Philippians (cf. 1.29f.; 3.10), the specifically instrumental view of it here is worth comparing with Col. 1.24, as K. Barth does.

The little phrase **now as always** is easily overlooked. The word **now** occurs over 60 times in the Pauline corpus, and frequently denotes for him the present not in any neutral or banal sense, but with the highly charged connotation of the divinely significant Now, the *kairos* of God's action and human opportunity to respond and act. Sometimes this is the 'now already' of Christ as opposed to the time before his coming (e.g. Rom. 3.21; 5.9; Col. 1.22); sometimes the 'still now' which awaits the world to come (e.g. Gal. 4.25; cf. Tit. 2.12). In all these cases, however, Paul views the present not as the insignificant shadow of the past or of the future, but as the moment to receive and to participate both in what God has already done through Christ and in the kingdom he is about to complete. Past and future together imbue the 'now' with a powerful significance: 'Now is the acceptable time; now is the day of salvation'; 'now is the moment for you to wake from sleep: salvation is nearer to us now than when we first believed' (2 Cor. 6.2; Rom. 13.11; cf. Heb. 3.7–11). There is for Paul no time like the present moment to know Christ and to make him known. To understand the spirit of this idea, it is worth comparing the eschatologically charged sense of the present in Qumran's *War Scroll* (1QM) or Pesharim (commentaries on the prophets, e.g. 1QpHab 7.1–14). On a less obviously eschatological note, grasping the opportunity of faithful witness in the face of danger is a notion amply attested in texts that would have been familiar to Paul (Esth. 4.14f.; Dan. 3.17f.; 2 Macc. 6.24ff.; cf. *m.Abot* 1.14). On the point of martyrdom, Rabbi Akiba (d. *c.* 135) is later reported to have been delighted that 'now at last' he had the opportunity to love God 'with all your soul', as Deut. 6.5 requires: see *b.Ber.* 61b [*bar.*]. Writing to Rome around AD 110, Ignatius of Antioch rejoices on the point of death that 'now I am beginning to be a disciple' (*Rom.* 5.3), while Polycarp gives thanks for 'this day and this hour' of his martyrdom (*Mart. Pol.* 14.2). At stake here is a far richer sense of the present moment – more sacramental, less fatalistic – than in Horace's call to 'seize the day', *carpe diem* (1.11.8, justly returned to fame by the film *Dead Poets' Society*). The contrast with the Pauline assurance about the 'Now' as the moment of salvation could hardly be greater (cf. Clement of Alexandria, *Protr.* 9: 'today' is an icon of eternity). See further G. Stählin, *TDNT* 4: 1112–23; Lincoln 1981: 101 and *passim*; Luz 1968; Weder 1993; also Bultmann 1952: 274–8, 348.

Whatever it takes, **whether by life or by death**, Paul lives for the exaltation of his Lord. At the same time, he *looks forward* to this exaltation in either case with **eager expectation and hope!** Life and death, although charged in his mind with symbolic and theological significance, are here most plausibly understood in physical terms, as referring to the possible result of his trial. Although on balance Paul suspects he may well live and be released (1.24f., 27), he is sure that life and death can equally contribute to the advance of the gospel and the greater glory of Christ. The apostle's steadfast witness to the end is certainly in view; but, given the idea of Christ's exaltation in Paul's body through death, there may also be an initial allusion to the resurrection, to be followed up explicitly in 3.21 (cf. K. Barth). Either way, therefore, Paul remains confident of deliverance (v. 19), which does not depend on whether he lives or dies.

21 Although it was not Paul's primary purpose, the discussion of the last three verses has introduced the earnest question of his attitude in the face of death. Given the unquestionable seriousness of a capital trial, as well as the Philippians' concern for him, he sees fit to add some further reflections specifically on this subject. In his frank and somewhat introspective weighing up of the relative merits of death and continued life, Paul in fact employs a rhetorical device (*sunkrisis*, 'comparison') which in ancient Hellenistic writings is sometimes applied to life and death (although in pagan texts it usually carries a tone of profound pessimism about human life). The emotional appeal of this comparison is heightened when he first intimates a preference for death and then resolves the apparent indecision in favour of continued ministry. Its function is to give Paul's readers closer insight into his deliberations on the matter, offering them access to his own Christ-like example of preferring a life of service to others (cf. p. 228 below). See further Vollenweider 1994.

As the emphatic first word suggests, Paul's tone becomes even more personal as he affirms what is clearly one of his most deeply felt convictions, palpably forged on the anvil of doubts and trials (cf. 2 Cor. 1.8f.; 7.5): **for me, living is Christ and dying is gain**. In its originally oral presentation to the Philippian church, this is a statement whose parallel structure and assonance would further enhance the rhetorical effect. Paul knows that he may well be found guilty, and that his desire for Christ's glorification might well exact the ultimate price. But although he knows something of the human struggle with death (cf. 2 Cor. 1.7f.), it is not an experience which he faces with fear or despair. 'To live is Christ' – that, reasonably enough, is the epitome of Paul's whole life as a Christian. About a decade earlier he had put it similarly in Galatians: 'It is no longer I who live, but it is Christ who lives in me' (Gal. 2.20; cf. Rom. 8.10); in Colossians, likewise, the new life of Christians is 'hidden with Christ in God' – an idea not incompatible with Phil. 3.20 – so that Christ now 'is your life' (Col. 3.3f.).

Interpreters have been greatly exercised over whether 'to live' here refers to the present bodily existence or to life in the more comprehensive, spiritual sense which Paul uses e.g. in 2.16; 4.3 (see O'Brien 119–22). Two observations suggest that the debate may be somewhat pointless: first, Paul's explicit references to his captivity as well as to his 'body' (v. 20) and 'flesh' (vv. 22, 24) leave no doubt that he faces a courtroom decision of *physical* life and death, and that this is the matter about which he wishes to set his readers' minds at ease. If to live this present life is already 'Christ', to join him more fully in the life to come can only be a further advantage. Secondly, however, if it is true on the earthly plane that 'to live means Christ', the eschatological reference of vv. 19–20 and 23 clearly implies *a fortiori* that 'life' in the fuller sense, too, can only be life in Christ.

The Christian's life on earth means belonging to the risen Christ – and *therefore*, to pass through death, as he did, in order to be with him in the life he now lives can only be **gain** (*kerdos*, lit. 'profit'), indeed 'far better' (v. 23). (Because of this explicit comparison, Droge & Tabor 1992: 121 suggest a possible word play in the phrase 'to live is Christ' (*to zén christos*), whose pronunciation in Koiné Greek would have been very similar to that of *to zén chréstos* ('life is good').) Socrates also thought of death as a likely 'gain' (*kerdos*: cf. Plato, *Apology* 40C-D; cf. earlier Aeschylus, *Prometheus* 747–51; Sophocles, *Antigone* 463–4), and so did much of Platonic and later Gnostic thought, in which death was commonly seen as liberating one from imprisonment in a miserable bodily existence (cf. Antin 1974; Palmer 1975). See further *NW*, pp. 655–65.

But Paul's description of death as 'gain' does not mean that like the Stoics he regards life and death as indifferent (*pace* Jaquette 1995: 110–20 and 1996) or his present life as mere drudgery and misery. Here, after all, is a man who is uncommonly sure *and joyful* about his present calling, as no epistle makes clearer than Philippians. If he uses accessible contemporary language to discuss the reasons why *for Christians* the joy of life in Christ is surpassed only by the life with Christ to come, this does not mean for a moment that he shares the presuppositions about living and dying held by his pagan contemporaries. Death is not 'gain' in the sense of escape, but in the sense of 3.8(ff.): 'gaining' more of Christ who is already our life, and entering into full participation in his resurrection. What matters, therefore, is not inner detachment from *adiaphora* so much as to discern *ta diapheronta* ('what really matters', 1.10), the most important of which is a life with Christ to the glory and praise of God (cf. v. 11).

Death rather than godlessness, incidentally, could clearly be thought an advantage from a Jewish perspective, too: see the above examples (p. 86) as well as 1 Macc. 2.29–38; 6.43f.; Josephus' account of Masada and many other episodes in the *Jewish War*, Bk. 7 and *passim*; and the second-century rabbinic injunction that one must suffer death rather than commit bloodshed, idolatry, or fornication, *b.Sanh.* 74a [*bar.*]. Such examples should give pause to those interpreters of Philippians who have long dismissed out of hand Ernst Lohmeyer's admittedly somewhat fanciful and one-sided discussion of Philippians in relation to the theme of martyrdom. Could it be that in addition to the reasons given, Paul regards his possible martyr's death as evangelical 'gain' and 'advance' precisely because, as in the Jewish parallels, he understands it to be a matter of the ultimate witness to Christ (cf. the rabbinic use of *qiddush ha-shem*, lit. 'sanctification of the Name', as a technical term for martyrdom)? Cf. Lohmeyer, who in this respect is followed by O'Brien, R.P. Martin and Collange.

Albert Schweitzer 1953: 135–8 (cf. Lohmeyer 64) made the more specific suggestion about 1.21–3 that the expectation of 'being with Christ' after death is exclusively a martyr's hope; this has found recent support in Müller 64–9, on the basis of the martyrs' accounts in 2 & 4 Maccabees and of patristic evidence (cf. further Otto 1995, Treiyer 1996). While the context of martyrdom here is of course undeniable, a restrictive view in Paul is made unlikely by passages like 2 Cor. 5.8 and 1 Thess. 4.14. More significantly, in discussing eschatology Paul consistently speaks in terms of the corporate hope of Christians and never employs a separate category of martyrs.

22 Having raised the two options of 'living' and 'dying', Paul now briefly (and a little disjointedly) comments further on each of them. His syntax here is convoluted, and the full-scale commentaries offer detailed discussion of many different interpretative suggestions. It may well be that the grammatical deterioration reflects something of Paul's own inner conflict on the matter! 'Living' and 'dying' are exclusive alternatives (as indeed they are for Hamlet); and not only is the outcome unresolved, but from Paul's Christian perspective it is by no means clear which of the two options is to be preferred, which one would mean the greater evangelical 'advance'. If he is to remain alive **in the flesh**, i.e. in his earthly existence, **that would mean fruitful labour** (lit. 'fruit of labour') for the gospel. A few years previously he had anticipated, and now presumably found, such fruit of his work in Rome (Rom. 1.13); but he had also set his sights on a field which still remained to be harvested, namely Spain (Rom. 15.28); it could be that this is still his wish here (but see below on v. 26).

Lightfoot and others opt for extending the condition in various ways: 'If [or: what if ...?] remaining alive in the flesh would mean fruitful labour, then I cannot say what I shall choose.' Although in some ways a more elegant solution, this seems on balance to go further against the grain of an already distended syntax, as the majority of recent commentators conclude.

Logically, we might now expect 'and if I am to die ...' But Paul has already told us that dying would be 'gain'; instead, therefore, he breaks off and exclaims, **And which I shall choose I cannot say!** The phrase here translated 'I cannot say' has been the subject of some debate. The verb (*gnōrizō*) literally means 'to disclose' or 'make known'. But since it seems unlikely in context that Paul should *refuse* to reveal what is a clear preference in his own mind (see also vv. 23f.), a number of interpreters opt for the rare but less awkward alternative meaning 'to know'. The sentence then could read, 'I do not *know* which I shall choose'. But, since none of the verb's many other uses in the NT carries this meaning, it seems preferable to avoid it if possible. The intention is in any case fairly clear from the context: while he may have his personal preference (vv. 21b, 23), Paul has faced a genuine uncertainty as to which of the two options would bring a greater advance for the gospel. An appropriate and idiomatic English reading is 'I cannot tell'. (So e.g. the REB; somewhat less plausibly, Lohmeyer, followed by O'Brien, supposes that Paul means he has 'nothing to declare' about this matter from the Lord. Another feasible alternative is to construct the sentence as question and answer ('And what shall I choose? I cannot say'); but the meaning is hardly affected.)

There is no need to tone down this language of deliberate choice (*haireomai*) in favour of a vague preference – 'all other things being equal', as it were: in the end, the resolution of Paul's deliberation in this passage is precisely that he chooses to forgo his personal 'desire to depart and be with Christ' (1.23) in order to remain with the Philippians for their 'progress and joy in the faith' (1.25). In this respect this passage, like a number of others in the letter, has an important paradigmatic function: Paul's reasoning invites imitation and foreshadows the example of Christ in 2.5–8 (see also pp. 122, 228 below).

At the same time, it need not strike us as odd that the imprisoned Paul should even consider the possibility of 'choosing' to die rather than to live. His situation was in some ways comparable to that of other prisoners awaiting trial in the Graeco-Roman world. Unlike Seneca or a number of well-known contemporaries, Paul is not likely to have given serious thought to suicide (*pace* Droge 1988, Droge & Tabor 1992: 113–28; Jaquette

1994; cf. the more balanced picture in Vollenweider 1994; Wansink 1996: 96–8 and *passim*). A more promising formal similarity exists with the celebrated figure of Socrates, who was remembered as having said that he would 'choose' (*haireomai*) death rather than to betray his beliefs (e.g. Xenophon, *Apology of Socrates* 9; Plato, *Apology of Socrates* 38E; Epictetus, *Discourses* 1.9.24; cf. Wansink 1996: 120–22). Of course the difference *vis-à-vis* Socrates' view of the good life is most evident in the fact that, as we have seen, Paul's criterion of choice is to subordinate his personal preference to the 'progress and joy' of his fellow believers. In this respect there is no real parallel, and Paul's reasoning owes more to the trial of Jesus than to that of Socrates (see 2.5–8).

23 Paul is thus **torn in two directions** (lit. 'hard pressed', 'hemmed in between the two'): from his own perspective, death seems by far the better alternative: it would be 'gain' for him, because through sharing in death and resurrection it would bring him yet more of Christ (cf. 3.8ff.). Life or death is not in any case his personal choice; but if it were, his own passionate **longing** (*epithumia*, a word which tends elsewhere to denote selfish, forbidden desire; but contrast 1 Thess. 2.17) is **to depart and be with Christ**. This idea again seems entirely in keeping with 3.7–14, although its precise meaning in Paul is virtually impossible to determine. The word **depart** (*analuō*) may originally have been military or naval metaphor meaning to 'break camp' or 'hoist anchor'; Paul seems to be following its popular Hellenistic usage to denote death. It is, however, important to distinguish Paul's usage from the Greek idea of the soul's departure from the body, of which there is no mention here. The phrase 'to be **with Christ**' has received a great deal of scholarly attention, both as a distinctive Pauline phrase denoting a quasi-mystical participation in Christ and in relation to a host of possible Hellenistic (e.g. *HCNT* 482) or, more plausibly, Jewish backgrounds (see O'Brien's excursus on the subject, 132–7; cf. Wedderburn 1985 and p. 52 above on 'in Christ'). In any case, the phrase clearly denotes both the present union of Christians with Christ *and* (in our context) the future destiny of Christians in perfected fellowship with him.

So the plain interpretation is that Paul prefers death, which would mean being with Christ. That, he says emphatically and without doubt, would be **better by far** (lit. 'much rather better') – presumably because it would mean to have 'gained' Christ fully and to share in the power of his resurrection.

While the plain meaning is relatively clear, this verse in fact gives rise to a host of interpretative questions. Some of these are primarily exegetical, but others bear on the lively effects of this passage in later Christian life and thought (see Bockmuehl 1995).

Following C.H. Dodd 1953, it has often been suggested that at some point between 1 Corinthians 15 and 2 Corinthians 4–5 Paul changed his mind about whether he would still be alive at the parousia (perhaps as a result of the crisis related in 2 Cor. 1.8–9?). Prior to this, Paul unselfconsciously includes himself when discussing those who will be alive on that day (1 Cor. 15.51f.; 1 Thess. 4.15–17), while referring to deceased Christians simply as those who have 'fallen asleep' (e.g. 1. Thess. 4.13; 1 Cor. 11.30; 15.6, 18, 20, 51). Indeed in 1 Thess. 4.17 (cf. 5.10) the phrase 'we shall be with the Lord forever' relates specifically to the parousia, rather than (as here) to death. Beginning with 2 Corinthians, and without in any way surrendering the idea of Christ's coming, Paul speaks both of resurrection at the parousia (Phil. 3.20f.; 2 Cor. 4.4) *and* of an apparently immediate heavenly presence with Christ after death (2 Cor. 5.1–10 and the present verse; cf. Walter 1996: 63f.). (An immediate presence with the Lord after death is incidentally taken for granted in Polycarp's subsequent letter to Philippi, 9.2.)

More recently, however, scholars have become more reluctant to accept developmental readings of Paul's eschatological thought (but see e.g. Schnelle 1989: 37–48 and *passim*). Our evidence is very limited, and all the extant letters are written by the mature Paul, between 15 and 30 years after his conversion. What is more, the same co-existence of belief in future blessedness at death leading eventually to eschatological resurrection is also found in Jewish apocalyptic sources, e.g. *1 Enoch* 70.1ff. and 102.4–105.2 *passim* (cf. O'Brien; Gnilka 88–93; Hoffmann 1978: 81–155; note also B. F. Meyer 1989).

But can these two thoughts really be logically reconciled? And, supposing they can: does Paul assume, as Irenaeus (*Haer.* 5.31.2) and others went on to do, that the departed Christians now exist in an intermediate state between death and resurrection? And if he does, is that intermediate state a kind of unconscious soul-sleep, a state of suspended animation until the parousia? Are dead believers awaiting the resurrection in purgatory, a place of purification and punishment for venial sins, as especially Western Catholics have argued? Or are the departed simply and completely dead, body and soul, until the resurrection? These issues have generated a host of different answers in two thousand years of interpretation. At the end of the day, however, the questions persist – perhaps because they demand the impossible: a description of transcendence and eternity in immanent temporal terms. As poets and children know well, transcendent reality can be known only through metaphor. 'When we've been there ten thousand years ...,' wrote John Newton in a famous paradox, 'we've no less days to sing his praise than when we first began.' Perhaps the most exegetically comprehensive and theologically satisfactory solution is to say that for Paul the dead pass into a kind of time beyond time, where judgement and resurrection and full knowledge of the risen Christ are seen to be a present reality, even while they are still anticipated on earth.

The truth is, however, that Paul does not directly address himself to these kinds of questions, which in fact to some extent miss the point of this passage altogether. Paul is not interested in the metaphysics of some twilight world between death and resurrection. Instead, for him it is clear that the one supreme good in life and death is to be in Christ and with Christ, to be a part of his triumphal defeat of evil, sin and death in all its forms. To be so identified with Christ in his death and resurrection, however, means in turn that life and death are equally the spheres of fellowship with him. Paul affirms that no one and nothing that God has created and redeemed is beyond the reach of his love (Rom. 8.31–9). To depart and be with Christ on the other side of death, therefore, can only be 'gain', 'better by far'. And however else this 'gain' may be specifically envisioned, for Paul it can mean nothing less than 'to know Christ and the power of his resurrection', and to attain to 'the prize of the heavenly call of God in Jesus Christ' (to use language from chapter 3). It is thus quite appropriate to suggest that death has become for him a call to be with Christ; Ambrose rightly concluded that 'to live is Christ' must also mean 'where Christ is, there is life, there is the kingdom' (*Commentary on Luke* 10.121, MPL 15: 1834A, cited in *CCC*, §1011). In his excursus on this subject, Collange writes, '"To die" and "to be with Christ" are therefore in large measure synonymous. Life with Christ after death is no problem for the apostle; it flows like a pure spring from the victory of Easter.' For further discussion see Kreitzer 1993a, 1993b; Harris 1983; Hoffmann 1978; Stemberger 1972; Lincoln 1981.

24 While Paul's personal preference is to be with Christ immediately, remaining alive on earth is **more** necessary for the sake of his continued ministry to the Philippians and others. For the advance of the gospel (note the reiteration of the word **progress** in v. 25 following v. 12), Paul gladly postpones his personal desire on behalf of his vocation to bring the gospel to the Gentiles. Yet again, he sets the example of the kind of Christ-like behaviour which he will encourage among the Philippians in the next section (note 2.4–5).

25 The realization that staying alive for now is more important gives Paul confidence that he will indeed stay alive to strengthen the faithful. This confidence is initially surprising, especially in view of the ostensible uncertainty he has just expressed about what the future might hold. Various explanations have been proffered for this apparent change of heart, including sudden revelations in the course of writing the letter.

The difficulty disappears, however, if one reads these verses as continuing the assessment of his 'second option', that of staying alive, **for your sakes** (v. 24). From his own point of view, the preferred choice seems clear. Looking at it from the perspective of his churches, however, he is **fully convinced** that there is indeed a need for his continued work. How can he **know** that he will remain alive? His certainty here is conditioned by what he perceives to be **necessary**, and thus somewhat less strongly worded than that of verse 19: there, he had the sure knowledge of deliverance in Christ. Here, there is no divine revelation about his staying alive and being released; but given the need for his ministry to the Philippians, Paul feels sure that he will indeed **remain** alive **and continue** his ministry **with** them and *for* them. The word **all** reiterates the inclusive note of 1.3f.: he will not take sides in the apparent personal wranglings at Philippi.

The purpose of Paul's continued work is the Philippians' **progress and joy** in (lit. 'of') the faith, which is presumably the 'progress of the gospel' (v. 12) applied specifically to the Philippians. Progress is the objective quality, while joy is its appropriation in personal experience. (The relationship is similar, if secular and trite, in the modern greeting-card wish of 'success and happiness'.) The twin themes of Christian progress and joy, which have characterized Paul's description of his own situation since 1.12 (cf. v. 18 (2x); v. 4) will also guide his concern for the Philippians throughout the remainder of the letter. Their progress in the faith goes hand in hand with joy in the faith, a connection worth noting. Faith that is not joyful wilts away.

The faith could here denote either the trusting human response to the gospel or the corresponding *object* or content of belief (which one can contend for as 'the faith of the gospel', 1.27, and which can be proclaimed, Gal. 1.23; cf. e.g. 1 Tim. 4.6; Jude 3); quite possibly both are meant. That the Philippians in fact needed such progress in their Christian lives seems a plausible conclusion from 1.27–2.1.

26 The result of Paul's continued labour may indeed be that he will be able to see the Philippians again, so that their **jubilation**

(or 'boasting') in Christ will abound. 'To boast' in this context means to regard as a source of strength and encouragement. Paul himself in 2.16 expresses his desire to 'boast' and be proud of the Philippians on the day of Christ. Here, Christ is that source of strength and encouragement, as expressed through Paul's ministry and the progress of the Philippian church; **in Christ Jesus**, therefore, denotes both the ground and the mode of their jubilation (cf. p. 152 above). This source of boasting alters the very definitions of what the surrounding Graeco-Roman culture holds to be worthy of shame and of pride (cf. Witherington 1994: 47–9, citing H. Moxnes).

Not only does Paul think he will survive his present ordeal, but his phrase 'remain and continue with you' in the preceding verse turns out to mean that he may soon be free to visit his churches in the East! Paul says **when I come to you again** – though a more literal translation would be 'through my being with you again', which in itself leaves unclear whether this eventuality is as yet merely possible, or plausible, or likely. Verses 27 and 2.17 suggest that Paul's visit is in any case by no means certain.

The question of Paul's envisioned release and travel plans has a significant bearing on our understanding of his biography. If he is writing from Caesarea, there is nothing inherently surprising about his desire to visit Philippi upon his release, presumably *en route* to Rome. If, on the other hand, he is writing from Rome (which on balance is more likely, cf. pp. 30–32 above), then we have evidence here that he may have changed his plan, or at least his timing, of a proposed trip to Spain. Romans 15.23–8 did not envision further ministry in the East; but the present verse, along with Philemon 22 (dating perhaps from around the same time), suggests a change of mind. His two or more years in detention may have left the apostle keen to refresh his existing relationships before setting out for new pastures in the far West, which according to *1 Clem.* 5.7 (*c.* AD 96) and later church tradition he may eventually have reached. (Defenders of the authenticity of 1 Timothy also sometimes invoke a further period of ministry in the East after his Roman imprisonment.) However, this is not in fact a serious difficulty, since there are other indications that his plans were adaptable to changing circumstances (e.g. 1 Cor. 16.8; 2 Cor. 1.16, 23; Acts 16.6–10; 19.21–2; 20.3; cf. 2 Tim. 4.13).

This verse ends the section of Paul's personal news and notes. From here, he goes on to exhortations to the church at Philippi, for which 1.12–26 will repeatedly turn out to be paradigmatic. (See also below, p. 228 for the theme of Paul's example in 3.17 and 4.9.) Paul's own joy at the 'progress of the gospel' has now brought him quite naturally to motivating the Philippians in their own 'progress and joy in the faith'.

III WORTHY CITIZENS OF THE GOSPEL (1.27–2.18)

Although all the emphasis so far has been on Paul's seemingly unruffled relationship with the Philippian church, this clearly does not mean that there is no need for exhortation and encouragement to grow. Verses 24–6 prepared the readers for this subject, which occupies Paul from here until the end of chapter 2. (In 2.19ff., a separate paragraph, he discusses the part which the travels of Timothy and Epaphroditus will play in this task of encouragement.) Rhetorically and logically, this section is really the centrepiece of Philippians: it spells out in the most fundamental terms what the 'progress of the gospel' means at Philippi. (D. F. Watson 1988: 65–7 calls this the *narratio*, 2.1ff. the *probatio*; cf. O'Brien and others.)

Paul begins with two short sections on fortitude in the midst of suffering (vv. 27–30) and on unselfish unity (2.1–4); this in turn leads into his famous poetic passage on the example of Christ's humble obedience (2.5–11) and finally to an admonition to exemplary conduct in the world (2.12–18). But the whole section 1.27–2.18 hangs together in terms of Paul's opening exhortation to live lives worthy of the gospel. Another heading for the body of the letter might be 'Christian citizenship', since this distinctive and comprehensive theme is prominent in verse 27 and recurs in 3.20 and probably in 2.15.

A   STEADFASTNESS IN SUFFERING   (1.27–30)

(27) Always remember one thing: live as worthy citizens of the gospel of Christ. In doing this, whether I come and see you or hear about your situation from a distance, you will stand firm in one Spirit, striving side by side in one accord for the faith of the gospel. (28) And you must not be in any way intimidated by your adversaries: this will serve as God's proof to them, both of their destruction and of your salvation. (29) This is because to you it has been granted not only to believe in Christ, but even to suffer on his behalf: (30) you are engaged in the same struggle which you yourselves saw me have and which you now hear that I have.

In Greek, verses 27–30 make up one long and somewhat inelegant sentence, which for purposes of translation requires disentanglement and paraphrase. But as many commentators note, the theme or rubric both for this paragraph and for the section as a whole is clearly marked in the first verse.

27 Always remember one thing. The first word of this new section, the adverb *monon* literally meaning 'only', grabs the readers' attention by dispelling other thoughts and placing special weight on the statement that follows. We here follow the commentators' usual route of offering a paraphrase: 'now the important thing is this: ...' (O'Brien); 'whatever may happen, whether I visit you again or not, ...' (Lightfoot; cf. Calvin); etc. What really matters is not what may happen to Paul but whether Christ is honoured at Philippi. As Paul dictates, one can imagine him pacing about and raising his index finger to make this point (cf. K. Barth) ...!

The translation **live as ... citizens** takes seriously the reference to citizenship which the verb *politeuesthai* originally carries in the Greek. While it could be used more broadly of one's public 'walk' or lifestyle, the explicit recurrence of the citizenship theme in 3.20 and its importance for the social setting of Philippi make it likely that we should identify it here. Given the peculiar position of Philippi as a Roman colony with full Italian legal status (see above, p. 4), an appeal to the privilege of citizenship would be particularly poignant. Roman citizens and colonies around the empire prided themselves on their élite status; according to Acts 16.37f., Paul himself appealed to his citizenship while in Philippi. The word *politeuesthai* here carries the dual sense of exercising the rights and public duties of free and full citizenship. It is likely, therefore, that Paul deliberately chooses this term (used only here; but cf. *politeuma* in 3.20 and *politeia* in Eph. 2.12), as carrying rather more punch at Philippi than his more common words for 'walk' or 'conduct' (cf. also Schenk).

Hellenistic *Jewish* usage of the same verb provides an interesting backdrop to this discussion. In passages like LXX Esther 8.12[p]; 2 Macc. 6.1; 11.25; Josephus, *Vita* 12 and even Acts 23.1, the term is used to describe simply the practice of a Jewish *way of life*, and some interpreters for this reason have supposed that the meaning of the word is identical to 'walk' (e.g. H. Strathmann, *TDNT* 6: 526, 534). Against this it is worth stressing, however, that in all these references the adoption of a Jewish lifestyle is conceived as a deliberate, publicly visible, and (at least in the broad sense) *politically relevant* act which in the context is distinguished from alternative lifestyles that might have been chosen instead. Paul and other NT writers repeatedly apply this notion to a reference point of transcendent citizenship, as in 3.20 (see below, p. 233; cf. Gal. 4.25f.; more clearly Heb. 11.10, 16;

13.14). Significantly, the same terminology of 'worthy Christian citizenship' reappears in Polycarp's letter to Philippi (5.1f.) and in the *Epistle to Diognetus* 5.9. It had a profound effect on patristic thought, above all on Augustine (see further Bockmuehl 1995).

It is worth noting, however, that Paul neither highlights his own Roman citizenship nor in any way presupposes that of his readers; indeed by writing in Greek he is clearly appealing to a wider audience than that of the Latin-speaking highest echelons of Philippian society. The rhetorical force of Paul's language is to play on the perceived desirability of citizenship in Roman society at Philippi, and to contrast against this the *Christian* vision of enfranchisement and belonging.

Christians, then, are to adopt a way of life that is in keeping with their corporate citizenship as constituted in Christ and the gospel. Against the colonial preoccupation with the coveted citizenship of Rome, Paul interposes a counter-citizenship whose capital and seat of power are not earthly but heavenly, whose guarantor is not Nero but Christ. Philippi may be a colony enjoying the personal imperial patronage of Lord Caesar, but the church at Philippi is a personal colony of Christ the Lord above all (2.10–11). The exercise of their common citizenship, therefore, must be **worthy** of his gospel, which is as it were the 'constitution' of that kingdom (cf. K. Barth).

In saying this, Paul does not of course assert some sort of innate 'worthiness' of the citizens. Instead he merely insists that, having been incorporated as citizens and thereby *made* worthy, their conduct now is to be *appropriate*, in keeping with this new status and dignity (cf. Leo the Great, quoted in *CCC*, §1691f.). The logic here is in fact typically Pauline, and repeated countless times in his ethical passages. For Aristotle, practice makes perfect and doing constitutes being: the virtuous person becomes so by the practice of virtuous acts. For Paul, by contrast, being precedes and entails doing. (And only then can doing in turn confirm being, as e.g. in Phil. 2.12f.) His ethics is that of an eschatological *noblesse oblige*; 'live what in Christ you already are'. 'You *are* citizens of heaven; therefore live accordingly, in a manner that is worthy of your king.' Similar arguments, taking their point of departure in the language of dying and rising with Christ, new life in the Spirit, etc. occur in Rom. 6, Gal. 5, Col. 3 and elsewhere.

The practical substance of what it means to live worthy of the gospel in Philippi is now explained in the remainder of this section, perhaps especially as illustrated in 2.5–11: to live by the gospel of Christ means above all to live by the *example* of Christ.

Verse 27b in Greek continues with a grammatically incomplete purpose clause: literally, 'in order that (*hina*), **whether I come and see you'** or not. (In addition to the incomplete *hina* clause, the two alternatives separated by the conditional *eite* ('whether') are also without apodosis; for this usage cf. e.g. BDF §446, 454.3.) For the Philippians, the result of living in a way worthy of the gospel will be a corporate Christian existence that stands firm and united, and which is entirely independent of Paul's absence or presence with them. Just as Paul's deliverance and the progress of the gospel are not affected by his circumstances, so also a gospel-centred lifestyle in Philippi can stand on its own two feet – irrespective of whether Paul lives or dies. (See already on 1.7 above; cf. Schlosser 1995b.) The phrase **your situation** is equivalent to 'my situation' in 1.12. Paul may well expect to **hear** about the Philippian situation when Timothy returns from his imminent mission (2.19ff.).

The Philippians are to **stand firm in one Spirit**. 'Spirit' here could be the human spirit, in parallel with **in one accord** (lit. 'as one person', 'in one soul'); on balance, however, Phil. 2.1 along with Pauline usage elsewhere (esp. 1 Cor. 12.9, 13; cf. Eph. 2.18; 4.4) favours a reference to the Holy Spirit (cf. Fee 1994: 743–6). Paul's phrase here is not perhaps entirely unambiguous (cf. e.g. Rom. 12.11; 1 Cor. 5.3; 6.17; Col. 1.9; 2.5), but the overall intention is clear. Christians may not be immune from human experiences of conflict, antipathy, or 'personality clashes' (euphemistically so called); but just as the new ground of their existence is now the gospel of Christ, so they will seek instead, and indeed through their partnership in the one Spirit (2.1), to be standing firm in unity and **striving side by side** (*sunathlountes*) for the one gospel. The vocabulary here suggests the joint exertion of athletes or soldiers working as a team; both metaphors would be very familiar at Philippi. The same constellation of 'standing' and 'striving side by side', incidentally, occurs again in the conflict passage at 4.1, 3. (At the same time, Aristotle *Nic. Eth.* 9.8 links the 'one soul' expression with friendship.)

The Philippians are contending **for the faith of the gospel**. This phrase could be taken instrumentally, i.e. 'by means of the faith' (so e.g. Calvin); more likely, however, is the translation here offered, which follows most other commentators in reading a so-called dative of advantage. **The faith of the gospel** (a phrase found nowhere else in the NT) may mean either the faith whose content is the gospel, or faith that arises from the gospel. The former is perhaps a little more likely in view of the use of 'faith' in v. 25. But the distinction is in any case immaterial, since Paul's elliptical phrase probably encompasses both meanings. Christians are to contend for gospel-based faith.

28 This is the first direct mention of opponents at Philippi, and it joins the theme of unity to that of steadfastness in adversity. Who might these adversaries be?

Many commentators opt for the convenient identification with the *Judaizers* mentioned in 3.2. This is certainly not impossible. The present context, however, offers no hint of supporting evidence. On the contrary: while the opposition here in 1.28–30 is clearly acute, threatening intimidation and causing actual suffering, the wholesale satirical admonition in 3.2 to 'beware of the dogs, evildoers and mutilators' has almost a note of the perfunctory about it, as we shall see. The Judaizers are people who have plagued his ministry at every turn; while there is nothing to suggest that they were a threat specifically at Philippi, which in any case was not a significant Jewish centre, years of painful experience (perhaps even at nearby Thessalonica: cf. Acts 17.5–7; 1 Thess. 2.16) have taught Paul to be wary and to pre-empt any hostile 'take-over bid' as far as possible. The Philippians must clearly know what Paul is talking about when he inveighs against 'the dogs'; and they will know that their activities impinge on the Pauline mission at Philippi as elsewhere. Nevertheless, the lack of detail and specific evidence of actual interference at Philippi suggests that, unlike 1.28, the warning tone of 3.2 is perhaps a little reminiscent of Cato the Elder (234–149 BC), the Roman senator who famously ended all his later speeches with the words, 'And meanwhile, it is my opinion that Carthage must be destroyed.' The sentiment in 3.2 is one of acute but seasoned vigilance in the face of persistent danger.

A stronger case can be made for *pagan* opposition. The adversaries are apparently from outside the Christian community, and are of the same kind as those who confronted Paul when he first came to Philippi (v. 30) – i.e. more likely pagan, especially linked with the authorities. There is a good deal of evidence to suggest that Christianity could have been viewed as a threat to the political fibre of Philippi, whose character and self-understanding as an Italic colony under exclusive Augustan patronage were at this stage intimately bound up with Roman imperial religion (cf. Introduction, pp. 3, 6). The introduction of alien religious practices combined with new and competing external loyalties (both to a different religious 'Lord' and to a different organizational structure and leadership) was immediately suspect. From this point of view, conflicts between religion and the state were by definition evidence of *false* religion and dangerous to political stability. Acts 16.20f. suggests that Paul's mission was perceived to be just such a menace to the integrity of the Philippian polity and citizenship, and it is easy to see why the same sorts of people would perceive the ensuing Pauline church to present the same sort of threat: Christians, who explicitly defined their citizenship (1.27; 3.20; cf. p. 97) and their locus of supreme sovereignty (2.9–11) to be elsewhere, must necessarily incur the odium of being 'un-Roman' enemies of the public order (cf. already the polemic of Acts 16.20–21). Serious persecution of Macedonian Christians is intimated in 2 Cor. 8.1f.; 1 Thess. 1.6; 3.3; 2 Thess. 1.4; 1 Thess. 2.14 shows that it may well emanate from pagans. (See further Bormann 1995: 217–24; Pilhofer 1995: 137–9.)

But whoever these people are, whether pagan or Jewish, Paul is concerned that his presence or absence should make no difference to the Philippians' confident Christian citizenship in the midst of such adversity. The rare Greek verb 'to intimidate' (*pturō*) is elsewhere used of startling horses into a stampede: an apt exhortation not to be frightened or panicked into retreat by the strength of opposition.

The next phrase is difficult. **'This'** (*hētis*), which grammatically anticipates the word **proof** (*endeixis*), most plausibly refers back to the disposition which Paul has just encouraged in the Philippians: their spiritual unity and teamwork for the gospel, and their fearlessness in the face of opposition. Such demeanour on the part of Christians is in itself a clear enough indication that their enemies' efforts are doomed to fail. The steadfast endurance of another Macedonian congregation is similarly described as 'evidence' of God's purposes in 2 Thess. 1.5. Paul's language here does not of course require that this 'proof' is necessarily recognized by the opponents, merely that it pertains to them. Paul's eschatological certitude here is the same that was at play earlier in discussing his own situation, vv. 19ff.

God himself enables the Philippians' steadfast unity; it is **God's proof** (lit. 'a proof ... and of your salvation; and this [is] from God': the latter clause modifies not just 'salvation', but both the 'proof' and the reality which it signifies). He himself will ensure that they win through to the end, to **salvation** – a victory against which their opponents are fighting a losing battle. Just as God's grace in Christ progresses unstoppably to final deliverance, so the enemies of that same grace are on the road that leads eventually but surely to **destruction** and judgement on the 'day of Christ' (cf. 2 Cor. 2.16). As always in Scripture, the promise of God's victory and of the vindication of his faithful people necessarily include the defeat of his enemies. The same Pauline terminology of contrast between those who are in the process of being saved and those who are on the highway to disaster occurs side by side in 1 Cor. 1.18. And while it is clearly possible to be 'airlifted', as it were, from the latter road to the former (e.g. 1 Cor.

6.11; Col. 1.12; and cf. Eph. 2.3; 5.8), there can be no doubt as to where the two tracks lead. Modern readers who object to such harshly polarized and uncompromising language are inclined to forget that the two terms here are not arbitrarily, but necessarily complementary: if **salvation** is in any meaningful sense the victory of justice and the good, it must necessarily entail the **destruction** of the machinery of injustice and evil.

All the while, as K. Barth notes, it is important to bear in mind that the fight is not reactionary, against the adversaries, but *for* the faith of the gospel, v. 27.

29–30 These verses offer a surprising explanation of *why* Paul thinks that Christian steadfastness in adversity is God's proof of salvation. It is because the suffering of Christians is inherently, indeed almost by definition, related to that of Christ! The passive **it has been granted** (*echaristhê*) suggests that both **to believe** in Christ and **to suffer** as a result of it are in fact the gift of God's grace (*charis*) – the same grace in which Paul and his readers were in 1.6–7 said to be partners. The Greek here shows quite emphatically, if somewhat clumsily and untranslatably, that this gift of grace is profoundly related to Christ: lit., 'it has been granted to you on behalf of Christ, not just to believe in him but also to suffer on his behalf.' Not only apostolic proclamation takes place on behalf of Christ (so e.g. 2 Cor. 5.20); the same is true of Christian suffering.

In a widely attested Jewish and early Christian view, the righteous sufferings of believers are never in vain, but are in the purposes of God imbued with a powerful moral, and in some sense redemptive, significance (see already Ps. 116.15; cf. e.g. Isa. 53; Wisd. 2; 2 Macc. 6–7). While Christians saw this perspective uniquely fulfilled and vindicated in Christ, that did not prevent them from seeing their own sufferings *on behalf of* Christ as also making a positive, albeit derivative and participatory, contribution within the redemptive plan of God. It is significant that Paul uses the same language of Christian suffering for Christ (*huper Christou*; so also 2 Cor. 12.10; cf. Col. 1.24; Acts 9.16) as of Christ's suffering for us (*huper hêmôn*: e.g. Rom. 5.8; 8.32; 2 Cor. 5.21; Gal. 3.13; 1 Thess. 5.10).

This positive view of Christian suffering was also adopted by Paul, who clearly saw his own suffering for Christ as a privilege. In 3.10 he speaks of his longing to participate in Christ's sufferings. Other important passages include 2 Cor. 4.10f. about manifesting in his body both the death and the life of Jesus, and Col. 1.24 about completing in his own person the full measure of the messianic sufferings. This cannot of course be seen as a triumphal idea; rather, in 2.17 Paul goes on to speak of it in terms of sacrifice – again a striking metaphor in view of the language used elsewhere of Christ's death (e.g. Rom. 3.25; 1 Cor. 5.7; cf. Eph. 5.2). This idea of Christian suffering on behalf of Christ is intimated in sources ranging from Acts 5.41 to the second-century accounts of martyrdom (e.g. Polycarp: *Mart. Pol.*, 14.2; Eusebius, *Hist. Eccl.* 5.1.23 on the martyrs of Lyon).

Here, the Philippians are privileged to share in the same persecution for the gospel which they witnessed during Paul's time at Philippi and which he is still experiencing in his present captivity. (The word **struggle**, *agōn*, is another athletic or military metaphor; cf. v. 27 and 2.25. See further Krentz 1993, Geoffrion 1993 and Peterlin 1995: 160–65 on the significance of such imagery in the Philippian context.) There is ample evidence of the suffering which Paul repeatedly experienced in the course of his missionary work in Macedonia. The incident in Acts 16 may in fact represent only the tip of the iceberg: Paul himself elsewhere mentions severe difficulties at Philippi (1 Thess. 2.2) and in Macedonia more generally (2 Cor. 7.5). Evidently not all was smooth sailing after the conversion of the Philippian jailer! (On this same note of shared suffering it is interesting that in Col. 4.10 Aristarchus, if identical with the one in Acts (e.g. 27.2), is a Macedonian fellow prisoner of Paul; cf. Phlm. 24.) Since the present trials of Paul and the Philippians are likely to have a common origin in distinctly Roman religious and political opposition, the nature of their struggle may be **the same** not just generally, as a struggle for the same gospel, but quite specifically. Logically and rhetorically, this assertion of a parallel experience would once again seem to justify a paradigmatic understanding of 1.12–26.

For Paul as for the Philippians, then, this suffering on Christ's behalf represents something of the 'participation in his sufferings' of which 3.10 will go on to speak. At the same time, the practical content of this active relationship with Christ is also part and parcel of the positive appropriation of the example of Christ, as urged in 2.5–11. It is interesting that Paul's proposed response to external adversity highlights as the key obstacle not weaknesses of doctrine, but weakness of the knees and flawed relationships! But then again, chapter 2 of course will illustrate the necessary interdependence of sound doctrine (2.5–11) with Christian harmony (2.1–4) and fortitude (2.12–16).

B HARMONY AND UNSELFISHNESS (2.1-4)

The next paragraph resumes the theme of unity, which appeared most recently in v. 27b.

(1) For this reason, if indeed there is in Christ any encouragement at all, if any consolation of love or fellowship in the Spirit, if any compassion or mercy, (2) then make my joy complete by being like-minded – having the same love, united in heart and mind. (3) Do nothing based on selfish ambition or conceit, but in humility consider each other better than yourselves: (4) look out not for your own rights, but actually for those of each other.

Paul logically links this material with the preceding paragraph (*oun*, **for this reason**, 'therefore'), suggesting that the categorical call to Christian citizenship in v. 27 is still the overall concern. And like 1.27–30, these four verses form a single sentence in Greek. This in itself suggests that the sentence 'works' and 'flows' best if it is seen as spoken rather than written word – designed not as a piece of literature so much as for the original oral performance in public reading (and before that, presumably, in dictation).

In light of the massive debate about the nature of 2.5–11, we should note that even here there is already a widely recognized poetic rhythm in Paul's language – though nobody finds here a pre-Pauline 'hymn'. On other grounds, too, it is in many ways artificial to separate this paragraph too clearly from 2.5–11. Despite the seam at 2.5, the two are intricately interwoven in terms of language, logic and subject matter, as we shall see: the first relates to the second as the Christian mind to the mind of Christ. Both rhetorically and theologically, 2.5–11 shapes and illustrates 2.1–4. At the same time, several of the themes of this paragraph recur throughout the letter.

1 If indeed there is in Christ any encouragement... The 'if' (which occurs four times in the Greek of this verse) does not of course designate a doubtful proposition but one that is certain. Many interpreters prefer to translate 'since ...' or 'as sure as...'; this is grammatically possible and also makes good sense of **for this reason** (*oun*), confirming a logical link with Paul's preceding remarks. In 2 Cor. 5.17, a similar verbless clause beginning with the parallel words *ei tis en Christô* is not conditional ('should anyone be in Christ') but inclusive and indefinite ('whoever is in Christ'). If the conditional sense is in any sense to be retained here, this could be in terms of ironic understatement: 'if Christ means any encouragement at all ... [as of course he does]'.

A slight textual uncertainty besets the indefinite pronoun (*tis* or *ti*) underlying the word **any** throughout this verse. NA[27] and most commentators assume the reading as suggested, which creates a slight problem only in relation to 'any compassion or mercy', where the masculine pronoun *tis* does not agree with the adjacent noun *splangchna* in either gender (neuter) or number (plural); but this loose usage could easily be due to a rhetorical desire for more consistent assonance throughout this chain of qualities. Beyond this, however, a few MSS show a tendency to use consistently the masculine pronoun (*tis*), while others favour the neuter (*ti*). Hawthorne, following BDF §137.2, accepts the conjecture that the original reading was consistently *ti*, and translates 'if in any way [I have shown you].... .' On balance, however, the inconsistent usage of NA[27] enjoys the best MS support and should be accepted.

Paul is firmly convinced of these realities of the Christian life, and he knows that the Philippians are, too: he is rehearsing common ground. That in turn has a kind of leverage effect on the apodosis of this condition in verses 2–4: 'since all these things are of course abundantly provided in Christ, then of course how much more should you be of one mind, etc.' The appeal is deliberately emotional, both in terms of the rhetorical effect and in much of its vocabulary as well – words like 'encouragement', 'consolation', 'love', 'fellowship', 'compassion', 'mercy'. It is relevant that all these terms relate not to the life of the individual but to the corporate life of the church. The Christian community at Philippi is here reminded of the resources of encouragement and compassion that are found in their life together in Christ – the Christ whose self-giving service is about to be rehearsed in 2.5–11.

Given the context of suffering which Paul has just introduced in 1.29–30, it is entirely understandable why such encouraging language should be felt appropriate here as part of his plea for unity and mutual respect. There has been considerable debate among scholars about the precise meaning of these terms; the different options are most thoroughly expounded in O'Brien 167–76. However, the impassioned moral and spiritual appeal of passages like 2.1–11 is too easily left threadbare by excessive analysis (cf. K. Barth); they speak the soaring, unanswerable language of a Bach cantata, which is best understood by being heard out to the end – and then heard again. Brief comments will suffice to let the text expound itself.

First, and most importantly, the tone is set by the idea of

encouragement (*paraklêsis*) **in Christ**, which is then supplemented by three other terms in apposition. Contrary to how it is commonly understood today, the word 'encouragement' here does not denote an unqualified and morally vacuous affirmation but contains the ideas of both consolation and strengthening. (Even the English word once meant to give someone courage.) Commentators are divided between 'exhortation' and 'comfort', but perhaps this is in any case a false alternative. Union with Christ (being **in Christ**, cf. p. 52), even in the midst of suffering, opens up a treasury of consolation and strength.

The next two items are constructed in parallel and seem to belong together: 'if any **consolation of love**, if any **fellowship in** (lit. "of") **the Spirit**'. The first phrase is best understood as the consolation that is offered by love; 'consolation' (*paramuthion*) is a near synonym of the word 'encouragement' above (*pace* Lightfoot, who has 'incentive'). The abstract and unqualified usage initially leaves one wondering whose love is intended. But Paul speaks in any case of love that is 'in Christ'; the whole thrust of the argument, moreover, shows it is life in Christ which provides the resources that in turn make Christian love and unity possible.

The term **fellowship in the Spirit** lends itself to a range of quite different interpretations, ranging from 'spiritual partnership' to 'participation in the Spirit'. The same phrase occurs in 2 Cor. 13.13. The word **fellowship** (*koinônia*, cf. 15; 3.10) in any case denotes not togetherness so much as a *partnership* of common interest, forged and empowered by the Holy Spirit.

Regarding the word **Spirit** (*pneuma*), commentators here generally fall in line with their earlier reading at 1.27. Ambiguous passages like this can allow an inevitably autobiographical element to enter exegesis here. One suspects that many interpreters unwittingly approach unspecified references to 'spirit' according to temperament and churchmanship, taking either a maximalist Pentecostal line that identifies the third person of the Trinity as often as possible, or applying Ockham's razor to the point where one does not recognize the Holy Spirit unless it is absolutely unavoidable. In Philippians there is no doubt that Paul uses the word both of the human (4.23) and of the Holy Spirit (1.19; 3.3), leaving only 1.27 and 2.1 in any doubt. On the balance of the argument at this point and especially of Pauline theology in general, a reference to the Spirit of God is here at least impossible to exclude. The Philippian partnership with Paul involves their prayers and God's supply of the Spirit of Jesus (1.19), and the corporate Christian existence is marked by worship 'in the Spirit of God' (3.3). Elsewhere, Paul specifically regards Christians as baptized 'in one Spirit' into one body and 'made to drink of one Spirit' (1 Cor. 12.13); and in a famous Trinitarian formula, now known to many Christians as 'the Grace', he speaks of 'the grace of the Lord Jesus Christ, the love of God, and the fellowship of the Holy Spirit' (2 Cor. 13.13). Thus, while it also undoubtedly entails a human partnership among the Philippians, this fellowship of which Paul speaks has its source and origin 'in Christ' and therefore pertains to their participation in the 'Spirit of Jesus Christ' (cf. 1.19). (Some commentators (Fee; Witherington 1994: 61f.) go so far as to say that the first three 'if' clauses constitute a specifically Trinitarian structure of the passage, relating respectively to Christ, God the Father, and the Holy Spirit; but this seems unlikely on several grounds, including the omission of 'God' from the second clause and the awkward presence of a fourth.)

The last conditional clause presents two near-synonymous terms that appear without qualification: **if any compassion or mercy**. Both appeal unabashedly to the emotions, yet both arise from Christ himself: to be in Christ means to have one's heart moved to tender affection for others. Compassion and mercy as essential divine qualities are also affirmed elsewhere in Paul (e.g. Rom. 12.1); indeed it is precisely God's compassion in Christ which enables Christians to show the same to others (2 Cor. 1.3f.; cf. Col. 3.12). And just as Paul longs for the Philippians with the 'compassion of Christ' in 1.8, so he expects them to be transparent in their disposition towards each other. John Chrysostom offers a comment which, although homiletical in intention, powerfully captures the intended effect of Paul's statement on the Philippian context: compassion and mercy should become the Christian counterpart of a status symbol. 'As the children of the wealthy have an ornament of gold about their neck, and never put it off, because it exhibits a token of their high birth, so should we too wear mercy ever about us' (Introductory Discourse on Philippians).

In the present context, these qualities of being 'in Christ' are powerfully illustrated by the imminent reference to the story of Christ himself, in 2.6–11. This manner of reasoning is indeed thoroughly Pauline: 'compassion' and 'mercy' similarly appear as part of the Christian disposition in Col. 3.12f., where forgiveness of one another is also grounded in the example of Christ (cf. Rom. 15.7; cf. Eph. 2.4; 5.2; also 1 John 4.11).

First, however, Paul sets out to mount his appeal on the basis of these resources that are richly available in Christ. After this series of four powerful, mutually reinforcing 'if' clauses, he now arrives at the 'then', the apodosis and implication, which is phrased in the imperative. 'If these benefits of life in Christ have any relevance at all, then. ...' This appeal is also expressed in a series of appositional and nearly synonymous statements, calling for unity buttressed by mutual deference.

2 Make my joy complete. In a telling expression of the personal warmth of their relationship, the opening imperative – indeed the only imperative – of Paul's exhortation here is the kind of roundabout and tactful appeal that might preface a request between two friends who are concerned for each other's welfare. What Paul asks has to do with the Philippians' relationships amongst each other; but he himself takes a keen personal interest in them as their pastor and friend. Their progress in the faith, expressed in unity and harmony (cf. earlier 1.25, 27), will fill up his own measure of joy – and, given their bonds of friendship, that in itself should be incentive to pursue it. Paul has already expressed his delight and further desire for the Philippians' progress in faith (1.3–11). The completing or (lit.) 'fulfilling' of this joy, however, will finally take place on the day of Christ, as he intimates in 1.6 and goes on to make clear in 2.16.

Despite the enthusiastically affirming tones of 1.3ff., it is clear that the main obstacle which remains to Paul's joy over the Philippians is concern about a lack of love and harmony among them. It is not evident from these brief phrases that disunity is already an acute and critical problem in the church (*pace* Peterlin 1995: 59–65 and *passim*, whose otherwise well-informed account manifests some of the pitfalls of 'mirror-reading' Pauline letters). Since apart from 4.2–3 we lack explicit evidence for divisions within the Philippian church, Paul's language here may merely identify what he considers to be a serious risk – heightened in his mind because of the evident tensions among the church in Rome (1.15, 17; 2.20–21). Caird 129, commenting on the similarity of wording between this passage and 2.21, quite plausibly surmises 'that the warnings of vv. 1–4 were occasioned by the behaviour of the Christians in Rome and not by what Paul had heard of those in Philippi' (cf. ibid., p. 117). Paul's remarks here do in any case cast a shadow forward to 4.2–3, and must be read with a view to that passage as well.

The Philippians, then, are encouraged to counteract any disunity by **being like-minded – having the same love, united in heart and mind**. The initial subordinate clause (lit. 'that you should think the same thing') is elaborated by a series of participles, which in fact continue through to verse 4. The meaning of these phrases in the present verse is virtually identical, as is also indicated by the matching recurrence of the verb 'to think'

(*phroneō*) at the end of the verse – literally, 'think the same ...
thinking the one thing'. Indeed it is intriguing that the present
letter accounts for nearly half of all Pauline uses of this verb: it is
used to describe Paul's attitude to the Philippians (1.7) and theirs
to him (4.10), as well as to highlight fundamental human disposi-
tions which from a Christian perspective may be either appropriate or misguided (2.5; 3.15 (2x), 19; 4.2). The biblical use of this
term is concerned not with intellectual effort as such, but with a
moral and spiritual orientation or 'mind-set'. Having the 'same
mind' means in this sense to have the same priorities and be
united in purpose (cf. 1 Cor. 1.10); it refers to attitude as much as
to intellect.

Paul's emphasis on Christian unanimity here aims not at the
flattening of different points of view, but at a commitment to
likeness of aim and purpose. It is this alone which can foster
genuine consensus amidst diversity. The imposition of a veto or
decree, by contrast, can of course be equally divisive whether
administered by an élite or by a 'majority'. The actual *content* of
this 'sameness' of mind is about to be spelled out in 2.6–11, which
recounts the 'mind' of Christ (v. 5).

Having the same love must mean to share the kind of love
which has the same source (love's consolation is 'in Christ', v. 1),
motivation and object. Verses 3–4 go on to illustrate what happens where this is not the case; 2.5–11 serve to indicate that love
which is 'in Christ' will be attuned to the paradigm of 'the mind of
Christ'. Sharing the same mind and the same love is bolstered by
being engaged in 'the same struggle' (1.30) on Christ's behalf –
participating together in 'the fellowship of his sufferings' (3.10).

Our translation **united in heart and mind** (lit. 'together in
soul having the same mind') can either be taken as a hendiadys
(e.g. Collange) or separately; the meaning is little affected. The
first of these terms (*sumpsuchos*) is virtually identical to 'in one
spirit' (*mia psuchē*) in 1.27, though here it is concerned with
internal unity and there with an external threat.

3 In Greek, the sentence begun in v. 1 continues with further
participial modifiers, turning in these next two verses from a list
of general positive qualities to two more specific contrasts in the
form 'not A but B'. First, there is a call to avoid **selfish ambition**
and **conceit**. The former was used previously in 1.17 (see p. 77)
to characterize the self-seeking behaviour of Paul's rivals in
Rome, in contrast with those who proclaim Christ out of love.

The noun rendered 'conceit' (*kenodoxia*, lit. 'vain glory, empty
boast') occurs only here in the New Testament, although it is
commonly understood in Hellenistic Greek as referring to people

with an inflated sense of themselves, projecting an image but lacking its substance. For Christians, it is linked with arrogance and pride, as is implicit in the contrast with humility in this verse, and explicit in some second-century Christian catalogues of vices (e.g. *1 Clem.* 35.5; Hermas *Mand.* 8.5). In Gal. 5.26, Paul connects the corresponding adjective (*kenodoxos*) with an attitude of competitiveness and envy, which may suggest why the two words are linked here. The pursuit of prestige and self-fulfilment is incompatible with Christian love and unity.

In relation to both terms, it is somewhat ironic that in recent years, perhaps especially since the demise of socialism, the notion of competition seems in public discourse to have lost any undesirable connotations as a motto for human interaction. The New Testament writers, by contrast, distinguish quite sharply between competition for virtuous (e.g. Mark 9.35; Rom. 12.10; 1 Thess. 4.18; 1 Cor. 14.12; Heb. 10.24) and for selfish ends. In Galatians 5.13–15 Paul himself appears to formulate a stark choice between 'becoming slaves to one another in love' and 'biting and devouring one another'. Here in Philippians, he is about to illustrate this contrast further by means of the example of Christ, who did not exploit his own advantage (2.6) but served as a slave (2.7).

Instead of pursuing their own prestige, that strangely addictive and debasing cocktail of vanity and public opinion, the Philippians are called to **humility** (*tapeinophrosuné*), the 'lowliness of heart' which agrees to treat and think of others preferentially. The centrality of this word is one of the paradoxes of early Christian ethics which made little sense in the first century, and perhaps makes even less today. In secular Greek it is rarely used, and then in a derogatory sense to denote servile weakness, obsequious grovelling or on the other hand mean-spiritedness (e.g. Epictetus *Discourses* 3.24.56; see W. Grundmann in *TDNT* 8:1–27).

The Old Testament and contemporary Judaism had a more positive place for humility: Moses is singled out for his humility (Num. 12.3), and lowliness and humility before God are positively encouraged (e.g. Ps. 25.9; 149.4; cf. 2 Chr. 7.14; Prov. 3.34; Isa. 57.15; 66.2; Zeph. 3.12). Not unlike Paul in our passage, the Qumran sectarians had a vision for a community marked by truth and humility, compassionate love and upright intent (1QS 2.24–5; cf. 3.8–9; 4.3; 5.3, 25). The biblical view of humility is precisely *not* feigned or grovelling, nor a sanctimonious or pathetic lack of self-esteem, but rather a mark of moral strength and integrity. It involves an unadorned acknowledgement of one's own creaturely inadequacies, and entrusting one's fortunes to God rather than to one's own abilities or resources. (It stands to reason, therefore, that while humility before God does not *require* that one is poor or suffering external affliction, it is more likely found in those who are. On the other hand, the key social distinctive of the Judaeo-Christian as opposed to the Greek view of humility is precisely its non-hierarchical intent: it governs relations between people who are in principle equals, and is not a cliché for excessive deference to superiors.) Humility has in that sense an 'ex-centric' orientation, taking its focus outside oneself, and finding its power in the power of God. *God* is the one who humbles the proud but lifts up the humble (1 Sam. 2.1–10; Luke 1.46–55), to whom alone he reveals himself (cf. Ps. 25). As both 1QS and the New Testament writings show, humility in this sense creates corporate identity, community and solidarity.

The New Testament writers inherited this concept and continue to use it in its Jewish sense (e.g. Matt. 18.4; Luke 1.51–3; 14.11 par.; Jas. 4.6, 10; 1 Pet. 5.5–6). Beyond that, however, paradigmatic references to the humility of *Jesus* occur at several pivotal passages in the gospels (see e.g. Mark 10.45 par.; Matt. 11.29), and had a palpably formative influence for the early Christian notion of humility (cf. e.g. 2 Cor. 8.9; Eph. 5.2; 1 Pet. 2.23).

In Paul, perhaps the most illuminating parallel of the clash between the Greek and the biblical mentality is 2 Cor. 10.1, where he contrasts the Corinthians' apparently negative (secular) view of humility with the 'meekness and gentleness of Christ'. It is thus the humility of Christ which sustains Christian humility not just before God but before other people. Both the destructiveness of human pride and the true freedom of humility are known in the example of Christ, and so Paul's call for humility in the church can only be understood when one recognizes its specific link with the example of Christ in the following verses: Christ, too, 'humbled himself' (v. 8). It is significant for our passage that in Col. 3.12–15 humility is thought to be one of the prerequisites for love and peace among Christians. (Similarly Eph. 4.1–3; cf. Thomas à Kempis, *Imitation of Christ* 1.7, 'The humble live in continuous peace, while in the hearts of the proud are envy and frequent anger.') Far from being oppressive, therefore, the Christ-like humility commended in 2.5–8 is a liberating eschatological source of power, peace and communion (see Wengst 1988: 45–53; *pace* Briggs 1989 and Schottroff 1996: 43–6; cf. Koperski 1996: 336f., Osiek 1995: 243).

Like the twofold use of the verb 'to think' in verse 2, the two participles translated **consider** in this verse and 'look out for' in verse 4 refer to an attitude of heart and mind required for love and unity in the church. The participle translated **better** derives from the verb *huperechō* 'to surpass', found also at 3.8 and 4.7. Considering **each other better than yourselves** is not of course a matter of condescending to offer the occasional polite compliment to one's fellow Christian while continuing to bask in the untroubled assurance of one's own superiority. Nor, on the other hand, is it to grovel in a perpetually self-doubting or self-despising inferiority complex. It means to think and speak more highly of others than of oneself, to value their needs and their achievements before one's own; to give preference to each other without distinction – not only to the good, the strong or the beautiful (cf. K. Barth).

Choosing to build up others by deference and service: what this means is defined first and foremost in the example of Christ, about to be introduced in 2.5–11. Specifically, this exhortation is also illuminated by its possible social *Sitz im Leben* at Philippi, which as an imperial colony in Macedonia assigned a high value to questions of Roman social status and rank, even beyond the distinction between citizens and non-citizens (cf. e.g. Pilhofer 1995: 85–92, 122–34, 142–4). The presence of such status considerations in Roman Philippi would give considerable 'bite' to Paul's call to *consider others better*. This issue is noted by several commentators with reference to Merk 1968: 177–8. Cf. also Bormann 1995, *passim;* Garnsey 1970: 221ff.

Regardless of their ancient setting, however, these instructions should not be thought to have been any more congenial to the first century than they appear to us today, incited as we are by popular opinion makers to set our individual 'choices' and 'needs', and those of our 'communities' (which too often means special interest groups), before the good of others. It would be a profound misinterpretation to assume, as later critics did, that Paul's notion here is grounded in some sort of sickly masochism or unworldly philanthropic dream. Instead, he merely assumes that the road to peace must pass through unquestioned respect for the integrity and dignity of the other person. That, at any rate, had been Paul's recipe for the divided factions in the church at Rome a few years earlier, whom he also exhorted to imitate Christ in mutual acceptance and to 'pursue what makes for peace and for mutual upbuilding' (Rom. 14.19; cf. 15.6). The letter to the Ephesians similarly links humility, patience and 'bearing with one another in love' for the attainment of peace (Eph. 4.2–3). As the example of Christ in 2.5–11 goes on to demonstrate, true humility is a mark not of weakness but of strength.

4 Verse 4 provides another participial restatement of the nature of this Christian humility, and the final modifier of the call for like-mindedness in verse 2. To regard others as better than oneself means to **look out for** *their* **rights** (lit. 'the things of others'), and not just for one's own: to invest one's best creative effort and energy in securing and maintaining other people's best interest. A well-known motto among the early rabbis was, 'Let your friend's honour be as dear to you as your own' (*m.Abot* 2.15, R. Eliezer ben Hyrcanus). The secret of unity and like-mindedness, once again, lies in mutual unselfish interest in building others up – enabling them to achieve and enjoy 'things that they scarcely thought possible for themselves' (I.H. Marshall). This in turn erects, as John Chrysostom says with a view ahead to 4.5, a 'double wall of gentleness', which allows nothing hurtful to intrude (cf. similarly Polycarp *Phil.* 10.1: 'anticipating one another by the gentleness of the Lord').

Before summing up this paragraph we must pause for a brief textual note on 2.4, which was mentioned in the earlier discussion of the text of Philippians (Introduction, p. 40) and is pertinent to the interpretation. Readers who are comparing Bible translations will note that, while most translate, 'Let each of you look not *only* ...', but *also* ...', the NRSV offers a less accommodating rendering: 'Let each of you look not to your own interests, but to the interests of others.' The difference comes down to the omission of the single Greek word *kai* ('also') in the Western manuscript tradition and several Latin versions: the NRSV rendering follows this omission, whereas most other translations include the word. The issue is quite difficult to resolve on standard text critical principles, so that commentators are divided; even NA[27] represents the uncertainty by including the doubtful word in square brackets. External criteria of strong early and widespread support for the *kai* would suggest its authenticity. Internal criteria are more difficult to assess: one could argue on the one hand that a scribe might introduce this word to make the statement less radical. Its secondary removal, on the other hand, is equally conceivable on the Pauline precedent of 1 Cor. 10.24 ('Do not pursue your own interest, but that of the other'; cf. 10.33) along with the explicit 'not ... but ...' structure in verse 3.

Perhaps there is in the end little difference either in grammar or in practice: morally, Paul's point certainly is not self-neglect or self-loathing but a genuinely unselfish investment of ourselves for the good of other people. Grammatically, it is significant to note the absence of *monon* ('only') from the negative clause: Paul exhorts the Philippians to **look out not** [rather than 'not *only*'] **for your own rights**. In the absence of *monon, alla kai* properly serves to denote 'contrastive emphasis' (Louw & Nida 1989: §91.11), meaning 'but actually' or 'but rather' – not 'but also' (cf.

similarly LXX Ezra 2.15; Job 21.17; Isa. 39.4; 48.6; Ezek. 18.11; Wisd. 14.22). Either way, then, the emphasis here is on 'the other', on the peace and unity of the community as achieved when its members prioritize not their own private welfare but that of their brothers and sisters (cf. Müller 86f.). Paul does not operate by the neo-pagan presupposition that I cannot love others until I love myself. This is not of course because he hates himself: indeed the Christian life for him takes as its very starting point the fact that Christ 'loved me' and 'loved us' (Gal. 2.20; Rom. 8.37). Rather, and precisely for that reason, Paul sets out not to find himself but to find Christ – and 'to be found in him' (3.10). This is the only basis on which he and his readers can be freed to 'look out for each other's rights'.

Christian humility, then, can be properly understood and practically feasible only 'in Christ', and that in two ways. First, only personal dignity that has been incorporated and reconstituted in his cross and exultation (2.8–9) can *afford* to regard others as better than itself; and, second, Christ's own example both defines humility and assures its vindication and reward. Chrysostom shrewdly captures Paul's perspective when he says, 'There is nothing so foreign to a Christian soul as arrogance.' That is precisely what the following verses go on to demonstrate.

C   THE MIND OF CHRIST   (2.5–11)

Paul now proceeds to illustrate the Christian disposition by appealing in exalted, poetic language to the example of Christ himself. (Note that the following translation follows the versification of the Greek text; English translations generally take the last line of verse 7 with verse 8.)

(5) This is the attitude you should have among yourselves, which is also in Christ Jesus.

> **(6) While he was in the form of God,**
> **he did not think he needed to take advantage**
> **of this equality with God.**

> **(7) Instead, he emptied himself**
> **by taking the form of a slave**
> **and being born in human likeness;**

> **and, having appeared in human shape,**
> **(8) he humbled himself**
> **and became obedient as far as death**

> **– all the way to death on a cross.**

(9) And therefore God highly exalted him
and granted him the Name
        that is above every name,

(10) so that at the name of Jesus
'every knee shall bow',
        of those in heaven, on earth and under the earth;

(11) and every tongue shall confess
that 'Jesus Christ is Lord',
        for the glory of God the Father.

Verse 5 introduces a paragraph which, from the perspective of Christian theology and the 'effective history' of Philippians, is easily the most important in this letter (cf. Bockmuehl 1995: 75–83). It also (and for only partly related reasons) happens to be a passage which in the twentieth century has been the subject of an uncontainable deluge of scholarly debate, quite possibly more so than any other New Testament text. Other passages in the NT are of similar poetic grandeur and force; others have been similarly influential in the history of the church; but few if any have over this past century received even a comparable amount of scholarly attention. (In that respect at least, contemporary biblical scholars tend to gather like vultures over a suspected carcass.) Fifteen years ago, one well-known monograph on Philippians 2.5–11 and its modern history of interpretation had a bibliography of five hundred items; at least another hundred items could now easily be added (R.P. Martin 1983; cf. Rissi 1987, Hofius 1991 and recent commentaries).

In a treatment of this limited nature we can of course only highlight some of the key issues and suggest a way through the jungle which will at least indicate Paul's basic theological purpose in the passage. Students looking for further detail will be well served by recent full-scale critical commentaries (O'Brien offers 85 circumspect and tightly argued pages; cf. Müller's commentary as well as his 1988 article), monograph treatments like those by R.P. Martin 1983 and Hofius 1991, and the plentiful secondary literature they discuss. On the other hand, readers who are more interested in continuing the running exposition of Philippians are perhaps best advised to take note of the four questions raised below, and then to turn forward to p. 126 for the exegesis of the passage.

In addition to a number of knotty exegetical problems to be examined individually, several important issues have been raised about the passage as a whole – in particular about verses 6–11, which clearly belong together. Four questions are worth briefly addressing in turn:

(1) Are vv. 6–11 best understood as an early Christian *hymn*?

(2) Is Paul quoting vv. 6–11 from a previously existing Christian source?

(3) If so, was this source originally composed in Greek or in Aramaic?

(4) What is the religious background assumed by vv. 6–11?

(1) The striking poetic features of this passage were first expounded by J. Weiss in 1897 (cited in O'Brien 189), and then taken up in the commentaries of Plummer and others. Since then, they have been the subject of a large amount of further discussion, and a majority of scholars have long assumed that we are dealing in these verses with an early Christian 'hymn'. Detailed work has provided different analyses of the passage's poetic pattern, including the number and layout of the strophes. Some of the proposals have involved the omission or relocation of various phrases to accommodate a particular structure, thereby supporting interpretations in terms of one or another competing christology (kenotic, adoptionist, highlighting Adam or the servant of Isa. 53). Determined in part by the question of a pre-Pauline source (see below), these efforts have at times been guided by the desire to identify an aesthetically streamlined, supposedly original form of this 'hymn' – stripped, for instance, of the reference to the cross in v. 8 (on which see below).

Everyone agrees on the fact that exalted, lyrical, quasi-credal language is employed in these verses. There is an undeniable rhythm here, combined with typically poetic tension, repetition and a Hebraic-sounding parallelism (e.g. v. 7b, 8b), although occasional proposals to identify a clear meter have been forced and implausible (e.g. Eckman 1980; cf. the critique in Schenk 194). The issue at stake of course is whether the passage constitutes a 'hymn'; and this is largely a matter of definition. A minimum criterion might be actual liturgical use, whether in musical chant or in public credal recitation, prior to the writing of Philippians. Posed in these terms, however, the question is immediately reduced to a matter of speculation. Despite continuing assertions of this 'hymn' being *sung* in one setting or another (so e.g. Hengel 1995: 289; R. P. Martin 1992: 41; Minear 1990; cf. Karris 1996), we have in fact no contextual evidence of such use; nor is the passage ever cited in this connection in Christian literature of the first or second century. The book of Revelation presents us with a number of actual hymns (4.8, 11; 5.9, 12f.; 7.12;

11.17; 15.3f.) and the context of several other passages indicates their plausible or likely liturgical use (e.g. Luke 1.46–55, 68–79; Acts 8.37 *v.l.*; Rom. 10.9; 1 Cor. 12.3; 16.22; Eph. 5.14; 1 Tim. 3.16). Nevertheless, the existing evidence is too limited to permit any definite conclusions about the specific identification, setting and use of first-century Christian hymnic texts. A passing reference in Ephesians 5.19 certainly attests the *fact* that Christians used 'psalms and hymns and spiritual songs'; and we have some indication of early Christian liturgical poetry from the Septuagintal *Odes*, the *Odes of Solomon* and the *Apostolic Constitutions*; cf. also Pliny the Younger's report of Christians in Asia Minor 'saying' a hymn to Christ 'as if to a god' (*carmenque Christo quasi deo dicere: Letter* 10.96). But in the absence of a clearly controlled and documented typology we have no way of identifying such a hymn in our case with any degree of confidence. (For a similar criticism of the 'hymnic' identification see Schenk 193–5; cf. Basevi & Chapa 1993; Kennel 1995. On hymns in early Christian worship more generally see Hengel 1995; R. P. Martin 1992.)

Perhaps another telling argument *against* a 'hymnic' reading of this passage is the observation that scholars have advanced at least half a dozen mutually incompatible proposals of how the different stanzas are to be arranged and divided. Some of these in fact depend on surgery on the text as it stands, involving various omissions or rearrangements. (What is more, most scholars acknowledge that on any reconstruction this text could constitute only a hymnic *fragment*, since the subject is not explicit but introduced in v. 6 by the relative pronoun *hos*, 'who'. Note, however, the role of this same *hos* in introducing similarly solemn christological affirmations, e.g. in Rom. 3.25; 4.25; 8.32; 1 Cor. 1.30; Col. 1.13; 1 Tim. 3.16.)

This lack of agreement about the very form and outline of our passage suggests that, even though poetic *style* and credal *language* are undoubtedly present, it is unwarranted and potentially misleading to call it a 'hymn' in the absence of evidence for its liturgical usage. (Cf. Fee 1992 and Hooker 1978, though the latter does on balance prefer to see here a 'poem' rather than prose. Note also that REB, somewhat exceptionally, does not print this text in a poetic layout.)

(2) Closely related is the question of *authorship*. In 1928, E. Lohmeyer published the first edition of his commentary and a monograph on Phil. 2.5–11 entitled *Kyrios Jesus*. Noting several unusual features of the vocabulary, style and theology of the passage, as well as its apparent integrity and independence from the flow of Paul's own argument, Lohmeyer concluded that

verses 6–11 were originally a Jewish-Christian liturgical hymn which Paul merely quotes in order to buttress his own argument. Since then, variations on Lohmeyer's basic thesis of a pre-Pauline source have been followed by a large majority of scholars; Schenk (175, 210, 336) even proposes that the Philippians had composed the passage themselves!

Nothing in the context indicates that Paul is quoting anything or wants his readers to think that he is. Nevertheless, the same is of course true of many Pauline quotations from the Old Testament, which would have been clear as such to him, and perhaps in many cases to his readers. In assessing the material, therefore, it is important to consider several other criteria, above all a number of unusual words and ideas. Only here does Paul use the word *harpagmos*, which denotes an action of greed paraphrased in our translation as 'making the most of' something; more significantly, he does not elsewhere speak of Christ's incarnation in terms of 'self-humbling' (*kenoô*, v. 7; *tapeinoô*, v. 8), of his 'form' (*morphé*, v. 6–7), or indeed of his becoming a 'slave' (*doulos*, v. 7). Several other linguistic points have been made. Theologically, too, scholars have noted the lack of reference to the resurrection or the parousia; some have also argued on structural grounds that the reference to the cross in v. 8 is secondary, having been added in by Paul (so e.g. among recent commentators Schenk 191 and Müller 105).

A detailed refutation of these and other arguments would exceed our present purposes. Suffice it to say that the linguistic arguments are particularly inconclusive, since they prescribe for Paul a narrowness of style and vocabulary that one would not dare to impose on any other author. Many other, indubitably authentic passages also contain *hapax legomena* (words used only once). Given the very limited extent of Paul's surviving literary output, such evidence really leads nowhere – especially if one considers that it is precisely in poetical or lyrical contexts that one might well expect an author to resort to unusual language.

The theological points are indeed more interesting; but here, too, one should not confine Paul to a straitjacket that he himself clearly does not don elsewhere: in the case of issues such as the Law or eschatology, one readily finds him adopting a variety of seemingly incompatible approaches, without any need to assume inauthenticity or self-contradiction. Here, the theme of the incarnation as the pre-existent Christ's self-humbling is in fact confirmed to be Pauline at 2 Cor. 8.9 (so rightly I.H. Marshall 1993: 129). The resurrection is absent from other passages about the incarnation and the cross, and vice versa (cf. e.g. Rom. 10.6–15; Gal. 2.20f.; 1 Thess. 5.10). Similarly, the postulate of a secondary insertion of the cross is really a matter of doubtful conjecture; in fact, a number of scholars emphatically *include* it in their reconstruction of the 'hymn' (see below on v. 8). The resurrection, on the other hand, is arguably implicit in Christ's exaltation, since the flow of the narrative clearly requires this as the reversal of the downward direction that ended in death. On this point there is, moreover, a certain circularity in the 'pre-Pauline' view of 2.6–11: if the passage is in fact Pauline, there is really no problem in the wider context of Philippians, since the resurrection of Christ does occur explicitly in 3.10 and the parousia in 1.10; 2.16; 3.20f.

The several untypical ideas and terms in the passage must of course be acknowledged. Nevertheless, they could well be the result of its poetical style: one might compare 1 Cor. 13, which also contains nine Pauline *hapax legomena* and a number of unparalleled ideas. Alternatively, we might be dealing with an 'intertextual' attempt to evoke certain well-known Christian traditions and concepts which Paul and his readers shared in common (cf. e.g. Heb. 2.9; 5.8–10; *Asc. Isa.* 3.13–18). Neither assumption requires pre-Pauline authorship. (Similar examples of a tacitly reassuring allusion to Christian tradition may be present in Rom. 1.3f. and 3.25f.; see also Meeks 1991 on the possible influence of Johannine thought on Phil. 2.6–11.)

However one decides this question, one important methodological consideration must surely govern all cases of possible pre-Pauline quotations: the exegete is duty-bound to accept that Paul uses all his material because in his opinion it says what he wants, and that he means what he says. Modern readers of Philippians will do well to recognize that these lines would have formed a seamless part both of Paul's continuous *dictation* of the letter, as well as of its intended oral delivery (cf. Fee 194 n. 6). It simply will not do, therefore, as a number of commentators have presumed (including my own predecessor in this series), to interpret such passages only in relation to their imagined original setting – as though Paul or his letter had nothing to do with them. Statements about the supposed *setting and background* of such 'pre-Pauline' texts are, with very few exceptions, doubly speculative. Even where there is good reason to suspect pre-Pauline material, therefore, responsible interpretation will focus its efforts on the meaning of the text within its present context. What matters is how a text is now heard by its author and his readers – even though in Paul's case that of course may well at times amount to at least two different things (cf. Jas. 2.14–26; 2 Pet. 3.15f.; Acts 21.21). What *else* a quotation may or may not have meant in its own supposed original setting is in strictly exegetical terms irrelevant for the interpretative task at hand – just as the historical Maher-shalal-hash-baz (Isa. 8.1ff.) could be said to have little bearing on the meaning of Isaiah 7.14 in Matthew 1.23. In our case it is particularly significant that a good many verbal and conceptual links can be shown to connect the passage quite specifically with its immediately preceding (esp. 2.1–4) and following (2.12ff.) context.

In the absence of persuasive evidence to the contrary, therefore, the interpretation of Philippians 2.6–11 may for all practical purposes proceed on the assumption that these are the words of Paul. (Several other recent authors have also failed to find compelling reasons for a pre-Pauline origin: e.g. Carson, Moo, Morris 1992: 318–19; Fee; O'Brien; Silva; I.H. Marshall 1993: 129; Wick 1994: 178–180. Hengel 1995: 289 allows for this possibility; cf. also Basevi & Chapa 1993: 343. On the methodological assumption that Paul means what he says, see also the sage comments of Fee 192 n. 3.)

We can now deal rather more briefly with the two remaining questions.

(3) E. Lohmeyer argued that this passage was originally composed in Aramaic; several other scholars since then have presented a variety of proposed retranslations into Aramaic (e.g. recently Fitzmyer 1988), though occasional counter-arguments have also been voiced. Given Paul's own native Hebrew and Aramaic background, however (2 Cor. 11.22; Phil. 3.5; cf. Acts 21.40; 22.3; 26.14), these and other Semitisms should not be surprising, least of all in such a lyrical and highly charged religious text as this. What the feasibility of such efforts *does* demonstrate is not so much a pre-Pauline Palestinian Christian origin (*pace* Fitzmyer 1988: 483), but that the passage is composed in language indebted to that tradition and should in the first instance be read against that formative background.

(4) A wide range of possible religious backgrounds has been proposed for the ideas in Philippians 2.6–11. This contextual question of course becomes rather more pressing for those who suppose both that the hymn is pre-Pauline and that its original meaning and setting are vital for its interpretation. Given our limited knowledge of pre-Pauline Christianity and of its christology, this has left scholars the freedom to differ radically as to the likely background of the 'hymn': whether mainstream Jewish and Old Testament views of the Suffering Righteous or of Adam; whether Hellenistic Jewish Wisdom speculation, pre-Christian Hellenistic or Jewish Gnosticism, the Iranian Heavenly Redeemer

myth, etc., or even combinations of a number of settings (e.g. Seeley 1994). The various options are well covered in the second-ary literature (e.g. O'Brien 193–8, 263–8; R.P. Martin 1983 *passim*).

If, on the other hand, we are primarily interested in the meaning of the passage in its present context, the problem of ascertaining its original *Sitz im Leben* is immediately far less acute; if one assumes Pauline authorship, it disappears. One is then still left with the issue of the conceptual background to Paul's own thought, and perhaps to that of the Philippians. But this problem is no more serious than for any other Pauline text; the answers are likely to be commensurable, and will apply for the letter as a whole. We have tried to outline something of the Philippian context in the Introduction. As for Paul himself, his writings are best seen as the product of his religious and cultural formation in Palestinian and Diaspora Judaism on the one hand, and of his experience as a missionary to Gentiles on the other. We shall leave more specific observations for the exposition of 2.5–11, to which we must now turn.

5 Verse 5 begins a new sentence, following the series of sub-ordinate clauses that dominated the syntax of 2.1–4. But rather than being set apart both from 2.1–4 and 2.6–11, this verse constitutes an inextricable link between the two passages. Paul resumes the fourfold emphasis in 2.1–4 on the right Christian **attitude** (*phroneô*, cf. v. 2 (2x); also *tapeinophrosuné*, 'humility', and *hégeomai*, 'consider', in v. 3), thus preparing for the descrip-tion of the mind of Christ, who did not 'consider' (*hégeomai*, v. 6) equality with God something to be exploited, but 'humbled' himself (*tapeinoô*, v. 8). What is more, verse 5 is many ways the linchpin of the whole argument of 1.27–2.18: the key to a citizen-ship 'worthy of the gospel of Christ' is in fact none other than to adopt the mind of Christ. (Some would even argue that 2.6–11 represents a rendition of that gospel of Christ: see O'Brien 204 n. 4, citing Mengel 1982: 245.)

However, even if the place of verse 5 in its context is agreed to be fairly clear, its meaning is open to different interpretations and has been the subject of considerable debate. A literal translation would be, 'Think this among yourselves, which also in Christ Jesus.' Alternatively, the verb could be read not as imperative but as indicative: 'You think this ...'. The latter option receives support from a widely attested, but probably secondary manu-script variant which inserts a 'for' (*gar*) to provide a smoother link with the preceding verses – thus grammatically ruling out an imperative. However, Paul's whole point in the preceding and following verses is to urge the Philippians to *adopt* a new disposition towards each other; so most interpreters accept the imperative as required by the context. Syntactically, too, the opening word **this** is here best understood as gathering up verses 2–4 and linking forward to the **which** of v. 5b, while the verb *phroneô* ('think', here rendered *have this attitude*) explicitly picks up verse 2. The grammatical links are determined by the theological nexus of the Philippian Christians' incorporation into Christ.

A more serious problem remains, however: the literal translation shows that one also requires a verb to be supplied in the relative clause. The main proposals boil down to two: 'Have this attitude among yourselves,'

'which *was* also in Christ Jesus' (the 'ethical' reading).
'which *you have* in Christ Jesus' (the 'kerygmatic' reading).

The most notable supporters of the latter reading include Käsemann 1950 and R.P. Martin 1983. These writers suggest that Paul is encouraging the Philippians to adopt in their relationship with each other the disposition that is already (or at least *ought* to be) theirs in their relationship with Christ. The interpretation is based on two assumptions. First, the following, pre-Pauline 'Christ-hymn' of 2.6–11 must be interpreted in line with its supposed original context; and however that may be construed, 2.6–11 taken in isolation has a *doctrinal* (and hence 'kerygmatic') rather than any obvious ethical function. Secondly, Käsemann in particular objects to the 'ethical' interpretation on the grounds that it is impossible: verses 6–11 speak of incarnation, death on the cross and exaltation to heaven, none of which can be understood as an ethical example to follow.

In reply, it must be said that the insistence on a pre-Pauline setting really begs the question of how Paul himself is using the phrase here. And on this level the close parallels especially between 2.6–11 and 2.1–4 clearly suggest that he is wanting to draw *ethical* consequences for the attitude of Christians from the example of the attitude displayed by Jesus. That this is not an alien thought to him is easily demonstrated by passages like Rom. 15.2f., 7 or 2 Cor. 8.9 (cf. Col. 3.13; Eph. 4.32; 5.2, 25), where participation in Christ is similarly put to moral use in terms of the imitation of his example. (The same idea is reiterated in Polycarp's letter to Philippi, 8.2; 10.1.) See further the useful methodological observations of Fowl 1990 and Kraftchick 1993a on the ethical interpretation of narrative.

It is of course true that imitating the incarnation, or even the moral attitude behind the incarnation, seems a somewhat problematic notion in several respects – not to mention the exaltation, vv. 9–11. Nevertheless, we must acknowledge the possibility that it may seem so more to the modern interpreter than it did to Paul. The rhetorical purpose of his argument is in any case concerned not to persuade his readers to try and discern a vague similarity, but firmly to posit an analogy. Such 'imitation' of Christ (for this term compare 1 Thess. 1.6; 1 Cor. 11.1; Eph. 5.1), therefore, amounts not to the replication of particular actions but to the emulation, *mutatis mutandis*, of equivalent attitudes. For the rabbis, the imitation of God, explicitly enjoined in Deut. 13.4, meant to emulate his merciful and gracious attributes (*Mek. Beshallaḥ* 3 on Exod. 15.2 (L. 2:25: Abba Saul, 2nd cent.); *b.Sot* 14a). Here, then, just as Christ was not proud and self-serving but humbly served others, obedient until death, so the Philippians should not be selfish but humbly devoted to others (2.2), obedient (2.12, 14f.) and steadfast in their suffering for him (1.28–30; cf. 2.17f.).

God's response to such obedience, too, is analogous to the example of Christ: just as Christ was vindicated in his eschatological exaltation (2.9–11 – N.B. this is no longer his action, therefore no longer an example to be emulated), so those who adopt the mind of Christ may confidently expect to be vindicated with him and by him (1.6, 19; 3.10–14, 20f.). In this respect, *being* 'in Christ' (cf. above, p. 52) engenders *doing* in accord with his example.

Without wishing to deny the 'kerygmatic' significance of being **in Christ**, therefore, this leaves us in the present context with a primary stress on some version of the 'ethical' interpretation, the first of the two options outlined above. On this reading, there is an explicit appeal to the example of Jesus, which probably requires that one supplies a form of the verb 'to be' (Lightfoot's reading, 'as Christ Jesus *thought* in himself', is somewhat too periphrastic). Given the past tense narrative that follows, most interpreters of this persuasion have opted for a straightforward historical reference to 'the mind-set … which *was* also in Christ Jesus'. This interpretation, a version of which was eloquently argued by Moule 1970: 265, is certainly possible and will not miss Paul's point by much. (See further Fowl 1990: 77–101, Hawthorne 1996: 167–72, Hurtado 1984 and Larsson 1962 on the imitation of the story of Christ.)

Finally, however, a grammatical consideration suggests the possibility of a further refinement of this reading. In NT Greek, verbless subordinate clauses most naturally reflect the tense of the main clause (e.g. 1 Cor. 8.6; Heb. 2.10). Grammatically, therefore, the simplest reading is to supply the *present* tense of 'to be': 'have this attitude amongst yourselves, which *is* also in Christ Jesus'. While it leaves intact the moral analogy with the narrative that follows, this reading has the advantage that the indicated attitudes of the mind of Christ are seen to be not just a past fact of history but a *present reality*. (Cf. also REB: 'what you find in Christ Jesus'.)

Four substantive arguments also favour this perspective. (i) It seems strongly implied in the way in which Paul grounds the Christ-like attitudes he encourages among the Philippians in the present accessibility of life 'in Christ' (2.1; cf. 4.1–2). (ii) The layout of 2.6–11 appears to make certain statements about the time before and after the incarnation which are of necessity beyond and outside time. For Paul, as for contemporary Jewish apocalyptic thought, God's messianic designs, though realized in history, have a certain timeless existence in eternity; a good illustration of this is Paul's notion of a heavenly mystery concealed for eternal ages, but now made manifest in history (1 Cor. 2.6–16; Col. 1.26f.). (iii) The ongoing reality of Christ's interest in the good of others seems strongly implied in a number of Pauline and other NT texts. Despite his exaltation to heaven, Paul evidently believes that Christ still intercedes for us even now (Rom. 8.34; cf. Heb. 7.25; John 17): the love of him who 'loved us' is now an ongoing and eternal fact (Rom. 8.35–9; 2 Thess. 2.16f.; 2 Cor. 1.3–5; 5.14). Here in Philippians, not only is the 'compassion of Christ' still a present reality (1.8; cf. 2.1), but he himself is 'near' as the ground of all joy and gentleness (4.4f.), in every aspect of life (1.21). (iv) Finally, this translation may narrow the gap between the usual two options: although 'in Christ Jesus' still relates to the agent whose attitude the Philippians should emulate, there is on this reading a clearer acknowledgement that the reality of his example embraces both past and present.

In some sense, therefore, the 'mind-set' of unselfish compassion which Paul encourages in the Philippians 'is present' in Christ Jesus both historically and eternally. This belief, indeed, could be said to follow from the continuity of the 'Jesus Christ of history' with the 'Jesus Christ of faith' that is implied in the resurrection: for Paul, the one who 'was buried' (1 Cor. 15.4) is present as the one who was raised. This alone enables a present *participation* in, rather than mere remembrance of, past saving events (1 Cor. 10.16). A similar principle may underlie the Johannine notion of the scars of the risen Jesus, John 20.20–26; and of the lamb standing in heaven 'as if it had been slaughtered', Rev. 5.6; cf. 13.8.

Thomas Aquinas quite reasonably sees in this verse an encouragement for Christians to acquire in their own experience the disposition that is already theirs in the example of Christ. In an intriguing homiletical exposition, he then goes on to show from Scripture how this task of experiential appropriation is to be accomplished for each of the five senses: to see Christ's glory and thus become enlightened (Isa. 33.17; 2 Cor. 3.18), to hear his wisdom and so become happy (1 Kgs. 10.8; Ps. 18.44), to smell the grace of his meekness and therefore run to him (Cant. 1.3), to taste the sweetness of his mercy and remain always in God (Ps. 34.9), and to touch his power and thus be saved (Matt. 9.21).

6 The christological passage (the 'hymn') itself, then, comprises verses 6–11. Given its poetic character, the literary structure is particularly worth noting.

The poetic structure of 2.6–11

The outline of this passage is now generally recognized as falling into (a) verses 6–8 dealing with Christ's action of humbling himself, and (b) 9–11 with God's action of vindicating and exalting him. Beyond that, however, conflicting detailed outlines have been proposed. For an interpretation of the passage within its present context, it will be important not to accentuate literary form at the expense of content. Thus, taking into account both considerations, we may offer a fairly basic compromise solution, which is also reflected in the translation given above. (This analysis represents a modification of Hooker 1978: 158f., who has been followed by several other commentators.)

(a)	6a-c	3 lines on Jesus' attitude in his original state
	7a-c	3 lines on his attitude in becoming human
	7d-8b	3 lines on his attitude in his passion and death
	8c	reiteration and turning point: his death on the cross
(b)	9a-c	3 lines on God's response of exalting him
	10a-c	3 lines on purpose (i): his dominion over all creatures
	11a-c	3 lines on purpose (ii): his worship by all creatures.

Scholars of various persuasions have noted that the reference to the Cross in verse 8c is in some ways the odd one out: the literary rhythm appears to slow down and grind to a halt at this point. So, of course, does the narrative of Christ's descent to death. As a result, it seems appropriate to acknowledge the special status of this line as the pivot and turning point between the two halves, 'crowning' Christ's humiliation and as a result ('therefore', v. 9) meriting his exaltation.

This is of course only one possible structural analysis among many. In any case, however, O'Brien 192 is right to note that as long as we acknowledge a contingency of form on content, 'a correct understanding of the hymn is not dependent on its correct versification'. This point is strengthened still further if the literary character is in any case best seen not as formal poetry but as lyrical, exalted prose (so e.g. Fee 1992). With that in mind, we may turn to the interpretation of verse 6.

Exegesis of 2.6–11

Verse 6 begins in Greek with the relative pronoun 'who' (*hos*), which in its present context clearly identifies Christ as the subject. In 2 Cor. 8.9 we find a similar pattern: a moral appeal to generosity is linked by a relative pronoun to the story of Christ. Here, Paul's narrative appeal to the 'mind' of Christ begins with his pre-existent state as one who already enjoyed equality with God.

What does it mean to say Christ **was** (lit. 'existing') **in the form of God**? Although it originally denoted the visible outward appearance of a person or object, the word **form** (*morphē*, only Phil. 2.6f. and Mark 16.17) could also come to mean the distinguishing characteristics that correspond to this appearance. Here, it is worth noting from a literary perspective that **the form of God** is parallel with **equality** (lit. 'being equal') **with God**; at the same time, it has its counterpart in verse 7 in the phrase **the form of a slave** (*morphē doulou*), which in turn is further paralleled by **in human likeness**. In this context, these phrases suggest the linguistic contours within which to understand the term **form of God**. Among the majority of scholars there is still widespread agreement that we are dealing with Christ's state or condition in relation to God, *prior to* his state or condition as a servant. In some sense, **equality with God** interprets **in the form of God** (cf. Wright 1986: 344; Hawthorne 84). Beyond this, however, interpretations of the term *morphē* have varied from God's 'essential attributes' to his state or mode of being, from his 'glory' to his 'image'.

New Testament and Septuagintal usage is not a great deal of help in resolving the problem, since in the NT the word is used only here and in the longer ending of Mark (16.12), where it describes the visible 'form' of the resurrection appearance on the road to Emmaus. The relatively rare LXX usage of *morphē* has not proved a great deal more helpful. Job's night vision in Job 4.16 suggests that *morphé* is something visible to the eyes, while Isaiah 44.13 makes it clear that the 'form of a man' means the physical human shape. Visible shape or appearance is clearly also what is intended in several references in Daniel (4.36; 5.6, 9, 10; 7.28) and in the Deuterocanonical books (e.g. 4 Macc. 15.4; Wisd. 18.1; cf. Wisd. 7.10; 11.17; Sir. 9.8; 4 Macc. 8.10). Conversely, despite an undeniable conceptual proximity of *morphé* to the terms of 'image' or 'glory' they are in fact by no means synonymous (cf. W. Pöhlmann in *EDNT* 2: 443; Steenburg 1988; Fee 204 n. 49, 209 n. 73; note also Fowl 1990: 53f. on the visual meaning of *morphé*).

Various other conceptual backgrounds have been proposed, but no entirely obvious or satisfactory explanation has as yet emerged, in part because no fully plausible Hebraic or Hellenistic setting has been demonstrated. Dibelius 74 plausibly related the term to the German word *Gestalt* (shape, form), stressing the primarily mythological origins of the notion of a divine 'form'. Similar terminology certainly occurs in Greek religion, magical papyri and Gnostic texts (cf. J. Behm, *TDNT* 4: 746–8; also Müller 93f.); but many of these texts relate explicitly or implicitly to the classic mythological legends, while later ones often show syncretistic Jewish influence. Given the Jewish-Christian tenor of our passage, a direct dependence on such pagan material must be deemed highly unlikely.

Our working hypothesis here will be to read the word *morphé* quite straightforwardly in terms of the visual characteristics of a person or object: that, at any rate, applies equally well to the two uses of the word in vv. 6–7. Philo of Alexandria also generally employs *morphé* in this sense. His treatment of one biblical passage in particular opens up an intriguing possibility which has not been widely explored. In his *Life of Moses* 1.66, Philo describes how Moses approached the burning bush (Exod. 3) and saw in the midst of the fire

> a most beautiful form (*morphé*), not like any visible object, an image supremely divine in appearance, shining with a light more brilliant than that of fire. One might suppose this to be the image of Him Who Is (*eikona tou ontos*); but let us call it an angel.

Philo clearly goes beyond the LXX in suggesting that what Moses saw in the bush was something which, although on balance best regarded as an angel, nevertheless manifested a 'form' which in every significant respect could easily be taken to be that of God. One senses that his desire to safeguard the transcendence of God's 'form' (cf. Wisd. 18.1) leaves Philo somewhat tentative, and in any case he does not explore the word *morphé* along these lines elsewhere. Nevertheless, this glimpse leaves open the possibility that the notion of God's 'form' could belong to the context of Jewish traditions about mystical ascent to heaven and about the heavenly appearance of God – traditions with which Paul himself may show some measure of familiarity (cf. e.g. Rowland 1982: 378–86; Schäfer 1984; also Segal 1990: 34–71, Morray-Jones 1993 and Scott 1996; but note the critique of Morray-Jones in Goshen Gottstein 1995).

Of potential interest in this regard is a group of first-century BC texts in the Dead Sea Scrolls known as the *Songs of the Sabbath Sacrifice*. This material shows a sustained interest in the worship offered by heavenly beings in the immediate presence of God. Here, reference is made, for instance, to (i) the 'form' (*tabnit*, translated *morphé* in LXX Isa. 44.13) of the divine throne chariot (4Q405 20–21–22.ii.8); (ii) the glorious 'form' (*tabnit*) of the leaders in the realm of spirits (4Q403 2.3); (iii) the blessing offered to the captains of 'the form of God' (*tabnit elohim*): possibly 'the form of divine beings' (4Q403 2.16); as well as to 'every form (*tabnit*) of wondrous spirits' (11Q17 5–6.2), who again are closely associated with *elohim*, 'God' or 'divine beings'. Although it is not the only term used in this connection, the word *tabnit* is particularly interesting in this regard, since rather like *morphé* it refers most typically to the visible, three-dimensional shape or design of an object. Its biblical precedents in relation to heavenly realities include Exod. 25.9, 40 and Ezek. 8.3, all three of which are passages used in later mystical texts. God's *tzelem* and *demût*, both of which can mean an image or likeness in either two or three dimensions, are regularly predicated of man (see Gen. 1.26f. 5.3); but human beings are never said to be in God's *tabnit*. A passage in the Talmud in fact intimates the relationship to 'image' by saying that man's being made 'in the image (*tzelem*) of God' means 'in the image (*tzelem*) of the likeness (*demût*) of his form (*tabnit*)' (*b.Ket.* 8a); the 'form' according to this text concerns God's true appearance, while his image and likeness remain at one remove. (Cf. the formulation in Ezek. 1.28b, 'the appearance of the likeness of the glory of the Lord'.)

The same interest in the form of God continues in mystical texts of later centuries. On the Jewish side, they develop an increasing interest in the anthropomorphic 'measures' and dimensions of the divine body, which was apparently inspired by the descriptions of the body of the Beloved in the Song of Songs. (Fishbane 1992 highlights the use of concepts like God's 'measure' *middah* or 'form' *tzurah* in Tannaitic midrashim, and compares this with Eph. 4.13 and *passim*; Mopsik 1994 similarly relates that passage to the later *Shi'ur Qomah*. See further Cohen

1983.) Similar interests in the divine form are present in the Slavonic *2 Enoch* (13.3–10) as well as in Valentinian and other forms of Gnosticism with their distinctive concern for divine *morphai*, 'forms'.

The full details of this argument would take us beyond the scope of this commentary (see further Bockmuehl 1997). Suffice it to say that the **form of God** probably means simply the visual characteristics of his heavenly being, which Christ shared but took on the characteristics of a servant. Such an interpretation may be underlined by the complementary contrast which Paul draws in 3.21 between two kinds of body, (lit.) the human 'body of our humiliation' and Christ's heavenly 'body of glory' (cf. also 1 Cor. 15.40, 44; and note Stroumsa 1983.) This reading of *morphé*, then, strongly confirms our passage's emphasis on Christ's pre-existence (in this respect Calvin and others rightly compare John 17.5); and it does so by linking the text with a well-established Jewish mystical tradition which could speak of God and heavenly beings in unabashedly visual and even anthropomorphic terms.

Christ humbled himself because he **did not think he needed to take advantage of this equality with God**, lit. 'he did not consider it *harpagmos* to be equal to God'. At the heart of this phrase is another rare and highly disputed term, which has been the subject of at least twenty different interpretations. The fullest recent study of *harpagmos* has been that of Wright 1986 (cf. 1991: 62–90, including a useful tabular arrangement on p. 81); little would be gained by rehearsing his thorough analysis here. For our purposes the different variations may be summed up under three main categories, all of which are semantically possible: (i) Christ did not think that the state of being equal to God consisted in 'snatching' or 'getting', but rather in self-giving; (ii) he did not consider equality with God, which he already enjoyed, a prized possession to be retained and selfishly exploited; or (iii) he did not consider such equality a prize or treasure to be snatched or gained (but which he did not yet possess). To use the Latin tags which have often been applied to the different interpretations for convenience: (i) views *harpagmos* predicatively, as the *action* of snatching itself (*raptus*). Options (ii) and (iii) both see it as denoting the prize which is the *object* of that action: (ii) takes it as a present possession to be used for oneself (*res rapta, res retinenda*), while (iii) identifies the prize as something still to be acquired (*res rapienda*).

A decisive argument against (iii), arising from our earlier discussion of the 'form of God', is that the context precisely does *not* suggest that there was still some higher status to which the

129

pre-incarnate Christ might possibly have aspired. This reading also fails to explain why, had there been such a thing, it would have been wrong to aspire to it.

Interpretation (i), by contrast, makes better sense of the exegetical and theological context: equality with God was for Christ not concerned with snatching, pursuing 'selfish ambition' (2.3) and 'looking out for his own interests' (2.4), but divinity in its very nature meant giving and self-emptying (so e.g. Moule 1970; Bruce 1981: 271f.; Hawthorne 85). Despite its considerable advantages, however, three slight queries weigh against this reading. The first is the idea that a divine being should have been thought, even hypothetically, to consider 'snatching' at something that was not already his. Secondly, this proposal may also tend to weaken the logical force of Christ's example, on which Paul's exhortation draws in 2.5 and throughout the letter. If the point is the more abstract one that Christ did not consider divinity to consist in acquisitiveness, the practical analogy with the Christian life is less obvious than if it is interpretation (ii), that he did not treat who he was and what he had as a means to selfish ends. The latter, finally, may also explain more readily why v. 6 requires the strongly adversative *alla* ('but, instead') in v. 7: reading (i) could just as easily have been followed by 'therefore'.

Interpretation (ii), then, is a closely comparable but on balance somewhat more satisfactory solution: Christ did not consider his existing divine status as a possession to be exploited for selfish interests. The rhetorical context of our passage (2.1–5; 2.14, 21 etc.) gives this reading considerable exegetical and theological advantages; these are further buttressed by philological research suggesting that in secular usage to consider something a *harpagmos* means to exploit fully something that is already in one's possession (see Wright 1986; O'Brien; Fee, all of whom cite Hoover 1971). The force of the sentence, including the contrastive *alla*, can then be seen as structurally equivalent to a common NT description of the work of Christ: he did not come to please himself, but to bear the burdens of humankind (Rom. 15.3; Mark 10.45 par.; cf. Rom. 8.32; John 12.47).

At the end of the day, it must be highly doubtful that Paul or his audience would have tied themselves in knots over this word even remotely as much as his interpreters have done. It will suffice to conclude, as Silva 117 does, that 'v. 6 is simply concerned to state negatively what the main verbs in vv. 7–8 state positively': Jesus refused to act selfishly with regard to his pre-incarnate state in relation to God; **he did not think he needed to take advantage**, to make the most of it. We should recall that this is the attitude Paul had in view when in verse 3 he used the same verb ('think, consider') in 'consider each other better than yourselves'.

Unlike the human (and perhaps especially the Philippian) tendency to use status and privilege to one's own advantage, Christ did not regard his position as something to be selfishly exploited.

A number of scholars have seen in this verse, as well as in verses 7-8, a deliberate contrast between Christ and the story of the Fall of Adam in Genesis 3. The argument is roughly this: Adam was in the image of God (Gen. 1.26f.; 5.3) but *did* snatch at equality with God (cf. Gen. 3.5); where Adam was disobedient, Christ was obedient, etc. Aside from a general, though not inevitable, predisposition in favour of seeing *harpagmos* as a prize to be acquired (i.e. (iii) above), the underlying assumption tends to be that 'form' in Phil. 2.6 is interchangeable with 'image' in Genesis (and 'glory' elsewhere). On this reading, the present passage represents another instance of the 'first Adam – second Adam' theme, which Paul develops clearly in Rom. 5.18-19; 1 Cor. 15.45-7 (and hints of which have been seen in other passages as well, including Col. 1.15; 2 Cor. 4.4).

This suggestion, too, has given rise to a large amount of secondary literature, which is reflected in the full-scale commentaries (e.g. O'Brien's excursus, 263-8). Key proponents of an Adamic reading have included Cullmann 1963: 174-81, Dunn 1980: 174-81, Hooker 1978 and Murphy-O'Connor 1976: 25-50 (and 1996: 227); cf. somewhat differently Wright 1991a: 57-9, 90-5.

Two significant inter-connected issues require attention: (1) does Paul intend a parallel with Adam? And (2) if he does, is the parallel chiefly concerned with the earthly Jesus?

(1) Regarding the first issue, it is easy to see the intriguing potential in this text for a contrast between Christ and Adam; and interpreters have in fact suggested this connection ever since Irenaeus (*Haer.* 5.16.2-3; cf. 3.22.1, 3-4). In the wider terms of Pauline theology, too, such an Adam vs. Christ polarity seems entirely suitable and appropriate.

Nevertheless, the passage has proved remarkably resistant to any positive demonstration of verbal or other specific parallels with the text of Genesis 3. In the Genesis story, it is Eve rather than Adam who receives the proposal to be 'like God' (Gen. 3.5; LXX has 'like gods'). This 'likeness', moreover, is expressed specifically in terms of the knowledge of good and evil, which was in fact acquired (Gen. 3.22), rather than in terms of being 'equal to

God'. Neither 'form' (*morphē*) nor 'equality' (*isos*) are ever mentioned in the Genesis text. As we have seen, the suggested identification of 'form' with 'image' (or even 'glory') is not only lexically hard to substantiate, but would appear to falter on the repetition of the word in v. 7 ('form of a slave'); cf. Wanamaker 1987; Steenburg 1988. The language of 'existence' (*huparchōn*) in the form of God hardly applies to Adam, and the parallel is made highly unlikely by the notion of *taking on* the 'form of a slave'.

(2) The second question is to some extent dependent on the first, as is the urgency with which it must be asked. If there is a sense in which Christ undoes what Adam did, where is this act to be located? Those who affirm the Adamic scenario here vary as to whether they see verse 6 taking place in heaven (the pre-existently human Second Adam) and only verses 7–8 on earth, or all of verses 6–8 predicated of the incarnate Christ. Although parallels to the former idea have been sought in 1 Cor. 15.47 and in Philo of Alexandria, an eternally pre-existent *human* Jesus seems difficult to establish in Paul and to square either with the assertions of v. 6 or with the implied *movement* to humanity in v. 7. The second option has in recent times been strongly championed by Dunn 1980: 174–81, who argues that even v. 6 must be read in Adamic terms of the human Jesus, and that therefore there is here no mention of pre-existence or any prior temporal reference at all: Jesus' exaltation is not his 'return' to heaven but the restoration to the human 'Second Adam' of the glory which the first Adam lost.

Despite attracting a good deal of interest, it is probably fair to say that Dunn's interpretation has failed to win the day. It seems unable to accommodate the most likely reading of 'the form of God', and of the term *harpagmos*, in relation to 'equality with God'. It also, as a result, disrupts the natural flow of Christ being first in that 'form' and then 'born in human likeness' and taking the 'form of a slave' (cf. Wanamaker 1987). The whole language and logic of verses 6–8 suggest a movement from a divine to a human state, which Christ did not 'have' but '*took*' (*labōn*). And while acknowledging that Paul was perhaps untroubled by the metaphysical intricacies of 'pre-existence', we may accept with the vast majority of interpreters since antiquity that the most natural reading of this and other passages (e.g. Col. 1.15–17; 1 Cor. 8.6) will associate Christ with a time *prior* to Adam. (It is in any case worth stressing that early Christian advocates of the Adam typology did *not* assert it as an alternative to a pre-existential reading of our passage.)

Two things may be said by way of summary of this discussion.

First, Paul's evident fondness for the Christ–Adam polarity elsewhere may indeed have coloured his presentation of Christ's
attitude in this passage, too. This seems especially plausible if one
considers that Paul has placed, and arguably composed (cf.
pp. 117–20 above), verses 6–8 in deliberate antithesis to the self-
centred human behaviour decried in 2.3–4 and 2.21. Secondly,
however, the text nevertheless offers insufficient evidence to
establish an *explicit* link, or even a deliberate allusion, to Adam.
The only demonstrably intentional contrast is between Christ and
the Philippians, and parallels with Adam are just as likely to be
the result of accustomed ways of Pauline thinking about sinless
Christ and sinful humanity.

The arguments here are obviously complex and intricate, and
scholarship has yet to reach a consensus on this matter. The
problem is, however, that the undeniable counter-analogy
between Philippians 2 and Genesis 3 *in general* is not easily
pinned down in *particulars*. Cf. also Fowl 1990: 70–73.

7 Verses 7–8 now spell out the humility which Christ chose in
place of the self-serving attitude rejected in verse 6: **instead, he
emptied himself**. The verb *kenoô* can mean either literally 'to
empty', or metaphorically to 'deprive' or 'make of no effect' (cf. 1
Cor. 9.15; 2 Cor. 9.3; Rom. 4.14). Interpretations of the phrase
abound, in part because no obvious parallel usage has come to
light. The best initial approach is again a syntactical one, which
shows that the three verbal phrases of verse 7 stand in parallel.
Christ's 'emptying himself' has everything to do with **taking the
form of a slave** and **being born in human likeness**. Probably
the best grammatical understanding is that the second and third
phrase express the mode and manner of Christ's self-emptying,
which has a further parallel in self-humiliation (v. 8). Christ's
incarnation and voluntary death on the cross, then, were the way
in which he showed that 'being equal to God' was for him not a
possession to be exploited for selfish ends; instead, it led him to
deprive himself and serve others. In this way, v. 7 in turn sheds
light on the meaning of v. 6.

Some English translations begin verse 6 with '*although* he was
in the form of God', thereby suggesting that Christ took on the
'form of a slave' *despite* his status of equality with God. It is worth
noting, however, that this is not present in the Greek text; nor is
there any explicit assertion that Christ *gave up* the equality with
God to take on the form of a slave. Instead, the text just as easily
allows for a reading which takes Christ's self-humbling as an
expression of his divinity (i.e. almost '*since* he was in the form of
God'). There is no sense that Christ *exchanged* the form of God for

the form of a slave; instead he *manifested* the form of God in the form of a slave (so rightly Bruce 70; O'Brien; Koperski 1996: 333; and see below).

Although the grammatical form is necessarily tenuous and one must be careful not to overstate the case, there is in fact a rich tradition of Jewish interpretation according to which God personally identifies with the suffering and affliction of his people. Even the biblical precedent is suggestive: He 'knows and sees' their slavery, and 'comes down' to deliver them personally (Exod. 3.7f.); he places his dwelling in their midst and walks among them (Lev. 26.11f.; cf. 16.16). The *Qere'* reading of Isaiah 63.9 is particularly evocative: 'He was afflicted in all their affliction', a notion richly developed in rabbinic Judaism (see *b.Sot.* 31a; *b.Taan.* 16a; *Exod.R.* 2.5; cf. *b.Sot.* 5a; P. Kuhn 1968: 82–92 and *passim*; Goldberg 1978: 211–19 on *Pes.R.* 36.8). On this reading, therefore, it is precisely *in God's character* to humble himself and to minister to his people for their redemption. Both the pre-existent heavenly form and the self-humbling incarnation equally display what it means to be God. (Cf. further Moule 1970: 273–4; Wright 1991a: 90 and *passim*; O'Brien 214–16.)

Christ emptied himself and took **the form of a slave**. This is another difficult phrase, which commentators find easier to illustrate than to explain. It has been taken to mean a number of things (cf. e.g. R.P. Martin 1983: 169–96); four possibilities are worth examining.

(1) Christ *gave up* the 'form of God' and his equality with God to take on the 'form of a slave'. This interpretation, once popular in the so-called 'kenotic' christology of the late nineteenth and early twentieth centuries, is now on the whole discredited. It presumes a literalistic reading of Christ's 'self-emptying' and fails to recognize that the 'emptying' is in fact explicated by the participles of 'taking' and 'becoming', rather than by cancelling who and what he was, viz. 'in the form of God' and 'equal to God'. The flow of the Greek is, 'existing in the form of God, ... he emptied himself ...'. There is no notion of 'exchanging' one thing for another; instead, the divine 'form' adopts the human, so that the human embodies the divine, both veiling and (as the Fourth Gospel stresses) revealing it. (See also Bruce 70; cf. Pöhlmann in *EDNT* 2: 443 on the immutability of the two 'forms' here in view.)

(2) Another suggestion whose support has waned is that in the incarnation Christ became a slave to demons, until by his cross he defeated them. Its advocates have tended to draw on passages like 1 Cor. 2.8; Col. 2.15, 20, and especially on the later Gnostic

heavenly redeemer myth. This idea, however, finds no positive support in the present passage, and in its developed form is now generally agreed to belong to a later time and another setting.

(3) A few writers have proposed that **the form of a slave** is equivalent to a simile: Christ divested himself of his power and his rights to the point where he became to all intents and purposes 'comparable to a slave' (so Moule 1970: 268; cf. Bruce). Christ's being in the 'form of God', however, meant not that he was 'comparable' but rather that he was 'equal to God'. The distinction may be a fine one; but it seems on balance more likely that Christ is here said to have *been* a metaphorical slave, rather than to have been *like* a literal one. In any case it is true that the word *doulos*, as in 1.1, carries vividly evocative overtones in a Graeco-Roman setting and would set the stage for the imminent reference to crucifixion, a punishment popularly associated with slaves.

(4) One common interpretation, developed especially by L. Cerfaux 1959 and J. Jeremias 1963, has linked the passage with the 'Servant' of Isaiah 53. The argument is not only that there is a general similarity between the work of the Servant and that of Christ, but that the words 'slave', 'emptying' and 'death' (v. 8) are deliberately reminiscent of Isa. 53.12: he 'poured himself out to death'.

There are, however, a number of well-known problems with this reading. The LXX in Isa. 53.12 does not in fact use the words 'empty' or 'slave' (but rather *pais*, 'servant' or 'son'); nor does it employ the term *morphé* to speak of the Servant's appearance. What is more, a clear allusion to Isa. 53.12 at this point would introduce a structurally awkward and implausible reference to Christ's death (vv. 7a, b) before his incarnation (7c, d) and a further reference to the cross (8b, c).

Nevertheless, others have brought intriguing additional evidence to bear. Contrary to the assertions of some (e.g. K. H. Rengstorf in *TDNT* 2: 266f.), *doulos* is in fact used interchangeably of the Servant in a number of passages (e.g. Isa. 42.19; 48.20; 49.3, 5). It is also found consistently in the important early second-century translation of Aquila, who moreover does speak of the 'form' (*morphé*) of this 'slave' in 52.14 and 53.2. Given Paul's choice of language, this latter piece of evidence is particularly suggestive of a possible link with the Jewish interpretative traditions surrounding Isaiah 53.

In the end, a direct dependence of this passage on the LXX of Isa. 53 clearly cannot be demonstrated (so rightly Hooker 1978; cf.

Hofius 1991: 62). Nor is it structurally likely that v. 7 intends a definite reference to Isa. 53.12. Nevertheless, the general point remains well taken, and is supported by the evidence of other ancient versions: the self-effacing humility of Jesus in taking the 'form of a slave' and accepting death is described in language resembling the passage about the despised appearance of the suffering Isaianic Servant. There, it is precisely the Servant's abject self-humbling on behalf of others which becomes divinely instrumental for their redemption and his triumphant exaltation (cf. Isa. 53.5–6, 10–12). As in verse 6, the literal and (here at least) concretely visual connotations of the word *morphé* are significant, especially given Aquila's rendering. A general connection with Isaiah 53 also fits well within the broader biblical and post-biblical Jewish interpretative tradition of the righteous person whose obedience and suffering are rewarded in vindication (e.g. Wisd. 2; 2 Macc. 6–7; etc.). Perhaps rather like the subliminal presence of the Adam–Christ contrast in Pauline discussions of human obedience or disobedience, this varied but coherent tradition of the Servant may be assumed implicitly to shape the way in which the story of Christ's righteous suffering would be told. See further Krinetzki 1959; Wagner 1986; Wright 1991a: 59–62; Hübner 1993: 328f.; also Hofius 1993 *passim*.

One additional possibility worth pondering is that this indirect hermeneutical underpinning of our passage may be further enhanced by a christological reading of Psalm 8. This approach, already facilitated by the LXX superscript 'for the End' (*eis to telos*, 8.1), is explicitly attested in Hebrews 2.6–9 (but cf. also 1 Cor. 15.27; Eph. 1.22): Christ the 'human being' and 'son of man' was made 'for a little while' lower than the angels (Hebr. 'God'), but because of his suffering and death he has now been 'crowned with glory and honour', and God has 'put all things under his feet'. The Psalm begins with an emphasis on the 'name' of the 'Lord' (*kurios*) as wondrous in all the earth (8.2, 8.10); his majesty 'has been exalted above the heavens' (LXX v. 2). Cf. further Hays 1993: 127 and *passim*.

However we interpret this phrase, then, Christ's **taking the form of a slave** is best understood as his voluntary descent from the highest status, 'equality with God', to the lowest, that of a slave, giving up all his rights and privileges in order to serve. Quite possibly this should be understood within the Old Testament and Jewish notions of the suffering righteous servant of God. Beyond that, the possibility cannot be ruled out that Paul's reference to 'Christ *Jesus*' (v. 5) deliberately alludes to the attitude affirmed of Jesus in the gospel tradition: he came 'to serve and give his life as a ransom' (Mark 10.45 par.; note *doulos* in v. 44 par.), he was among his disciples 'as one who serves' (Luke 22.27), and he invited others to learn from his humility (Matt. 11.29). The Fourth Gospel presents Jesus' washing of his disciples' feet as his example of servanthood (13.15–16), and commentators since John Chrysostom have cited it to illustrate the present passage. (Note further the slave in the parable of Luke 14.16–24, who in its original setting may have been understood to be Jesus. In light of our earlier comments about the timeless reality of Christ's attitude, it is also interesting to note the allusion in Luke 12.37 to his *future* service on his return as Lord.)

Christ's self-emptying is further expressed in **being born in human likeness**, lit. 'in the likeness of human beings'. The term 'likeness', as in Romans 8.3 ('in the likeness of sinful flesh'), does not denote that Christ was only 'like' human beings but did not become fully human, as Gnosticism later thought. Nor should one see in this phrase a deliberate suggestion that in some aspects Christ was *unlike* human beings (*pace* Fee 213). Instead, it is now widely agreed to mean, 'he came into the same conditions of human life as the rest of us' (thus e.g. Ziesler 1989: 204 on Rom. 8.3; cf. Loh & Nida 59). This is also suggested by the plural 'human beings': he was not only abstractly like *a* human being (though this is the reading of the Gnostic Marcion and a few manuscripts influenced by him; cf. also LXX Ezek. 1.5), but like human beings collectively. Both his birth and his humanity, then, were fully human – and v. 8 shows that his death was, too. **Being born** (lit. 'having become': for a similar use cf. Rom. 1.3; Gal. 4.4) human may be contrasted with how he eternally **was** (lit. 'existed') in v. 6. Drawing together various strands of Pauline thought, Irenaeus writes, 'The Son of God was made man, assuming his ancient handiwork into his very self' (*Haer.* 4.33.4; cf. 3.16.6; 3.18.1).

The next line (verse 7d) is difficult to assign with confidence either to the preceding or the following sentence. Nevertheless, the beginning of a new sentence is suggested by the opening **and** (which grammatically links the main verb 'emptied' with the next main verb 'humbled'), along with the poetic structure and the flow of the argument. Having once **appeared in human shape**, Christ now submits to death on the cross. In this way the first set of three lines deals with Christ's pre-existent state, the next with his becoming man, and the third with his obedience to death. The word **shape** (*schéma*), which in the NT occurs only here and in 1 Cor. 7.31, completes the triplet of phrases denoting the 'form', 'likeness', and 'shape' of Christ's humanity. Of the three words, it is probably the most general in meaning, referring to the visible human appearance of Jesus. (Bengel's old distinction may not be far off the mark in associating 'form' with an object in and of itself, 'likeness' in its relation to another, and 'shape' to its visual aspect.) The cumulative effect of these words is to stress that Jesus humbled himself to become human, and indeed lowly, *through and through.*

The verb here translated **appeared** means literally, 'he was found'. In its passive use here, however, it has to do not so much with discovery but with what in French is expressed by *se trouver*: the way a person's circumstances turn out in the event, rather than what is the case in principle.

8 Within the observable events of history, then, Jesus was born as a man – and *as such,* **in human shape** (not as a powerful or invulnerable heavenly being) he **humbled himself**. This latter term relates closely to the vocabulary and the attitude encouraged in verses 3–4, and stands in parallel to 'he emptied himself' in the previous verse, as the final downward step of self-abasement. It is significant that this verb is not in the passive, but in the active aorist tense with a reflexive pronoun, suggesting a voluntary historical act of self-humbling. This historical groundedness of Christ's humanity and self-humbling may well be significant for the moral point Paul is trying to derive, especially in light of the fact that the Philippians are being exhorted to love and unity in the midst of real adversity (1.30).

Christ **became obedient**. Here the word *genomenos*, earlier translated 'being born', recurs a second time. Having 'become' like human beings by being born, Christ now **became** obedient, as a human being. He was, in other words, not so by definition, *a priori*, but became so in taking up the form of the servant, and in his everyday moral decisions and actions (cf. Heb. 5.8; Luke 2.51–2; Rom. 5.19; see also Manzi 1996 for a comparison of Phil. 2.6–11 with the 'solidarity' theme in Heb. 5.5–10). This dimension is indeed essential for Paul's hortatory purpose: Jesus can serve as a moral example only if his obedient humility was voluntary rather than either automatic or enforced. (It will not do to say, as e.g. Bloomquist 1993: 166 does, that submission and suffering here as elsewhere in Philippians merely amount to acquiescing in the inevitable.) Chrysostom comments, 'He is lowly minded who humbles himself, not he who is lowly by necessity.'

Just as we were not told explicitly whose slave Christ was, so there is no indication of the one *to whom* he was obedient. There is certainly no warrant for assuming obedience to demons or to death, as some commentators have proposed. Elsewhere in Paul, obedience applies frequently to God, Christ and the gospel. An implicit reference to God's will seems most plausible, since Paul understands Christ's death on the cross as being in response to God's will (Gal. 1.4; cf. Matt. 26.42 par.; Heb. 10.10). It is on the strength of Christ's obedience to God that God in turn exalts him in verses 9–11; and it is that same obedience to God which, arguably, Paul goes on to commend to the Philippians in verse 12.

Christ's obedience was unconditional and unlimited: it went as far as it could, to the end of his life, **as far as death**. This is the ultimate expression of faithfulness and obedience in the suffering righteous, similarly illustrated in the cases of Isaiah 53.12, the Maccabean martyrs, and later figures like Akiba, Ignatius or Polycarp (see p. 86 above; in that respect at least it is not true, as Lohmeyer and others have claimed, that only a divine being could die as a matter of obedience, rather than of necessity). Within the canonical context of Philippians, the specifically christological dimension of this phrase is perhaps most clearly illustrated in the prayer at Gethsemane (Mark 14.36 par.).

Paul appends a final reiterating phrase (an *anadiplosis*) which causes his poetry, and with it the story of Christ's self-humbling 'in the form of a slave', to shudder to a halt: **all the way to death on a cross**. Not even in death did he choose his own preference, perhaps a zealot's 'honourable' option of suicide or death in battle. Instead, he endured a shameful execution reserved for slaves and rebels, 'the most cruel and abominable form of punishment', as Cicero called it, a shocking and offensive topic unsuitable for polite conversation (cf. Hengel 1977: 1–10). Crucifixion was equally reviled by Jews, for whom it fell under the curse of Deut. 21.23, and who were horrified that Hasmonean rulers nevertheless brazenly introduced it as a Jewish punishment on a large scale (cf. Josephus *Ant.* 13.380–83; *B.J.* 1.97–8; 4QpNah 1.7–8; cf. 11QTemple 64.9–13). This shamefulness of the cross of Jesus was something which the early Christians faced consciously (Heb. 12.2; 1 Cor. 1.18, 28; cf. Gal. 3.13); it may also account for the relatively late appearance of the cross as a Christian symbol.

Structurally, then, this phrase is not extraneous to the passage but is singled out as the deliberate climax at least of verses 6–8 (so e.g. Hofius 1991: 106f., Hengel 1977: 62f., and commentators including Caird, Bruce, Fee, O'Brien). It has the effect of an arresting musical syncopation, marking the end of the downward narrative but leaving one on the edge of one's seat for what comes next. These words stand out both syntactically and thematically, drawing attention to the centrality of the cross as both the climax of Christ's exemplary humility and the final purpose of the incarnation itself. What is more, it is precisely in his shameful death that his unique significance for the Christian message lies: Christ died not a noble death or for a good person, but a scandalous death for the ungodly (Rom. 5.7–8; 1 Cor. 1.23). This is where Graeco-Roman comparisons and parallels fail to do justice to Paul's emphatic little phrase *thanatou de staurou*: Christ did more than just 'make the Philippians into his friends' (so Stowers 1991: 120 in comparing Lucian's *Toxaris*; cf. earlier L. M. White 1990; contrast the telling criticism of this parallel in Bormann 1995: 166–7 n. 25).

The prominent position of the cross in this context of exhortation may also imply something of its meaning to the apostle personally, as Lightfoot thought with reference to Tertullian: while Paul's own life was now at stake for the gospel, nevertheless his own humiliation still did not match that of his Lord. His Roman citizenship meant that he himself was highly unlikely to be crucified (but cf. Hengel 1977: 39–45).

This reference to the cross is of course very brief, without explanation. Here is not the place for Paul to reflect on its atoning significance (though that may well be understood), as indeed he does not speak of Christ's ministry before it or his resurrection after it. The point is simply that the cross serves as the crowning expression of his humble obedience and service of others.

9 Verse 9 begins the second half of this christological narrative, and with it the scene changes dramatically from humiliation to vindication. The subject agent changes, too: from Christ humbling himself to God exalting him. The starkly simple, almost staccato statements of verses 6–8 now give way to grammatically and thematically rich descriptions, underpinned by unmistakable biblical allusions to divine splendour. The counterpart to unlimited obedience and ultimate humiliation is unlimited vindication and ultimate exaltation: Christ is raised to the highest position in heaven.

The inclusion of these three verses might be thought inappropriate, given the contextual concern for Christ's humility as an example to the Philippians. Theologically, however, his exaltation is in fact equally important – not indeed in the sense of a reward, but rather as the moral counterbalance to the acceptance of suffering. Theodicy requires that innocent suffering should be vindicated: only thus can it be meaningful, and only so can God be seen to be just. From the Christian perspective, suffering is never an end in itself. It always stands in a necessary relationship to God's justice. The same logic is already implied in Jesus' daring and emphatically theological rather than proverbial statement, 'all who humble themselves will be exalted' (Matt. 23.12 par.). It applies even to his own suffering, a point which Paul elsewhere dramatically underscores by affirming that Christ's suffering and death on the cross would *not* by itself bring salvation: 'If Christ has not been raised, your faith is vain' (1 Cor. 15.17; cf. Rom. 4.25). And therefore no theologically meaningful appeal to Christ's example can be based on his death alone. The ethical force of the passage, then, is safeguarded first in the proof of divine sovereignty and justice, and secondly by the promise of participation in his heavenly life that results from being 'in Christ' (cf. 3.21: the same power which here makes all things subject to him is the one which conforms our bodies to his). It is on the strength of Christ's exaltation that believers at Philippi have the assurance that their suffering, too, will be vindicated and brought into conformity with his glory.

For this reason, verse 9 begins with **and therefore**: 'that is why' the just and loving Father exalted him. Given God's character, he will respond to the humble obedience of Christ. The logic of this **therefore** of vindication is paralleled in Isaiah 53.12 as well as in other descriptions of the faithful believer's deliverance (e.g. Ps. 18.24; Isa. 50.7; 61.7; Ezek. 37.12; cf. more generally Hofius 1991: 41–55, on celebrations of God's lordship in passages of thanksgiving). There may possibly be a note of reward here, but primarily the focus is on God's vindicating righteousness, towards which Jesus' act is one of faithful trust (cf. below on 3.9).

God **highly exalted** (*huperhupsōsen*) Jesus, indeed the word **him** is placed in an emphatic position: he who 'humbled *himself'*, he is the one whom God now exalts. Paul stresses only the fact, not the process of this exaltation, which elsewhere might involve resurrection, ascension and sitting on the right hand of God (e.g. Rom. 8.34; Eph. 1.20); here, abject servanthood gives way immediately to sovereign lordship as its counterpart (cf. similarly Heb. 1.3; Luke 24.26). This verb, which occurs only here in the NT, literally means he 'super-exalted' him. In its simple form the LXX uses it of the Servant in Isa 52.13, although 'super-exaltedness' describes God's position in Psalm 96(= 97).9 and frequently in the apocryphal Song of the Three Young Men, Dan. 3.52–90 (LXX and Theodotion). This LXX usage, along with the context, suggests that the verb should be understood in absolute ('most highly') rather than comparative terms ('more highly'): Christ is lifted up with the kind of exaltation that befits his divine station.

God **granted him** the supreme name. The verb here suggests that this was God's gracious gift and sovereign decision, rather than a right or entitlement. In the ancient world, and in Judaism in particular, a **name** was of interest for what it signified, and not simply as a label. Names frequently retained an active association either with their meaning (e.g. Matthew = Mattai, short for Mattatyahu, 'the Lord's gift') or with an important ancient personage (e.g. Mary = Miriam), or both. This could be true both for given names (like 'Simeon') and especially for adopted names (like 'Cephas'/'Peter'), which often denote someone's nature or character.

Scholarly interest here, therefore, has understandably focused on what this name **above every name** might be. Most assume with a kind of Anselmian certainty that there can be no greater name than *kurios*, 'Lord', which in the Greek Old Testament represents God's ineffable name (*YHWH* in Hebrew). C.F.D. Moule, on the other hand, has argued that on straightforward syntactical grounds the very next verse declares that name to be 'Jesus': it is **the name of Jesus** to which everything and everyone is subject (Moule 1970: 270). However, it is perhaps not entirely clear whether all shall bow to him because Jesus *has* the name above every name, or because 'Jesus' *is* that name. By sprinkling one's quotation marks somewhat differently, it is equally possible to read in verse 11 the universal confession that Jesus Christ is 'Lord', i.e. *YHWH*. What is more, in assuming the highest name to be 'Jesus' one creates the slight awkwardness that the exalted name here appears quite specifically to be granted upon his exaltation, not at birth (the 'therefore' makes the granting of the name dependent on what goes before, rather than part of it). A similar perspective seems to be taken in Eph. 1.21 (closely related and possibly dependent on Phil. 2.9: cf. e.g. Hofius 1991: 76–92), and in Heb. 1.4. This perspective is, moreover, compatible with the suggestion that Psalm 8 may have contributed to the assertion: it is precisely the divine name *YHWH* which is exalted over all things (see p. 136 above; Ps. 8 is similarly used in later Jewish mystical speculation about the divine name: e.g. Schäfer 1981: §391; cf. *b.Shab.* 88b [R. Joshua b. Levi, 3rd cent.]).

The precise issue is difficult to decide with certainty, and is perhaps in any case a storm in an exegetical teacup. What is clear is that it is *Jesus* who receives this name, that to his name all creatures are subject, and that he is *kurios*: 'Lord', *YHWH*. There can indeed be no greater or more powerful name than that: God's own name is exalted above everything (cf. e.g. Ps. 8.1; 138.2; 148.13).

It is significant that several of the Jewish mystical texts cited earlier in relation to verse 6 also show an interest in the mighty names of God and of his heavenly agents – including Metatron, the exalted Enoch and divine vicegerent. We know from various Dead Sea documents that the Essenes had an intense interest in the glorious and transcendent names of the heavenly beings (e.g. 1QM 9.15f.; 1Q19[= Noah] 2.4; 4Q544[= 4Q^{c}Amram^b ar] 3.1–2; cf. also Josephus, *B.J.* 2.142). In another first-century BC document, an archangel suggestively named Yahoel bears the name and power of God (*Apoc. Abr.* 17); and Metatron, whose name according to the Talmud is 'like the name of his master' (*b.Sanh.* 38b), according to a later passage explicitly bears the divine name, 'the little *YHWH*', *3 Enoch* 48.7. Even Philo of Alexandria called the Logos, God's firstborn son, an archangel 'of many names', one of which is 'name of God' (*Conf.* 146). It is quite plausible, therefore, that in the Palestinian Christian traditions whose language Paul reflects in 2.6–11, a reference to the 'name above every name' would have been well understood. (The later *Midrash on Psalms* 9.6 (ed. Buber, 42a) specifically addresses 'your name that transcends all names'; cf. Hofius 1991: 27f., 109–11, who also notes later Gnostic interest in the same subject. Gnostic use of this and other parts of our passage is frequently attested by the church fathers (see the discussion in Bockmuehl 1995).)

Paul's conviction here, then, is that Jesus has received the name of God himself, which is above the names of all created beings not just on earth but in heaven. Although this is a supremely Christian theological statement, its consequences include important applications in the Graeco-Roman social context of Philippi. If Christ the servant has become the Lord above all, then this has a dual effect, both of endorsing loyal service to masters and rulers, and of denying that any human lord could take the place of ultimate authority. In other words: if Christ is worshipped as *kurios*, then that title and that worship must be denied to Caesar, who also claimed it in the official Emperor cult (note e.g. Acts 25.26) – and whose characteristic ambition was apotheosis rather than kenosis and 'obedience unto death'. (With death approaching in AD 79, Vespasian famously, if perhaps tongue in cheek, exclaimed, 'I think I am becoming a god!' Suetonius, *Vespasian* 23.4.) While the storm of the coming Neronian persecution may still have been some way in the future at the time of writing, for Paul the most vivid political memory in this respect would quite likely be that of Caligula (AD 37–41), who solicited worship as *kurios* and attempted to place his idol in the Temple at Jerusalem (cf. Seeley 1994: 68–71). For Gentile readers accustomed to divine hero myths and to public religious veneration for the Emperor and other supposed god-men, the affirmation of Jesus as *Lord* and as *Saviour* (3.20) presented the alternative between Christ and paganism in a way that was both accessible and posed in the starkest possible terms. (On the hero myths note e.g. Knox 1939: 220–26 and 1948; H. D. Betz 1996 argues that the early Christians deliberately avoided associating their christology with the ancient hero cults.)

Although in a general sense this political implication of Christ's lordship would apply throughout the Roman Empire, in the first century it was especially true in a place like Philippi, a colony under personal imperial patronage. (Wright 1991b: 206–7 usefully compares the rebel Judas the Galilean, who insisted that he would accept 'no master but God', Josephus, *B.J.* 2.118.) Even apart from the specifically political threat of such a claim, however, it is significant to note the broader clash in social presuppositions: Roman society generally treasured 'upwardly mobile' values rather than an attitude of humility and self-emptying. See e.g. *NW* §5 on 2.7; cf. Wengst 1986: 434–7, 1988: 49–51; Bormann 1995: 217–24 and *passim*. (At the same time it is true that Stoic writers like Seneca and Dio Chrysostom could be similarly critical of political leadership that did not express itself in selflessness and service, although in Graeco-Roman practice such behaviour tended to be clad in the conventions of reciprocally advantageous public benefactions. Cf. Seeley 1994: 61–8; Bringmann 1993; also *HCNT* 479–80 on the pagan *Letter of Hippocrates* and the Gnostic *Corpus Hermeticum* 1.12–15.)

Does this assignment of 'the name above every name' imply that Christ is more highly exalted after the crucifixion than before the incarnation? It is certainly true that there seems to be a difference between 'before' and 'after': there is no reason to think that the end is just a restoration to the beginning. Instead, although Christ was 'equal to God' from the beginning, he acquired the 'name above every name' with his exaltation. The humiliation and triumph of the incarnation, in other words, make an identifiable difference even within the Godhead. While there is no suggestion of a change of *being*, there is nevertheless a change of *name* and of *function*: at his exaltation Christ becomes Lord of all and receives the name above all. A similar thought is implied in Romans 1.3–4: here, although the *fact* of Christ's divine sonship has no clear beginning, it is only at his resurrection that Christ is confirmed as 'son of God *with power*'. In Matthew 28.18, too, it is clearly at his resurrection that Jesus has received 'all power in heaven and on earth'; and Acts 2.36 affirms that God has 'made' the Jesus who was crucified 'both Lord and Messiah'.

10 Verses 10–11 are phrased in parallel, and present God's twofold purpose in exalting Jesus. Verse 10 is a kind of midrash

on Isaiah 45.23 LXX, where God says, 'By myself I have sworn ... :
to me every knee shall bow and every tongue will confess to God.'
This powerful statement of universal rule, which in Rom. 14.11
applies to God, is here transferred to Jesus. It is particularly
significant for christology that the context of this same passage in
Isaiah affirms both the *uniqueness* of God's sovereignty and the
universalism of his extension of salvation to the whole world (Isa.
45.22, 24). This is not a replacement of God with Christ, but
simply a recognition that he who from the beginning shared the
'form of God' and 'equality with God' (v. 6) has now been granted
the name of God and shares in receiving the worship of God from
all creatures. (See above, p. 82 for an earlier example of so-called
'intertextual' use of the OT. The specifically doxological and
liturgical implications of Isa. 45.23 in this context are further
highlighted by its use in two ancient synagogal prayers, the '*Alênu*
and the *Nishmat Kol Hay*, recommended by the Mishnah for use
at the end of the *Haggadah* service on Passover: Elbogen 1993: 96;
cf. Hofius 1991: 48–51 and see *m.Pes.* 10.7.)

At (lit. 'in') **the name of Jesus** is grammatically a little
unclear. Among other things, it could mean worship offered (i) 'in
his name (but to God)', (ii) whenever his name 'Jesus' is pronounced, or (iii) 'in honour of his name'. The first option can be
dismissed in light of the confession of verse 11 ('Jesus Christ *is*
Lord'); the second stands and falls with C.F.D. Moule's identification of the 'name above every name', as discussed above. The
third does makes good sense both grammatically and in the
context. Septuagintal usage, however, suggests that worship 'in
the name of' God actually means that it is offered *to* God (e.g. LXX
1 Kgs. 8.44; Ps. 43.9(= 44.8); 62.5(= 63.4); 104(= 105).3). Bowing
one's knee 'in the name of' Christ is comparable to raising one's
hands 'in the name of' God (so LXX Ps. 62.5). The meaning of this
phrase, in other words, is equivalent to Isa. 45.23: **every knee
shall bow** *to* Jesus (cf. similarly Lightfoot). All will be subject to
him and pay him honour, in the traditional position of abject
reverence adopted to acknowledge a person of awesome authority (e.g. Gen. 41.43; 2 Kgs. 1.13), and especially God (e.g. 1 Kgs.
8.54; 19.18; 2 Chr. 6.13; Ezra 9.5; Ps. 95.6; Dan. 6.10). By applying
Isa. 45.23 to Christ, Paul suggests that divine worship will be
offered to Jesus as both Messiah and Lord.

'Every knee' is further specified to mean the knees **of those in
heaven, on earth and under the earth**. This is a conventional
description of the universe, following contemporary Jewish and
Christian cosmology; it includes every creature, human and
otherwise (cf. e.g. Rev. 5.13; Ps. 148). The Greek adjectives here
could be neuter, referring more generally to 'all things' in these

different spheres; but their 'bowing of the knee' requires at least that rational beings are included. More specifically, the reference is to angelic beings, to human beings and to the dead: 'under the earth' is more likely to refer to the realm of the dead than that of demonic powers, as Hofius (1991: 123–31) has shown, since the latter usage appears to be unattested. (It is interesting, none the less, that the demon of the Philippian slave-girl, as in other NT and early Christian texts, is exorcised by the *name* of Jesus: Acts 16.18.) Christ is the one to whom everyone will be subject. Cf. also *NW* §§3–7.

At the same time, the **so that** (Gk. *hina*) suggests that this bending of the knee to Christ is God's purpose and *intention*, even if it has not yet been accomplished. There remains, as many commentators recognize, an eschatological tension here, which is not fully resolved: many at present do not participate in this reality. For Christians, of course, the acknowledgement that 'Jesus Christ is Lord' forms part of their basic orientation and confession (cf. Rom. 10.9; 1 Cor. 12.3). And the Church already joins in the heavenly adoration offered by the angels (cf. 1 Cor. 11.10; 13.1; Eph. 2.6; 3.10; Rev. 5.6ff.; an idea also present at Qumran, e.g. in the *Songs of the Sabbath Sacrifice*). One day, however, that acknowledgement of Christ's lordship will be offered by all creatures everywhere. It is in keeping with the eschatology both of Deutero-Isaiah and of the NT (including Isa. 45.23 in Rom. 14.10–12) that the coming of God's final rule is considered to be not just a pious wish but an unstoppable certainty. In the same way, too, this universal worship is inevitable: many will 'bow the knee' to him in joyful adoration, though some who were his enemies may find themselves doing so in shame (cf. Isa. 45.24).

11 Verse 11, closely following on from the previous verse, completes the christological passage. It offers the second half of God's purpose in exalting Jesus, again drawing on Isaiah 45.23 and combining it with a Christian confession: **every tongue shall confess** or 'acknowledge', **'Jesus Christ is Lord'**. Confessing with the tongue is the verbal complement to the bodily movement of bowing the knee. Both together give expression to the inward response. (With its linguistic connotations, the term **tongue** may also include the *Gentile* contribution to this confession of Jesus as Messiah and Lord; cf. Isa. 45.20, 22.)

The meaning of the word **confess** (*exomologeō*) is hotly and widely contested, being taken to denote either 'admit and acknowledge' or 'confess with thanksgiving'. While it is true that the Septuagint typically employs the term of the confession of praise and thanksgiving, it can occasionally be used of acknowledging something against one's will (most clearly in 2 Macc. 7.37, a martyr's prayer that Antiochus will be forced to acknowledge that God is One). This rather sober sense of confession on God's terms, with or without one's consent, also appears to be present in Romans 14.10–12, which quotes Isa. 45.23 in the context of certain judgement. The Isaiah passage itself also seems to envision the confession of God's lordship from both a positive and a begrudging frame of mind (see v. 24). In Hebrew, 'all who were enraged against him will come to him and be ashamed'; in the Greek, 'all who separate themselves shall be ashamed'.

Given that Romans 14 clearly shows Paul to understand the context of Isa 45.23, the balance of probability must be that he does so here. Thus the 'confession' of verse 11 should be seen as an 'open acknowledgement' of Christ's sovereignty. It is undoubtedly true that this will be a matter of praise and thanksgiving for a great many in heaven, on earth and among the dead. Nevertheless, the context both of the quotation and possibly of Philippians as well (1.28; 2.15; 3.18f.; cf. Rom. 16.20; Col. 2.15) seems to allow that there may be some for whom this confession will be a matter of shame and an acknowledgement of defeat (see the extensive argument of O'Brien 243–50).

Jesus Christ is Lord resembles the important early Christian confession, 'Jesus is Lord', which along with faith in Christ's resurrection was thought to offer assurance of salvation (see Rom. 10.9; 1 Cor. 12.3; cf. Acts 2.36; 10.36; 2 Cor. 4.5; Col. 2.6; Jude 4). Given what we said earlier about 'the name above every name' and about the appropriation of Isa. 45.23, it is clear that **Lord** (*kurios*) is here understood as in the LXX, to represent the divine name *YHWH*. Here, however, we hear that this confession is to be offered not just by the Church but by 'every tongue'. This, then, shows the Church's worship and confession eschatologically anticipating that which is soon to be offered by all the created universe: the acknowledgement of the true nature and sovereignty of God in Christ.

Moreover, as we also saw earlier (p. 143), this assertion introduces into the daily reality of Christian life at Philippi a profoundly double-edged political point: one who confesses *Jesus* as Lord enters at once into the same freedom to serve that he himself exercised, to promote the welfare of others rather than one's own. At the same time, one who says 'Jesus Christ is *Lord*' cannot also agree that 'Caesar (or any other human potentate) is Lord': a Christian is forbidden to render to other powers, or to require from them, the allegiance that belongs to Christ alone. This conviction is unmistakable in the accounts of the early Christian martyrs.

This worship and confession of Jesus is **to the glory of God the Father**. Here is a fitting conclusion, not just to verses 9–11 but to the entire passage. It serves as a kind of doxological exclamation mark: in brief but typically Pauline fashion, this phrase brings the whole argument under the heading of the greater glory of God. Similar devices occur in Rom. 15.7; 1 Cor. 10.31; 2 Cor. 1.20; 2 Cor. 4.15. The immediate reference is Jesus' installation as Lord of all; but it is appropriate to take it in the broader sense of affirming that both his humiliation and his exaltation occur to the glory of God the Father. 'God was glorified in the humiliation of Christ as much as he is in his exaltation' (Bruce 80). Conversely, all this 'high' christology emphatically enhances rather than diminishes the glory of God, firmly securing the unequivocally monotheistic orientation of Paul's thought. It is distinctive of apostolic Christianity that its devotion to Christ refocused, but was in no way intended to compromise, its belief in the One God of Israel. (See 1 Cor. 8.6; cf. Rom. 3.20; Gal. 3.20; Eph. 4.6. Cf. further Hurtado 1988, 1993: 565; Bauckham 1992; Holtz 1985; Kreitzer 1987: 157–63.)

Summing up briefly, Paul presents in Philippians 2.6–11 the theological and christological centrepiece of his letter. In a 'divine nutshell' he describes the work of Jesus Christ from the perspective of eternity, and in so doing offers a radically Christ-centred re-affirmation of Jewish monotheism (cf. e.g. Wright 1991b: 205–7). Nevertheless, this is no christological high-wire act or esoteric speculation. The whole purpose, in keeping with 1.27–30 and 2.1–4, is to commend to the Philippians the Lord's example as the ultimate paradigm for their own steadfastness in adversity and harmonious unity amongst each other. Paul points them to the pre-existent Christ's self-giving humility and uncalculating service of humanity, all the way to death on a cross, and to God's powerful vindication of his faithfulness by exalting him to the highest place in heaven, so that his unchallenged Lordship may be universally acknowledged. This is the secret of a 'citizenship' that is worthy of the gospel (1.27). We noted in 2.5 that numerous verbal and conceptual links connect this passage with its immediate and wider context. In the verses that follow, Paul now encourages his readers to integrate this perspective into their way of life at Philippi.

D   PRACTICAL IMPLICATIONS   (2.12–18)

Verses 12–18 constitute the final paragraph of the long section comprising 1.27–2.18. The christological passage of verses 6–11 finds its application first in the call to a serious common pursuit of

the Christian life, empowered by God and marked by the obedience that also characterized the life of Jesus (vv. 12–13). This
obedience is then concretely applied in a threefold exhortation to
the Philippians: to be faithful without complaint in their relations
with each other (v. 14); to show integrity in their witness to the
outside world (vv. 15–16); to rejoice in their sacrificial offering of
their faith to God, of which Paul's own life and ministry form a
part (vv. 17–18).

**(12) And so, my dear friends, as you have always obeyed:
continue working out your own salvation with fear and trembling, not just when I am with you but all the more now in my
absence; (13) for God is the one who is at work in you to
produce both the desire and its fulfilment, for the sake of his
will. (14) Do everything without grumbling and bickering,
(15) so that you may become blameless and pure, children of
God without blemish in the midst of a 'crooked and perverted
generation' among whom you shine like lights in the world,
(16) as you continue holding fast the word of life; this gives me
reason to be proud on the day of Christ, in that I did not run or
toil in vain. (17) However, even if I am being poured out as a
libation over the sacrifice and priestly service which is your
faith, I am glad and rejoice with all of you – (18) and in the
same way you too must be glad and rejoice together with me.**

12 Although Paul switches from the heights of christology to the
practical reality of Christian ethics, he clearly regards what now
follows as arising from what he has just said: **and so** (*hôste*)
begins a new sentence by offering an inference from the preceding argument. The topical links are not difficult to identify: they
include the continuing themes of unity (2.2–4; 2.14), salvation in
the midst of adversity (1.28; 2.12, 16), and Christian citizenship in
the face of a hostile public (1.27–30, 2.15f.). There is also a specific
verbal link between the word 'obey' in this verse and Christ's
obedience in verse 8.

Formally, the main clause of verse 12 is 'continue working out
your salvation with fear and trembling'. Two dependent clauses
modify it: 'as you have always obeyed' and 'not just when I am
with you but all the more now in my absence'.

But first, Paul warmly addresses the Philippians as his **dear
friends** (lit. 'my beloved'). It is a term which befits his friendship
with the Philippians, and is reiterated in the fuller exhortation of
4.1 ('my brothers and sisters whom I love and long for'). However,
Paul uses a similar address in exhortations to the strife-torn
church at Corinth (1 Cor. 10.14; 15.58; 2 Cor. 7.1; 12.19) and even

to the Christians in Rome, most of whom he has never met (Rom. 12.19). His relations with Philippi are indeed particularly affectionate, as the addition of the personal pronoun **my** indicates. His love for *all* Christians, however, roots not in their familiarity or inherent attractiveness but in Christ himself (note 1 Cor. 16.24; 1 Thess. 3.12).

Before Paul presents his exhortation, he matches his affectionate address with an affirming vote of confidence: **as you have always obeyed**. Unlike for instance the church at Corinth (2 Cor. 10.6), the Philippians have actively participated in the gospel 'from the first day until now', and Paul is convinced that God's good work in them will continue (cf. 1.5–6). 'Obedience' was just mentioned in verse 8 in relation to Christ, and it is his example on which Paul now builds. As in the earlier passage, no indication is given of the one to whom this obedience is due. In this context at least, it is unlikely to mean obedience to Paul, as some have suggested (e.g. NRSV, Vincent). While obedience does occasionally apply to the word and ministry of the apostles (e.g. Rom. 15.18; 16.19; 1 Cor. 5; 2 Cor. 2.9, 10.5–6; Phlm. 21; 2 Thess. 3.14), in its absolute form in the present context it is best seen as obedience to God and to the gospel – what Paul elsewhere calls 'the obedience of faith' (Rom. 1.5; 16.26).

One should not of course set up a false polarity between the authority of the gospel and that of the apostolic ministry: those who obey the apostolic proclamation indirectly respect and heed the apostolic office. And even in a letter to friends, which does not mention the word 'Apostle', that is still what Paul remains and what implicitly gives his instructions to the Philippians the weight and authority which they clearly carry. Nevertheless, the primary point in this context would seem to be Christ-like obedience to God, and by extension to the gospel of Christ.

The very notion of obedience grates on modern sensibilities, as does Paul and Timothy's self-description as 'slaves of Jesus Christ' in 1.1. It would have been no more palatable to ancient tastes: Graeco-Roman ethics, conditioned to formulate its ideals in the intellectualist terms of a morally autonomous individual, could not regard 'obedience' as a virtue (cf. Frank 1976: 395–8); even early patristic writers do not discuss it very frequently. It was only the theological anthropology of Christianity's Jewish roots which provided the framework for a view of obedience as a Christ-like character quality to be commended.

It is of course true that a Christian understanding of obedience cannot be squared with an absolutism of human autonomy and an inalienable supremacy of individual 'rights'. But if liberty means to be free from evil and oppression, free to live in peace and justice with God and fellow humans, then there is nothing inappropriate about choosing freely to bring one's life into conformity with the gospel of Christ, the very source of true freedom (cf. on 1.1 above). And that is really what Paul means by obedience: conforming oneself to the gospel – what elsewhere he calls 'obeying the truth' (Gal. 5.7; cf. Rom. 2.8). It would make sense to say that in this respect the Philippians have **always obeyed**, namely they have faithfully continued since the first day of their obedience to the gospel until now. Their freedom consists not in individual autonomy but in a relationship with Christ.

In this verse, such Christian obedience is expressed in a phrase that initially sounds most un-Pauline: **continue working out your own salvation with fear and trembling.** Paul's use of the verb 'to work out' (*katergazomai*) is consistent throughout his writings (20x) and always means 'to bring about' or 'to achieve'. In view of this, some have suggested that the word 'salvation', earlier used in 1.19 and 1.28, must be intended not in its theological sense but to mean deliverance or well-being more generally (as e.g. at Mark 3.4; Acts 27.34 and in secular usage). On the other hand, a number of commentators especially of a Protestant bent have been preoccupied with the need to see here a concern for eternal, *individual* salvation.

As on both previous occasions in this letter, however, it is best not to reduce the term **salvation** too readily either to the individual and spiritual or to the corporate and social realm. Three facts must be affirmed together: (i) the NT notion of salvation encompasses deliverance from all forms of evil, oppression and injustice, whether due to visible or to invisible forces. (ii) It is never concerned either purely with the individual or purely with the corporate dimension, but directly addresses both individuals and the body of Christ which together they constitute and to which they belong (note especially Rom. 12.5). (iii) As the work of God, salvation concerns both the present experience of 'being saved' (1 Cor. 1.18; 15.2; 2 Cor. 2.15) and a future and permanent reality. While Christian experience may anticipate it in the here and now, salvation always ultimately relates to the final and transcendent consummation of God's purposes for the world (note 1 Thess. 1.9–10; Rom. 13.11; cf. further Caird 1994: 118–35; Fee 235 and n. 23).

In this context, the corporate dimension is clear from the exhortations to unity and steadfastness in 1.27ff. and again in 2.14–16. The individual concern is safeguarded by the reciprocal 'each other' of 2.3–4, the reflexive pronoun here in 2.12 ('your *own* salvation'; cf. 2.3–4), and arguably the plural 'lights' in verse 15. The challenge is both to 'each of them' and to 'all of them' (cf.

Bruce). Similarly, 'deliverance' may have a temporal relevance just as in 1.19 and 28 it related to deliverance from adversity for Paul and for the Philippians. At the same time, however, the eternal and transcendent dimension applies just as on both earlier occasions: here it is raised by the earnest reference to 'fear and trembling' (on which see below; cf. also 2 Tim. 4.18 for a similar combination of temporal and eternal 'salvation').

The present tense of the verb suggests a sustained, ongoing effort: '**continue working out** your own salvation'. This is in fact not as remote from Paul's thought as might seem to be the case (even though similar notions in post-apostolic documents have traditionally been assigned by liberal Protestant exegesis to the onset of 'early Catholicism' and the loss of the pure Pauline vision). As we noted, Paul tends to speak of salvation as something that is either occurring in the present (e.g. 1 Cor. 1.18; 9.22; 15.2; 2 Cor. 2.15) or still to come in the future (e.g. Rom. 5.9f., 10.9f.). The one apparent exception in the undisputed letters, Rom. 8.24f., merely confirms the general rule by defining past salvation explicitly in terms of hope and expectation (similarly Eph. 2.5, 8 with 2.7; contrast 2 Tim. 1.9; Tit. 3.5, but note I. H. Marshall 1996b on 1 Tim. 4.16; 2 Tim. 2.10 etc.). Here in Philippians, the future dimension is evident in 3.20. As for active human engagement in the divine work of salvation, Paul urges the Christians at Rome to wake up and grasp hold of the fact that 'salvation is nearer to us now than when we first believed' – a fact which requires practical dedication to a Christian lifestyle (Rom. 13.11–14; cf. the notion of 'confirming your call and election' in 2 Pet. 1.10). It is God who saves – but there is a human responsibility to *take hold* of that salvation, as even Phil. 3.12 makes clear (cf. 1 Cor. 9.24; 1 Tim. 6.12).

Perhaps the best clue to this present 'working out' of salvation at Philippi, however, lies in the realization that Paul urges it **not just when I am with you but *all the more* now in my absence**. If their 'working out' is now even *more* necessary, this may be because the apostle himself is now unable to contribute to it. Paul sometimes speaks of his work quite unselfconsciously as driven by the desire and purpose to 'save' people (Rom. 11.14; 1 Cor. 9.22). Doubtless he means by this not that he personally saves them but merely that his purpose is to 'get them saved' (cf. 1 Cor. 9.22 with 10.33). At the same time, he gives no indication that his own ability to do so is somehow unique. Indeed, a similarly elliptical use of language seems to be present when he encourages even wives and husbands of unbelieving partners to consider that they may 'save' each other (1 Cor. 7.16). In a later text, the next generation of Christian leaders is encouraged to 'save both yourselves and your hearers' (1 Tim. 4.16; cf. also Jas. 5.20; Jude 23). Given that such language about 'salvation' is evidently not exceptional, we should consider the possibility that Paul simply encourages the Philippians to take on for themselves the work he used to do among them: 'Since I cannot now personally work in your midst to "save" you, you must show your Christian obedience all the more by continuing to work out your *own* salvation.' Rather like Christian citizenship (1.27; 3.20), salvation is realized both in receiving it and in working it out, taking an active share of responsibility for its implementation.

Fear and trembling is a common biblical phrase describing the response of due reverence in face of a major challenge, and especially in the presence of God and his mighty acts. The only other uses of the phrase in the Pauline corpus are in relation to human beings (2 Cor. 7.15; Eph. 6.5), although in both cases an ultimate reference to God or Christ is likely (so also LXX Exod. 15.16). Paul does not imply cowering in terror, but with due awe and reverence taking seriously the responsibilities of Christian obedience and Christian citizenship. Here, fear and trembling are the appropriate disposition precisely *because* 'God is the one who is at work within you', verse 13. There is quite probably an element of admonition in this phrase: it contrasts with a casual Christianity's approach of ignoring God in practice and 'treating him as if he didn't matter' (I.H. Marshall).

The Philippians' exercise of their obedience should not be dependent on the apostle's presence or absence. Within this context, **when I am with you** (lit. 'as in my presence') should be understood not just retrospectively, but as a general reference to Paul's presence: whether he is at Philippi (as in the past and possibly again in the future, 2.24) or not, the Philippians should continue to progress in their salvation and to advance the gospel.

13 The hearty, spirited exhortation of verse 12 is now theologically grounded (note the opening **for**, giving the reason). The power to do all this is in fact not their own but God's: **for God is the one who is at work in you**. Ruffled Protestant feathers can take comfort ...! In Greek, the sentence in fact begins emphatically with *theos*, **God**, clearly placing the stress on his agency rather than ours. It is God's power which 'energizes' Christian citizenship to work out its salvation (*energeō*, twice in this verse), just as that same power (*energeia*, 3.21) will complete his work at the parousia.

Theologically, the relationship in verses 12 and 13 between God's saving work and his moral demand is both thoroughly Pharisaic and thoroughly Pauline. On the one hand, the free will and accountability of individuals are fully compatible with the sovereign work of God. R. Akiba famously said, 'Everything is foreseen, yet freedom of choice is given; and the world is judged by grace, yet all is according to the amount of the work' (*m.Abot* 3.19). On the other hand, the characteristically Pauline dimension of verses 12–13 emerges in the eschatological balance between the theological 'indicative' and the moral 'imperative': the accomplished fact or 'indicative' of new life by God's grace gives rise to and empowers its practical realization (the 'imperative') in the demand to live out that new life. Paul's letters express this same relationship both in the broad sweep of the argument and in detail. Ethical sections of his letters are linked to preceding doctrinal ones by a logical 'therefore' (e.g. Rom. 12.1; Col. 3.1; cf. Eph. 4.1); similarly, the grace of the gospel undergirds the moral demand of the gospel sometimes within the same sentence: 'If we live by the Spirit, let us also walk by the Spirit' (Gal. 5.25; cf. 1 Cor. 5.7f.; Col. 3.3, 5). R. Bultmann famously brought this perspective to a point as 'Become what you are!' (Bultmann 1952: 332f.). Paul's Greek phrase here in Phil. 2.12 aptly (if untranslatably) captures this by stating that God himself 'energizes' or 'works' (*energein*) the Christian's 'willing' (*thelein*) and 'working' (*energein*).

God, then, produces in the Philippians **both the desire and its fulfilment** (lit. 'both the willing and the achieving'). One is reminded of the extensive discussion in Romans 7–8: life without Christ leaves us able only to desire (*thelein*) but not to do (*katergazesthai*) what God commands (Rom. 7.15–22), but the coming of Christ means that the righteous requirements of the Law come to fulfilment in us as we live according to the Spirit and not the flesh (8.4, 13). Through his Spirit, God empowers Christians to discern, desire and do the will of God. **God is the one** who accomplishes this work; yet he does so **in you**, in the Philippians. The same confidence was present in 1.6; see above.

All this occurs **for the sake of his** (lit. 'the') **will**. As in 1.15, this phrase has occasioned a certain amount of debate as to whether human or divine good will (*eudokia*) is in view. Grammatically, however, God is the subject of the sentence and the most plausible reference must be to him, as e.g. in Eph. 1.5, 9. (Cf. further Matt. 11.26 par.; G. Schrenk, *TDNT* 2: 742–5; and see above on 1.15.) It is thus for God's own purpose and pleasure that he empowers the Philippians to work out their own salvation in practice.

14 After spelling out his call to a Christ-like obedient life in verses 12–13, Paul goes on in verses 14–16 to apply this same theme more concretely to their particular situation, in their relationships both internally and with outsiders. These three verses constitute a single sentence in Greek.

Verse 14 recalls the exhortation to unity in 2.3f., and again makes us wonder whether or not a 'live issue' of disunity is at stake in Philippi: **do everything without grumbling and bickering. Everything** includes the whole spectrum of what it means to 'work out one's salvation'; similar comprehensive statements appear in 1 Cor. 10.31 and Col. 3.17. **Grumbling** denotes dissatisfied complaining against other people (cf. Acts 6.1; 1 Pet. 4.9), while **bickering** here refers to petty disputes and questionings. Both are signs of lacking humility, as K. Barth rightly points out in reference to the earlier part of the chapter.

One of the difficulties is that of determining whether Paul refers to 'active' grumbling at Philippi; and if so, whether the Philippians are bickering against God or amongst each other. Paul's terminology offers an evocative allusion to the **grumbling and bickering** of Israel wandering in the desert, in which context the LXX uses these words frequently. That this subject occupied his mind is certainly clear from its explicit recurrence in 1 Cor. 10.10. Yet even in the Old Testament examples, the Israelite complaints are directed against God as much as against Moses (e.g. Num. 14.2–3; 20.2ff.; 21.5; Deut. 1.27; Ps. 106.25). The mere use of such terms does not help to indicate whether the Philippians are grumbling against outsiders, against each other, against their leaders or against God – or indeed whether Paul is simply offering a routine reminder in commonplace OT language. A problem of internal unity is certainly possible in 2.2–4 (see our comments there and cf. Peterlin 1995); a quarrel of uncertain magnitude is explicitly addressed in 4.2–3.

It is difficult to know if Paul wants to draw an explicit parallel with Israel in the desert: quite possibly the situation at Philippi merely evokes in his mind the traditional terminology associated with such behaviour. If, on the other hand, the parallel with the wilderness wanderings is deliberate and acute, it would seem reasonable to suppose that Paul has in mind complaints not just against God but also against the Christian leaders at Philippi. Perhaps this is in any case the most common way in which dissatisfaction in the church expresses itself. Quite plausibly Euodia and Syntyche are a particular focus of such discontent, even though they themselves apparently enjoy positions of respect and honour in the church (4.2–3). Might this unrest be a reason why bishops and deacons are so mysteriously singled out in Paul's prescript at 1.1 (cf. Silva)? We shall likely never know.

Aquinas tersely observes that while you cannot exist without sin, you can without grumbling!

Suffice it to say for now that the negative expression of Christlike obedience is here seen in the avoidance of grumbling and bickering, just as in 2.3 Paul inveighed against selfish ambition and conceit. These things, then, are not minor blemishes of morality, peripheral human weaknesses in an otherwise flawless Christian spectacle. Instead, they are part of what marks the great watershed of the Christian life, 'the scene of the decisive Christian "Either–Or" (K. Barth): either one belongs to Christ and henceforth adopts the mind of Christ, or one does not.

15 The purpose and result of laying aside such grumbling and bickering are **that you may become blameless and pure**. This language begins to alter the perspective from a strictly internal one to a consideration of the Christian witness to the outside world. As people who are united and publicly at peace with one another, Christians will seen to be innocent and above reproach.

This blamelessness will thus come to characterize them not just on the future day of the Lord (cf. 1.6), but already in their public life here and now: they will be **children of God without blemish in the midst of a 'crooked and perverse generation'**. Christians are God's adopted **children** by virtue of their participation in Christ (Rom. 8.14–17; Gal. 3.26; 4.5–6; cf. Eph. 1.5); this assertion corresponds to the reality of God as their Father (cf. 1.2; 2.11; 4.20; see p. 56 above). In the Old Testament, the word translated **without blemish** is used of ritually spotless sacrificial animals, but can also be applied to the sincere and godly believer (e.g. Ps. 15.2; 18.23; 37.18; in the NT cf. Col. 1.22; Eph. 1.4; 5.27).

Next, however, Paul borrows a phrase from a textually problematic passage in Deut. 32.5. There, Moses uses the same terms to describe Israel's unfaithfulness to their God: literally, 'they have dealt falsely with him; they are not his children because of their corruption; they are a crooked and perverted generation' (cf. also Deut. 32.20). Based in part on tendentious translations like that in RSV and NIV ('they are no longer his children'; contrast NRSV), many commentators continue to interpret Paul's use of this passage as replacing Israel with the Church. As a consequence, the 'crooked and perverted' generation is taken to refer specifically to the rejection of the Jews and to Paul's Jewish adversaries as addressed in 3.2, while Christians are now God's true children. (So e.g. Collange, O'Brien, Hawthorne.)

Several good reasons, however, make it unlikely that Paul really intends here such a fundamental statement about the fate of

Judaism as a whole. It seems far-fetched to infer such a reading from Paul's apparent source in Deut. 32.5, where both the Hebrew and the LXX text are highly problematic, but where the context does not really allow for the proposed reading. Whatever else it may mean, the LXX paraphrase, which could be punctuated in a number of ways, does not seem to assume an end to Israel's sonship: 'they sinned not against him: blemished children, a crooked and perverse generation. [v. 6] Do you thus repay the Lord, O foolish and unwise people? Did not he himself, your father, acquire you, make and create you?' The implication in the Palestinian Targum (*Neof.*, *Targ. Ps.-J.*) and certain Christian lectionaries (cf. Göttingen LXX) is that the children's blemish and sin are 'not against him but against themselves'. Similarly, early rabbinic discussion quite reasonably read v. 5 as involving a question: 'Is the corruption his? No, his children's is the blemish' (e.g. *Sifre Deut.* 308 (R. Meir); *Exod.R.* 42.1).

Philippians contains not a single explicit reference to the Old Testament; nor is there any indication or indeed likelihood of intimate familiarity with it on the part of Paul's readers (cf. p. 9 above). It seems improbable, in the absence of contrary evidence, that Paul could in any case assume a specific awareness of a link with Deuteronomy 32 on the part of his readers.

In all the other NT allusions to Deut. 32.5 (Matt. 12.39; 17.17 par.; Acts 2.40) the speaker makes not a judgement about 'Israel' as a whole but about the faithlessness among his contemporaries (Matt. 12.40–41; Acts 2.39). In these contexts, Deut. 32.5 serves merely to draw a parallel with the generation of the wilderness upon whom God's judgement fell. The rhetorical purpose of the allusion to Deut. 32.5, then, is most likely the usual biblical appeal not to behave like the generation in the wilderness (note further 1 Cor. 10.1–11; Ps. 78.8; 95.8–11; cf. Num. 32.13; Deut. 1.35; 32.20).

Here in Philippians, the phrase 'children ... in the midst of a crooked and perverse generation' is paralleled and illustrated in the following subordinate clause by 'lights in the world'. This makes a more general reference to non-Christian contemporaries at Philippi far more plausible than a wholesale dismissal of Judaism.

Paul himself evidently believed that various promises including 'adoption' continued to belong to faithful Israel, even if its ranks were now swelled by faithful Gentiles, and that these promises were irrevocable (Rom. 9.4; 11.29; note also his use in Rom. 9.25–6 of Hos. 1.10 (=LXX 2.1) but *not* of Hos. 1.9). See also our discussion of 3.2ff. below.

On balance, therefore, Paul can be said to describe the result of harmony among the Philippian Christians as enabling Christians to become God's irreproachable children living among their corrupt contemporaries.

In this situation, the Philippians are encouraged to **shine like lights** (*phôstéres*, i.e. luminaries or stars) **in the world**. Like the reference to a 'crooked and perverted generation', this has loose connections with a number of Old Testament texts, but without any specific dependence. We may compare Isa. 42.6; 49.6, where Israel as the Servant of God is to be 'a light to lighten the Gentiles'; this is applied to Christ in Luke 2.32 and to the Pauline mission in Acts 13.47 (and cf. 26.23). The LXX of Dan. 12.3 describes the age of the resurrection when 'those who understand shall shine like luminaries (*phôstéres*) of heaven, and those who strengthen my words like the stars of heaven for ever and ever'. Paul's phrase **in the world** is interesting in this regard: it could be due to an alternative translation of the Hebrew word *'ôlam* in Dan. 12.3, in its post-biblical sense of 'the world'. If so, we would have additional evidence that the passage from Daniel is foremost in Paul's mind.

Christian lives, then, are to bring God's light into a dark world, thereby exercising the eschatological ministry of the righteous. Paul's interest in **the world** clearly goes beyond the local application to Philippi. It may well carry a hint of the more cosmic significance of the Christian mission and of the Church that is suggested elsewhere (e.g. 2 Cor. 5.19; Eph. 3.10; 1 Tim. 3.16; cf. Beare).

Two phrases in this verse are also reminiscent of Jesus' words in the Sermon on the Mount. Matt. 5.45 encourages unselfish behaviour among disciples for a similar purpose: 'so that you may become children of your Father in heaven'. The light symbolism recurs in Jesus' teaching about the disciples as the light of the world, who should let it shine before others (Matt. 5.14–16). Christians are called 'children of light' in 1 Thess. 5.5; Eph. 5.8 and John 12.36; this term also strikingly resembles the self-designation of the Qumran sectarians (e.g. 1 QS 1.9; 2.16; 1QM 13.5, 9), to which Jesus may be alluding in Luke 16.8 (cf. Flusser 1988).

16 Paul's sentence continues in this verse with the disputed phrase **as you continue holding fast the word of life**, which is probably best seen as dependent on the purpose clause of the previous sentence: 'so that you may become blameless and pure ... as you continue holding fast ...'. The expression **the word of life** has no precise parallels in Paul's writings, but is clearly a reference to God's word in the life-giving gospel, which the Philippians received from Paul (cf. 2 Tim. 1.1, 10; also 1 Thess. 2.13; Heb. 4.12; 1 John 1.1; Ps. 119.107).

It is the term *hold fast* (*epechô*), however, which raises several difficulties. First, it should probably be taken with v. 15, rather than with what follows (as the traditional verse division and some translations suggest). Secondly, however, scholars are divided on the meaning of this verb, which can be either 'to hold fast' or 'to proffer'. (Field 1899: 193–4, followed by Silva 149, notes the Syriac translation 'because you are to them in place of life', and considers as a third possibility the later Greek idiom *epechô logon*, meaning 'to correspond'; but this appears not to be attested prior to the third century AD.) The second of these would indicate a missionary dimension of the Christian life, which arguably is already present in the notion of the Philippians shining as 'lights' to the world. The first has the advantage of being more clearly connected with the overall theme of steadfastness in the face of adversity. On balance, the absence of comparable evangelistic usage of this verb in other early Christian texts should incline us to the translation as given: the Philippians are to continue 'holding fast' the word of life, just as they stand firm and live their lives in a manner worthy of the gospel (1.27).

This blamelessness and steadfastness of the Philippians in turn gives Paul once again **reason to be proud**, a theme we discussed earlier in relation to 1.26 (cf. also 2.2: 'make my joy complete'; cf. 4.1). On this occasion, Paul's 'boasting' is explicitly eschatological, oriented towards the coming **day of Christ** (see on 1.6, 10 above). His rejoicing then will be because the Philippians' lives are proof that he did not **run or toil in vain**. 'Running' is one of Paul's favourite athletic images to describe the Christian life (cf. Rom. 9.16; 1 Cor. 9.24 [3x], 26; Gal. 2.2; 5.7; 2 Thess. 3.1), and his concern not to fail or run **in vain** is similarly present in Gal. 2.2 (cf. 2 Cor. 6.1; 1 Thess. 3.5). In chapter 3, Paul will go on to offer a very personal testimony to his own desire to strain forward to the heavenly prize (Phil. 3.12–14). Similarly, **toil** or 'hard work' repeatedly describes both Paul's ministry (e.g. 1 Cor. 4.12; 15.10; Gal. 4.11; Col. 1.29) and that of others (e.g. 1 Thess. 5.12; 1 Cor. 16.16; Rom. 16.6, 12).

Given Paul's emphasis on the example of Christ and its parallels with the Isaianic righteous Servant (cf. p. 135), one intriguing possibility is that he may see *his own* apostolic work and suffering in partial analogy to the same Old Testament antecedents. The Servant is concerned that he may have 'laboured in vain' and his 'toil' is before the Lord (Isa. 49.4 LXX); his task is to bring 'light' and 'salvation' to the Gentiles (Isa. 49.6 LXX; cf. 55.4–5); and he 'pours out' himself to death (Isa. 53.12 Hebr.; cf. Phil. 2.17). Perhaps Paul's close sense of union with Christ even in his sufferings (3.7–14; cf. e.g. 2 Cor. 4.10f.; Col. 1.24) allowed him to draw a derivative, participatory comfort and assurance from some of the same OT passages which he believed to refer to his Lord.

There is, as a number of writers have pointed out, a distinct expectation of judgement here: Paul is aware that the quality of his own work for the gospel will come under scrutiny on that **day of Christ**. At times he shows an awareness that this could be a painful experience for leaders who have laid unreliable foundations (1 Cor. 3.10–15; cf. 1 Cor. 4.1–5; also Jas. 3.1). Nevertheless, here as elsewhere, he feels assured that the Macedonian churches will be his pride and joy on the day of Christ (cf. 1 Thess. 2.19–20; but also 2 Cor. 1.14).

17 Verses 17–18 conclude both this paragraph and the entire section 1.27–2.18 on a different note. Paul here uses a common sacrificial metaphor to show how both his own ministry and that of the Philippians serve together for the glory of God – regardless of how his present circumstances turn out. Although verse 17 begins with an adversative conjunction (**however**), its connection with the preceding argument is safeguarded by the fact that it further elaborates on Paul's hope of 'boasting' in the Philippians on the day of the Lord, and indicates that even his possible death cannot affect this. (O'Brien suggests the conjunction has 'ascensive' force, marking a progression.)

The imagery of this verse is that of sacrifice, which would have been well known and understood as a regular public practice throughout the Roman empire. (One of the difficulties for the contemporary student, by contrast, is that the practice of sacrifice has so completely vanished from our experience; as a result, biblical interpreters are poorly equipped to bring to life either that reality or indeed the wealth of associated religious imagery.) It is unclear whether Paul has in mind Jewish or pagan sacrificial practice, but the language of a libation or drink offering was sufficiently commonplace in the ancient world to allow us to leave the reference quite general. Both in Judaism and in pagan religion, sacrifices were often completed by pouring out a libation of wine or oil over the offering or at the foot of the altar. Paul affirms that the Christian faith of the Philippians constitutes a sacrifice to God, for which his own ministry serves as the accompanying libation.

Such metaphorical language is not unique in Paul's descriptions of the Christian life and ministry. In Romans, the apostle speaks of himself as a priest of the gospel bringing the offering of the Gentiles to Jerusalem (15.16; cf. 1 Cor. 9.13–14); and he invites his readers to present themselves to God as 'a living sacrifice' (12.1; cf. further Eph. 5.2; 1 Pet. 2.5). The figurative or spiritual understanding of sacrifice is found already in the Old Testament, where it repeatedly occurs in the Psalms (e.g. 50.14; 51.17; 119.108; cf. Prov. 16.6; 21.3) and occasionally in the Prophets (cf. Amos 5.21-4; Hos. 6.6; Isa. 1.11-17). It is reflected in the LXX (e.g. Ps. 4.5; 26(= 27).6; 49(= 50).14; 106(= 107).22; 115.8 (= 116.17)). Second Temple Judaism saw the growing acceptance of a view which later became dominant in rabbinic Judaism, that prayer and good works and the study of Torah are equivalent to sacrifice (e.g. Sir. 35.1; Tob. 4.10f.; 12.9; Dan. 3.39f. LXX; cf. *m.Abot* 1.2; *A.R.N.* 4 [S. 11a]; etc.).

One difficult question is whether Paul's self-description as a libation refers specifically to his possible death or merely to the exercise of his ministry. It can be shown that the language here used does not denote a sacrificial pouring out of *blood*, so that there is in any case no *literal* allusion to martyrdom (cf. Collange, citing A.-M. Denis). Noting the present tense of **I am being poured out** (*spendomai*), some have argued on this basis that Paul's image denotes his own ongoing ministry on behalf of his churches, with no reference to his death. This could also seem more in keeping with his apparent confidence about a future visit (v. 24).

However, it is perhaps more likely that Paul's view is a more comprehensive one: his work and ministry, whether in life or in death, is a drink offering **being poured out** to complement the sacrifice of the Philippians. A number of considerations suggest that Paul's possible martyrdom is at least included in his imagery here. He has already alluded to it in 1.20ff. and will do so again in 3.10. The conditional **if** in this clause seems to suggest something that is not just happening in any case, as for the last thirty years of his life, but which is an imminent possibility. Greek papyrus evidence suggests the execution of a prophet of Apollo could be seen as a libation (cf. *BAGD*), and Seneca spoke of the suicide required of him in similar terms (Tacitus, *Annals* 15.64; 16.35). Perhaps most tellingly, two passages that are most likely dependent on this verse assume without hesitation that 'being poured out as a libation' means to be put to death: see 2 Tim. 4.6; Ignatius, *Rom.* 2.2.

The Philippians, then, are seen as priests offering their own sacrifice of faith to God. (Cf. Lightfoot; note the term **priestly service**, *leitourgia*, although in non-sacrificial contexts this can simply denote a public service or duty, as in 2.30; cf. 2.25 *leitourgos*, 'minister'.) It is true that in 4.18 Paul associates this same image of sacrifice with the monetary gift he has received from Philippi. However, the breadth of this metaphor elsewhere (cf. Rom. 12.1 and see above) suggests that, contrary to recent interpretative fashion, its meaning in this rather general statement should not be restricted to financial connotations. The 'sacrifice' and 'priestly service' of the Philippians are first and foremost about the Christian life of **faith**, not about money – although generosity in the latter can of course be an appropriate expression of the former (cf. 4.18; 2 Cor. 9.12).

Paul's own ministry by life or by death is a libation being poured out to complement and complete the sacrifice of his friends at Philippi. It is that which leads him to say, **I am glad and rejoice** (lit. 'I rejoice and co-rejoice') **with all of you**: his joy is that he makes a contribution to the sacrifice they offer, just he has previously identified their faith and progress in the gospel as a cause for joy (1.4f., 25; cf. 2.2; 4.1, 10). It is intriguing to note that Paul sees himself as an addition to *their* sacrifice, rather than vice versa – a perspective on the 'mind of Christ' which not all subsequent Christian leaders have taken to heart.

18 Verse 18 simply encourages the Philippians to adopt the same view of the matter. It may seem odd that Paul finds it necessary to urge that they should **rejoice together with me**, having only just said that he rejoices together with all of them. But it is clearly a theme which this letter reiterates again and again: their 'progress and joy in the faith' (1.25) is something which has begun, but which Paul wants emphatically to encourage. This mutual joy is the aim and purpose of the preceding instructions. (See also p. 228 on Paul's appeal to his own example.)

The theme of rejoicing and encouraging others to rejoice is further reflected in 3.1 and 4.4. Paul's attitude in this regard resembles that of Moses in early rabbinic literature, who is said both to have rejoiced and to make others rejoice (e.g. *Sifre Deut.* 303 on 26.14; *m.M.Sh.* 5.12). It also calls to mind the rabbinic view of the one who does the work of God 'for its own sake': 'he makes both God and humankind rejoice' (*m.Abot* 6.1 *v.l.*, R. Meir).

Together, verses 17–18 are the perfect illustration of Bengel's justly famous summary of the entire letter: 'I rejoice; you, too, rejoice!' (*gaudeo, gaudete*: Bengel on 1.4).

In verses 13–18, Paul has once again sounded the note of joy in the midst of suffering, which we encountered earlier in 1.12–26 and at the beginning of the present section, in 1.27–30. This theme of course has nothing to do with a pathetic and pseudo-Christian satisfaction in feeling miserable: what Paul describes is joy *in spite of* suffering, not joy because of suffering. Nor, on the other hand, do we find here the sort of knee-jerk triumphalism in adversity which self-righteously treats all criticism and opposition as reinforcing the heedless certitude that 'we' are saved while all others are damned. Instead, Christian joy in affliction takes its source and occasion in the example of Christ, whose past service and suffering and exaltation (2.6–11) are the sole assurance of our own future victory (3.20f.).

Paul's brief statement of shared joy about the Philippians' common life and witness in Christ leads on to verses 19–30, which speak of travel plans on the part of the assistants despatched in both directions. Even though the Philippian church must now work out its own salvation in the apostle's absence (2.12), their continuing mutual encouragement is greatly aided by these trusted friends whom they can send to each other.

IV PLANS FOR RENEWED FELLOWSHIP (2.19–30)

Paul's news and plans pertain first to his long-standing assistant Timothy, the co-sender of this letter (1.1), and then to Epaphroditus, who had been delegated to present the Philippians' financial gift to Paul. He himself may come before long (v. 24; cf. 1.26), but in the meantime he expects to send them first (it seems) Epaphroditus (vv. 25–30) and then Timothy (2.19–24), once his own circumstances have become clearer (v. 23).

Since such 'travel narratives' are typically found near the beginning or the end of ancient letters including those of Paul (e.g. in Rom., 1 Cor., Col., Phlm.), it is frequently argued that Paul was at this point intending to draw his remarks to a close. Some have cited this as significant evidence in support of the argument that 3.1ff. is part of a different letter (see above, p. 20). However, it is now increasingly accepted that Paul's descriptions of his own or his friends' travels are so varied in nature and purpose that no strictly formal and structural definition of a so-called 'travelogue' can be developed. What is more, this particular passage in some ways has more in common with Paul's 'letters of commendation', which also occur at various points in his correspondence (e.g. 1 Thess. 3.23; 1 Cor. 16.15–18; 2 Cor. 8.16–24; Rom. 16.1–2). (The term 'travelogue' was proposed by Funk 1966: 264–74 and has been adopted by a number of commentators, although Funk's view of it as a clearly defined formal entity is now widely doubted. See further O'Brien; Fee, esp. n. 3.) Although it might be thought to beg certain questions, D.F. Watson 1988 regards the rhetorical classification of this section to be that of *digressio*.

This is in any case a much lighter and more 'newsy' section of the letter, with no major theological conundrums. Nevertheless, the relationships here discussed constitute part of the day-to-day reality of Christian living which the preceding section addressed theologically and ethically. We shall see that Paul's description of these two friends reveals a number of features that parallel his commendation of the 'mind of Christ' in 1.27–2.18.

A TIMOTHY   (2.19–24)

(19) I hope in the Lord Jesus to send Timothy to you shortly, so that I too may be encouraged at hearing your news. (20) I have no other kindred spirit like him, who will so genuinely care for your welfare. (21) (All the rest pursue their own interests, not those of Jesus Christ.) (22) But Timothy's proven character you know, that like a child with his father he served together with me for the cause of the gospel. (23) I hope, therefore, to send him as soon as I have a clearer idea about my situation. (24) And I am in fact confident in the Lord that I myself will soon be coming, too.

19 Since Paul is indisposed, **Timothy** will represent him. We discussed his uniquely close relationship with Paul in relation to their joint appearance in the letterhead, 1.1. Here we may just remind ourselves that his proposed mission to Philippi is something of which he had already gained a good deal of experience: he had already been sent to Macedonia more than ten years earlier (1 Thess. 3.2f.; cf. Acts 17.14; 18.5; 19.22), to Corinth on several occasions (1 Cor. 4.17; 16.10), and according to the Pastoral Letters and Eusebius to Ephesus as well (1 Tim. 1.2f. and *passim*; *Hist. Eccl.* 3.4). Timothy, then, is an 'old hand' on the Pauline team, and already well known to the Philippians (cf. v. 22). He will be sent to them **shortly**, once Paul's Roman circumstances have become clearer (v. 23). (Such a mission would also be compatible with an Ephesian origin of Philippians (cf. Acts 19.22), but this is unlikely on other grounds: see the Introduction, p. 27.)

Even this relatively routine piece of planning, however, is conducted **in the Lord Jesus**: not merely, as some have suggested, because events at Rome may overtake Paul's plan and prevent him from carrying it out. It is certainly true that this and all plans are dependent on the Lord's will (cf. 1 Cor. 4.19; 16.7; Jas. 4.15); but here as in 1.8, 14; 3.1, **in the Lord** is more than a limiting condition or a fatalistic 'just in case' insurance policy. Instead, it is **the Lord Jesus** who grounds his **hope** (cf. p. 84 above); he is the one with whom and through whom these plans are conceived, and he is the one who carries the sovereign responsibility for their outcome. **In the Lord Jesus**, therefore, constitutes both a proviso and a guarantee. The proviso is that the sovereign Lord is in charge of these plans; and his purposes may differ from Paul's. The guarantee is the same: **the Lord** is in charge, who is sure to see to final completion the good work that he has begun (1.6; cf. 1.19, 3.20f.).

The purpose of sending Timothy is apparently to obtain a reliable account of the situation at Philippi: to receive news about their 'progress and joy in the faith' (1.25), their unity and steadfastness in adversity (1.27ff.) – and perhaps their resolution of simmering conflicts (2.14; 4.1–3). Just as the return of Epaphroditus will bring the Philippians joy and presumably news of Paul (v. 28), so Paul hopes that through Timothy's mission he **too may be encouraged**. Although Philippi enjoyed excellent road connections and the proximity of a fine harbour at Neapolis (modern Kaválla), Timothy's round trip could easily take three months, especially if other churches were to be visited (cf. p. 31 on travelling times). This alone suggests that Paul's situation, while serious, is at least not immediately threatening: he looks forward to Timothy's news on his return.

20 Two reasons indicate Timothy's suitability for this mission. The first is given in this verse: Paul has **no other kindred spirit like him** in Rome, no one like-minded or (lit.) 'equal in soul'. The emphasis could be that Paul has (i) no one *like Timothy*, of his calibre; (ii) no one *like Paul* in his fundamental commitments; or (iii) no one who is equally concerned for the Philippians. The context indicates a preference for (ii), although (i) and (iii) follow from it: the point of the contrast between Timothy and all the others is that he shares a Christ-centred loyalty to the gospel in close partnership with Paul (vv. 21f.). And no one **so genuinely cares** for the Philippians. The verb 'to care' (*merimnaō*) is used again in 4.6 in the sense of 'to worry'. Here, in the future tense, it indicates the active interest and practical care that Timothy will show for the Philippians: in a positive sense, he is 'anxious' for their welfare. The NT repeatedly highlights this 'true' or 'genuine' quality of Timothy: he is called Paul's 'true son' in 1 Tim. 1.2, and Paul says of him that 'he does the work of the Lord just as I do' (1 Cor. 16.10). There may be an implicit sense that Timothy has Paul's full endorsement and represents him, although no formal delegation of apostolic authority is indicated; indeed verse 24 could suggest the opposite.

Here, Paul dispatches his letter of commendation ahead of Timothy's visit, since the time is not quite ready to send him.

21 This verse presents a parenthetical comment in Paul's commendation of Timothy, almost as a footnote to the previous verse. Nevertheless, it seems an astonishing statement: **all the rest** (lit. 'everyone') **pursue their own interests**. Who are *all* these others around him? Paul is presumably not making a statement about all other Christians at Rome, especially after his positive remarks about '*most* of the brothers and sisters' in 1.14, who apparently even send their greetings in 4.22. Instead, there must be an implied contrast between Timothy's character and some others, who might have been thought suitable as Paul's potential partners or even emissaries in place of Timothy. Alternatively, the apostle's slightly jaded tone may betray disappointment at co-workers who have abandoned him: 2 Tim. 4.10, if an authentic reminiscence of Paul's Roman detention, implies that among those who left Paul stranded in prison was Demas, another former associate with Macedonian connections (cf. Phlm. 24; Col. 4.14).

The conjunction *gar* (lit. 'for') introduces a justification of the previous statement: Paul has no one like Timothy, since other young Christian leaders at Rome prefer to pursue their own self-advancement. We heard earlier about those who 'preach Christ out of selfish ambition' (1.15, 17). This verse, then, suggests that Paul's rivals may have included some of the more prominent evangelists with a present or past ministry in Rome – and perhaps that his feelings about them were not always as generous as in 1.15–17. None of them care sufficiently about the church at Philippi – or, accordingly, about the cause of Jesus Christ. Selfishness may well have prevented the others from volunteering an arduous journey to support the work of an apparent apostolic 'loser' now in Roman detention, whose future was uncertain at best. (Cf. Rapske 1994: 288–98 on the shame commonly associated with Roman imprisonment.)

The explicit contrast with other potential assistants shows Timothy to be even more outstanding and exemplary: while the others pursue **their own interests**, Timothy is anxious for that of the Philippians and, by implication, for the cause **of Jesus Christ** and the gospel. As he reflects on Timothy's rare excellence of character, therefore, Paul finds himself musing how many are religious only for their own interest (cf. Bengel).

22 Timothy's **proven character** is well known to the Philippians, since his ministry in Macedonia goes back many years. This character has been acquired, honed and demonstrated in his long-standing teamwork with Paul, which is characterized by their common service for the gospel. (Note the relationship between 'endurance' and 'character' in Rom. 5.4.) Herein, then, lies a second reason for sending him (cf. v. 20): his proven track record.

When Paul speaks of his spiritual fatherhood (1 Cor. 4.15; 1 Thess. 2.11), motherhood (Gal. 4.19; 1 Thess. 2.7) and parenthood (2 Cor. 6.13; 12.14) of various churches and individuals (e.g. Phlm. 10), this relates primarily to his having brought them to faith. Paul's father–son relationship with Timothy, however, would appear to carry an additional, more affectionate and personal dimension – grown over many years of friendship between an older and a younger man labouring at the same task. Such a relationship is also reflected in the Pastoral Epistles, where Timothy is addressed as 'my child' (1 Tim. 1.18; 2 Tim. 2.1). For the Philippians, his filial loyalty and common cause with Paul are also a guarantee that he will be trustworthy in carrying out his task just as the apostle would. Similar relationships appear to exist between teachers and students in Jewish wisdom literature (e.g. Prov. 1.8ff.; 2.1; 3.1, 11, 21 and *passim*; see further Matt. 23.8f. and *b.Sanh.* 19b).

Service of **the gospel** here must mean service of the cause of the gospel, as well as service of Christ as the one it concerns; cf. our comments on 1.5, 7, 12, above.

Within the larger argument of the letter, Timothy seems to be commended as a positive example to the Philippians: the language used of him, as indeed of Epaphroditus in v. 25–30, may well be deliberately evocative of the attitudes set out in 1.27–2.18, especially in 2.5–11. He has at heart the interests of others (cf. 2.4), the cause of Jesus Christ (cf. 2.5) and the gospel (1.27). Here in verse 22, he is said to serve the gospel as a **slave**: the verb (*douleuô*) is closely linked with Christ's own service in the form of a 'slave' (*doulos*) in 2.6. His service as a servant of Jesus Christ **together with** Paul was already affirmed in 1.1.

23 Recapitulating the subject of verse 19, then, Paul hopes to despatch Timothy once his present situation becomes a little clearer. Timothy is the man for the job: literally, Paul says 'this one, then, I hope to send'. Paul cannot send him, however, until he has **a clearer idea about my situation**, presumably concerning either a sense of the likely verdict or at least the precise charges and the time frame envisioned for the trial. Only then will he know what news and instructions to send with Timothy to Philippi. Alternatively, it could be that in his present uncertain situation Paul still needs Timothy precisely because there is no other like-minded assistant available (cf. v. 20).

24 Verses 23 and 24 syntactically belong together: the Greek adds particles indicating that 'on the one hand' Paul is going to send Timothy; but 'on the other hand' he is **confident** that he himself **will soon be coming too**. We heard in 1.19 of Paul's certainty ('I know') that his present circumstances will turn out for his deliverance, and in 1.25 of his conviction that he will 'remain and continue' with the Philippians because it is necessary for their joy and progress in the gospel. In addition, however, the question of his martyrdom has already been mentioned a couple of times (1.20–23; 2.17) and will in a slightly different form be raised again in 3.10. This verse, therefore, comes a little unexpectedly. It seems particularly peculiar that he 'hopes in the Lord' to send Timothy, but is *confident* **in the Lord** (cf. 1.6, 14, 25) that he will soon be coming himself. (Both Timothy's coming and his own are subject to the same proviso that they will occur **in the Lord**; see on v. 19.) He expects to come **soon**; this must in any case mean a matter of months at least, since he appears to have every intention of awaiting Timothy's return (2.19). Perhaps, too, Timothy's mission is intended to look after the work in Macedonia just in case Paul's release is not in fact imminent (cf. Caird).

What is the basis of this expectation? Perhaps he is secretly hopeful that the capital charge against him, though grave, may be dismissed in the end, because his accusers will not manage to mount a proper case (cf. Acts 28.18–19; Rapske 1994: 188f.). Or perhaps his conviction that he is still needed for the work of the gospel among the Philippians (1.25) has increased his assurance. (It is worth noting his emphasis on 'I, too': Timothy's visit, although bearing his full endorsement, is no substitute for the arrival of the apostle himself, who clearly remains the senior partner in their relationship and the prime focus of the Philippians' concern; cf. 4.10.)

Paul's stated desire to visit Philippi upon his release confirms that he has changed his travel plans since the writing of Romans; see on 1.26 above.

B   EPAPHRODITUS   (2.25–30)

Epaphroditus, the courier of the Philippians' gift to Paul, is coming even before Timothy, quite possibly as the bearer of the letter (so e.g. the letter subscript in the Majority Text and Codex 075). Paul's commendation of him, if slightly different in tone, is also strongly positive.

(25) Meanwhile, I consider it necessary to send you Epaphroditus, my brother and co-worker and fellow-soldier, who is

also your envoy and minister to my need. (26) He has been longing to see you all, and distressed that you had heard about his illness. (27) He was indeed so ill that he very nearly died. But God had mercy on him – not only on him but on me, too, so that I might not suffer one sorrow after another. (28) I am therefore sending him sooner than expected, so that you may rejoice again when you see him, and that I may be less sorrowful. (29) So welcome him in the Lord with all joy, and hold such people in honour: (30) for he came close to death for the work of Christ, having risked his life in order to make up for the service you were unable to render to me yourselves.

25 Epaphroditus is someone the Philippians know as one of their own: he is the man they sent to Paul with their financial gift to minister to his need (cf. 4.18). Paul says he *considers it necessary* to send him back. The Greek here uses the aorist, normally associated with the past tense (i.e. 'I considered it necessary'): this is the so-called 'epistolary aorist', relating Paul's present course of action to the tense that will be appropriate from his readers' perspective (cf. v. 28). Epaphroditus is coming now and apparently serves as the bearer of the letter; the Philippians are urged to give him a warm welcome in verses 29–30.

We know nothing more of Epaphroditus than what we learn here and in 4.18. His name is related to the cult of the goddess Aphrodite, and he is therefore most likely a convert from a genuinely pagan family background. (He should be distinguished from Epaphras in Col. 1.7; 4.12 and Phlm. 23, who bears a short form of the same name but comes from Colossae in Phrygia, i.e. southwestern Asia Minor.)

Epaphroditus is described in generous terms that resemble the commendation of other Pauline fellow workers and letter bearers, particularly in Romans 16. Some scholars claim to detect in this pattern a formal convention, suggesting that it serves a quasi-official purpose of giving Epaphroditus an apostolic 'reference' letter. And it is clearly true that a sender's endorsement of his courier or emissary was an important reassurance in an age without public postal services or telecommunications. (Cf. Murphy-O'Connor 1995 on the practical issues Paul faced in writing letters.) Nevertheless, the genuine warmth of Paul's words about Epaphroditus suggests that they are more than simply perfunctory.

Paul relates to Epaphroditus as his **brother**, a **co-worker** and a **fellow-soldier**. The first term describes fellow Christians in general, but here probably includes a special note of personal affection. The second is used to describe not Christians in general but active partners in ministry (e.g. 1 Cor. 3.9 Paul and Apollos; 2 Cor. 8.23 Titus; Rom. 16.21 Timothy), who are seen as fellow workers not just with Paul but 'with God' (1 Cor. 3.9; 1 Thess. 3.2). The third term, finally, is a military term denoting a 'comrade in arms' which appears only here and in Phlm. 2. Given Paul's language of 'struggle' and 'conflict' in 1.27, 30, as well as his use elsewhere of military imagery for his work in conditions of adversity (e.g. 1 Cor. 9.7; 2 Cor. 10.3), it is safe to see here a confirmation that Epaphroditus, like Paul, has had his commitments tested in the face of genuine conflict. (Cf. further 1 Tim. 1.18; 2 Tim. 2.3–4 regarding Timothy.) We do not know the nature of these conflicts, but they may include his coming close to death for the Christian ministry (v. 30).

Epaphroditus' role was to be the Philippians' **envoy** (*apostolos*: see below), and the supplier of Paul's need. The word **minister** (*leitourgos*) generally designates someone who discharges a public service; while the LXX frequently relates this specifically to priestly service (cf. *leitourgia* in 2.17), there is no indication of priestly connotations here (cf. v. 30). Epaphroditus is a messenger charged by his church with the official duty of looking after Paul's needs while in Roman custody. This **need** was clearly in part financial, and a significant part of Epaphroditus' responsibility was to deliver the gift of the Philippians (4.18). Nevertheless, Paul's sorrow about the lack of friends in Rome (2.21) and his reference to the 'needs' of the Philippians suggest that their emissary's task may have been defined more broadly: to make himself available to the apostle for personal and material assistance during this time of uncertainty. (So Bengel and many modern commentators.) Despite Paul's reluctance to speak of his need in 4.11, it remains true that as a Roman prisoner he would have relied to some extent on provisions from his friends (cf. Acts 24.23 on Paul in Caesarea; Rapske 1994: 209–16, 369–92 *passim*).

This is also suggested by several indications that the Philippians may have thought his task to be incomplete and did not expect him back so soon. The first of these is in the present verse: Paul says that he, not Epaphroditus, considers it **necessary** for his Philippian helper to return. This sounds almost apologetic, as if giving Epaphroditus' termination of service the official approval it would not otherwise have had. No reason for the decision is given (v. 26 by itself seems insufficient; but see vv. 27–8). Paul's Philippian assistant has not resigned or deserted; nor has he been fired: the apostle does not say he is sending him 'back' (cf. Gnilka on v. 29, O'Brien 333 n. 26). Indeed the value of his stay is underlined by the fact that Paul speaks without the slightest hint of criticism, affirming instead that Epaphroditus' service is fully 'completed' (v. 30).

On a linguistic note, the use of *apostolos* (**envoy**) for Epaphroditus suggests that in Paul's vocabulary the term had not yet exclusively assumed the quasi-technical meaning which it carries in Paul's self-description elsewhere as an 'apostle of Jesus Christ' (1 Cor. 1.1, etc.). Instead, it retains its original meaning of 'appointed emissary': as Epaphroditus is for the Philippians (cf. similarly 2 Cor. 8.23), so Paul is the 'emissary' of Jesus Christ, commissioned not by a church but by the risen Lord himself (note 1 Cor. 9.1; 15.7, 9).

26 Epaphroditus has been keenly **longing to see** his home community again after an extended absence. More than simple homesickness accounts for this longing, however: he has been distressed that the Philippians had learned of his illness. If his readers had any suspicion that Epaphroditus had failed or been disloyal to their commission, Paul means to dispel such thoughts. Their friend has been **distressed** that they might think his illness had left him unable to carry out his task: the verb *adémoneó* here describes anguish due not so much to shock (*pace* Bruce, O'Brien *et al.* citing H. B. Swete) but to the perceived inability to change a state of affairs (it is so used in Symmachus Ps. 60.2(= 61.3); 115.2(= 116.11); Aquila Job 18.20; and arguably even in Mark 14.33–6 par. Matt. 26.37–9; cf. Josephus *Ant.* 15.211).

Paul's reference to this unspecified illness has given rise to much scholarly speculation. Did Epaphroditus contract it on his way to Rome or once he got there, perhaps in sharing Paul's detention? (Only the former would apply on the assumption of a narrowly financial assignment, as in this case his mission could be threatened only by his failure to arrive in Rome.) Was the illness itself the occasion of 'risking his life' (v. 30), or did he 'very nearly die' in the course of pressing on to Rome (cf. Caird)? We shall probably never know. What is clear is the following outline: some time after leaving Philippi, Epaphroditus became so gravely ill that word of it got back to Philippi, whether at his own or someone else's initiative (though there is no evidence that it was Paul's). The very success of his mission seemed in doubt. The Philippians perhaps hear only now that in fact he came near to death, most likely while already at Rome (v. 27). He has perhaps recovered only within the past couple of months, evidently not long enough to send word of this back to Philippi. He is keen to see his friends again and to put their minds at ease.

An Ephesian or Caesarean setting of Philippians has sometimes been inferred from the relative ease and frequency of communications that may be assumed by verse 26: Epaphroditus' journey to Paul, a messenger's journey to Philippi to bear news of his illness, and so on. To alleviate the perceived difficulty and compress these journeys into a shorter time frame, some have suggested in answer to these questions that Epaphroditus' message to Philippi might have been sent while he was still *en route* to Rome, and that in any case no reply from them was required for him to suppose that they might be worried. But the difficulty of communication is in any case exaggerated. Since Philippi was located on the Via Egnatia, the main artery of roads connecting Rome with the Eastern Empire, relative ease of communications was assured, possibly with the assistance of Christian friends travelling on business (e.g. those mentioned in Rom. 16.3, 6, 7, 10b, 11; note also the evidence for frequent Jewish contact both between Palestine and Rome and around the diaspora, e.g. Barclay 1996: 421–4). If Epaphroditus left Philippi even six or nine months ago, there is no difficulty. (See further p. 31 above, and cf. Witherington 1994: 79f.; Fee 36f., 277f. and nn. 28–31.)

27 If this reconstruction approximately fits the facts, the remainder of this paragraph falls into place relatively easily. Epaphroditus really was at death's door: this much confirms the fears at Philippi, and yet it shows both that he was not lacking in commitment and that on his recovery Paul has good reason to send him home (note the 'therefore' in v. 28).

By God's grace Epaphroditus has now been restored. Paul mentions only the fact that **God had mercy on him**, but tells us nothing more about either the disease or the manner of its healing. This divine **mercy**, regularly associated with the deliverance of his people and of individuals in the Old Testament (e.g. LXX Exod. 33.19; Ps. 6.3; 9.14(= 13); 50.3(= 51.1)), is the same quality that characterizes Jesus' healings and exorcisms in the gospels (e.g. Mark 10.47f.; Luke 17.13.; cf. Mark 5.19; Matt. 15.22; 17.15). There is no contradiction in saying that a martyr's death in the Lord's service is 'gain' (1.21) and yet that recovery from mortal illness is a sign of divine mercy.

Paul, too, has experienced Epaphroditus' recovery as God's mercy, since his death would have left him with **one sorrow after another** (lit. 'grief upon grief'). It is clear why the death of his 'fellow-soldier' would have caused him sorrow – but what was the earlier sorrow to which this would have added? It was probably not Epaphroditus' prior illness, as some have supposed: Paul's language in v. 28 about being 'less sorrowful' (*alupoteros*, a comparative) suggests that his sorrow is now merely reduced, not abated. The apostle's sadness preceded his friend's arrival and is not removed by his departure. It pertains to his own situation: not, we may assume, his captivity *per se*, which he described in such positive terms in 1.12–14, but the selfish rivalry of some Christian leaders (1.15, 17), which has left him without any allies other than Timothy (2.20–21; cf. Col. 4.11).

28 This, then, identifies the explicit reason for wanting Epaphroditus to return **sooner** rather than later. The literal translation is either 'more urgently' or 'more swiftly'; but in either case it is clear that what Paul means is 'as soon as possible', and therefore **sooner than expected**. This course of action has several advantages: it allows Epaphroditus after his brush with death to be restored to his family and friends, and to set the church at ease both about his personal circumstances and about the success of his mission (cf. v. 26). Just as the Philippians' concern for Paul's well-being moved them first to send Epaphroditus and then to worry about the possible failure of his mission, so his concern for their welfare now impels the apostle to have him return (cf. 1.7, lit. Paul's 'thinking about you all' with 4.10, lit. 'your thinking about me'). Knowledge of their renewed joy at seeing each other again will reduce Paul's continuing sorrow and disappointment at the behaviour of some of his fellow Christians at Rome (2.21; cf. 3.18). Given the previous reference to his 'grief' (*lupē*) in v. 27, there is thus no need to relate Paul's expectation of being **less sorrowful** (*alupoteros*) to the Philippian church's supposedly divided allegiance to Paul (*pace* Peterlin 1995).

29 Having thus explained his action, Paul encourages the Philippians to **welcome** Epaphroditus **in the Lord** and **with all joy**. To urge the warm reception of a courier has on the one hand an aspect of polite and requisite convention. Here, however, his wish comes with a genuine warmth (cf. similarly Phoebe in Rom. 16.1–2). One might have thought this to be an unnecessary injunction for a man who was clearly one of their own and in any case the subject of much concern. There is no need to assume that something has seriously gone amiss in their relationship (*pace* some commentators). Nevertheless, Epaphroditus' return is likely to be unexpected and sooner than intended: it might well evoke among the Philippians a bittersweet mixture of feelings, both of relief and of disappointment that from their perspective the journey had not been an unmitigated success. Paul's words may anticipate that the fleeting delight over a safe reunion could too easily be drowned in an over-hasty lapse into humdrum routines of familiarity and, perhaps, of lingering reproach. But to forestall all this, Paul urges that Epaphroditus be received **in the Lord, with all joy** and **in honour**. Significantly, the present tense of the verbs for 'receiving' and 'holding in honour' suggests that it should be an *enduring* welcome (cf. O'Brien). But Paul is clearly wanting to extrapolate: it is not just Epaphroditus, but **such people** generally who should be honoured. Once again, those who stake their ambition on the example of Christ in 2.6–11 will find themselves in conflict with the values and presuppositions of the secular path to power. By saying that it is people like Epaphroditus whom the Philippians should **hold in honour** (*entimous*), Paul at once contradicts Graeco-Roman society's pervasive culture of rewarding the upwardly mobile quest for prestige and public recognition (*philotimia*). The Church instead will prize and value those who aspire to the mind of Christ.

30 People like Epaphroditus, then, should be held in honour (cf. Stephanas in 1 Cor. 16.15–18). He has put his life on the line and nearly died (v. 27), but Paul brings that fact into explicit connection with **the work of Christ**. This is equivalent to the 'service for the gospel' which Paul earlier commended in Timothy (v. 22). The work is Christ's: he began it and he will complete it (1.6). Meanwhile, however, he has also assigned it to his people: Christian participation in the work of Christ is an essential part of that 'working out of one's salvation' of which 2.12 spoke. The late first-century Rabbi Tarfon was remembered as saying, 'The day is short; the task is great; the workmen are lazy; the reward is great, and the Master is insistent. ... It is not up to you to complete the task, but neither are you free to neglect it' (*m.Abot* 2.20f.). Epaphroditus has devoted himself to the God-given task, both on his own account and on behalf of the Philippians. His willingness to expend himself in the service of others, to risk his life and come **close to death** (*mechri thanatou*) for the 'work of Christ' echoes something of the 'mind' of Christ himself, who was 'obedient to death (*mechri thanatou*)' (2.8).

At the same time, he has in fact been able **to make up for** (lit. 'fill up' or 'discharge fully') **the service** which the Philippians were unable to render in person. This raises an issue to which Paul returns in 4.10: during their long separation, the Philippians have been unable to express fully their active partnership in the apostle's ministry. It was only Epaphroditus, in bringing their gift and offering his assistance, who has now 'discharged' that deficit on their behalf, unselfishly risking his life in the process. Epaphroditus, therefore, personally completes the priestly **service** (*leitourgia*) of the Philippians, as a part of the sacrifice of their faith to which 1.17 referred.

Both Timothy and Epaphroditus, then, are here commended in terms which show that they embody something of the attitudes Paul encouraged in 1.27–2.18, especially in relation to the example of Christ (2.5–11). In self-giving service of others for the work of the gospel, each of them in different ways has adopted the 'mind of Christ Jesus'.

V INTERIM CONCLUSION: REJOICE! *(3.1)*

It is clear that we have reached the end of a section. This new verse moves on from the commendation of Epaphroditus and Timothy. Given the last two paragraphs, we are now in some ways ready for the conclusion of the letter. It seems plausible to end with the commendation of various people and the so-called 'travelogue', which occur near the end of other letters as well. And so it makes good sense that the apostle writes, **Finally**.

Nevertheless, this verse gives rise to numerous problems of understanding, perhaps the most vexing of which is that the letter does *not* in fact end. Since it seems implausible to attach 3.1 specifically to the commendation of Epaphroditus, we are left with several options, the three most important of which are as follows: (i) chapter 3 in its entirety is a new section; 3.1 is not a conclusion, but belongs to the first paragraph of this new section. (ii) 3.1 (or 3.1a) does begin a conclusion, but it continues most logically in 4.1, *after* the inserted letter fragment 3.1b (or 3.2)–21. (iii) 3.1 (or 3.1a) is indeed a kind of conclusion following from what precedes, but it stands on its own. After this Paul begins a new section, whether by design or in a change of plans.

Option (i) is certainly respectable, but leaves the abrupt change of tone between 3.1 and 3.2 particularly difficult to account for (see below on the word **finally**, 3.1). Recent attempts to do so, whether based on formal rhetorical or linguistic considerations, still seem tainted with an inherent arbitrariness of method (see pp. 20ff., 38ff. above). Rhetorical devices may indeed have a useful part to play in the interpretation of chapter 3, as we will see. Nevertheless, the prescriptive use of rules of formal rhetoric to improve Paul's rambling oratory is best resisted.

Option (ii) is in many ways the neatest and simplest, especially given the apparently smooth connection of 3.1 with 4.1. The arguments against this option were presented at some length in the introduction (see pp. 20–25), and we shall not rehearse them here. In the absence of clear textual and historical evidence, the biblical critic's wielding of the scalpel is generally more dangerous to the patient than the application of Ockham's razor to the critic's hypotheses.

The last option (iii) is arguably the most untidy – but not of course for that reason less likely as an interpretation of Paul's argument. There is a sense in which **finally** here indicates a conclusion of what has gone before, even if not necessarily the end of the letter. In 1 Thess. 3, too, Paul discusses Timothy's travels before apparently concluding, 'Finally' (4.1) – and then going on to introduce several important new subjects in the remaining two chapters. Prescriptive rhetorical or structural assumptions about the form of Paul's argumentation can too easily force it into a straitjacket that denies him the freedom to say, 'Ah, and one more thing … That reminds me. …' Yet that may be precisely what he does in 3.2. He begins to conclude in 3.1 – and then goes on concluding for some considerable time. An important additional matter comes to mind – triggered perhaps by the word 'safeguard' in verse 1: 'Oh, and speaking of safeguards, you must remember to beware of the "dogs". …'

On this reading, then, Paul's initial train of thought is interrupted after 3.1, which remains an unfinished conclusion. For one reason or another, it gives way to a further thought, which may well be triggered by these words themselves or by continuing reflection about the preceding subject matter. Alternatively, he could have reached the point of conclusion and taken a break, during which time he heard alarming news about the activities of Judaizers either in Rome or, less plausibly, in Philippi (see below on v. 2). Either way, however, verse 1 cannot easily be incorporated into the following section and must stand as an interim conclusion of what precedes.

A remaining question is whether 3.1 should be seen as appended to 2.19–30 or placed separately, as a more general conclusion to the argument thus far. The arguments in this regard are finely balanced; and since a new section is in any case about to begin, it probably does not matter greatly how one decides. Nevertheless, it may be best to see the verse as a *general* conclusion to 2.19–30: Paul desires the Philippians to rejoice in verse 28 and instructs them to receive Epaphroditus 'with all joy in the Lord' in verse 29. It is therefore not surprising if Paul in 3.1 recapitulates in the same terms and even comments on the fact that he is repeating himself. What is more, the exhortation to joy in this concluding statement appropriately parallels that of 1.27–2.18 (see 2.17f.), and arguably that of 1.12–26 as well (cf. 1.25f.). The same exhortation next occurs in 4.4, following the section 3.2–4.3. Joy links all the different themes of the letter together.

(3.1) And finally, brothers and sisters, rejoice in the Lord! I do not find it troublesome to write the same thing again, but for you it is a safeguard.

The term **finally** (*to loipon*) has understandably been the subject of considerable debate. Its precise range of meaning is difficult to represent in English, but literal translations would include 'and as far as the rest is concerned', 'and beyond that', even 'and henceforth' (cf. French *d'ailleurs*, German *im übrigen*). It is certainly correct that its meaning to some extent depends on the context (so O'Brien), but on that assumption it will end up being conveniently adapted to justify one's prior reconstruction of the argument at this point. Its function is best seen as transitional: *to loipon* introduces a further thought, whether short or long, in resolution or progression from what has gone before. What the word's Pauline and wider usage does *not* lead one to expect is a transition into what amounts to a rhetorical flame-thrower: 'and beyond that, rejoice in the Lord ...: beware of the dogs!' It is the effect of this sudden polemical eruption in v. 2 which suggests that while the word may introduce a new thought, it was not *this* new thought which was initially uppermost on Paul's mind when he said *to loipon*, **Finally**. Something has caused him to change course.

Paul once again addresses the Philippians in a familiar way as his **brothers and sisters**, a term we discussed earlier in relation to 1.12 (see p. 73).

The term **rejoice**, too, comes as no surprise, since the theme of joy has been repeatedly stressed. Although its literal meaning is 'rejoice', by itself the word *chaire* (pl. *chairete*) had come to mean 'hello' or, less commonly, 'good-bye'. A fair (if not unanswerable) case can be made that this is how it functions in 2 Cor. 13.11, which introduces a conclusion remarkably similar in form to that found here: 'finally, brothers and sisters, farewell (*loipon, adelphoi, chairete*)!' Translations and commentators have occasionally tried to read the present verse accordingly: 'finally, farewell in the Lord' (e.g. Beare, citing E.J. Goodspeed, also on 4.4). However, the undeniable importance of the theme of Christian joy in 2.17–18, 28–9 and elsewhere makes it most unlikely that 'joy in the Lord' should suddenly acquire a different meaning. Instead, Paul wants the Philippians to rejoice in 2.28–9 and does not mind saying it once more in this verse; similarly in 4.4, where again he repeats himself explicitly. (Wick 1994: 57–8 proposes that this call to rejoice, standing as it does exactly half way through the epistle, could be said to form the rhetorical centre of the letter; but this insight must be balanced against the overarching theological importance of 2.5–11.)

Their joy is **in the Lord** because he is both its occasion and its source. See on verses 17–18 and 29 above, and more generally p. 59. Such joy in the Lord is independent of adverse circumstances – and even of selfishly minded people (cf. 1.18)! For the Philippians, it must also be independent of what happens to Paul (2.17f.).

Paul's next few words have long puzzled his interpreters: 'to write the same things to you is not troublesome for me, but safe for you.' (According to LSJ, the adjective *oknéron* denotes that which causes one to shrink or hesitate, hence **troublesome**. Contrast Reed 1996, who argues that *oknéron* is part of a polite epistolary hesitation formula; but his examples do not seem altogether apposite or persuasive in this context.)

What, first of all, are the *same things*? Is Paul pointing forward to what he is about to say, or back to what he has just said? This is a problem faced equally by advocates of the letter's partition and by those favouring integrity. Four possible solutions may be distinguished.

(1) One recurring interpretation is that Paul's repetition occurs in the verses that follow: the phrase **the same thing** points forward to his warning about Judaizers, about which he has warned the Philippians in a previous letter or letters. That Paul wrote other letters to Philippi is certainly possible, even if there is little positive evidence to support it (see above, p. 22). And his repeated conflict with those who attempted to make Jewish observance mandatory for Gentiles is of course well known from Galatians, Romans 14–15, or Colossians 2.

This interpretation, however, is beset with several difficulties. First, there is in fact no clear reference to previous letters (unlike e.g. 1 Cor. 5.9; 2 Cor. 7.8; 10.9). Previous correspondence would have been sent before Epaphroditus' arrival and therefore many months ago; one might in that case expect a more explicit mention of such a document. Secondly, it is significant that Paul literally says he is writing 'the same things' (*ta auta*), not that he is writing 'once again' (*palin*). The subject of his repetition, therefore, is more likely to be something in the present communication – and thus something other than the Judaizers, who have not been mentioned before.

(2) Another possibility is that 'the same things' refers to an earlier *oral* instruction, perhaps taken by a previous messenger or else to be delivered simultaneously by Epaphroditus or later Timothy. This is certainly conceivable. However, Paul makes no specific reference either to such an oral instruction, which might in any case be suspect as not coming from Paul's own hand and therefore carrying a lesser authority (cf. Gal. 6.11; 2 Thess. 3.17). What is more, he does refer specifically to *writing* **the same thing again**, which would be an odd way of referring to an accompanying oral message. Finally, the only known specific message entrusted to an individual at Philippi is in fact included in writing, in 4.2 (see the discussion there).

(3) A third, somewhat more viable option combines aspects of the first two and is espoused by many recent commentators. On this view, Paul refers in general to previous instructions in the course of his ministry among the Philippians, when he had frequent occasions to refute the claims of the Judaizers in the terms outlined in 3.2–11: his denial that Gentiles are required to convert to Torah observance, drawing in part on his own experience of coming to faith in Christ as a strict Pharisee; and the sharp contrast between that view and his affirmation of justification by faith in Christ alone. It is certainly true that these were important aspects of Paul's missionary practice, and the very brevity of his descriptions in 3.2–3 suggests that this is not the first time that the issue is being raised (see also on v. 18 below).

Once again, however, we stumble over the fact that Paul refers to '*writing* the same thing', which on this account has not yet been mentioned in this or any known previous letter. In referring to his own previous instructions, Paul is generally more explicit, rehearsing particular incidents or 'reminding' his readers (e.g. 1 Cor. 4.17; 11.23; 15.1; 1 Thess. 3.4; 4.6; 2 Thess. 2.5; cf. Gal. 3.1). Here in Philippians it is particularly significant that in 3.18, where Paul does allude to a previous communication, his language is again unmistakably clear: he recalls those enemies of the Cross about whom he 'often used to tell' his friends (*hous pollakis elegon humin*). Here in 3.1, there is no such reference to another discourse, but merely to 'writing the same things'. (Fee repeatedly stresses the supposedly asyndetic syntax of 3.1–2 as tying these sentences closely together; but while this is a valid point within v. 2 (cf. O'Brien 347), the contrasting particles in the subordinate clause of 3.1b (*men* ... *de*) do in fact allow for a natural break after v. 1).

(4) The most likely reading, therefore, is to see **the same thing** as a subject or subjects (pl. *ta auta*) which Paul has previously raised *in this letter*. Since the first two chapters nowhere refer to Judaizers, the theme in view is most likely Paul's constant exhortation to *joy* in the midst of affliction. Paul has given previous explicit exhortations to joy in 2.18 and 2.29; and he will 'say it again' twice in 4.4.

It is important to stress the fundamentally *oral* context of this communication. Paul's congregational letters, perhaps more obviously than, say, Philemon or the Gospel of Luke, were understood by both author and recipients to be intended first and foremost for public reading before the church (cf. Fee 16f. and nn. 46–8, citing Achtemeier 1990). Both writer and audience were well accustomed, too, to the informalities of style or structure which this oral form of communication may necessitate or at any rate accommodate, and which are sprinkled throughout Paul's writings. What every public speaker knows to be indispensable, however, is clarity of sequence and reference. He or she may refer to communications outside the present discourse, such as 'what I told you before' or 'what you wrote to me' (1 Cor. 7.1). But when Paul reiterates an earlier exhortation to joy and then says, 'I don't mind repeating myself,' hearers of a live oral presentation will in any case detect a backward, not a forward reference. Whether this is what his dictation 'really intended' is of course a matter about which certainty may not perhaps be had. But what his audience was likely to hear, and what his long experience arguably told him they would hear, is a renewed call to rejoice in the Lord. This, then, is an interpretation which fits with both the context and the argument of Philippians; and it is on balance the most plausible reading.

There is, however, one obvious objection to our proposed reading of joy as the subject of Paul's reiteration. While Paul may not mind repeating it, it is rather less clear why joy should be **a safeguard** (lit. 'safe') for the Philippians. Many interpreters for this reason prefer a version of options 1–3 above: it is easier to see why the apostle might want to take every precaution against the Judaizing opponents who have dogged his ministry for so many years, and whose current efforts at Rome possibly account for the sudden outburst of 3.2. Joy, on the other hand, is less obviously 'safe'. This objection clearly has some merit, which is partly why option 3 in particular was described above as a viable alternative. However, it remains a subsidiary point; and as an argument for a reference to Judaizers it stands and falls with the overall validity of the case for reading 3.1 in the light of 3.2.

What might be said in defence of *joy* as a **safeguard**? Caird 132, in a homiletical vein, remarks that 'joy of any kind is a safeguard against the utilitarian attitude which judges people and things wholly by the use that can be made of them' (cf. similarly Bruce, Hawthorne). Morally and theologically, one would not of course take issue with this statement. It is well worth pondering. On the exegetical level, however, it appears to assume, with Lightfoot, that joy is a 'safeguard' against the disunity and selfish ambition which Paul noted earlier on in this letter. This is subject to two criticisms: first, Paul addresses himself to the problem of congregational strife neither in the immediately preceding nor in the following section; indeed he last mentioned it in passing in 2.14. His hearers would therefore have no contextual indication that this is the particular safeguard he has in mind. And secondly, Paul's own overall argument clearly and repeatedly suggests that the remedy for selfish ambition is not joy so much as Christ-like humility (so rightly O'Brien).

The preceding context in fact refers to no particular danger against which joy might be a 'safeguard': the term seems to be used in an absolute, non-specific sense. This leads us to propose that Paul understands joy in the Lord to be *inherently* 'safe' *(asphales)*, by definition a bulwark against all manner of dangers. Such a view is indeed supported by a wealth of evidence not commonly noted by commentators. Nehemiah 8.10 famously encapsulates the fundamental conviction that 'the joy of the Lord is your strength'. Joy is likewise linked with God's strength in Ps. 81.1 and 1 Chr. 16.27 ('strength and joy are in his place'). Mount Zion is the joy of all the earth because God has shown himself a 'sure defence' within her citadels (Ps. 48.2–3); similarly, the king in particular rejoices in the security of the Lord's strength (Ps. 21.1; cf. 63.11). The individual believer, too, repeatedly takes refuge in the Lord, rejoicing in him and resting secure (5.11; 16.9; 64.10; cf. Hab. 3.18–19; Zeph. 3.17). Negatively, abandoning one's joy and stronghold in the Lord's service and seeking it elsewhere will lead to disaster (Deut. 28.47; Ezek. 24.25). In the Dead Sea Scrolls, joyful praise is said to afford power over demons (4Q510 1.4–8; 4Q511 *passim*; cf. *T. Sol.* 1.5–8; 3.5–7; 25.9).

The relevance of a spiritual quality like joy to the issue of 'safeguards' is further illustrated by several comparable uses in the LXX of Paul's word *asphales* ('safe'). Those who hold fast to wisdom, the tree of life, are 'safe' as are those who hold on to the Lord (Prov. 3.18; cf. Wisd. 7.23), while the hearts of fools and the ungodly are not (Prov. 15.7; Wisd. 4.3). Security rests in God, who protects Israel 'safely' (*asphalôs*) like a father his children (2 Macc. 3.22; 3 Macc. 7.6). In 2 Macc. 15.7–16, Judas Maccabaeus arms his men with the 'security' (*asphaleia*, v. 11) not of shield and spear, but of a well-chosen exhortation to trust in God, which leads them all to rejoice (*euphrainô*, cf. LXX usage in Isa. and Pss.). On the basis of these examples, it is not difficult to see how an exhortation to joy in the Lord might be regarded as a 'safeguard'.

What Paul is saying in verse 1, therefore, is that he does not mind repeating his call to joy in the Lord because it is this which will serve them as a safeguard in every situation – including of course such external and internal threats as the rest of the letter goes on to address.

VI SERVANTS OF CHRIST AND ENEMIES OF THE CROSS (3.2–4.3)

Verse 2 on any reckoning represents a sharp and sudden change of tone. It introduces a new section, which begins without any syntactical markers or links to what has just gone before. There is no 'and' or 'therefore' or 'moreover', but simply: 'Beware of the dogs'. The section introduced by this statement relies on sharp contrasts to make its rhetorical points: its emphatic indictment of Judaizing opponents (3.2–4a) is driven home by the contrast between Paul's own former (3.4b-6) and present (3.7–14) way of life. This in turn is presented as an example to emulate (3.15–21), contrasting Paul's own pattern against that of the 'enemies of the Cross' (3.18), and their goals and priorities (3.19) against those of the commonwealth of God (3.20–21). After a summary statement (4.1) Paul appends an appeal for unity among two prominent women at Philippi, which is to be facilitated by a third individual in their midst (4.2–3).

A THE 'DOGS' (3.2–4a)

The first paragraph explodes with a bitterly satirical attack on a group of enemies. Something has triggered in Paul's mind an acute awareness of the threat emanating from the Judaizing party. Although the discontinuity with 3.1 is indeed jarring and surprising, there are no ultimately cogent reasons for supposing that Paul could not turn from the one to the other. The interruption could have been a thought flashing through his mind as he imagined the scene of Epaphroditus' welcome at Philippi.

Perhaps the continued animosity between Euodia and Syntyche caused him alarm as he considered the damage his opponents could do in a divided church. Alternatively, disconcerting news may have reached him of the activities of Judaizers in Rome or elsewhere (though probably not in Philippi, as Lightfoot thought: the attack is too unspecific in character, and unexpected news from Philippi would surely have been acknowledged as such). All sorts of things could have happened, which might lead him to return to dictation and stress a concern suddenly more urgent than it seemed before. Precisely what transpired we will never know. But if, say, a government minister sat down one evening to begin writing a letter to her constituents, it is not difficult to imagine how abruptly different her tone might be the next evening if in the meantime her government had suffered a serious political setback, or if slanderous allegations had been raised against her in the press.

Who, then, are these adversaries, described as 'dogs', 'evil workers' and 'the mutilation'? It was sometimes thought in the past that they could be three different groups, but the syntax suggests that Paul in fact describes the same people from three different angles. These verses, in any case, are one of Paul's clearest and most blatant attacks on those who attempted on the basis of Christianity's Jewish origin to impose a full regime of Jewish law observance on Gentile converts to Christianity. His tone and passion are reminiscent of Galatians, written the better part of a decade earlier, and to some extent of 2 Cor. 10–13 – a connection highlighted by those commentators, such as Friedrich 131–4, who favour an Ephesian origin of this letter (note also Lüdemann 1989a: 108). In addition to undoubted similarities, however, several of the challenges in 2 Corinthians seem rather different. Unlike the case in Philippians, Paul speaks there in acute self-defence against challenges to his apostolicity and self-presentation; circumcision, on the other hand, does not seem to be the central point of contention. At the same time, here in Philippians the polished formulations and cadences of his invective suggest that Paul's thoughts have had time to mature, and he knows precisely what to aim at. He may well have used these or similar words before, and in different contexts, whether in Galatia, Corinth or elsewhere.

As we saw above on 1.28, the remarks here are quite possibly a general warning, rather than being directed against specific individuals at Philippi: indeed Paul gives no clear intimation that the threat to this church is either acute or locally resident. His tone certainly implies that the Philippians know perfectly well who is meant by 'the dogs': Christian Jews, quite possibly from

Palestine (3.5), travelling between diaspora communities to persuade Gentile Christians to become full Jewish proselytes. But the specific application to Philippi remains extremely vague and short on detail, as Lüdemann 1989a: 103–9 rightly points out. Thus, the immediate occasion that gives rise to Paul's outburst here could just as easily be some event at Rome or some news about a church other than Philippi.

It is important to read the meaning of these statements in the painful polemical context in which they are spoken, rather than to take them as a general and definitive assessment of Jewish Christianity or of Judaism, as has often been done. One should not ask people to appraise the merits of their marriage either on their honeymoon or just after a serious row. Both are instructive about the characters involved and may lend colour and perspective to our view of them; but neither will give the outsider a particularly accurate impression. Similarly, if we wish to hear Pauline Christianity on the subject of its relationship with Judaism, we should begin neither in the heat of battle (Gal. 3) nor at a later time when the problem seems to have disappeared altogether (Eph. 2). Instead, a good place to start is when its founding Apostle finds himself having to offer to a fresh audience a considered statement of the problem as it presents itself after twenty years of Christian work. Such a statement does indeed survive in the form of Paul's letter to Rome. And the questions asked there are precisely those which must be answered if we are to understand the balance of Paul's convictions: 'What advantage has the Jew? Do we overthrow the Law? Does the blessing of Abraham extend to the Gentiles? Has God rejected his people? Has Israel stumbled so as to fall?' (cf. Rom. 3.1, 31; 4.9; 11.1, 11). A full assessment should begin there, as arguably the closest we can get to the centre of Paul's convictions, and work outwards to the more placid or polemical periphery. (Cf. similarly Dunn 1994.) In Philippians 3 as anywhere else, therefore, it will be necessary to draw on Paul's other reflections about similar subjects, in order to elucidate what he is saying – and what he is not saying.

(2) Watch out for the 'dogs', watch out for the evil 'workers', watch out for the 'mutilation'. (3) It is *we* who are the circumcision, who serve by the Spirit of God and exult in Christ Jesus and put no confidence in the flesh (4) – even though I, too, have grounds even for confidence in the flesh.

2 The Greek of this sentence creates a striking linguistic and acoustic effect: three times Paul repeats his warning to 'watch out', and each time he adds an article and an object beginning with the letter 'K' (*tous kunas* ... *tous kakous ergatas* ... *tén katatomén*). The form of this verse, along with its abrupt opening, is clearly calculated to prick up the ears of his audience. The verb translated **watch out** (*blepete*) literally means 'look at' or 'pay attention to'; when used in warnings, however, it can acquire the rhetorical sense of 'beware' (*pace* Kilpatrick 1968, Caird, Hawthorne).

All three of the terms Paul now introduces appear to be satirical word-plays on characteristic technical terms used by his opponents. Insiders often forget how quickly their religious language acquires a meaning all its own; the practical effect of 'insider talk' is often to reinforce boundaries between insiders and outsiders, or even to create exclusiveness unawares. Modern Christian examples range widely according to churchmanship, from 'words of knowledge' to the 'hypostatic union', from 'getting into the Word' to 'venerating the Presence'. Paul is at any rate intimately familiar with the issues, and he derides the religious chauvinism inherent in his opponents' slogans.

First, then, **the dogs**. This word has of course served as an insult in many cultures and languages since antiquity, presumably because of the shamelessly aggressive and slovenly habits which were perceived to characterize the semi-domesticated dogs roaming the streets of many countries until relatively recently. Some have thought of Paul's term as a general insult of this kind; an explicit association also existed with the Cynic school of philosophy. The specifically Jewish context of Paul's invective, however, is made clear by the third term 'mutilation' (see below), and is in any case explicit in verse 5. The characteristically Jewish connotations of the word 'dog' may therefore be a better guide here.

In the Old Testament, dogs are associated with indiscriminate and base behaviour: they eat refuse, including dead animals (Exod. 22.31) and the bodies of unburied people (e.g. 1 Kgs. 14.11; 21.23f.; 2 Kgs. 9.10, 36; Jer. 15.3), and may even return to their own vomit (Prov. 26.11; cf. 2 Pet. 2.22). A 'dead dog' denotes an utterly worthless and objectionable person (2 Sam. 16.9; cf. 2 Sam. 9.8; 2 Kgs. 8.13). Deut. 23.15 appears to refer to male prostitutes as dogs; Israel's leaders are described as lazy but ravenous dogs in Isa. 56.10f. A metaphorical use to designate evildoers is also implied in Ps. 22.16, 22; in Ps. 59.6, 14 the reference is to evil enemies who may well be *Gentiles* (cf. v. 5). (In Israelite literature the notion of dogs as pets or companions does not occur prior to the book of Tobit (5.16; 6.1; 11.4), although the discovery of a cemetery with 700 buried dogs at Ashkelon may suggest a more positive view of the animals among Phoenicians in the Persian period: see Wapnish & Hesse 1993.)

In the post-biblical period, the objectionable qualities of dogs appear to be concentrated in their aggressive disregard for any semblance of moral decency or distinction between clean and unclean. A metaphorical application to people suggested itself: the term came to be used of pagans, who also did not know how to distinguish between pure and impure, sacred and profane (e.g. Exod. 22.31 in *m.Ned.* 4.3; *m.Bek.* 5.6). In a rabbinic tale featuring Akiba in discussion with Tinneius Rufus, Roman governor of Judaea at the start of the Bar Kokhba Revolt (AD 132), Akiba relates a dream in which he named his two dogs Rufus and Rufina (Tanḥ. *Terumah* 3, 100a, on Exod. 25.2). This application was apparently followed by Jesus, too (Mark 7.27f. par.). As a result, just as meat consecrated for sacrifice in the Temple must be kept from straying dogs, so sacred truths and practices must not be exposed to pagans: see 4QMMT 61–2; cf. Matt. 7.6; *Did.* 9.5 on the Eucharist; *Ps.-Clem. Hom.* 2.19. Certainly 'dogs', Gentiles and the impure would have no part in the coming redemption. Purity is increasingly applied both in the literal *and* in the metaphorical, moral sense which then comes to dominate in the New Testament (Rev. 22.15; cf. Gal. 5.19–21; Eph. 5.5; Rev. 21.27; Isa. 35.8f.; 52.1; *Ps. Sol.* 17.26–30).

This Jewish background, then, offers a clue to Paul's usage, which will gradually be confirmed as we progress through this passage. He attacks those who, from the imagined superiority of their Jewish status and practice, reject fellowship with Gentile Christians whose indifference to the purity laws makes them like dogs. From this perspective, the Gentiles cannot become part of the people of God without converting to Judaism: only full Jews can be full Christians; others are 'dogs'.

It would be ironic if, as seems possible, these opponents are themselves Jewish only by conversion, not by birth (see below on verse 5). As Gentiles who have undergone the rigours of conversion specifically in order to join the people of God, their hostility to Pauline Christianity could then be seen to manifest a characteristic convert resentment at being told their costly decision was pointless and unnecessary. (A comparable attitude towards Christianity seems to have characterized the proselyte Aquila in the second century.) That Paul's adversaries are Christians seems likely both from their vested interest in the circumcision of *Gentile* believers, and perhaps especially from the apparent danger of their being accepted as examples in the church at Philippi (cf. e.g. Gnilka 211; I.H. Marshall; Lüdemann 1989a: 106; Witherington 1994: 89f.). Paul and other Jewish

Christians clearly did experience opposition from fellow Jews (e.g. 2 Cor. 11.24; 1 Thess. 2.14; cf. Acts 14.19; 21.27ff.), but the NT offers little positive evidence of concerted non-Christian Jewish efforts to proselytize purely *Gentile* churches. While it is true that in Macedonia one must allow for the possibility of local interference in Paul's Gentile mission on the part of Jewish agitators emanating from Thessalonica (cf. 1 Thess. 2.16; Acts 17.5–7, 13), focused non-Christian Jewish counter-missionary activity among Gentile churches is difficult to substantiate at this stage (but note Justin *Dial.* 17.1; 47.3; 108.2; cf. p. 10 above on the question of Jewish proselytism).

For Paul, by contrast, Christ's work among the Gentiles is itself holy and pure (Phil. 1.1, 10; cf. e.g. 1 Cor. 3.17; 7.14; Col. 1.22; also Eph. *passim* and the frequent reference to Christians as 'saints', i.e. 'holy ones'), and in Christ God's call has gone out to the Gentiles to pursue holiness and flee impurity (e.g. 1 Thess. 4.7; 2 Cor. 7.1). If there are any dogs, therefore, it is *the opponents*: it is they who despise and dishonour what is sacred.

The adversaries are further referred to as the **evil 'workers'** (*kakous ergatas*). The Psalmist repeatedly speaks of 'workers of iniquity' in describing God's enemies and his own (e.g. Ps. 5.5; 6.8; 14.4; 28.3; cf. Prov. 10.29; Hos. 6.8; Job 31.3; 34.8, 22; also Luke 13.27). It could be that this is what is meant here, although there is no close LXX parallel to Paul's phrase, and the present context does not refer primarily to *moral* wickedness.

Two more specific interpretations must also be considered. Some have suggested that Paul's term may generally designate evil *missionaries*, since the term 'workers' is occasionally so employed in the gospels (e.g. Matt. 9.38 par.; 10.10 par.), and it may represent early Jewish-Christian usage. Using similar terminology, Paul himself speaks of Jewish-Christian false apostles in Corinth as 'deceitful workers' (*ergatai dolioi*), who falsely present themselves as ministers of 'righteousness' (2 Cor. 11.13, 15). For the derivation of this possible self-description we may compare several OT passages (e.g. Ps. 15.2 'worker of righteousness'; LXX Isa. 32.17 'works of righteousness'). The term 'worker' may well be a self-designation of the Judaizing opponents envisioned in Philippians as well, although Paul is not necessarily referring to the same people: indeed the Corinthian emphases on charismatic presence (2 Cor. 10.10; 12.12), rhetorical polish (11.6), financial support (11.8f.; 12.13) and heavenly visions (12.1ff.) are not mentioned here. Nevertheless, the similarity is intriguing, especially considering that these are the only two occurrences of the word 'worker' in the undisputed Pauline epistles (contrast 1 Tim. 5.18; 2 Tim. 2.15).

A second possibility, not necessarily incompatible with the first, is that there may be a deliberate pun on the opponents' claim to be doing the so-called 'works of the Law' (*erga nomou*). It has recently become clear that this phrase 'works of the Law', which occupies Paul's polemic against Judaizing Christian opponents in Romans (2.15; 3.20, 27f.; cf. 9.32) and Galatians (2.16; 3.2, 5, 10), had in conservative Jewish circles become a watchword to describe the practices prescribed in the Torah, especially those which distinguished Jew from Gentile and the observant from the non-observant. A passage of particular importance in this respect is 4QMMT 113, which uses the phrase 'works of the Torah' (*ma'aśê ha-tôrah*) in describing various aspects of Jewish practice as understood by the Qumran sect. (Although 4Q174[Flor] 1.7 is sometimes mentioned in this connection (e.g. by Flusser 1996b: 158; Dunn 1997: 150, citing older English translations based on DJD 5.53), the correct reading there is *ma'aśê tôdah*, i.e. 'works of thanksgiving': see Brooke 1985: 108; Steudel 1994: 44; cf. García Martínez 1996: 136. A somewhat different usage emerges in the frequent early rabbinic expressions of 'working' or 'toiling' in the Torah' and 'working in the commandments' as referring to study and practice: e.g. *m.Abot* 6.1–2, 4; *b.Ber.* 17a.)

Such 'works of the Law' were not in the first place understood as good works intended to earn salvation, as the Reformers thought, but as a practical mark of fidelity to the Torah, confirming the distinction between those who were part of the covenant and those who were not (cf. Dunn 1990: 183–241 and *passim* in partial refinement of E. P. Sanders 1977, 1983). That is to say, from the perspective of insiders these 'works' were not precondition so much as *proof* of membership. A number of scholars have begun to argue that Paul's repeated references to 'works of the Law' are a critical reaction against the first-century Jewish view in which such 'works' and 'working' functioned in this way (cf. Abegg 1994; Dunn 1990: 219–25 and 1997; also Flusser 1996a and 1996b: 157f.). In practice, of course, much of this distinction is in the eye of the beholder – not least when, in confronting supposed 'outsiders' like Gentile Christians, the difference between an outward manifestation of membership and an imposing entrance requirement or status symbol could quickly become imperceptible. Precisely there of course is the rub of Paul's argument: works of law, the 'badge' of grace and covenant membership, had in his view become an exclusive ethnic 'boast'. And there, too, one might argue, lies the abiding validity of the Reformational view: the Pauline statements do have a wider relevance for theological anthropology and the doctrine of salvation – though

not, to be sure, for the supposed antithesis of 'legalistic' Judaism
vs. Christianity as the religion of grace. (Cf. also the useful
argument of I.H. Marshall 1996a, who approaches the Pauline
view of 'works' from the perspective of its development in
Ephesians and the Pastoral Epistles.)

It is difficult to decide with certainty between the several
interpretations we have considered; quite possibly elements of
more than one may be present. Most likely, in any case, Paul
refers to a contemporary expression of Jewish piety which his
Judaizing opponents had turned into their own battle standard,
highlighting the true Israel's faithfulness to the Torah in contrast
to non-observant Pauline Christianity. It is precisely their insistence on the exclusive, covenant-defining function of Jewish
legal practices which in the light of Christ's coming makes these
adversaries **evil workers**.

Finally, the term **'mutilation'** (*katatomé*), which on any reckoning is the least disputed. It is clearly a sarcastic play on the
word *peritomé* ('circumcision'), possibly echoing a contemporary
anti-Semitic slur about the practice. Paul's attack on his opponents' interest in circumcision here sounds only marginally more
subtle than that expressed some years earlier in Gal. 5.12. Physical circumcision of the male foreskin has been the visible sign of
the covenant with Abraham (Gen. 17.10–24; cf. Acts 7.8) for Jews
throughout the ages. From very early times, it had been understood as having a metaphorical significance: both the Law and the
Prophets speak of the need for a moral and spiritual 'circumcision
of the heart' expressed in love for the Lord and obedience to his
commandments (Deut. 10.16; 30.6; Jer. 4.4; Ezek. 44.7). The same
theme continued to be developed in the post-biblical period,
although even allegorical interpreters like Philo and the author of
the *Epistle of Aristeas* made it clear that the allegorical meaning of
circumcision by no means implied that the literal was no longer
required. In suggesting that outward circumcision is worth nothing without circumcision of the heart (Rom. 2.29), Paul closely
echoes the attitude of Jeremiah, to whom Jews uncircumcised in
heart were no better than pagans from the surrounding nations,
and equally under God's judgement (Jer. 4.4, 9.25f.; cf. similarly
1QS 5.5, etc.). Paul's sarcastic term *katatomé* is related to a verb
describing the religious self-mutilation of the adherents of paganism (LXX Lev. 21.5; 1 Kgs. 18.28; Isa. 15.2; Hos. 7.14; cf. H.
Koester, *TDNT* 8: 110f.). In other words, circumcision that is not
of the heart is no better than ritual pagan laceration.

Although he was often understood differently by Jews and
Jewish Christians (cf. Acts. 21.21), Paul never spoke out against
circumcision and law observance on the part of Jews; indeed he

thought it valuable (Rom. 3.1) and encouraged Jews to continue in it after they became Christians (1 Cor. 7.18). Acts 16.3 suggests that Paul even arranged for the circumcision of Timothy, who was legally a Jew. Circumcision was not for Jews incompatible with Christian faith (note Rom. 4.12).

But Paul insists that his own message of salvation for Gentiles is the valid 'gospel for the *uncircumcised*' (Gal. 2.7), who inherit the promises to Israel by virtue of faith in Christ alone. In this respect his ministry is in keeping with the landmark decision reported of the so-called Apostolic Council, which resolved precisely that Gentile believers in Christ did not need to become full proselytes to Judaism (Acts 15, esp. vv. 1, 5, 9, 19). In a later captivity epistle, Paul suggests that for Gentile believers baptism is the equivalent of circumcision (Col. 2.11–13). On the other hand, since conversion to Judaism implies the obligation to accept and keep the Torah, for Gentiles to become circumcised means that the gospel and the coming of Christ are of no benefit to them (Gal. 5.2f.). According to Paul's gospel, therefore, in Christ there is no advantage in being circumcised (1 Cor. 7.19; Gal. 5.6; 6.15; Col. 3.11).

One additional dimension of Paul's long struggle against the 'circumcision party' is worth noting at this stage, since it runs as an undercurrent through the entire passage, 3.2–11. For a Gentile Christian, one of the attractions in becoming circumcised might appear to be a certain social status and security: Christianity was not an officially tolerated religion (*religio licita*), and was therefore perceived as a potential threat not just by Judaism but by the Roman state as well. Only the imperial cult and the various ethnic religions under Roman rule, including Judaism, enjoyed the sanction and protection of the state. Uncircumcised Gentile Christians, however, were not a legally recognizable entity. 'Persecution for the cross of Christ' (Gal. 6.12) could therefore arise for Gentile Christians from the Roman state for Roman reasons; and for Jewish Christians like Paul, who advocated fellowship with Gentiles and thus the dismantling of Judaism's ethnic boundaries, from the synagogues for Jewish reasons (for the latter see e.g. 2 Cor. 11.24; cf. Acts 21.21, 28ff.). In a city like Philippi with at best a very limited Jewish population, persecution from the local synagogue would have been less of an issue, even if Jewish or Jewish-Christian travellers from Thessalonica and further afield must have passed through Philippi regularly. But the opprobrium of the Roman state was in any case a serious consideration for the citizens of this Italic colony, so that the appeal of the Judaizing message would not have been lost on the Gentile believers there. (Documentary evidence that harassed Christians were attracted by Judaism's official status is admittedly hard to pin down explicitly, but in addition to our present text it may be implicit in the fear of assimilation displayed in much of the early Christian anti-Jewish literature (e.g. *Barn.* 3.6; Justin, *Dial.* 8.4, 47.3; cf. Horbury 1992: 323–7). A more explicit instance is in the late third-century *Martyrdom of Pionius* (ed. Musurillo 1972), with its concerned appeal to persecuted Christians not to 'yield in despair' (14.16) to the Jews who are 'calling some of you into the synagogues' (13.1).) Cf. also Tellbe 1994.

3 Consistent with the view on circumcision just described, Paul affirms emphatically that **we**, all those who have faith in Christ, **are the circumcision**. He is not saying that uncircumcised Christians are the 'true' (allegorical) circumcision and Jews are not, or that Christianity has replaced and invalidated Judaism, much as that has become a popular view in subsequent centuries. And the contrast in this passage is not between Christianity and 'Israel' or Christianity and 'the Jews', despite many commentators. It is specifically between covenant membership as defined according to Paul's gospel and as defined according to his Judaizing opponents, as verses 4–6 go on to show.

What Paul is saying is again in keeping with Romans 4 and Acts 15: faith in Christ places Gentile believers on the same footing before God as Jewish believers, co-opting them into the Abrahamic covenant which circumcision symbolizes. That covenant, however, cannot in any case be straightforwardly identified with physical circumcision, as Jeremiah already pointed out (Jer. 9.25f.). This fact makes a nonsense of the claims of the opponents, who stake their superiority and supposedly exclusive covenant membership on their group identity as 'the circumcision' (see Gal. 2.12; cf. Col. 4.11; Eph. 2.11; Tit. 1.10). For Paul, by contrast, it is those who have faith, the circumcised in heart, who are the real 'circumcision' – regardless of whether they are Jewish and physically circumcised or Gentile and physically uncircumcised (note again Rom. 4.11–12; cf. Rom. 2.28–9). Theologically speaking, **we ... are the circumcision**, the people of the covenant of Abraham – which of course was predicated on faith (Gen. 15.6, 18) before it was ever linked with circumcision (Gen. 17.10). The righteousness credited to Abraham before his circumcision, therefore, pertains in Paul's view to all who share his faith (Rom. 4.9–12).

Three characteristics distinguish Paul and his churches from the circumcision party; they are best understood as giving not the reasons *why* Christians are the circumcision, but what characterizes their lives as the circumcision in contrast to their opponents (cf. O'Brien 359f.). All three phrases base Christian life in a relationship of faith in the grace of God rather than in human merit, and the third serves as a contrast to the first two.

First, Christians **serve by the Spirit of God**. The LXX and the NT use the word **serve** (*latreuō*) exclusively in a religious sense, for the service of God or of pagan gods (the only exception is Deut. 28.48). It corresponds to the Hebrew word *'abad* (cf. the noun *'abôdah*), which in contemporary and Rabbinic Hebrew frequently means either priestly service or in the transferred sense 'worship' and 'prayer' (cf. similarly Luke 2.37; Acts 26.7; Rev. 7.15; 22.3). NT and Pauline usage, however, also retains the sense that all of life should be an act of service and worship to God: to present oneself to God as a continual living sacrifice is the appropriate kind of spiritual 'service' (Rom. 12.1; cf. Luke 1.74; Acts 24.14; 27.23). This is deliberately reflected in our translation.

Once again the contrast is not between Jewish and Christian service of God, much as that continues to be suggested by the commentators; indeed Paul himself affirms that 'the service' (*latreia*) of God, like the promises, pertains by origin and irrevocable divine endowment to Israel (Rom. 9.4; cf. 11.29; Acts 24.14). Instead, the contrast is between the true circumcision whose service is empowered by and directed towards the Spirit of God, and those whose service is narrow-mindedly focused on their 'works of the Law' as defining their service and status before God. It is the Spirit of God who characterizes the Christian existence and makes the service of God possible, enabling believers to 'walk by the Spirit' and to worship appropriately (Rom. 8.1–14; Gal. 5.16, 25).

While the overall sense of Paul's phrase is clear, there are one or two grammatical and textual uncertainties. First, the text as it stands could be translated either 'serve *by* the Spirit of God' (with most translations and commentators) or else simply 'serve the Spirit of God', an option that commentaries tend to overlook. However, the consistent NT usage of the word, whether used with an indirect object or absolutely (Luke 2.37; Acts 26.7; and probably here), is of worship directed either to God himself or pagan gods. Its use of the Spirit (or even of Christ) would be unparalleled. The instrumental or modal function of the Spirit, on the other hand, even without the article, is thoroughly Pauline (Rom. 8.13f.; 1 Cor. 14.2; Gal. 5.16, etc.; cf. Phil. 2.1); and it is this which must therefore be the preferred understanding here: Christians worship through the Holy Spirit.

(Some have suggested a conceptual parallel with John 4.24:

since God is Spirit, those who worship God must 'worship him in spirit and in truth'. In Romans 1.9, Paul writes, 'I serve (*latreuô*) God in *my* spirit.' Here, however, it is clearly the Holy Spirit who is in view.)

On another note, a wide range of MSS supports an interesting textual variant, reading 'who serve God (*theô*) by the Spirit', rather than 'by the Spirit of God (*theou*)'. What is more, the important early papyrus p⁴⁶ omits the word 'God' altogether, although this was not widely followed. The omission is probably accidental. The reading *theô*, which also appears to underlie the KJV, may well be a deliberate adaptation in line with conventional usage and theology: it makes explicit that 'God' is the one being served. The weight of textual evidence for this, although strong and widely distributed, nevertheless does not extend to the most important early MSS.

The second characteristic of the true circumcision is that they **exult** (lit. 'boast') **in Christ Jesus**. The idea of boasting was earlier encountered in 1.26 and 2.16, where Paul used the noun rather than the verb (see above). Here, the point is specifically about the need to boast or exult *on the right basis*. This is a theme which is richly anticipated in the prophetic insistence that the only justified boasting is in one's relationship with God (Jer. 9.23–4, a passage which Paul adapts to the form 'Let the one who boasts boast in the Lord': see 1 Cor. 1.31; 2 Cor. 10.17). God himself is his people's 'boast' (Deut. 10.21), and the only valid 'boasting' is rooted in God's work and not one's own (cf. R. Bultmann, *TDNT* 3: 646–8).

This same contrast is clearly intended here, as this *exulting* in God's work **in Christ Jesus** is immediately contrasted with placing **confidence in the flesh**. The former marks the true circumcision of the heart, which finds the ground and object of its boast in God's work of redemption. Putting confidence in the flesh, on the other hand, is the action of those who define themselves and other people in terms of their human merit, status and achievement. The Judaizing opponents do this with their insistence that outward Jewish observance, not faith in Christ, is what makes people members of the covenant and gives them standing before God. (Elsewhere, Paul uses similar language to criticize those who, like the sophists, put confidence in rhetorical skill and self-presentation; see 1 Cor. 1.31–2.5; 2 Cor. 10.12–18 and cf. Forbes 1986; Lim 1987.)

The negative corollary to what Paul has just said about the true source of boasting, therefore, is that Christians put no **confidence in the flesh**. They do not, in other words, rely on human strength. The word 'flesh' is used by Paul in a variety of meanings generally concerned with physical humanity, quite often as apart from God or in contrast to him. This is also consistent with its meaning in many OT texts and in contemporary Judaism (note e.g. Gen. 6.3; Isa. 31.3; 1QH 7.16–26). As such, 'flesh' is often (but by no means always) associated with sinful and unregenerate behaviour and desires, seen as characteristic of human beings without God and in need of redemption (e.g. 1 Cor. 15.50; Gal. 5.16, 19; Rom. 13.14). These negative connotations of 'flesh' are frequently contrasted with the new life in Christ, which is characterized not by its fallen humanity but by the Spirit of God (e.g. Rom. 8.4–13; Gal. 3.3; 4.29; 5.16f.; 6.8; cf. John 3.6; 6.63). See further G. Barth 56f.; Brandenburger 1968; E. Schweizer in *TDNT* 7: 98–151.

Here, then, unlike their opponents, the true circumcision place their confidence not in human worth and work but in the Spirit of God. As we shall see, the Judaizers' confidence in the flesh finds its more specific focus in the specific privileges and merits which Jewish status holds for them. There is no need to restrict this narrowly to circumcision as that which relates quite literally to the 'flesh'. In fact, Paul himself goes on in verses 5ff. to give a comprehensive list of the human qualities of status and achievement which to the Judaizers seem to promise the benefit of a superior standing before God.

4 Paul insists at the same time that by the standards of his opponents he, too, might have reason to **put ... confidence in** such human qualities. (The present participle *echôn*, translated **I ... have**, indicates that Paul's reasons for such confidence 'in the flesh' are not merely a past reality.) He could easily outplay the Judaizers at their own game, and shows this in verses 4b-6. Nevertheless, as he explains further in verses 7ff., he has found something far better. To 'serve God' and 'exult in Christ' are a far better bet than to boast in one's achievements.

B PAUL'S NATIONALISTIC PAST (3.4b-6)

Salvation by faith in Christ is not a weak or degenerate doctrine, much as critics from Celsus to Nietzsche and beyond have tried to depict it so. For Paul, Christ is not a consolation prize or a crutch for one who could not hold his own in his former way of life. His rejection of human status and achievement is certainly not a matter of 'sour grapes'. Paul sets out, therefore, to use his own example in refuting the Judaizing position with its concomitant promises of enhanced religious and (at least implicitly) social prestige. To do so, he lists the impeccable Jewish pedigree by which he himself once set store, at a time when he adhered to a nationalistic position with great fervour and dedication. This personal example will serve as the negative backdrop against which to formulate his positive affirmation of faith in Christ in verses 7–11. It also confirms the continued influence on Paul's argument here of the example of Christ in 2.6–11.

The rhetorical effect of all this is considerable. While the opponents flaunt their (possibly only acquired rather than native) Judaism to enhance their status, Paul shows how his own Jewish credentials are flawless and superior to theirs – and yet to be disregarded in Christ.

(4b) If anyone else thinks of having grounds for confidence in the flesh, I have more: (5) circumcised when I was eight days old, from the race of Israel and the tribe of Benjamin, a Hebrew of a Hebrew family; regarding 'Torah', a Pharisee; (6) regarding 'zeal', a persecutor of the church; regarding 'righteousness' as specified by the Torah, without fault.

If the Judaizing opponents think they can establish their superiority over the law-free mission to the Gentiles on their human credentials, Paul can easily outdo them. He offers us in these verses a remarkably forthright testimony about his pre-Christian past, which in this form is unmatched anywhere else in his writings (but see 2 Cor. 11.22ff.; Gal. 1.13–14; 1 Cor. 15.9; cf. 1 Tim. 1.15). Nevertheless, while it offers us an important glimpse of Paul's own background and formation, its purpose is not autobiographical but polemical and paradigmatic: it is not Paul's person but the principles of the gospel which are at stake. The items cited are carefully selected to fit the present controversial setting, and must not be assumed to offer straightforward information about either Paul's life or his views before becoming a Christian. That being said, these verses still afford a fascinating perspective on the self-perception of the Saul of Tarsus who persecuted the fledgling church. See further Haacker 1975; Hengel 1991, 1997 (contrast the more sceptical remarks of Strecker 1995, who doubts Paul's pre-Christian links with Jerusalem).

5   The first four points identify Paul's credentials by birth, while the following three denote his own achievements. First, he was **circumcised** into the Abrahamic covenant when he was **eight days old**, as required for every male Jewish baby (Lev 12.3; cf. Luke 1.59; 2.21). This is also proof that he was no mere proselyte: humanly speaking, his status was always going to be superior to those who seek to gain merit before God through conversion. As a member of **the race of Israel**, Paul is identified from birth with the covenant people of God. This is the terminology by which Jews referred to their own nation, especially in religious contexts: others might call them Jews, but only they called themselves the children of Israel (cf. K.G. Kuhn, *TDNT* 3: 359–65; W. Gutbrod, ibid. 371f.). Paul is an insider by descent. More specifically, he is of **the tribe of Benjamin**. Paul mentions his tribe both here and in Rom. 11.1, a context in which he asserts his authentic allegiance and solidarity with the Jewish people. It shows his reputable descent: the patriarch Benjamin was a son of Rachel, and the only one of the twelve to be born in the land of promise (Gen. 35.16–18). From his tribe came Paul's namesake Saul, the first king of Israel; the choice of this name for their son may show something of the pride of Paul's parents in their Benjaminite heritage (Acts 7.58; 13.9; cf. 13.21). Only the tribe of Benjamin had remained faithful to Judah and the house of David after the death of Solomon, going into exile with them and returning with Ezra to resettle the land around Jerusalem. Esther and her cousin Mordecai the Benjaminite (Esth. 2.5) are remembered in the joyful annual feast of Purim.

Much of this may well not have been familiar to the apostle's Gentile readers at Philippi; but in a context of anti-Judaizing polemic that certainly does not render the mention of Benjaminite descent incidental to the argument (*pace* Pilhofer 1995: 125). At the same time, it is quite likely that in Philippi Paul's reference to his Jewish *phulé* or tribe will have struck a related chord with readers who were constantly aware that Philippi's Roman citizenship was intimately connected with membership in the ancestral Roman family of the *tribus Voltinia* (see above, p. 4).

What is more, Paul is **a Hebrew** of **a Hebrew family** (lit. 'a Hebrew of Hebrews'). While many Jews especially in the diaspora spoke only Greek and read the Scriptures in Greek, this is a term specifically denoting Jews who spoke Hebrew or Aramaic with one another and prayed and read the Scriptures in Hebrew (cf. also Acts 6.1; 2 and 4 Macc. *passim*; Philo, *Mos.* 2.32). (The reference is not always clear: although many Palestinian Jews especially in Galilee spoke Aramaic, the Bar Kokhba letters and other evidence suggest that Hebrew remained alive as a spoken language in and around Jerusalem at least until the time of the Second Revolt, AD 132–5.) Inscriptions in the diaspora indicate that **a Hebrew** was a Jew who maintained close connections with Palestine and the Hebrew language, and especially with religious traditions (cf. Hengel 1991: 4–6; and see e.g. *CIJ* I, No. 718 for Corinth and *JIWE* II, No. 112 for Rome). At least during Paul's childhood, his family was resident in the city of Tarsus in Cilicia, to which perhaps they had been taken as slaves in the aftermath of the Roman conquest of Palestine in 63 BC (cf. Barclay 1996: 382–3; Hengel 1991: 4–17). In this context, their acquisition of hereditary Roman citizenship (cf. Acts 22.28) may have been the result of manumission. Nevertheless, they had remained linguistically and culturally connected to the Jewish heartland; Acts suggests not only that he moved to Jerusalem early on and was educated under Rabban Gamaliel the Elder (22.3; 26.4), but also that other members of his family later lived there (23.16). Paul at any rate still regarded himself as a **Hebrew** (cf. 2 Cor. 11.22; Acts 21.40; 22.2; 26.14).

In addition to his valued Jewish inheritance, however, Paul himself became committed to a conservative Jewish way of life which he was prepared to defend at considerable cost to himself. His next three claims highlight his personal track record as a Jew. If the first four qualifications gave him a considerable inherited pedigree, he now shows three separate aspects in which he did not neglect this heritage or take it for granted but went to great lengths to safeguard it. These three areas are his denominational orientation, his commitment to the nationalist cause, and his level of Torah observance.

First, **regarding 'Torah'**, Paul was **a Pharisee**. The issue of practical law observance is more specifically highlighted in verse 6, while the present reference seems to designate the particular *approach* to the Law which Paul followed. Different 'sects' with different perspectives on the Torah are described by Josephus (*Ant.* 18.12–23; *B.J.* 2.120–65; cf. also Acts 26.5) and come to vivid expression in the gospels (e.g. Matt. 22.23ff., 34) and Acts (23.6–9) as well as in the Dead Sea Scrolls.

The name 'Pharisees' (*pharisaioi*) probably means 'the separated ones' (Hebr. *perushim*, Aram. *perishayya*), and basically refers to a group that assigned particular significance to the Jewish purity laws with their stress on the distinction of clean and unclean, being concerned to maintain in daily life the standard of purity and holiness required for the Temple. For this reason Pharisees needed to distance themselves from 'unclean' persons like non-observant Jews or Gentiles, and to maintain an exclusive table fellowship. They were a popular conservative movement focused on a keen interest in the study of the Torah and in guarding the national traditions against pagan and secular trends. According to Josephus, they numbered about 6,000 and enjoyed great religious popularity and influence among the masses (*Ant.* 13.288, 298; 17.42; 18.15); he highlights especially their 'strictness' or 'accuracy' (*akribeia*; cf. similarly Acts 22.3) in interpreting the Torah. See further Saldarini 1992: 289–91; E.P. Sanders 1992: 380–412.

Paul, then, describes himself as a Pharisee, that is to say a member of a widely respected group with a conservative approach to the study and practice of the Law. Acts 23.6 suggests that he had grown up in a Pharisaic family; but he had clearly adopted this approach for himself as well. One point worth pondering here is that Paul in no way suggests that he has ceased to be a Pharisee, just as he has clearly not ceased to be a Hebrew or indeed a Jew (see 2 Cor. 11.22; Rom. 11.1; Gal. 2.15; cf. Acts 21.39; 22.3). Grammatically, all the assertions up to v. 6 are in the present tense, even if his persecution of the Church clearly no longer applies (cf. Niebuhr 1992: 103). In a number of respects, including such matters as the exposition of Scripture, his belief in the resurrection and the judgement, and the importance of passing on and preserving tradition, he may well continue to hold Pharisaic views, even if his practice of purity laws and table fellowship was now more lenient than would have been acceptable to most Pharisees. The Lucan Paul's statement in Acts 23.6, although serving Lucan redactional interests and thus unverifiable, remains plausible at least in a polemical context: 'I *am* a Pharisee.' Luke's Paul had observed Passover and the Feast of Unleavened Bread at Philippi (20.6); he had taken a Nazirite vow (Acts 18.18), and in Jerusalem had undergone a ritual cleansing and offered sacrifices in the Temple (21.24, 26). This of course must be balanced against statements such as that he has become 'all things to all people' (1 Cor. 9.19–23), and references to his 'earlier life in Judaism' (Gal. 1.13–14). In any case our difficulty in assessing this matter is that Paul's letters reflect his teaching to Gentiles, but tell us relatively little about how he governed his own lifestyle as the Jew he still claims to be. (On Paul's Pharisaic heritage see further O. Betz 1977; Jeremias 1969 with a critique by Haacker 1971–2; Niebuhr 1992: 79–109; Becker 1989: 42–53; also Tomson 1990 *passim.*)

In the present context, Paul's claim to be a Pharisee is deliberate and well-placed: it would confirm his unassailable Jewish credentials in the face of his Judaizing opponents, some of whom may well have been Pharisees or Pharisaic sympathizers themselves (cf. Acts 15.15; Matt. 23.15).

6 While there were a number of well-known moderate rabbis, including Hillel and Paul's own apparent teacher, Gamaliel the Elder (Acts 5.34; 22.3), verse 6 offers evidence that Paul may have been particularly strict and radical in certain of his views. The second of his 'achievements' relates to **zeal**. Although this word can elsewhere mean envy or jealousy, and appears in Pauline lists of vices (Gal. 5.20; Rom. 13.13; 1 Cor. 3.3; 2 Cor. 12.20), it is used here in a positive sense of ardour or enthusiasm. (Indeed as such it can even be praiseworthy, when directed to the right ends: e.g. 1 Cor. 12.31; 14.1, 39; 2 Cor. 9.2; 11.2; cf. Tit. 2.14; 1 Pet. 3.13; Pol. *Phil.* 6.3.) Paul himself affirms that he had been extremely 'zealous' for the ancestral traditions of Judaism (Gal. 1.14), the careful preservation of which was another of the hallmarks of Pharisaism.

By the mid-first century, the term 'zeal' had in certain circles become something of a technical term in Jewish nationalist circles. The biblical high priest Phinehas was a particularly popular paradigm in this regard. His concern for the purity of Israel drove him to kill an Israelite man and his Midianite mistress; in return for this 'zeal for God' he was promised a covenant of eternal priesthood because he made atonement for Israel (Num. 25.6–13). This story became very influential in the post-exilic period. Psalm 106.31 asserts that Phinehas's action was 'reckoned to him as righteousness' for ever, while for Sirach 45.23 his zeal made him 'the third in glory' with Moses and Aaron and allowed him to make atonement for Israel. Phinehas is also presented as the rationale and inspiration behind the Maccabean revolt against pagan domination and syncretism (1 Macc. 2.26, 54); in 4 Macc. 18.12 he is specifically praised as a 'zealot' (*zélótés*). In the first century AD, there was in some circles an increasing sense that the purity and holiness of Israel must be safeguarded at any cost, and that Roman domination would need to be overthrown. There was considerable expectation of an eschatological cleansing of the land and Temple, including the expulsion of the Gentiles from the holy city (cf. esp. *Ps. Sol.* 17.21–30). By the 60s, this sentiment had developed into support for open rebellion, and among the factions eventually engaged in this were the so-called 'Zealots', described by Josephus as a group who adopted militant means but whose theology was basically Pharisaic.

Although the 'zealots' as an armed group in this narrow sense cannot be documented earlier in the century, it is clear that prior uses of the term 'zeal' or 'zealot' came to be closely linked with a fervent commitment to defending the purity of Israel's religious practice and of her communal institutions, even at the cost of life itself. The motivation of Phinehas enjoyed enduring admiration (see above; cf. e.g. Josephus *Ant.* 4.152–5; *m.Sanh.* 9.6; *Sifre Num.* 131; *P.R.E.* 47), and it may help to explain why 'zealot' fervour in the Jewish Revolt could be addressed both against pagan oppressors and against rival Jewish factions. Jesus' demonstration in the Temple, too, is understood as an act of 'zeal' in John 2.17; and the 'zeal' of the Jewish believers in Acts 21.20f. is seen in their dismay at the claim that Paul is apparently teaching Jews to abandon Moses, circumcision, and the Jewish way of life.

If Paul therefore appears to identify his persecution of the church as an expression of 'zeal' both here and in Gal. 1.13–14 (and cf. Acts 22.3–4), this seems to link his pre-Christian life to hard-line concerns for the national purity of Israel and its faithfulness to the Torah. In both passages, Paul himself clearly implies that his own approach was at the radical (and quite possibly violent: Gal.1.13, 23; Acts 9.1; 22.4; 26.10–11) end of the contemporary Jewish spectrum, though probably not in its militant expression of armed insurgency against Rome (cf. Hengel 1991: 63–8, 83–94). To be sure, Acts presents his persecution of the church as his individual initiative (9.1), in striking contrast to the words of moderation attributed to his rabbinic teacher, Gamaliel the Elder, in 5.34–9. Nevertheless, it probably arose out of a nationalist dedication to the purity of Israel, which he perceived Christianity to be threatening with its criticism of the Temple (cf. Acts 6.14 with 8.1), its openness to an inclusion of Gentiles, and arguably its endorsement of a crucified Messiah. The potentially militant nationalist leanings of the pre-Christian Paul may also find an interesting echo in Jerome's apparent preservation of a tradition that Paul's family originally hailed from the town of Gischala in Galilee, which in the first century became a well-known hotbed of nationalism (Jerome, *De Viris Illustribus* 5 (MPL 23.646); *Epist. ad Philem.* 23 (MPL 26.653); cf. Haacker 1975: 4–10; Riesner 1994: 134–5). See further Hengel 1989, 1991 *passim*; Légasse 1995: 379–87; also Horbury 1985 on the broader context of 'zeal' as a focus of communal cohesion in Second Temple Judaism).

In his encounter with Christ, Paul had come to see that while the national zeal of contemporary Palestinian Judaism was indeed for God, its assumptions were nevertheless badly misguided (Rom. 10.2). (It is interesting to note that, from their very different perspectives, Josephus and Yohanan ben Zakkai (the founder of the rabbinic movement) had apparently also arrived at a critical view of militant Jewish nationalism by the time of the revolt against Rome some years later.)

Paul had manifested this zeal to the point of becoming a **persecutor of the church**, a fact he confirms on several other occasions (Gal. 1.13, 23; 1 Cor. 15.9; cf. 1 Tim. 1.13). According to Acts, this persecution involved imprisonment, intimidation including the threat of murder, and attempts to extract blasphemy (8.3; 9.1; 22.4–6; 26.10–11). Since Paul's persecution in Acts follows on the heels of the execution of Stephen, it is sometimes suggested that he addressed himself especially to Hellenistic (i.e. Greek-speaking) Jewish Christians (note Acts 6.9ff.). While this is possible in Paul's case, it is difficult to show that Hebrew Christians were generally spared Jewish nationalist opposition; certainly by AD 62 even a conservative Jewish Christian like James the brother of Jesus could be executed on a trumped-up charge of transgressing the Law (Josephus, *Ant.* 20.200; cf. Bernheim 1997: 253–8). In Gal. 1.13 Paul himself admits that his intention had been to destroy the church. This degree of national zeal for Israel presumably goes considerably beyond that of his Judaizing opponents, but it serves to illustrate one possible logical extension of their attitude.

This verse is the first time in Philippians that Paul has used the term **church** (*ekklésia*). Its literal meaning is of an assembly or gathering, whether for secular or religious purposes; in the LXX it often denotes the gathering of the people of God (see Horbury 1997). Paul uses it exclusively as a collective term for believers in Christ, whether in specific reference to a particular local assembly or as a collective term for the universal Church, which is at times perceived as a heavenly reality (e.g. Col. 1.18, 24; cf. Eph. 2.6; 3.10). The reference to his persecution of **the church** in the singular here and in 1 Cor. 15.9; Gal. 1.13f. ('the church of God') represents the collective usage; we may contrast the description in 1 Thess. 2.14 of the same persecuted 'churches of God in Christ Jesus that are in Judaea'. (It is sometimes suggested that Paul's notion of the corporate solidarity of the 'body of Christ' may have been particularly stimulated by reflecting on the connection between his persecution of Christians and his Damascus road encounter with the risen Jesus, especially as reported in Acts 9.4. See e.g. S. Kim 1981: 252–6; Fung 1993: 78.)

Paul's seventh and final statement of his Jewish merits serves to sum up all the others: **regarding 'righteousness' as specified by the Torah, without fault**. 'Righteousness' clearly turns out to be the central point of contention, as is clear from the contrast Paul establishes in verse 9. The distinction between a righteousness according to the Torah and righteousness by faith in Christ is a key concern for Paul: this is evident, for instance, from his extensive discussion of it in Romans 1–11, where 'righteousness' is both a function of God's character and the state of being vindicated and morally upright before him.

Here, it is clear from the general tenor of verses 5–6 that we are dealing with a human quality of uprightness in relation to the requirements of the Torah: all the merits and achievements he has listed are part of what constitutes his faultless 'righteousness according to the Torah'. (Cf. 4QMMT 113, 117 on the performance of 'works of the Torah' being 'reckoned as righteousness'; see also on v. 9 below.)

Measured by Pharisaism's own strict standards of Torah observance, Paul claims that he was (or is? see below) **without fault**. Traditional Protestant exegesis has tended to cringe at this claim, on the Reformational assumption that the Law could not in fact be kept – a notion thought to be supported in Galatians 3 and especially in Romans 7. Paul, however, never makes such a claim (contrast Gal. 5.3, which is intended in all seriousness). Nor should Paul's claim to blamelessness be psychologically reduced to the subjective perception of his pre-Christian conscience (cf. rightly O'Brien, citing J.M. Espy, against R. Bultmann and others). As E.P. Sanders points out (in an admittedly somewhat idealizing account), within the Torah's own provisions of purification from uncleanness and sacrificial atonement for sin it was perfectly possible to lead a life that was righteous and did not contravene this system – especially with the benefit of Pharisaic legal interpretation (E.P. Sanders 1992: 190–240 and *passim*). Although there is important evidence of dissent from the mainstream view in texts like 1QS and *4 Ezra* (on which see Longenecker 1991, 1995: 29–32), the general Pharisaic assumption was clearly that one could indeed keep the Torah's 613 commandments, that it was a realistic system of law also in the sense that it provided its own regular procedures for the observant to receive absolution and purification. The Law as a way of life was widely thought to be feasible and practical: for most faithful Jews it would have been absurd to think that God had given a revelation that could not in fact be lived out. In this respect, too, Paul does not say he was 'sinless', merely that he was upright and blameless by the standards he was following.

One must not of course extrapolate from Paul's high pre-Christian view of his achievements to clichés about the legalistic self-righteousness of Judaism in general. It is possible that in this respect, too, Paul may well have gone beyond some of his contemporaries. True, a danger of such legalism exists in certain Jewish writings at this time, and past generations of Christian exegesis spared no efforts in collecting the evidence (cf. e.g. G. Bertram, *TDNT* 2: 645–8 although many of his texts are cited tendentiously). Nevertheless it remains true that many post-canonical Jewish writings, including the *Prayer of Manasseh*, the Dead Sea Scrolls (e.g. 1QS 11) and numerous rabbinic texts, display an awareness of the need for repentance and the availability of God's free grace (cf. also E.P. Sanders 1977). The fact that the pre-Christian Paul may have subscribed to a system of legalistic self-righteousness does not mean that 'Judaism' as a whole did; indeed in many cases quite the opposite is true. At the same time, it is not difficult to see how the increasing fervour for national purity and strict observance in certain circles might have attracted someone of Paul's pre-Christian disposition.

It may be noted that Paul as a Christian has not ceased to think that being blameless (*amemptos*) is possible; indeed he still affirms it of himself and expects it of Christians (Phil. 2.15; cf. 1 Thess. 2.10; 3.13). 'Righteousness', too, remains essential for his Christian understanding of life before God (note Phil. 3.9; Rom. 8.10; 14.17, etc.). What has changed is the *nature* of the righteousness which makes it possible, and the fact that it is granted and sustained by God (cf. 1 Thess. 5.23; Phil. 2.13; 3.9).

At the same time, the following verses suggest that this type of externally measured and nationalistically appropriated righteousness in the Law turned out to be wholly inadequate. This was not because Paul had been wrong to observe it and excel in it; indeed Acts and (to a lesser extent) the Epistles offer hints that he continued to regard himself, in some meaningful sense and in some important contexts, as observant (e.g. Acts 18.18; 20.6; 21.26; 26.5; cf. Rom. 9.3–5; 1 Cor. 7.19; 16.8; see Tomson 1990; Niebuhr 1992; *pace* Barclay 1996: 384–7). Instead, he has rejected the Jewish nationalism of his 'earlier life' (Gal. 1.13–14) precisely because in his encounter with Christ he discovered that the way of narrow national exclusiveness is not the one that God has chosen in Christ – and, perhaps, that the example of Abraham (Rom. 4; Gal. 3) shows this to have been God's intention all along. Bruce suggests an intriguing biographical comparison with the story of the rich young man who also claimed he had kept all the commandments throughout his life (Mark 10.20; cf. Acts 23.1), and yet was unable to accept the message of Jesus.

C   PAUL'S CHRISTIAN EXPERIENCE: TAKING HOLD OF THE SURPASSING GAIN   (3.7–14)

Paul's personal testimony continues, but now turns to the startling change in orientation that occurred when he encountered Christ. Having set up in verses 4b–6 the merits and achievements of his former way of life, he now explains how he has come to reject his old way of thinking in favour of the much greater advantage of knowing Christ and sharing in God's righteousness by faith. Using financial terminology, he describes how the apparent assets of his former life turned out to be a worthless investment, which he has now written off in light of the far greater gain of knowing Christ and entering into intimate fellowship with him.

(7) But these things that I counted as my assets I have come to

reckon as loss on account of Christ. **(8)** No, more: I consider them all to be loss on account of the far greater value of knowing Christ Jesus my Lord. For his sake I have lost everything else, and consider it rubbish so that I may gain Christ **(9)** and be found in him – having not my own righteousness derived from the Torah, but the one that comes through the faith of Christ, the righteousness derived from God on the basis of faith. **(10)** I want to know him and the power of his resurrection and the fellowship of his sufferings, adopting the form of his death, **(11)** if somehow I may reach the resurrection from the dead. **(12)** Not that I have already taken possession or am already perfected; but I pursue it so that by all means I may take hold of that for which Christ Jesus took hold of me. **(13)** Brothers and sisters, I do not consider that I have already taken hold of it. But one thing I do: forgetting what lies behind and stretching forward to what lies ahead, **(14)** I race towards the goal for the prize, which is God's heavenly call in Christ Jesus.

7 There is considerable uncertainty about whether the Greek text of this verse should begin with the word **but**, which is missing in several important early manuscripts. The meaning is, however, hardly affected, as the rest of verse 7 shows unambiguously (cf. also Hawthorne 135): the list of merits and achievements which seemed to be gains have been written off as losses on account of Christ. (Lit., 'what were to me profits, these I have considered for Christ's sake as loss'.)

The language here is that of the accountant: the word **assets** *(kerdē)*, here used in the plural, signifies the various 'gains' or 'profits', while the word **loss** *(zēmia)* collectively designates them as a liability, a financial write-off or forfeiture. This financial imagery should be noted very carefully. Paul's wholesale rejection applies not to the qualities and achievements listed but the *value* he had attached to them. In and of themselves he might now regard them as good, bad or indifferent: his misguided persecution of the church is something of which he is now ashamed (1 Cor. 15.9), whereas the Israelite inheritance is something which he continues to value in its own right as an important gift and responsibility (cf. Rom. 3.1–2; 9.1–5; 11.1). But in relation to God's audit in Jesus Christ, these things appear as liabilities. A luxury tour bus may be a vital asset to a tour operator; for an aircraft manufacturer, however, it is likely to be a non-performing investment to be written off – unless it can be made to support the company's main business. The value of assets is always assessed in the light of business objectives.

It is also instructive to note that in rabbinic Judaism the terminology of profit (*sakhar*) and loss (*hephséd*) could be applied to the observant Jewish life: one should balance the loss incurred by observing a commandment against the superior profit it entails (e.g. *m.Abot* 2.1). Perhaps Paul's use of this imagery began even before his conversion.

In becoming a Christian, however, Paul's central 'business objective' has changed. **On account of Christ**, his prior gains have turned out to be loss-making investments. Christ as the supreme gain has become the overriding concern of Paul's life. Faith in him has showed up self-righteous pride in his achievements for what it is: not profit but loss, not asset but liability, not light but darkness. On becoming a Christian, his previous balance sheet suddenly looked alarming.

8 Verse 8 begins a new and complex sentence that extends all the way to verse 11. Its function is to explain what Paul meant by counting all things as loss 'on account of Christ'. The sentence begins with a string of five reinforcing Greek particles, literally 'yes, however, indeed I even …' (cf. Silva 183). Paul repeats and strengthens his affirmation that he continues to **consider** (perfect tense in v. 7, present tense here) **them all** as **loss** for the sake of a **far greater value**. That surpassing greatness is here identified as 'the knowledge of Christ Jesus my Lord'.

The term 'knowledge' (*gnôsis*) was charged with religious and philosophical meaning in the Graeco-Roman world; it was rapidly becoming one of the buzzwords for access to desirable religious 'inside information', partly intellectual and partly mystical. In the New Testament period, the term understood in this way was apparently beginning to affect some of the Christians at Corinth (see e.g. 1 Cor. 8.1–2, 7, 10–11) and at Ephesus (1 Tim. 6.20–21). By the second century, such perspectives had developed into a complex variety of religious and philosophical systems generally known as Gnosticism.

However, 'knowledge of God' also had a long and rather different meaning in Old Testament and Jewish thought, where it referred to a close relationship with God on the part of his people (e.g. Jer. 31.34; Hos. 2.20) and of individuals within it (1 Sam. 3.7). This was a relationship of mutual faithfulness expressed on God's side by grace and election (e.g. Exod. 33.12; Isa. 43.1) and on the human side by love for God and obedience to his commandments (Hos. 4.1–2; 6.6). A similar view of the knowledge of God continues in post-biblical Jewish literature (e.g. Bar. 2.15, 31; Wisd. 15.3; *Sib. Or.* 3.693), including the Dead Sea Scrolls (e.g. 1QS 1.12; 4.22; 11.16–20).

Pauline usage is in keeping with the Jewish tradition (e.g. 1 Cor. 15.34; 2 Cor. 4.6; Col. 1.10; cf. Eph. 1.17). Here and in verse 10, Paul offers a glimpse of the passionate and mystical engagement which knowing God through Jesus Christ entailed for him. This is a relationship which is intimately personal, involving **my Lord**; and it is incomparably more valuable than anything else. To know Christ is to know the mystery of God, in whom all the treasures of wisdom and knowledge are contained (Col. 2.2f.; cf. Eph. 1.17; 3.19). Paul's knowledge of Christ here in Philippians must be seen against the background of the christological passage Phil. 2.6–11, which describes him as Paul knows him: the crucified one, the same who is now exalted in heaven and known from the point of view of the resurrection (cf. 1 Cor. 2.2; 2 Cor. 5.16). Paul speaks here in terms of *knowledge* rather than *love* of Christ, but from the Jewish perspective love for God implies knowledge of God, and vice versa (see esp. Ps. 91.14; cf. Hos. 6.6; also the parallel of knowledge and love in 2 Cor. 6.6; 8.7; Col. 2.2; Eph. 3.19). While biblical and post-biblical Jewish sources helpfully illuminate this concern for the knowledge of God, we will see in v. 10 that Paul departs from Jewish and biblical precedent by focusing this knowledge on a mystical participation in the death and resurrection of Jesus. (For a survey of various suggested backgrounds of the term 'knowledge of Christ' see further Koperski 1996: 20–59.)

Knowing Christ Jesus, then, describes the fundamental reality of Paul's life, the relationship which suffuses, empowers and motivates all that he is and does. This is Paul's profoundly personal appropriation of the mind of Christ and of what it means to be 'in Christ' (e.g. 1.13, 26; 2.1, 5) and 'with Christ' (1.23). References to Christ as Lord have of course occurred repeatedly since 1.2. Nevertheless, here is the only time in this or any of his extant letters that Paul uses the expression **my Lord** (but note his self-designation as Christ's 'servant' in 1.1, and cf. similarly personal language in Gal. 2.20; 2 Cor. 12.8–10). Just as the christological passage of 2.6–11 presented the objective theological reality of Christ as the *kurios* who bears the divine name *YHWH*, so this verse makes the astonishing claim that this same Christ is '*my* Lord'. In other words, the great doctrinal affirmations of 2.6–11 are here seen to shape the deepest realities of Paul's own life and self-understanding: the Christ Jesus who humbled himself to death on a cross and who was exalted as 'Lord' is the one whom Paul wants to know intimately and personally, in whose redemptive sufferings and resurrection he longs to participate body and soul (cf. vv. 9–11, 21). On this appropriation and interpretation of the exalted christology of 2.5–11 see most recently Koperski 1996: 324, 332 and *passim.*

For the sake of this Christ, Paul has sustained the loss of **everything else** (lit. 'all things', *ta panta*). Unlike the earlier 'all' (*panta*) in this verse, this refers not only to the specific assets of verses 5–7, but to anything else that might be thought to be an asset in addition or competition to Christ. In this verse he uses the passive form of the verb (*zémioô*) corresponding to the noun earlier translated as **loss** (*zémia*); the meaning here is to 'forfeit' or 'suffer loss' with regard to something, to see the value of an asset reduced to zero (cf. 1 Cor. 3.15 and the slightly broader definition in Aristotle, *Nic. Eth.* 5.7). Everything else has had to be written off as loss for the sake of gaining Christ. Lightfoot comments helpfully on the pronounced rhetorical effect of repeatedly reiterating key terms like 'gain', 'consider', 'loss', 'all things'.

Paul's language here may echo Jesus' teachings in several respects. Jesus warns people that it will profit them nothing to 'gain' (*kerdainô*) the whole world but 'forfeit' their soul (pass. *zémioô*, Mark 8.36 parr.); from this perspective Paul has done well to set **everything** else at nought for the sake of knowing Christ. The description of his coming to faith is also reminiscent of Jesus' kingdom parables about the person who ventures everything for the sake of the one pearl of great value or the field with the treasure in it (Matt. 13.44–6).

Paul has paid the price of writing off his previous assets, including presumably not just his own view of himself and his achievements, but his status in the Jewish community, friendships and relationships and all the social security of his life in Jerusalem. But he has done so willingly – not grudgingly and, as we saw amply documented in verses 4–6, certainly not out of a position of discontent or 'sour grapes'. In a further escalation of the 'profit and loss' statement first made in verse 7, Paul now drives home the point that his God-ward change in priorities has meant that compared to 'gaining Christ', anything else can only be so much **rubbish**. The image progresses here beyond a mere calculation of relative worth to one of emphatic rejection of one's liabilities. In relation to God's grace in Jesus Christ, self-righteousness and human pedigrees of race or class are not just worthless but positively detrimental and repulsive. The word used here (*skubala*) literally means 'dung' or 'refuse', sometimes in the sense of food scraps to be thrown away, but also in the sense of excrement. It is used only here in the NT. The famous tenth-century Byzantine lexicon known as the *Suda* regards the term as a contraction of 'that which is thrown to the dogs' (*tois kusi balomenon*). If this derivation was popularly known in earlier centuries, there could conceivably be another pun here on the adversaries of verse 2: the things which give them the arrogance to call other people 'dogs' are themselves mere 'scraps for dogs' (so e.g. Lightfoot). But we have no evidence that this etymological association was familiar in the first century (cf. F. Lang, *TDNT* 7: 445–7). In any case the reference is to that which is thrown away because it is filthy and objectionable. Proverbs 30.12 speaks of the man who is 'pure in his own eyes, yet not cleansed of his filthiness' (cf. Sir. 27.4).

It is once again evident that Paul's statement about **everything else** denotes not the absolute but the relative value of these things, i.e. with a view to his object which is to **gain Christ**. In relation to the knowledge of Christ, the consideration of other supposed assets is a hindrance rather than a help. Compared to that surpassing and eternal gain, every human merit or achievement fades into insignificance, indeed becomes an obstacle.

With the expression 'to **gain Christ**', Paul returns to the accounting terminology: the former assets have become losses because they have been replaced by the surpassing gain of a relationship with Jesus Christ. Elsewhere this verb is used of Paul's missionary efforts of 'winning' people for Christ (1 Cor. 9.19–23; cf. 1 Pet. 3.1), but here it must mean the 'gain' of the relationship further described in the following verses. Significantly, the Greek clause suggests a purpose that is still being worked out and has a future orientation: although for Paul it is already true that 'to live is Christ' (1.21), his 'gaining Christ' and 'knowing Christ' will be complete when he will 'be with Christ' (1.23; note 1.21 'to die is *gain*'), or when the Saviour comes from heaven and transforms Christians into his glorious likeness (3.20).

9 It is this gain that far outstrips Paul's losses, and which allows him to 'exult in Christ Jesus' (3.3) even now. For this reason the next three verses go on to elaborate fully on the benefits of this new relationship. The goal of 'gaining Christ' will mean first 'to be **found in him**'. The meaning of this verb (pass. *heuriskō*), as in 2.7, is to 'prove to be' or 'turn out to be' something. Just as Christ was 'found' as a man in 2.7, so Paul wants to share both his suffering and his resurrection in being 'found in him' (cf. v. 10). On the other hand, while it is of course true that Christians are already 'in Christ' (see 1.1 and *passim*), the present phrase also continues the purpose clause with its future orientation towards the day of Christ (cf. Lightfoot, Bruce). Paul's language remains intensely personal, concerned not now with theological truth in general but with whether he in particular will be 'found in Christ', fully united to him. Christians *are* 'in Christ', but they in turn must also be 'found' in him on the day of Christ (see above on 2.12–13).

Significantly, being found in Christ on the 'day of Christ' is still concerned with righteousness: the subordinate clause explains the *mode* in which one comes to be found in Christ (so rightly O'Brien). In verse 6, Paul listed among his former assets his 'faultlessness' regarding the 'righteousness as defined in the Law'. Just as 'zeal', rightly directed, is still encouraged as an appropriate quality for Christians (e.g. Rom. 12.11; 1 Cor. 12.31; 14.1, 39), so 'righteousness', here as elsewhere, remains a key concern for Paul. The contrast is merely between **my own righteousness** and the kind that derives from God and rests on faith. One is unacceptable, the other is to be adopted. The first of these two kinds of righteousness is defined as **my own** and as **derived from the Torah**. Each of these two phrases is paralleled by a contrasting quality of the second righteousness: **my own** stands in contrast with **through the faith of Christ**, and **derived from the Torah** (*ek nomou*) contrasts with **derived from God** (*ek theou*) **on the basis of faith**.

Paul's former righteousness is 'his own' (cf. also Rom. 10.3) in the sense that he acquired it; it is his own achievement, as verse 6 showed. Although in its own right it was 'faultless', it proved worthless in relation to knowing Christ. As we noted in relation to verse 6, self-righteousness based on the Law is inadequate not because it is impossible, but because God neither desires nor accepts it. Being busy establishing 'his own' righteousness had caused Paul both to fail to recognize the Messiah and to persecute the Messiah's people. (Cf. Koperski 1996: 236.)

This former self-righteousness is **derived from the Torah**. Paul does not here reject faithful Torah observance but rather the attitude which finds in the observance of the 'works of the Law' grounds both for self-confidence before God and for the exclusion of others. It is this attitude which was once his own, as verse 6 showed; it now appears to characterize the Judaizers, who 'put their confidence in the flesh' (v. 3f.) and who exclude others, calling them 'dogs' (v. 2; note also Gal. 4.17, 'they want to exclude you'; cf. Col. 2.18).

But in what sense could that sort of righteousness be **derived from the Torah**? In a general sense it is obviously so, since its very *raison d'être* is grounded in the commandments. However, a more specific connection may also be possible. The Qumran sectarians clearly believed that their distinctive law observance would be 'reckoned to them as righteousness' (4QMMT 117). It is significant that the same Scriptural phrase 'reckoned as righteousness' applies in the Bible not just to Abraham in Gen 15.6, which is so important for Paul in Romans 4.3ff. (cf. Gal. 3.6), but also to the zeal of Phinehas (Ps. 106.31, cited earlier on v. 6). God's imputation of righteousness to a person could clearly be thought to have its primary basis either in zealous works of law observance or in faith and trust in God; Paul's own understanding clearly moved from the former to the latter when he became a Christian. (Gen. 15.6 of course never meant for Paul a righteousness without the practice of good works, although Jas. 2.23 appears to be quoting it against a misguided Paulinism which did draw that conclusion.) The idea of righteousness 'derived from the Law' could also take a specific cue from Deut. 6.25, 'If we take care to observe this entire commandment before the Lord our God, as he has commanded us, it will be righteousness to us.'

In contrast to this self-made righteousness derived from the Torah is another kind of righteousness, introduced by an adversative **but**. Where the former state of righteousness was attained by human achievement, this one is the gift of God, which places the recipient in a right relationship with him. Instead of being 'my own', this righteousness is characterized, first, as being **through the faith of Christ** (*dia pisteôs Christou*). This is a literal translation of a much disputed Pauline phrase (cf. similarly Rom. 3.22, 26; Gal. 2.16; 3.22), which has been taken to mean either 'faith in Christ' (objective genitive) or the 'faith (or faithfulness) *of* Christ' (subjective genitive).

Until recently, the great majority of commentators and translations followed the former interpretation, despite periodic arguments to the contrary. (A notable early exception was Karl Barth.) Since the early 1980s, however, a number of significant new contributions have made for a renewed and lively discussion, which shows no signs of abating. The arguments are too complex to rehearse in detail here. (See O'Brien and Fee 325 n.44 for surveys from differing perspectives.) The main difficulty is that both translations, if consistently applied, make sense in the passages concerned, while the respective theological implications seem significantly different: in one case *pistis Christou* describes a human faith response, while in the other case it describes the faith and faithfulness of Christ. (The same broad inclusiveness of faith and faithfulness, *fides* and *fiducia*, is similarly present in the Hebrew term *emunah*.)

It is clear that 'faith *in* Christ' is certainly a theme affirmed both in Philippians (1.29) and elsewhere in Paul and the New Testament, regardless of how one decides these particular genitive constructions (e.g. Gal. 3.26; Col. 1.4; 2.5; Acts 20.21; 24.24; 26.18). What is more, an objective genitive is certainly grammatically *possible*; it occurs for instance in Mark 11.22 (*pistis theou*, 'faith in God').

Within the letters of Paul, however, the debate of recent years has shown up a number of telling observations. It is true and quite possibly significant that Paul does not use Jesus as the subject of the verb *pisteuein* 'to believe' (cf. e.g. Koperski 1993b); nevertheless, there is no case where *pistis Christou* (or equivalent phrases) unambiguously means faith 'in' Jesus Christ – even if Gal. 2.16 in particular could clearly accommodate that reading. Further, *every* other Pauline use of 'faith' with a genitive denotes the faith or faithfulness *of* a person, rather than faith *in* that person: a particularly telling comparison can be made between Rom. 3.26 *ton ek pisteôs Iésou* and Rom. 4.16 *tô ek pisteôs Abraam.*

The subjective genitive reading also agrees with Hellenistic Jewish usage, where the term *pistis* generally means 'faithfulness'. The Messiah in particular was to be characterized by his faithfulness. Perhaps the most important passage for Paul in this regard is Hab. 2.4 ('the Righteous One shall live by his faithfulness'), understood as a messianic prophecy in Heb. 10.37 and arguably in Rom. 1.17 (cf. further Campbell 1992: 209–11; Strobel 1961: 177–82). And just as in Romans the believers' *hupakoé pisteôs* ('obedience of faith': 1.5; cf. 10.16; 15.18; 16.19, 26) could be said to derive from Christ's own *pistis* (3.22, 26) and *hupakoé* (5.19), it is not unreasonable in Philippians to link Christ's *pistis* (3.9) and being *hupékoos* (2.8) with those same qualities in the believers (1.25, 27, 29; 2.12, 17; 3.9). (Cf. the comparable logic in Heb. 5.7–9.)

Within Pauline theology, moreover, the *instrumental* use of 'faith of Christ' (note **through**, *dia* + genitive) is most appropriately read as a divine rather than a human action: human faith is not itself the means of bringing about the righteousness 'derived from God', but merely the mode of its reception. It is certainly only the work of Christ which is in any theologically significant sense instrumental to the righteousness of God.

Like Rom. 3.22 and Gal. 2.16, then, Phil. 3.9 is best understood as referring to *two* kinds of faithfulness in relation to God's righteousness revealed in Christ: the instrumental faithfulness *of* Christ in his self-humbling death on the Cross (*dia pisteôs Christou*), and the responding faithfulness of the believer (**on the basis of faith**, *epi té pistei*; cf. Rom. 3.22 'for all believers', *eis pantas tous pisteuontas*; Gal. 2.16 'and we have believed', *kai hémeis episteusamen*). This distinction allows one to specify *both* the objective ground of righteousness and the subjective mode of its acceptance, while removing what otherwise seems a surprising and possibly redundant *second* reference to human **faith**. (See also Hooker 1989: 331–3 on the dimension of 'interchange' between the two kinds of *pistis*. Cf. further Hays 1983, Campbell 1992: 58–69, Wallis 1995 *passim*, and the literature cited in O'Brien and Fee. Recent statements of the contrary position include Koperski 1993b with 1996: 322 n.80; Stuhlmacher 1992: 344.)

This righteousness 'through the faith of Christ' is further defined as being **from God on the basis of faith**, in contrast to that which was **from the Torah**. God is its source and 'the faith of Christ' is the means by which it is revealed. It may seem odd that 'God' and 'the Torah' should here be set at loggerheads, considering that God gave the Torah. But despite Gal. 3.19 Paul is not here anticipating the second-century Gnostic view that the Law was evil or not given by God. Instead, the contrast is with 'my own' righteousness, which placed trust and confidence in 'works' of the Law without recourse to its author's desire for faith. We should note again the autobiographical element here, which is well captured by Bruce 115:

> It is good to do what the Law requires, but that is not the way to receive the righteousness that God bestows. Paul's trusted foundation of legal righteousness collapsed beneath his feet on the Damascus road ... ; but in that same instant he received through faith ... the new and durable foundation of righteousness freely bestowed by God's grace.

Paul is offering a description not primarily of 'Judaism' vs. 'Christianity' but of his own former and present way of life. It is in the first instance Paul who pursued his own righteousness, and Paul who then found faith. But the example does have a pointed relevance in illustrating the contrast between the Pauline gospel and the demands of the Jewish-Christian opponents.

Protestant scholars in particular have made much of the strongly contrastive language which Paul uses to distinguish his former life by **my own righteousness derived from the Torah** from his new Christian life of **righteousness derived from God on the basis of faith**. Thus, in addition to frequent claims about Paul's 'abrogation' of the Law, one of the more specific recurring suggestions about Pauline ethics is the assumption that Paul has rejected the practical legal application of Scripture (*halakhah*) in favour of a morality that is more purely spiritual and theological in nature (*haggadah*). (So e.g. Vielhauer 1979: 220; J.A. Sanders 1975: 373f.) This does of course have an element of truth, in the sense that Paul's ethics is clearly far less obviously 'halakhic' and less explicitly Torah-dependent than, for instance, that of the

Dead Sea Scrolls or the early rabbis. Nevertheless, it is also becoming increasingly clear that, however in the end one construes the complex topic of 'Paul and the Law' *theologically*, the Torah continues in practice to be both formative and normative for Paul's ethics (cf. Tomson 1990, Rosner 1994, Bockmuehl 1994–5). Indeed his writings even suggest (e.g. in Rom. 3.8, 31; 6.1, 15; cf. 1 Cor. 5–10) that certain antinomian challenges and misinterpretations of his theology tended to reinforce his intention to uphold the abiding moral validity of the Torah, which in any case he saw as attesting the truth of the gospel (e.g. Rom. 3.21; cf. 15.4). In the present passage, the primary shift for Paul is between different models of justification: 'my own, through the Law' vs. 'Christ's, through his faithfulness'. If there is a shift from the Torah to Christ as well, this is a matter of perspective and function rather than of outright termination and substitution: it is *the way* the Torah is seen to function in the light of Christ which is at issue. From being used to buttress Paul's own righteousness, it comes to witness to the true righteousness that is in Christ: from legalism to Christ-mysticism.

This new righteousness is brought about *through* Christ's faithfulness, but it is appropriated **on the basis of faith**. This phrase (*epi té pistei*) denotes the human response of trust in God's saving acts, as in the case of Acts 3.16 (its only other NT occurrence). It is equivalent to putting one's confidence not 'in the flesh' but in God (cf. verse 3). In Paul's case, this response of faithfulness included writing off all those assets which had propped up his 'own' righteousness, and relying instead on the faithfulness of Christ (cf. Silva 187f.).

10 Paul goes on to reiterate in passionate, vibrant tones the 'surpassing value' of knowing Christ (cf. v. 8). Describing his encounter with Christ is not for him a matter of dusting off a significant but distant biographical reminiscence, but a powerful confession of that which continues to be the foundation and sustenance of his life, motivating and invigorating every fibre of his being and every moment of his time: **I want to know** Christ (lit. 'so that I may know him', using an infinitive of purpose). This phrase is obviously equivalent to his earlier reference to 'knowing Christ Jesus my Lord' (v. 8), and it is also parallel to 'that I may gain Christ and be found in him' (v. 8–9). (Another, less plausible alternative is to see the knowledge of Christ in this verse specifically as the purpose of receiving the 'righteousness from God'. But this gives insufficient weight to the parallel with v. 8, on which verses 10–11 now expand.)

To 'know Christ', then, is the overriding and unfading ambition of Paul's life. As we saw above, this 'knowledge' is not to be understood in the sense of knowing a fact or a formula, but of a comprehensive and ever-deepening personal relationship with Christ, increasingly growing into union with him.

Given what has already been said about Christ in Philippians, it comes as no surprise that Paul's personal knowledge of him should include the desire to share his 'mind' and the pattern of his life, both in his self-humbling obedience to death and in his glorious vindication (2.5–11). Both elements are here expressly cited, and closely linked together: **the power of his resurrection and the fellowship of his sufferings**. This link is particularly close if, as seems likely, the best text agrees with those manuscripts that drop the articles before 'fellowship' and 'sufferings'. These are merely two aspects of knowing Christ, not two different modes to be separated, as Paul similarly makes clear to his opponents in Corinth (e.g. 2 Cor. 4.7–11; 12.9f.).

Some have suggested that the sequence of resurrection and suffering parallels that of Paul's call vision in Acts 9, where his encounter with the exalted risen Christ (vv. 3–6) precedes the call to suffer for him (v. 16). But this parallel is difficult to verify here; more likely the sequence is merely dictated by Paul's insistence that the suffering no less than the resurrection of Christ is a vital component of 'knowing' him. At the same time, because his union is with the one who was both crucified and raised, Paul can approach life knowing 'the beginning from the end', as it were. For Christians, living after Easter, the resurrection is therefore both the first word and the last, the beginning and the end (note verse 11). The 'fellowship of his sufferings' is always in the light of his past triumphant victory and our common glorious future.

What might be meant by **the power of his resurrection**? Many interpreters have seen here a genitive of origin, suggesting the power that belongs to the risen Christ, a power which he continuously exercises in the life of the Christian and of the church. While this is not impossible, the resurrection of Christ is never elsewhere seen as a sign of *his* power but rather of God's. Paul frequently affirms that it was God's power which raised Christ from the dead (Rom. 1.4; 8.11; 1 Cor. 6.14; 2 Cor. 13.4; Col. 2.12; cf. Acts 2.24; Eph. 1.20), and this is in keeping with standard Jewish views about resurrection as being by the power of God (cf. already Ezek. 37.12, 2 Macc. 7.9, 14; 4Q521 ii 2.12; and note the second benediction of the *Amidah* or *Prayer of Eighteen Benedictions*: 'you revive the dead, mighty to save'). Although the resurrection is implicit rather than explicit in Phil. 2.9, Christ's exaltation is there clearly identified as God's work. Paul's desire, therefore, is to experience personally the power of God that was shown in Christ's resurrection. Sharing in Christ's death and resurrection by virtue of incorporation into him is a typically Pauline thought (cf. similarly Rom. 6.1–11; 8.11; Col. 2.12f. etc.).

At the same time, Paul wants to participate in Christ's **sufferings**. This theme was already anticipated in Phil. 1.29f., and it features significantly in other letters (e.g. 2 Cor. 1.5; 4.10f.; 11.23ff.; Col. 1.24). For Paul, the participation in Christ's sufferings is an important dimension of being united with him. **Fellowship** (*koinônia*) in his sufferings means an active sharing, as in the two previous uses of the term (1.5; 2.1). Such active sharing in Christ's passion and death is part of the necessary eschatological suffering of the Messianic era which was believed to usher in the kingdom of God (cf. Rom. 8.18; cf. Acts 14.22; 1 Thess. 3.3 and the idea of end-time 'birth-pangs', e.g. Mark 13.8). O. Betz 1990: 207f. offers the intriguing hypothesis that Paul's notion of the 'fellowship of the Messiah's sufferings' may derive from his translation of the word *ḥaburatô* ('his wound') in Isa. 53.5 as 'his fellowship'; this reading is also attested in the *Targum Jonathan*, which understands the suffering Servant as the victorious Messiah intervening for his people (cf. further Ådna 1996). At any rate, to participate in Christ's sufferings was for Paul not a symbolic reference to baptism or a way of explaining occasional adversity, but a way of relating the constant, and in his view eschatological, experience of affliction and tribulation to Christ (see 2 Cor. 4.10f.; cf. 1 Cor. 15.31; 2 Cor. 1.4–11; 11.23–8). 'The sufferings of Christ abound for us' (2 Cor. 1.5); to suffer on behalf of Christ is to participate in these sufferings of the messianic age.

The context of persecution is thus clearly important for Paul's understanding of the knowledge of Christ (cf. Minear 1990; Koperski 1996: 292f.). There may also be an allusion here to the possibility of martyrdom – but only as something that, if it arose, would be an integral part of the overall experience of 'knowing Christ'. Suffering for Christ, as Paul wrote earlier, is for Christians proof of their future salvation and glory (1.29; cf. Rom. 8.17–18).

Adopting the form of his death means literally 'becoming conformed to his death', and alludes to the frequent Pauline conviction about the believer's mystical participation in and with Christ. Grammatically, this rare verb *summorphizô* could be understood either in a passive ('being conformed', i.e. by God) or a middle sense ('taking the form of'). (BAGD 786; see Hawthorne on the latter option, and cf. below.) Syntactically, this phrase is best seen as dependent on the infinitive of purpose at the beginning of the verse (**to know him**). It describes the mode or circumstance in which that knowledge is attained: Paul wants to know him 'as his form is becoming like that of Christ in his death' (cf. also Loh & Nida). If this is correct, then Paul's continual 'becoming like Christ in his death' may point not only to the participation in his sufferings but also to his subsequent resurrection. As we suggested above, God's power in the resurrection of Christ is equally relevant to the apostle's present suffering and to his own future resurrection (verse 11; similarly 2 Cor. 4.11; Col. 3.1, etc.; cf. O'Brien). To have a share in Easter Sunday means to have a share in Good Friday – and vice versa (cf. K. Barth).

This interpretation, however, also means that **adopting the form of his death** should not be understood too literally. What Paul has in mind is not death on the cross, which as a Roman citizen he was in any case most unlikely to face. Even the possibility of martyrdom, though undoubtedly on his mind, does not exhaust the sense here: it is at present a mere possibility, and would be a singular event, whereas Paul's present participle suggests that 'being conformed to Christ's death' is for him a definite objective as well as an ongoing process. More promising is the widely accepted interpretation of a symbolic participation in Christ's death: although typically associated with the incorporation into Christ's death and resurrection at baptism (e.g. Rom. 6.4–6; Col. 2.20; 3.3; Gal. 2.19f.), Paul can equally exhort those who are already baptized to 'put to death' the old humanity (e.g. Rom. 8.13; Col. 3.5). Existentially, too, the present reality of Christ's death was a daily part of Paul's experience as his minister, as we saw earlier (2 Cor. 4.10ff.; cf. 1 Cor. 15.31). (For the general theme of dying and rising with Christ see e.g. Tannehill 1967; Wedderburn 1987.)

This much is certainly appropriate and in keeping with Paul's theology elsewhere. However, one additional point may be worth pondering. The verb Paul employs (*summorphizō*) is a rare word, not attested prior to Paul, and would arguably have struck his audience as unusual. Its literal meaning is to 'convey' (active) or 'take' (middle) the same 'form' (*morphē*). What was the *morphē* of Christ's death? The christological passage in 2.7–8 would suggest that he had taken the *morphē* of a servant and *as such* became 'obedient to death'. (It is also worth recalling our earlier discussion about the *form* of the Servant who gives himself up to death in Isa. 53: see esp. p. 135.) In the present context, where Paul has given up 'putting his confidence in the flesh' for 'exulting in Christ Jesus' and in his faithfulness (3.3, 9), there is a reasonable likelihood that the apostle may be deliberately raising the issue of the 'form' of Christ's death to indicate that his own former motivation of pride has given way to one of Christ-like humility. An additional advantage of this reading is that it allows Paul to present himself as a meaningful example to all Christians

(3.15–17), rather than only or primarily to apostolic martyrs. It is in becoming like the 'form' of Christ's humiliation that Christians will also participate in the 'form' of his heavenly glory (3.21, note the use of *summorphos*).

11   Paul speaks in the present tense of being conformed to Christ's death and this is, as we have seen, to be understood in terms of participation in Christ and, perhaps, emulation of the 'mind of Christ'. Now, however, he turns to the subject of his own resurrection, as a *future* event: **if somehow I may reach the resurrection from the dead**. While God's power in the resurrection of Jesus is something which Paul desires to know by union with Christ already in his present life (cf. e.g. Rom. 6.4, 13; 2 Cor. 4.11), this passage refers quite clearly to a resurrection still to come.

The Greek construction **if somehow** (*ei pôs*) seems to express an unusual element of hesitation about the apostle's participation in the resurrection. Elsewhere he is far more emphatic that Christians may look forward to participating in this eschatological event (1 Cor. 15.49–53; 1 Thess. 4.16–17; Rom. 6.5; note also 1.23). Here, however, there is a degree of contingency often underrated by commentators: Paul's own resurrection is his earnest desire, rather than a *fait accompli*. While his future hope is not in 'real doubt' (*pace* Otto 1995: 330; see 1.23; 3.20f.), Paul's whole point here is to insist that for the Christian there is still a race to be run and a prize to be won (3.12–14; contrast 3.18–19). The expression **if only** repeatedly carries this sense of strong desire and hope for something that is not in the speaker's power to control: so the aim of Paul's mission is 'if somehow I might move my kinsfolk to jealousy and so save some of them' (Rom. 11.14; on a much more pragmatic note cf. e.g. Acts 27.12). A similar note of contingency was present in 2.12–13, where Paul's conviction about God's completion of his good work in the Philippians (cf. 1.6) was perfectly compatible with the call to 'work out your own salvation with fear and trembling'.

Contrary to what some Christian theologies have taught, salvation for Paul is not some metaphysical drama whose palpable reality or unreality in daily life is more or less irrelevant. It is not 'a tangent barely touching a circle'; nor is it merely an abstract language game for 're-imagining ourselves differently'. Instead, it is the sovereign gift of God in Christ which is accepted by faith alone and then concretely *embodied* (cf. 2 Cor. 4.10f.; Rom. 8.11) in the banal, sublime and excruciating realities of the believer's life – by 'the power of his resurrection and the fellowship of his sufferings'. The stage for the drama is here: that is the meaning of the incarnation. Resurrection, then, is for believers no doubtful and uncertain desire but the sure hope for what God in Christ has promised. Yet the only road to it is the race-track of the expectant, Christ-orientated 'mind' that Paul himself exemplifies: forgetting the pride in his own status and achievements and reaching forward to the heavenly prize of fellowship with Christ (vv. 13f.). There lies the contingency. As the Lucan Paul puts it, 'Through many tribulations we must enter the kingdom of God' (Acts 14.22).

The term **resurrection from the dead** is itself an unusually emphatic reference to the belief in a future resurrection which has not already happened. Paul's word for **resurrection** here (*exanastasis*) is in this form found nowhere else in the NT; the prefix *ex-* should be understood as intensifying. Similarly, this resurrection is literally described as 'out from among the dead'. Such emphatic language calls for explanation, and we may consider two options that have been proposed.

(1) Lightfoot and others have thought that Paul's phrase should be understood as a deliberate reference to the resurrection of the *righteous* (cf. Luke 14.14; 20.35; John 5.29; Rev. 20.4–6), as distinct from the general resurrection (so most recently Otto 1995). While there is no unequivocal Pauline evidence for such a distinction, it is in any case intriguing that virtually every other NT statement about a resurrection *from* (*ek, apo*) rather than *of* the dead refers either to the resurrection of Jesus or to a resurrection of particular righteous people (Lazarus in John 12.1, 9, 17 is a separate case, but conforms to this rule). It is certainly true that Paul's view of the resurrection is concerned first and foremost with that of believers (note e.g. 1 Thess. 4.16f.), whereas that of unbelievers is not explicitly addressed.

However, one should perhaps not systematize Paul's thought unduly. In 1 Cor. 15 we hear repeatedly about the resurrection *of* the dead (vv. 12, 13, 21, 42), and about the fact that 'in Christ *all* shall be raised'; nevertheless this resurrection *of* the dead involves Christ first, then Christian believers, and then (it appears) everyone else, vv. 23–6. Romans 11.15, on the other hand, arguably suggests that just as Israel's rejection has meant the reconciliation of 'the world', so their restoration will mean an equally universal resurrection '*from* the dead'. In Acts 24.15, Paul is reported to express his belief in a universal resurrection of *both* the righteous and the unrighteous, while Acts 4.2 associates faith in Jesus with the resurrection not *from* but *of* the dead. This suggests that the phrase in verse 11 should not be over-interpreted.

(2) Another suggestion has been that Paul's emphatic language here may be directed against specific proponents of an over-

realized eschatology, in which the resurrection is no longer a future but only a present reality (e.g. recently Witherington 1994: 91). That such people existed is clear from the opposition to them expressed in 1 Cor. 15.12; 2 Tim. 2.18. Nevertheless, two considerations make it highly unlikely that such a view is here at issue. First, the opponents in 1 Corinthians and 2 Timothy are more generally Hellenizing rather than strictly Judaizing, possibly in both cases with a Gnostic-like orientation. And secondly, the only known *Jewish* group to question a belief in the resurrection were the Sadducees; yet Paul's rhetorical strategy here is clearly geared to people with an admiration for Pharisaism, its halakhic concerns for purity and its keen concern for the Torah and 'works of Torah' (3.2, 5–6, 19). Pharisees and their supporters, however, believed in a bodily resurrection and a final judgement (see e.g. Acts 23.6; Mark 12.18, 28; Josephus, *B.J.* 2.162f.; *m.Sanh.* 10.1).

It seems clear, then, that the Judaizing opponents did not question belief in the resurrection as such. Nevertheless, Paul's emphatic phrase does seem to make better sense if he is implicitly denying an opposing alternative (cf. Gnilka). It also remains the case that this alternative is most likely one that cast doubt over the future resurrection, either from a pagan or a Jewish perspective.

Graeco-Roman religion certainly did not believe in resurrection. There was a widespread, but still sporadic, belief in the immortality of the soul, especially among Platonists, in Orphic and Pythagorean circles, and in the oriental mystery cults; but this had no official status and was not, for instance, accepted by major groups like the Epicureans and some Stoics. Belief in a resurrection of the *body* was a distinctively Jewish and Christian idea, which might easily meet with pagan incredulity or ridicule (see Acts 17.18, 32; cf. Oepke 1950: 932). Nevertheless, while opposition to Paul's statement from pagan quarters is of course theoretically possible, we have at this stage little positive evidence of pagan doctrinal resistance, and it seems in any case unlikely in the present context of *Judaizing* opponents.

A polemical front against a Jewish objection seems after all the most likely. Converts to Judaism or Christianity would of course tend to embrace the hope of resurrection as a desirable benefit of becoming part of the people of God. The Judaizers, however, questioned *Gentile* salvation, and by implication might easily leave Gentile Christians in doubt as to whether Paul's gospel could deliver either immortality or the resurrection of the righteous. Paul's emphatic statement should be seen to reinforce the conviction that this assurance does indeed belong to the Gentiles by faith in Christ – regardless of what doubts might be cast on it by their detractors.

12 In verses 12–14, Paul goes on to elaborate on the implication of the complex purpose clauses of verses 7–11. His desire to know Christ is not yet a fully accomplished reality, but it still motivates and energizes his life toward the supreme goal and prize of heavenly union with him. In two significant contrasting statements, he denies having already attained present perfection and affirms instead his ongoing single-minded pursuit of the ultimate prize. It seems plausible that this contrast, too, is intended to deny Judaizing claims to perfection.

Verse 12, then, begins with an important concession: **Not that I have already taken possession** (lit. 'not that I have already received'). The Greek has no object, and considerable debate has surrounded the question of which object might need to be supplied. Some have looked ahead to the 'prize' at the end of verse 13 and others have sought to give a variety of reasons why the object was deliberately omitted. Probably the most likely reading is to see the preceding verses 8–11 as identifying the 'greater gain' that Paul is still pursuing: knowing Christ and being found in him, having a righteousness based on his faithfulness that is rooted in God and is received by faith, and attaining to the resurrection from the dead. Paul has indeed already suffered the loss of his earlier merits (v. 8), and Christ did take hold of him (v. 11) on the road to Damascus: both affirmations are in the aorist tense, describing past experiences. But the third aorist verb is negated: while Paul enjoys union with Christ now, he has not yet **taken possession** of the promises; and he himself is not yet **perfected**.

An intriguing textual variant suggests that some ancient readers understood the object to be the righteousness by faith of which verse 10 spoke. Papyrus p[46] (our earliest collection of Paul's letters), along with Codex D and other representatives of the Western text, adds the phrase 'or have already been justified'. The suggestion that Paul might not yet be justified appears flatly to contradict his own doctrine of justification in Romans and Galatians, and a number of interpreters have therefore argued that it is the sort of statement which harmonizing later scribes would be more likely to drop than to insert into the text. (Cf. Silva 203f.). Yet references to justification in the future do occur in Rom. 2.13 and 5.19, and a scribe's explanatory insertion of this phrase is easily conceivable if he thought that the object of 'taking possession' was in fact the 'righteousness' of verse 10. For this reason it is best to give full weight to the strong manuscript support for the text as NA[27] has it.

Paul also does not think that he is already **perfected**. He uses this verb (*teleioō*) only here, and many commentators suggest that he is alluding to claims to perfection on the part of the opponents. In the past this terminology has sometimes been linked with beliefs of the mystery religions or of Gnosticism (e.g. Koester 1962: 324; Schmithals 1957: 319f.). However, a Jewish Palestinian use of similar terminology is firmly documented among the Qumran sect, who saw themselves as 'perfect' (*tamim*), i.e. having integrity before God and in their observance of the Torah (1QS 1.8; 2.2; 4.20f.; 8.20 and *passim*; see already Ps. 119.1, 80). It is possible that Judaizing opponents similarly used the language of present *possession* of the covenant and Israelite 'sonship' to attract proselytes to Judaism (cf. Rom. 4.11; 5.11; 8.15 and see on v. 3 above), especially given the fourfold repetition in verses 12–13 of cognate verbs for 'taking possession' and 'taking hold' (*lambanō*, *katalambanō*).

Contrary to what even he himself might once have claimed (cf. v. 6b), Paul now knows that he has not yet been perfected. Instead, he presses on in order to apprehend that which is his in Christ. While the verb **pursue** (*diōkō*) sometimes appears in the sense of 'persecute' (so e.g. in v. 6), Paul also uses it more positively of the eager pursuit of peace (e.g. Rom. 14.9), hospitality (Rom. 12.13) or good deeds (1 Thess. 5.15). Here, then, Paul speaks of a concerted, strenuous pursuit intended **by all means** (*ei kai*; cf. *ei pōs* in v. 11) **to take hold** of the heavenly prize. This is the first of three uses of the verb **take hold** (*katalambanō*) in verses 12–13. Both verbs are used in connection with the athletic imagery of a race in the related context of Rom. 9.30–31 (cf. v. 32), where Israel stumbles in pursuing (*diōkō*) God's righteousness 'as if it were based on works', while the Gentiles in fact apprehend it (*katalambanō*). (Note also 1 Cor. 9.24, another racing image which involves 'taking hold' of a 'prize'; the correlation of 'pursuing' and 'taking hold' can also have a military application, e.g. LXX Exod. 15.9; Lam. 1.6; Sir. 11.10.)

Paul's eager pursuit has as its goal to apprehend the very prize (cf. 14) for the sake of which **Christ Jesus took hold** of him on the Damascus road. As in Rom. 5.12; 2 Cor. 5.4; Phil. 4.10, the Greek expression *eph' hō* is highly contested. It could mean 'because of the fact that', *epi toutō hoti*, as most commentators propose. But while that cannot be ruled out, our translation here and at 4.10 accepts the argument of Fitzmyer 1993: 330 that a 'consecutive' reading is to be preferred to a causal one (cf. NIV; Fee 346 n.31 and 430 n.28). At the point of his coming to faith, Paul was drastically apprehended for the service of Christ (cf. Acts 9.1ff.; 22.1ff.; 26.12ff.).

13 Paul is clearly keen to impress on the Philippians his point that the race is not yet over. Deliberately arresting their attention with the familiar Christian address **brothers and sisters** (*adelphoi*: cf. 1.12; 3.1) to show that his own experience is relevant to them as well, he emphatically reasserts as his considered judgement that he is not one who has already laid hold of the victor's crown. He has not yet been perfectly found in Christ, and the opponents' claims to perfection are based on a false boast in the flesh, on self-righteousness rather than on faith. Paul's point resembles a proverb cited by King Ahab: 'One who puts on his armour should not boast like him who takes it off' (1 Kgs. 20.11). Faith for Paul has an essentially incomplete and future dimension (cf. 1.18–26; 3.20f.; Rom. 8.24f.). The resurrection from the dead is still to come.

Instead, Paul is concerned about only **one thing**, and that is the pursuit of the **prize** with the single-mindedness of the athlete for whom nothing else counts. **Forgetting what lies behind**, he cannot afford to look over his shoulder (cf. also Jesus' words about the ploughman, Luke 9.62; also 17.32). **What lies behind** may include the things written off as loss (vv. 5–7); but the present tense of **forgetting** suggests an ongoing concern to be unencumbered both by what may have been abandoned in the past and what has already been achieved, the part of the course he has already covered. His aim is entirely before him: the verb **stretching forward** (*epekteinomenos* (mid.)) vividly captures the image of the runner who strains and leans forward into the race, reaching for the goal with every ounce of his being.

14 The runner's course is straight for the **goal** and the victor's **prize** that awaits him and all those who finish the race. The word **goal** (*skopos*) is found only here in the NT; it denotes the finish line which the runner has in view (cf. *skopeō*, 'to look at', used in Phil. 2.4 and 3.17).

But what is the prize? It is evidently defined by the phrase **God's heavenly call in Christ Jesus**. This translation, however, already represents something of an interpretation; a literal reading would be, 'the prize of the above (or upward) call of God in Christ Jesus'. Some have suggested that this is a genitive of apposition, so that the heavenly call is *itself* the prize for which Paul contends, i.e. a calling to be with Christ in heaven (cf. Heb. 3.1; 9.15; cf. Col. 3.3–4; Eph. 2.6). While this understanding of the 'upward call' could be compatible with Paul's thought elsewhere, it seems at this stage to disrupt the metaphor in which the goal is a prize, not a calling. What is more, it is worth underlining that for Paul the word 'calling' (*klēsis*) normally denotes the divine act of calling itself, rather than that to which one is called (so rightly O'Brien).

Another common interpretation has been to try and relate the **call** to the public honouring of winners at the end of a race, as they are summoned to come forward and receive their palm branch. While the idea of receiving a heavenly prize or crown is not without parallel in early Christian literature (cf. 2 Tim. 4.8; Jas. 1.12; 1 Pet. 5.4; Rev. 2.10), this is not generally linked with the imagery of Hellenistic games. There is, moreover, no clear evidence that this honouring of the victor was indeed referred to as an 'upward call'. More significantly, perhaps, to continue the athletic imagery to the specific ceremony of honouring the victor would compromise Paul's typically *theological* use of the term 'calling' (Fee 349 n.49). Müller suggests a more promising but admittedly limited parallel with Philo, *Rer. Div. Her.* 70, where the spirit-filled soul is said to be 'called up' (*anô kaleisthai*) to God; cf. also *Plant.* 23f.

Finally, a third interpretation opts for a subjective genitive: the goal is the prize which *pertains* to the calling, i.e. to which the divine call invites and which it promises. This reading is consistent with Paul's usual understanding of 'calling' as that which summons someone to salvation by faith in Christ. In this connection, the word *anô* ('above') need not be understood as indicating an 'upward' direction, but merely the heavenly origin, nature and intention of God's call (cf. its use in Gal. 4.26; Col. 3.1f.). It is God who calls, and his calling is to his own kingdom and glory (1 Thess. 2.12; cf. Phil. 3.20f.).

Perhaps the interpretation of Paul's words should not be defined too precisely. It is God who calls in Christ Jesus, and he calls the believer into eternal fellowship with him. This is the prize for which Paul is still contending.

In this way, our paragraph closes with a subtle change of perspective. Having begun by stressing his own strategy of writing off bad investments in order to take hold of the surpassing gain of knowing Christ, Paul now acknowledges that the prize is in fact that for which Christ 'has made me his own': **God's heavenly call**. It is God who calls Paul in Christ, and who has already 'apprehended' Paul and made him his own. Paul's task is to reach out and grasp the prize for which he is already appointed.

D PAUL'S EXAMPLE APPLIED (3.15–21)

In verse 15 we finally discover Paul's rhetorical purpose in the intensely personal testimony of chapter 3 thus far: he now opens up his discourse to his readers by inviting them to participate and follow his example. Paul's own Christian experience was earlier introduced in a paradigmatic sense in 1.12–26 (see above, p. 73). Here, he explicitly invites his readers to imitate him and thus to mature in their personal appropriation of the life of Christ. This proper attitude is evidently so important that Paul asserts it twice over (vv. 15–16, v. 17), setting it into graphic contrast with the counter-example of the Judaizers (vv. 18–19). He then returns once more to the Christ-centred orientation which he shares with the Philippians (note the first person plural introduced in vv. 15–16 and resumed in vv. 20–21), and concludes on a note of buoyant eschatological expectancy and trust in the power of the exalted Christ.

Interpreters have opted for a variety of different paragraph divisions within this passage (e.g. at 3.17, due to the lack of grammatical connection with the preceding material). In every case, however, there is a clear continuity of argument, so that it seems best to treat this passage as one section, even if the layout of my translation acknowledges the presence of parenthetical remarks in 3.18–19.

(15) So therefore all of us who are mature should adopt this stance. And even if in any respect you think differently, this too God will reveal to you. (16) Only let us in any case keep in step with the standard we have already attained. (17) Join together in following my example, brothers and sisters, and keep your eyes on those who live according to the model you have in us.

(18) As I used to tell you often, so I tell you now with tears: there are many who live as the enemies of the cross of Christ. (19) Their end is destruction, their god is their belly and their glory is in their shame. Their mind is set on earthly things.

(20) Our commonwealth, indeed, is in heaven, and it is from there that we eagerly expect a Saviour, the Lord Jesus Christ. (21) He will transfigure our lowly body into a form like that of his glorious body, according to the power that also enables him to subject all things to himself.

Given his preceding argument, Paul appropriately returns to the intellectual language of 'mind' or 'attitude', which was earlier applied in connection with the 'mind of Christ' (2.5; cf. 2.2). Here, it applies – or so it would appear – to Paul's own attitude of desiring the righteousness of Christ and striving to know him, as distinct from the pursuit of one's own status and achievements.

15 Paul invites all who are **mature** to adopt this same perspective: of pressing on to gain Christ fully, relying on his achievements rather than on their own. The connection with the preceding race imagery is assured through the word **therefore** (*oun*). Paul's attitude is that which befits those who have put their trust in Christ. One of the disputed questions in this verse, however, is the meaning of the term **mature** (*teleios*, 'perfect, complete, mature'), which in Jewish contexts applies to those whose trust is sincerely placed in God and who follow whole-heartedly in his ways (e.g. LXX Gen. 6.9; 1 Kgs. 8.61; 11.4). At Qumran, the corresponding Hebrew word *tamim* came to be used almost as a technical term for the members of the community, who live faithfully by the Law as it is normatively expounded by the Teacher of Righteousness (cf. above, p. 221). The New Testament uses oscillate from the sense of moral integrity and whole-ness before God (e.g. in Matthew and James) to eschatological perfection (e.g. 1 Cor. 13.10), and to the notion of intellectual or spiritual maturity or 'adulthood' in several Pauline passages (e.g. 1 Cor. 2.6; 14.20). The latter concept may be influenced by the meaning of *teleios* in contemporary Hellenistic philosophical and religious contexts.

As in the earlier use of the verb *teleioō* in verse 12, there has been considerable debate about whether the occurrence of this terminology allows us to 'mirror-read' here an ironic reference to the language of the supposed opponents, who may have claimed perfection for themselves (O'Brien 435 n.89 and Fee 343 n.23 list some of the many advocates of this view). Commentators have been reluctant to accept a straightforward reading of the term *teleios* here, since Paul might otherwise appear to contradict his insistence in v. 12 that he was 'not yet perfected'. If the reference here is meant ironically, the effect would be to place the word in quotation marks: 'all those who are "perfect" should adopt this attitude'. Paul's sentence would thus convey a veiled polemic, addressed to the Judaizers and all those at Philippi who might find themselves attracted to their viewpoint.

However, the case for the ironic reading is weak. One repeat-edly finds Paul using related words in slightly different senses in the same context (cf. Bruce 124, and e.g. cf. Phil. 3.2; Rom. 12.3; 2 Cor. 4.8). Moreover, given the religious and moral usage specifi-cally of the Greek and Hebrew *adjective* in contemporary Jewish texts, the etymological connection with the verb *teleioō* in v. 12 should perhaps not be overrated – even if something of a word-play cannot be ruled out. What is more, as Fee shows very clearly, Paul's tone here is inclusive and not polemical. A 'straightfor-ward' reading is buttressed particularly by his inclusion of him-self among those who are *teleios*, and by the reference to **all of us** (*hosoi*, lit. 'as many as', a correlative conjunction which tends to be used inclusively: see BAGD 586). Finally, it is worth noting that Paul does not use *teleios* ironically anywhere else. Cf. also Lüdemann 1989a: 106f.

But in what sense are the Philippian Christians **mature**? As the preceding verses show, the 'maturity' or 'perfection' here in view is clearly expressed in Paul's conviction that he has *not* yet attained to the prize, but is still striving to do so by the righteousness that comes from the faith of Christ. That eschatological orientation is the stance of Christian faith, and it is the mark of maturity in Christ to **adopt this stance**, lit. 'think this'. (The verb *phroneō*, lit. 'to think' is similarly used in 1.7 and especially in 2.2, 5 in relation to the 'mind of Christ'; as O'Brien notes, the use of the subjunctive rather than the imperative shows Paul being tactfully inclusive.) Chrysostom aptly comments that for Paul what characterizes perfection is not to consider oneself perfect! Christian maturity, that is to say, is to run the race rather than to consider it over (cf. K. Barth).

In a somewhat obscure turn of phrase, Paul now suggests that even if the Philippians think differently on any point, **this too God will reveal to you** (pl.). This is evidently concerned not with a fundamental departure from the Christ-like pattern (the sentence begins with **and** (*kai*), not 'but'; cf. Caird 144), but with a difference in a particular matter (*ti*, translated **in any respect**). The eirenic tone shows that he is not seriously worried about this difference of opinion, and suggests it is not indicative of Philippian opposition to him. Even if some may dissent from these principles of maturity, Paul trusts that God will grant them the wisdom and insight to discern what it means to live the pattern of a life with Christ.

Fee identifies here an expression of a wider Pauline largesse in the context of friendship, concerned in general rather than particular terms to stress a tolerance of disagreements. This is certainly possible, and might amount to an expression of open-heartedness somewhat like 2 Cor. 6.11. But if that is what Paul means, he could certainly have expressed himself less ambiguously; and in any case one wonders if this does not leave his relationship with the Philippians looking rather too anachronistically 'laid back'. (See also above, p. 34, on the problems with a formal identification of Philippians as a 'friendship letter'.)

More promising may be Silva's observation (p. 206f.), following Lightfoot, LSJ and others, that the adverb *heterōs* can in Hellenistic Greek carry more distinctly negative overtones, best rendered 'amiss' or 'badly' (cf. e.g. Epictetus *Discourses* 2.16.16; Josephus *C. Ap.* 1.26). Paul has outlined the right Christian mind-set (*phronein*) in the preceding verses, and encourages the Philippians to join him in adopting it; if in any respect their attitude is inappropriate, God will soon disclose this to them. What such an inferior attitude might consist of was hinted at in 2.1–4 and is about to be explicitly addressed in relation to the dispute involving two leaders in 4.2–3.

God will reveal to the Philippians where their thinking has gone amiss. Paul consistently uses the verb *apokaluptō* and its cognate noun *apokalupsis* to denote divine communication, whether in the foundational revelation of Christ or the gospel (e.g. Rom. 1.17f.; 1 Cor. 2.10; Gal. 1.12, 16; 3.23), in ecstatic visions or prophetic disclosures (1 Cor. 14.6, 26, 30; 2 Cor. 12.1, 7; Gal. 2.2) or in the eschaton (e.g. Rom. 8.18f.; 1 Cor. 1.7; 2 Thess. 1.7). (See further Bockmuehl 1990: 133–56.) Interpreters who regard v. 15a as an ironic allusion to the views of Gnosticizing opponents have traditionally noted the apparently parallel preoccupation with prophecies and visions at Corinth. On this reading, Paul continues his irony by assuring the Philippians that if they have a different opinion, 'this too God will "reveal" to you' (cf. e.g. Gnilka 200f.; Lührmann 1965: 42f.; Lincoln 1981: 94). However, once again the context gives no indication of irony or pointed controversy, and even in the Corinthian setting Paul arguably never debases the currency of this key theological term by using it in a derogatory sense. Guillet 1981: 609 surely hits the nail on the head in asserting that, while Paul is perfectly capable of irony when faced with distortions of the gospel, his is not the sort of temperament that would dissemble his irony.

How, then, does Paul assume this 'revelation' will take place? Since we cannot be certain either about the subject of the disagreement or about the manner of the revelation, it is of course impossible to be precise. Even commentators who do not take the 'ironic' interpretation are generally evasive on this question or avoid it altogether. Given Paul's usage elsewhere, however, the future tense must refer to a divine disclosure to be given either at the eschaton or through the Spirit's activity within the ongoing life of the community. Of these, the latter is more likely: Paul's reference concerns a specific matter in Philippi, rather than the parousia and future judgement in general. If, despite their adoption of Paul's stance, the thinking of the church has gone wrong in any matter, even this (*kai touto*) God will reveal to them. Such corrective revelation is evidently a corporate rather than an individual phenomenon, and is perhaps best understood either in terms of the congregational 'revelations' of 1 Cor. 14 or possibly in the more general terms of a conviction quietly gained by the work of the Spirit (cf. Eph. 1.17; thus e.g. O'Brien, citing M. Turner).

One might also compare the important biblical notion of God's disclosure of the thoughts of human hearts, as a mark of the eschatological age (e.g. 1 Cor. 14.25; cf. Luke 2.35; 12.2; Rom. 2.16; 1 Cor. 4.5).

On balance, then, we find underlying this passage a doctrine of both the Spirit and the Church which is remarkably hopeful and robust: Paul trusts the Spirit to bring the Church to a knowledge of the truth, and to reveal to it the areas where its thinking is 'out of step' (cf. v. 16) with the 'pattern' (v. 17) of life in Christ.

16 Minor differences of perspective are of little concern, but (*plén,* 'except that') above all Paul wants to reaffirm the exhortation of v. 15: Christians must take care to **keep in step** (*stoicheō*) with what they have already attained. The Majority Text reads, 'to keep in step with the same *rule,* to have the same mind'; and although this does not have sufficient early MSS support, it does seem to capture the meaning here in an appropriately Pauline manner (cf. Gal. 6.16). However their differences may be resolved, Paul exhorts the Philippians not to jeopardize the progress in the Christian life which they have already made, but to continue in accordance with the same stance of striving to know Christ (vv. 4–14) which both he and they (N.B. 1st person pl.) have adopted. By stressing this task as a joint and common endeavour of 'keeping in step', Paul hints at the theme of unity, which is about to feature more prominently in 4.1–3 (cf. Collange, Beare).

17 Yet once more, for good measure, Paul reiterates his appeal for the Philippians to adopt and follow this pattern of life which his own story embodies: **join together in following my example** (lit. 'be fellow imitators of me' (cf. Fee 364f. n.10); the compound word *summimétai* may be Paul's own creation, as it has not been attested elsewhere). This call to imitate Paul should not come as a surprise: just as the example of Timothy and Epaphroditus was implicitly set forth in 2.12, 29f., so Paul sees no conflict in affirming the supreme paradigm of Christ himself (2.5–11) and commending his own Christian life as a visible pattern of discipleship (similarly 4.9; cf. above on 1.12–26, also 2.17f.). Only his own apostolic example can vouchsafe for his Gentile churches an authentic and personal expression of the life of Christ.

The same theme occurs repeatedly in his letters: 'Be imitators of me, as I am of Christ' (1 Cor. 11.1; cf. 1 Cor. 4.16; 10.32–11.1; 1 Thess. 1.16; 2 Thess. 3.7, 9; also Eph. 5.1). In a similar vein, Paul quite confidently commends 'my ways in Christ Jesus, as I teach them everywhere in every church' (1 Cor. 4.17). The authoritative source of his example is of course Christ himself, as set forth in 2.5–11 (and cf. p. 122). Beyond that, however, the imitation of a teacher's example is a classic didactic theme amply attested among secular Graeco-Roman educators (Jaeger 1939–45: 1.306f., 310), and in Jewish circles especially in Philo and the rabbis: disciples must not only learn their master's teaching, but also emulate his behaviour (e.g. Philo, *Virt.* 66; *Congr.* 70; cf. Kirschner 1986). This is the essence of the relationship between Jesus and his disciples, and Paul transfers the same to his relationship with Jesus and with his own churches. Not only are they to emulate the 'mind of Christ' (2.5–11), but Paul invites them to imitate their apostle as he himself imitates Christ (1 Cor. 11.1). See further de Boer 1962; Best 1988: 59–72; Brant 1993, Hawthorne 1996: 172–4 and *passim.* (Contrast the politically deconstructionist treatment of Castelli 1991: 59–117, who reduces the theme of imitation to a Pauline exercise of power and control. Given the christological substance of 2.5–11 and 3.7–14, her account arguably reads into Paul's language about Christ-like self-humbling and service almost exactly the opposite of what is actually said.)

Elsewhere, the object of imitation can be the founding churches of Judaea (1 Thess. 2.14) or even the Pauline churches of Macedonia (2 Cor. 8.1–6; cf. 1 Thess. 1.7). Here, Paul expands the paradigm quite generally to include all **those who live according to the model you have in us**. This obviously requires discernment, as vv. 18–19 go on to show. Nevertheless, Paul unambiguously asserts a **model** or 'pattern' (*tupos*: cf. 2 Thess. 3.9; Rom. 6.17; 1 Thess. 1.7) of the Christian life which Christians are to learn from the apostles (*hēmas* (pl.), perhaps representing the apostolic team) and from others who live by it. Some of these 'others' of course may well be Philippians, as Paul's comments on Epaphroditus suggest (2.25–30); but the scope of reference is undoubtedly wider.

18 Some, however, do not live by this model, but by a different one. The deliberate contrast in verses 18–19 with another pattern of life (note the repetition of the verb *peripateō*, 'to walk') lends additional force to Paul's exhortation to adopt the Christ-centred orientation which he has spelled out. If Paul's own example is the 'type' (*tupos*, v. 17) to be followed, these people present the 'antitype', whose example is positively 'harmful'. The **enemies of the cross** are a subject about which Paul regularly warned the Philippians during his ministry with them. And it is this warning which he now feels moved to reiterate **with tears**, no doubt because he has been powerless in his imprisonment to counter repeated news of this threat.

But who are these enemies? Are they Christians? Are they localized in Philippi or found more widely? Are they the 'dogs' of 3.2, or Paul's competitors in Rome (1.15–16; cf. 2.21), or external opponents at Philippi (e.g. 1.28)? Scholarly views have varied widely, and the matter is complicated by Paul's grammatically awkward sentence in verses 18–19. (The best reading is to take 'there are many who live …' (v. 18a) together with 'their mind is set on earthly things' (v. 19b): cf. Fee 368 n.26.)

Paul employs a distinctively third-person perspective in his statement that **many live** (lit. 'walk') a different way, and that he used frequently to tell his readers about them. This suggests that these people are not directly implicated in Paul's relationship with the Philippians (contrast his language e.g. in 1 Cor. 5–7). Nevertheless, they are not merely neutral outsiders but stand in some connection with **the cross of Christ** (an elliptical phrase denoting Paul's message *about* the Cross: 1 Cor. 1.17f.; cf. Gal. 6.12). They are evidently too close to the church for Paul to adopt a detached frame of mind: they cause him **tears** and grief (lit. 'weeping'), and he identifies them as *the* **enemies of the cross**.

19 If the word 'walk' in v. 18 points in an ethical direction, verse 19 confirms the identification of these enemies to the cross in terms of *false practice*: despite the assertions of many commentators, false teaching is never explicitly mentioned. It is evidently their way of life which denies the Cross. As the extended discourse of 1 Corinthians 1.18–2.10 suggests, to be an enemy of the Cross means to trust in human wisdom and power rather than in God's redemption accomplished through the apparent weakness and folly of the crucified Messiah. It is to adopt a stance, in other words, which is precisely the opposite of the one that Paul outlined in verses 4–14.

Four further descriptions follow. First, their **end** (*telos*: 'end' or 'goal') **is destruction**. Paul's goal, though he has not yet attained it or been made perfect (*teleioō*) is to share in Christ's resurrection; but these enemies are bound for disaster. The language of perdition here is the same as that used of the Philippians' enemies in 1.28 (see above, p. 101); there as here, it functions not as a curse so much as an observation of the end of the road on which people are travelling (cf. similarly Matt. 7.13; also Num. 24.20, 24 as interpreted in the *Targ. Neof.* and *Targ. Ps.-J.*). In the present context this statement, standing as it does at the head of this list, may well be calculated for its shock value, as Bengel thought: these people, who are so close to the church and so numerous (**many**) that their identification requires careful discernment, are in fact 'walking' on a path that leads to utter ruin.

Yet we are still no closer to an identification of who they are. More light might seem to be shed on this question by Paul's second and third phrase: **their god is their belly and their glory is in their shame**. These words, however, have been subject to a wide range of contradictory interpretations. Some, including e.g. Hawthorne and Müller 186–91, Mearns 1987 and Murphy-O'Connor 1996: 229, continue to take the view, found as early as Ambrosiaster and later in Erasmus and Bengel, that the opponents must still be the Judaizing 'dogs' of 3.2. On this reading, we should see in the words **belly** (*koilia*) and **shame** (*aischuné*) allusions to a preoccupation with dietary laws and circumcised genitals. But the immediate context suggests no other connection with Jewish Christians; Paul never equates Judaizing dietary observance with idolatry; and the respective terms are used nowhere else in this allusive sense. What is more, the Jewish-Christian proselytizers of 3.2–11 seem on the face of it most unlikely to subscribe to the moral laxity condemned in the 'enemies of the cross' of 3.18–19. A closer parallel exists with the Jewish apostates who in 3 Macc. 7.11 have abandoned faithfulness to the commandments of God 'for the sake of the belly', and with 'the servants of their belly' in *Gen. Wisd.* 17.5 (cf. 14.6; 15.7; also Sir. 37.5).

Others suggest that the **shame** is that felt at the last judgement by those who find themselves rejected: so e.g. Gnilka, O'Brien, and Silva, with reference to 1.20. But a link with 1.20 is by no means self-evident: there is no hint of an eschatological point of reference, and in any case the New Testament never uses the noun *aischuné* in relation to the final judgement. The twofold use of *peripateó* ('to walk') requires a moral application, as does the theme of imitation. This moral point is also safeguarded by the apparent allusion to Hosea 4.7 (LXX), where immorality causes God to turn glory to dishonour.

We are clearly at a disadvantage, given that the Philippians evidently knew very well whom Paul had in mind (v. 18b) and therefore needed no detailed reminder. In some ways, therefore, the most honest approach might be to plead ignorance, as Fee 372f. does. Pauline usage does, however, afford a few additional hints. The word *koilia*, which literally denotes the abdomen (incl. the womb), refers to visceral appetites in Rom. 16.18, and in 1 Cor. 6.13 it is used to make a point about sexual ethics (cf. Sir. 23.6). Shamefulness (*aischuné*), similarly, can characterize all sorts of unregenerate excesses, including sexual ones (e.g. Rom. 1.27): it generally denotes the immoral practices of the pagan, pre-Christian life which believers have left behind (Rom. 6.21; Eph. 5.12; cf. 2 Cor. 4.2; Jude 13).

Most plausibly, therefore, the 'enemies of the cross' should be seen as those who, while perhaps at one time converted to Christianity, now place their pride and trust in things opposed to the cross of Christ: the worship of their appetites and shameful practices. The logical progression in this chapter, from the rejection of legalistic righteousness to a commendation of trust in Christ and then a warning against licentiousness, is in fact a familiar one in Pauline theology (*pace* Silva 209). It is the same progression which shapes the argument of Galatians (note 5.13ff.); in a short-circuited antinomian form (omitting the third stage) it comes to haunt Paul at Corinth (1 Cor. 5–6) and James in addressing a perverted Paulinism (Jas. 2). Following hard on the heels of his reference to 'perfection' (v. 15), Paul's 'pro-active' warning here is designed to preclude the sort of moral nonchalance which has repeatedly proved attractive to some of his more urbane and avant-garde interpreters, from Corinth to California.

In other words, the enemies of the cross of Christ are those who have turned full circle: having abandoned the way of the cross, they have their **mind** once again **set on earthly things** rather than on God's 'heavenly call in Christ Jesus' (v. 14). This phrase, indeed, takes us back to what for Paul is the heart of the Christian life: a fundamental change of orientation to set one's mind on knowing Christ (cf. 2.2–5; 3.15).

After all is said and done, however, we will do well to recall that in the present context Paul's interest in these enemies of the cross is general and rhetorical rather than specific and sustained. They are evidently of no acute importance to Paul, and their sole appearance in this letter serves merely to give sharper definition to the Christ-centred orientation which Paul wants to commend to his readers. It is this concern which governs his argument both before and after the parenthesis of verses 18–19.

20 In response to these 'many' whose life pattern is inimical to the cross, verses 20–21 reintroduce the familiar theme of citizenship (cf. p. 97 above on 1.27) and apply it to the heavenward disposition of the Christian way of life. Christians set their minds deliberately and explicitly on the heavenly commonwealth of Christ the Saviour – the 'prize', as verse 14 put it.

Paul's language in verses 20–21 is marked with a poetical grandeur that has led some to postulate the presence of another hymnic fragment (cf. Reumann 1984). Most scholars, however, accept that these verses are so clearly integral both to the immediate argument and to Philippians as a whole that this proposal has little to commend it. It is of course true, as various commentators have pointed out, that these verses do show a number of significant linguistic and theological connections with 2.5–11 (and e.g. with 1.27). That, however, is evidence not so much for a pre-Pauline hymn as against theories of partition (cf. Fee 378 n.16; and see more fully O'Brien 467–72).

Several ancient manuscripts and modern versions alike expect Paul's sentence to begin with an adversative 'but' (*de*) rather than his causative 'for' (*gar*). His connection and emphasis, however, are perfectly reasonable, even if a little difficult to preserve in English: the link is at once contrastive *and* explanatory. The word order makes it clear that the stress is on **our commonwealth**, as distinct from that of the 'many' whose loyalties are to their own appetites and to earthly ambitions. The use of *gar* at the same time indicates a logical connection, offering the reason both for the call to imitate Paul (vv. 15–17, preceding the parenthetical vv. 18–19) and for the fact that those who serve earthly appetites and ambitions find themselves on the road to ruin. A logically similar connection is made in 3.3, 'for *we* are the circumcision' (although as we saw there is no reason to suppose that the contrast here must be with the same group of Judaizing agitators).

Commonwealth (*politeuma*) is a term whose explosive theological and political potency in this context are hard to exaggerate (cf. Introduction, p. 4 and see on 1.27 above). It manifests a depth of pastoral insight that is the fruit of Paul's long-standing familiarity with the Philippian context, while at the same time bringing to a point the pledge of allegiance that is at the very heart of the Christian life. The meaning of the term is somewhat diffuse, and combines the primary sense of a political entity ('state') as a whole with that of the active participation of the individuals who belong to it. While its meaning is thus not adequately represented by the notion of 'citizenship', it nevertheless circumscribes a Graeco-Roman notion of the state that certainly includes the civic rights, duties and responsibilities of its citizens. At the same time, the term *politeuma* could denote either the ruling class as a sovereign body or alternatively a variety of religious, ethnic or other associations within the larger *polis*: it frequently refers, for instance, to the citizens of one city living abroad. In a related sense it was often used of the *Jewish* community, in some cases with specific reference to its internal forms of self-government (cf. Lüderitz 1994: 194–202, 221f.).

The notion of living as a community in exile while belonging to a polity in another country easily lent itself to metaphorical applications. In this respect, Philippians 1.27 and 3.20 may also reflect the idea, first attested in Philo of Alexandria, that believers in God and his law are in fact native citizens of the heavenly promised land and thus merely temporary sojourners on earth (e.g. *Conf.* 78; *Gig.* 61). The New Testament strongly echoes this idea in Hebrews 11 (cf. possibly Gal. 4.26; 1 Pet. 1.1; see further Bockmuehl 1995: 83–7). It may also be worth comparing and contrasting this notion with the pagan (and non-eschatological) sentiments expressed by the philosopher Heraclitus, Philo's senior contemporary in Alexandria, who believed that after death he would become a citizen of heaven among the gods: *Letter to Aphidamas* 5 (quoted in *HCNT*, p. 482)).

This concept of belonging to 'another commonwealth' would inevitably ring loud bells for a Christian church in a city with the Roman imperial self-consciousness of Philippi. It is clearly for this reason that Paul introduces the terminology of 3.20 and 1.27, which we do not otherwise encounter in his writings. As repeatedly in 1.12–2.18, Paul here employs everyday language familiar from public political life to underscore points of relevance for the life of the polity that is the church and the Kingdom of God. Indeed, both in meaning and effect, the theological function of the term *politeuma* here is comparable to that of *basileia* ('kingdom') elsewhere in the New Testament.

The primary point of this language here in Philippians is not of course one of *Realpolitik.* It does not concern how Christians are to exercise their civic responsibilities in relation to the secular state, even if that may be indirectly implicated in 1.27 and 2.14 (Winter 1994 unfortunately has almost nothing on the present verse); nor, indeed, is there any evidence to support the view that in this and other passages about the parousia Paul is urgently concerned about the imminent destruction of Jerusalem (so Wright 1991b: 208–9). Instead, Paul's aim here is to call the Philippians to *forget* the human status and achievements that lie behind and to shape their lives and aspirations in keeping with the heavenly counter-commonwealth of Christ to which they now belong.

***Our* commonwealth**, says Paul, is **in heaven** (*en ouranois*, a plural possibly reflecting Hebraic usage). Significantly, it is not 'in *the Church*': as history confirms only too painfully, the confusion of Church and Kingdom is to the detriment of both. Nor, indeed, is the Philippian church simply an earthly colony '*of* heaven', as Lincoln 1981: 97–101 rightly stresses. Instead, and even while resident in an earthly *politeuma* like Philippi that finds its welfare and success in the imperial might of Rome, Christians stake their hopes and loyalties in a different commonwealth. It is **from there** that they **eagerly expect a Saviour**. Although their heavenly commonwealth already **is** (*huparchei*, lit. 'exists') an already present reality governing their lives, the Christian orientation is nevertheless one of forward anticipation, as vv. 12–14 already made very clear. As elsewhere in the NT, to affirm a present stake in the Messianic kingdom does not rule out one's expectation of its future coming. The notion of the Saviour and his commonwealth coming **from** heaven (*ex hou*) may in this respect be comparable to the apocalyptic belief in a future descent to earth of the new Jerusalem (e.g. Rev. 3.12; 21.2f.; cf. Horbury 1996: 219–21, also with reference to Rom. 11.26 and Gal. 4.25f.).

The term **Saviour** (*sōtēr*) has particularly poignant overtones for the Roman imperial setting of this letter. It is true that the same verb *apekdechomai* gives expression to eager eschatological expectancy elsewhere in Paul (e.g. Rom. 8.19, 23, 25; Gal. 5.5; 1 Cor. 1.7). And a particularly close parallel to the present sentiment occurs in 1 Thess. 1.9f., where the Christian life is described as a matter of conversion from idols to serve the living God '*and to wait for his Son from heaven*'. The word **Saviour**, however, is not used in that context, as indeed outside the Pastoral Epistles it is only rarely found in the New Testament (and nowhere else in the undisputed Pauline epistles; cf. I.H. Marshall 1996b) – despite its sound theological pedigree in the LXX (e.g. Deut. 32.15; Isa. 45.15, 21; Mic. 7.7; LXX Ps. 24.5 (= 25.5); 26.9 (= 27.9)) and certain Jewish writings (e.g. *Sib.Or.* 1.73; 3.35). It was a title commonly used for Caesar in the Roman Emperor cult (see e.g. W. Foerster in *TDNT* 7:1010–12; Witherington 1994: 99–102). Although one should probably not assume that this accounts for its relative unpopularity in the NT and certain other Jewish texts (so rightly O'Brien 462 n.120, citing Cullmann), the political overtones do resonate more clearly in the present context where Jesus is unabashedly named as both **Saviour** (*sōtēr*) and **Lord** (*kurios*). Drawing on a comparison of 3.20–21 with the earlier passage of 1 Thess. 1.9f., Bormann 1995: 218 suggests here a more politically radical understanding of the parousia: while the letter to pre-Neronian Macedonia expected Jesus to 'save from the coming wrath' (1 Thess. 1.10; 5.9), the Lord and Saviour of Paul's Roman captivity will subject all the powers to himself (2.10f.; 3.21). The **Saviour** here is none other than **the Lord Jesus Christ**, the same one to whom every knee will bow and whom every tongue will acknowledge.

21 This Saviour's saving power not only **enables him to subject all things to himself**, but also to **transfigure** lowly mortal bodies into a **form like** (lit. 'conformed to') his own. Much of the language still echoes 2.5–11; in addition to the points already mentioned, it is worth noting the compound words 'transfigure' (*metaschématizô*: cf. *schéma*, 2.7) and 'conformed' (*summorphon*: cf. *morphé*, 2.6–7), as well as the juxtaposition of 'lowliness' or 'humiliation' (*tapeinôsis*: cf. *tapeinoô*, 2.8) and 'glory' (*doxa*, 2.10). Significantly, the enemies' false 'glory in their shame' (v. 19) is here contrasted with the participation in the transcendent heavenly glory of the exalted Lord.

Just as Paul urged (2.5) and exemplified (3.10) a mind-set of sharing in Christ's sufferings, so the coming of Christ will bring for his followers a vindication like his own (2.9–11; 3.11; cf. Rom. 6.5). It is the parousia, in other words, which will complete for the people of Christ their full cycle of humility and service leading to a glorious exaltation with Christ. Passages as diverse as Rom. 8.19 and Col. 3.4 similarly, speak of the parousia as the 'manifestation in glory' of the people of Christ.

The way in which that vindication is accomplished is through the resurrection. Paul's discourse follows the general lines of the argument in 1 Cor. 15.42–57: the resurrection will not be a transition to a disembodied state, but a 'change' (1 Cor. 15.52), a 'transfiguring' of the whole person. What is unusual here is the description of how that resurrection is accomplished: Christ himself (not God or the Spirit, as often elsewhere) will change **our lowly body** (lit. 'the body of our humiliation') into the same **form** as his own glorious body (lit. 'conformed to the body of his glory'; cf. 3.10 'conformed to his death'). While 1 Cor. 15.49 speaks of the 'glory' of the resurrected body and asserts that Christians at the resurrection will bear the 'image' (*eikôn*) of the resurrected Christ (cf. Harris 1983: 108ff.), it is only here that the heavenly **body** of Christ is explicitly in view and seen as definitive of the resurrection. As we suggested in relation to the 'form' of Christ in 2.6, Jewish mystical thought is particularly instructive as a conceptual background to the notion of a divine heavenly body. (See above, pp. 126–9 and cf. Bockmuehl 1997.)

Clearly, then, the parousia remains a lively expectation even in this late Pauline letter. Paul affirms that at the return of Christ the mortal bodies of believers are to be transfigured into a heavenly body like that of their exalted Lord. The power at work in that transformation is the same as that by which Christ is able to subject the universe (*ta panta*, **all things**) under his control. It serves as a confirmation of Paul's high christology that the equivalent act of subjection was in 2.9–11 ascribed to God. In Ps. 8.7, understood messianically in various NT passages (e.g. Heb. 2.6–9; cf. 1 Cor. 15.27; Eph. 1.22), it is God who subjects all things under the 'son of man'; here it is by the power of the exalted Christ himself.

E   PERSONAL APPEAL TO TWO LEADERS   (4.1-3)

Commentators differ widely over the argument of the first nine
verses of chapter 4. Some would see the discourse of chapter 3
concluded quite adequately with 3.21, while others take verse 1 to
fulfil this function and regard verse 2 as beginning the letter's
concluding particulars. Equally well, of course, it could introduce
the conclusion to the letter as a whole, thus beginning a section
comprising the whole of chapter 4, or at any rate verses 1-9. Still
others adjust their outline of these verses to the requirements of
their chosen partition theory. The variations are legion, and not
worth discussing in detail here. Suffice it to suggest that the very
diversity of scholarly opinion may indicate the arbitrariness of
attempts to impose a clear outline on the argument of Philippians
(cf. Introduction, p. 20). Here we will take the view that 4.1-3 offer
a direct application of the principles of 3.2-21 to the situation in
Philippi, both in general and in particular.

**(4.1) And so, brothers and sisters whom I love and long for, my
joy and crown, stand firm in the Lord in this way, my beloved.
(2) I appeal to Euodia and I appeal to Syntyche to agree with
each other in the Lord. (3) Yes, and I ask you, too, my loyal
companion: help these women. They fought alongside me in
the gospel, along with Clement and my other co-workers,
whose names are in the book of life.**

1 Verse 1 admirably captures the spirit of Paul's relationship
with the Philippians throughout this letter, and should in itself
suffice to caution against theories of serious problems either
within the church or in their friendship with Paul. Twice in this
short verse he goes out of his way to assure these **brothers and
sisters** (cf. 1.12; 3.1, 13, 17) of his love, and he declares his desire
to see them again. Both sentiments are commonly expressed in
ancient letters of friendship (so e.g. Stowers 1991: 109; cf. 1 Thess.
3.6; 2 Tim. 1.4), and were first affirmed in 1.8 (cf. 2.12). The
Philippians are, moreover, Paul's **joy and crown**. The same
designation is used of another Macedonian church in 1 Thess.
2.19, where it carries eschatological connotations: they will be his
cause for joy (a case of metonymy: see O'Brien) and his victor's
wreath at the coming of Christ. Here, Paul's phrase is likely to
have both present and future application: even now, the Philippians are his pride and joy, and he feels sure that they will be
his 'boast on the day of Christ' (2.16). The term 'joy' of course is a
central theme of this letter (cf. p. 59 above, and see v. 4).

Compared to this outburst of affection, Paul's appeal is relatively simple: it is that they should **stand firm** by these principles

(lit. 'thus') **in the Lord**. Similar exhortations are regularly found
in other letters (e.g. 1 Cor. 16.13; Gal. 5.1; 1 Thess. 3.8; 2 Thess.
2.15; Eph. 6.13f.), and the present verse reinforces a comparable
call to steadfastness in 1.27. Paul's sentence in this case begins
with the conjunction *hôste* (**and so**), which typically serves to
introduce the application of an argument to its specific situation
(so e.g. 2.12). Thus, given the glorious hope he has just laid before
them in 3.20–21, Paul now calls them to display a steadfast
commitment to the Christ-centred orientation which he himself
exemplifies (cf. 3.7–17).

2   Verses 2–3 focus this application more specifically; Paul takes
the unusual measure of singling out two individual leaders in the
Philippian church. As in 3.18–19, the case at issue will have been
perfectly obvious to the addressees. To later readers, however, the
situation necessarily remains somewhat obscure, but has provided plenty of speculative grist to scholarly mills.

   Euodia and **Syntyche** are two leading and presumably influential women in the Philippian church, quite possibly with
responsibilities for sensitive aspects of the church's work –
whether in administration, hospitality, or oversight of pastoral or
financial matters such as the church's allocation of moneys for
the poor. These two leaders are engaged in a feud, and are
therefore specially exhorted to adopt this same attitude and to
agree with each other. Calls to concord were earlier made in
1.27 and 2.2, but this more specific exhortation to harmony may
well be intended to ward off potentially more detrimental consequences for the church's ministry, including the possibility of a
public row or even a lawsuit (cf. 1 Cor. 6.1ff.). Paul's counsel is
compatible with conventional secular perspectives on civic disunity (Winter 1994: 100f.); here, however, it is explicitly rooted in
an appeal to Christ (**in the Lord**), whose example in 2.5–11 has
featured repeatedly throughout chapters 2 and 3. Quite apart from
any pragmatic political damage caused by their dispute, these
leaders taint and jeopardize the Christ-like example which they,
like Paul, should be setting for the church (v. 19b).

   The fact is, of course, that we know nothing more about either
of these women, about their dispute, or indeed about the **loyal
companion** who is asked to mediate between them in v. 3.
Euodia and Syntyche are most likely prominent Gentile converts
(their pagan names carry connotations of good fortune), although
a Jewish Euodia is known from a later inscription at Rome (*JIWE*
II, No. 110); KJV mistakenly assumed the male (?) name Euodias.
As we saw earlier, women appear to have enjoyed considerable
social and religious prominence at Philippi (Introduction, pp. 5,

8). In the case of these two, we have no evidence of any miscon-
duct or abuse of office, such as Polycarp had reason to lament in
the Philippian presbyter Valens two generations later (*Phil.*
11.1–4). Scholars trying to shed light on their disagreement have
sometimes suggested that the unusually named 'Lydia' (Acts
16.14, 40) might actually be an unnamed 'Lydian woman', who is
here identified as either Euodia or Syntyche; but this is unlikely
for reasons explained above (p. 17). Similarly, the suggestion that
they were in fact an independent 'missionary couple' whose
dispute was with Paul rather than with each other (so d'Angelo
1990: 76) is made impossible by Paul's appeal to them as individuals (**I appeal to Euodia and I appeal to Syntyche**) and by the
fact that his language of concord here (*to auto phronein*) is the
same as in 2.2, where it clearly meant harmony among the
Philippians themselves (note 2.3b–4).

Nor, for the same reason, is it a likely solution to suppose that
Euodia and Syntyche are the respective leaders of two opposed
factions or even 'house churches' at Philippi. The problem is
fundamentally personal, and Paul's appeal is exclusively individual and personal (contrast the language of 1 Cor. 1–4; 6.1–8;
11.18–22). There is no reason to think that the situation is
fundamentally different from that envisioned in Acts 16.40, where
the church apparently meets under one roof. In this regard
Peterlin's (1995) cumulative construal of a major problem of
disunity on the basis of two or three explicit exhortations to
harmony would seem to be a case of considerable 'overkill'.
(Somewhat ironically, this ubiquitous Philippian disunity
becomes for him an argument for epistolary unity, p. 217!) Dahl
1995 is probably nearer the mark in suggesting that the tension
between these two friends is the only blemish on Paul's otherwise
genuinely warm and joyful relationship with the Philippians
(p.14), but that this has admittedly coloured his earlier remarks
about their need for Christian concord (p. 9f.; cf. Caird 149–50).

3 Without taking sides, Paul pleads with these two women
individually as friends, and describes them in favourable terms as
long-standing co-workers and fellow fighters for the work of the
gospel. This 'fighting alongside' (*sunathleō*, a gladiatorial term
continuing the athletic imagery of 1.27; 3.12–14) **in the gospel** is
an expression of what Paul earlier called the 'partnership in the
gospel from the first day' (1.5): these are the people who shared in
the struggles of Paul's ministry at Philippi. Cf. Malinowski 1985;
Geoffrion 1993; Krentz 1993.

There is thus no suggestion that they are among the 'enemies
of the Cross' in 3.18, or that either or both of them are opposed to

Paul. Indeed, Fee 390 cites P. Marshall 1987: 341–8 in commenting on the interesting fact that while Paul occasionally names friends, his enemies tend to remain nameless. Paul's tone seems in any case to suggest that the problem was not grave and could be amicably resolved between the two women before it grew into a serious division. It is of course true that Paul's public naming of the disputing parties raises the profile of this matter considerably; he may well regard it as the most significant problem to be addressed in the otherwise flourishing Philippian church, even though it cannot be said to be his main purpose in writing to them (*pace* Winter 1994: 101; cf. p. 33 above). Nevertheless, both women are warmly described as Paul's faithful co-workers from the beginning, and there is no indication that their particular dispute surfaces anywhere else in the letter – except inasmuch as they are subsumed under his general commendations of humility and concord (e.g. 1.27; 2.2–4).

Euodia and Syntyche, then, are Paul's valued and proven co-workers in the gospel, along with a certain **Clement**, about whom we know nothing – unless, as Origen and Eusebius thought, he is the later bishop of Rome (cf. Lightfoot 168f.; Chrysostom, periodically followed by other commentators, imagined that Clement must be the husband of Euodia or Syntyche). Unlike the two women he bears a Latin name, which is also attested on a second-century list of Philippian members of the cult of Silvanus (*CIL* 3:121 'Valerius Clemens'; cf. Pilhofer 1995: 108–12, No. 163/L002, although this name is not discussed there).

As with other manifestly peripheral enigmas in New Testament interpretation, endless speculation has surrounded the identity of the **loyal companion** (*gnésie suzuge*, lit. 'true yoke-fellow'), who is asked to **help** the two women to be reconciled (*sullambanô:* its only NT use in the sense of 'assist'). Serious scholarly suggestions have included Lydia, Luke, Timothy, Epaphroditus, Silas, an otherwise unidentified leader called Syzygos, or even the congregation as a whole. In both Jewish and Greek contexts *suzugos* occasionally means 'wife' (e.g. *T. Reub.* 4.1; cf. BAGD); Clement of Alexandria, Origen and Erasmus therefore supposed that Paul is here instructing his own spouse! The latter possibility, at any rate, would appear to falter on two grounds: one, the fact that the vocative *gnésie* is masculine; and secondly, the strong likelihood, at least at the time of writing 1 Cor. 7.7; 9.5, that Paul was unmarried.

The fact is quite clearly that we do not and cannot know the answer, but that the addressees almost certainly did. On the partition hypothesis, if 4.1 constitutes the seam between two letter fragments, it could be that the name of the 'yoke-fellow' was contained in a lost section of this fragment (so e.g. Schmithals 1957: 306, who thinks it was Timothy). The reference could be an aside in Paul's dictation, addressed to someone in his presence but inadvertently and clumsily taken down by the secretary. More likely the 'yoke-fellow' is in fact someone who is or will be in Philippi, in which case there would appear to be two plausible scenarios. Syzygos could be a name or nickname; but this usage has never been attested elsewhere. Alternatively, the readers could have understood *suzugos* as an unambiguous designation of one particular leader in the church, perhaps the apostle's main representative or the leading 'bishop' (cf.1.1). (Given the usage of 1.1, it is certainly conceivable that Philippi may have had its own local terminology for the emerging forms of indigenous church leadership. See above and cf. Pilhofer 1995: 140–47.) That person could of course be Timothy or else Epaphroditus, who in 2.25 was already described as Paul's co-worker (*sunergos*) and fellow-soldier (*sustratiôtés*), and the Philippians' 'apostle' (*apostolos*) and minister (*leitourgos*). If that is really Paul's intention, however, his expression seems unusually awkward and opaque, given that both these men are with him in Rome at the time of writing.

Further possibilities include Silas, Paul's former fellow prisoner at Philippi (Acts 16.19, 25); and Luke, whose likely Philippian connections we discussed earlier (p. 13) and whom Paul explicitly values as his fellow worker (*sunergos*: Phlm. 24; cf. Col. 4.14; 2 Tim. 4.11). Philemon and Colossians, along with the so-called 'we' sections of Acts, suggest that Luke was with Paul at an early stage of his Roman imprisonment, as we saw. Now, however, there is no mention of Luke – perhaps because he has returned to Macedonia? Of all these individuals, therefore, Luke may in some ways be the most plausible. At the same time, in a church well known to Paul there must have been other co-workers whose identity is obscure to us but perfectly obvious to him and his first readers. (On the basis of Acts 16, for instance, it would be just as conceivable that Paul appeals here to his early convert Lydia, in whose house the church meets, to exercise a calming and benevolent influence.) Any identification of the **loyal companion**, therefore, must remain speculative. More than this we cannot say.

Named or unnamed, feuding or harmonious, the names of all these co-workers at Philippi are written **in the book of life**. This term (some Greek texts render it 'the book of the living') refers to the heavenly membership roll of all who belong to eternal life. Although it appears only here in Paul's letters, the idea is intimated as early as Exod. 32.32 and Ps. 69.28 and was popular in apocalyptic literature, both Jewish (e.g. Dan. 12.1; *1 Enoch* 47.3; cf. 1QM 12.3) and Christian (e.g. Rev. 3.5; 13.8; 17.8; 20.12, 15; 21.27 (N.B. *not* 22.19, *pace* Lightfoot, Fee); Hermas, *Vis.* 1.3.2; *Sim.* 2.9; *1 Clem.* 53.4; cf. Luke 10.20; Heb. 12.23). The Book of Life is to be opened on the day of judgement, and only those written in it will enter the kingdom of heaven (e.g. Dan. 12.1; Rev. 21.27).

With this specific closing appeal, Paul rounds out his section about the authentic Christian orientation in 3.1–4.3. Paul has abandoned self-reliance and the trust in human status and achievements in order to rely solely on Christ's faithfulness and to share in his self-humbling death and glorious resurrection. The apostle thus exemplifies the Christian orientation by straining forward to take hold of the heavenly prize of fellowship with Christ to which he has been called. He invites the Philippians likewise to renounce both 'religious' (3.4–6) and 'secular' (*epigeia*, 3.19) human status, ambitions and passions, adopting instead the 'Christian mind' and staking their lives on the commonwealth of heaven. To stand firm in this common purpose, however, also means for them to abandon the self-righteous indulgence of personal squabbles, which will inevitably spill over and poison the life of the church.

VII CONCLUDING EXHORTATIONS, FORMALITIES AND GREETINGS   (4.4–23)

From here on, the whole of chapter 4 is geared towards the conclusion of the letter. But just as a clear overall argument of the letter has been difficult to discern all along, it is not easy to see how the remainder of the letter is structured. Everyone agrees that 4.10–20 constitute a separate paragraph on the practical support Paul has received from the Philippians; indeed a good many commentators have argued that those verses are an independent letter of thanks for their donation, with or without 4.21–3 (for a convenient list of scholars see the tables in Bormann 1995: 110, 115; cf. Introduction, p. 21 above). Verses 4–9, however, are somewhat less obvious to categorize. They appear to recapitulate and bring to a point several of the major practical themes of the letter in a series of aphorisms about the joy, peace and freedom of the Christian life. The familiar word 'finally' (*to loipon*, 4.8; cf. 3.1), here rendered **beyond that**, introduces a parting exhortation to seek moral wisdom and emulate Paul's example, leaving verses 4–7 with a commendation of three spiritual qualities of the heart and a corresponding promise. Verses 10–20 then present Paul's cautiously worded thanks for the Philippian partnership and for their financial gift, deliberately placed just before his closing greetings.

In terms of both style and substance, then, this paragraph *as a whole* may be seen as a Pauline *peroratio* or letter conclusion (cf. Fee 398 and n. 1): a series of pointed and 'staccato' imperatives typically introduces a wish of peace, greetings, and a final grace or benediction. Paul's formal farewell is somewhat extended in this letter, both in terms of the conventional ingredients and in relation to the insertion of 'additional' material in vv. 10–20 (a variation similarly encountered in 1 Cor. 15.16–18 and Col. 4.7–9, 16–18a). What is more, in this particular case the late and seemingly cumbersome placement of thanks may well find its rhetorical justification in ancient Graeco-Roman convention, as we shall see.

A   CHRIST'S JOY AND PEACE
IN EVERY CIRCUMSTANCE   (4.4–9)

The letter's themes of unity and a Christ-like mind were recapitulated in 4.1–3. Here, Paul employs two fresh sets of crisply memorable imperatives to bring to a point the moral and spiritual message of his letter – quite possibly in deliberate contrast to the factious spirit displayed by Euodia and Syntyche. The first (vv. 4–7) encourages the readers to find the source of their peace and joy in God alone, who in Christ is 'near' and sustains them in every circumstance. The second commends a list of virtues as fuel for the shaping of a Christian imagination (v. 8) and the example of Paul as the model for Christian practice (v. 9).

(4) Rejoice in the Lord at all times. Again I will say: rejoice! (5) Let your gentleness be known to everyone. The Lord is near. (6) Do not worry about anything, but in every situation let your requests be known to God through prayer and petition with thanksgiving. (7) And so God's peace, which surpasses all understanding, will guard your hearts and thoughts in Christ Jesus. (8) Beyond that, my brothers and sisters, occupy your thoughts with whatever is true, noble, just, pure, pleasing or admirable, yes, if there is anything of moral excellence or praise. (9) And practise these things, which you learned and received and heard and saw in me. And the God of peace will be with you.

4 While the delicate diplomacy of 4.2–3 was in some sense also a 'concluding matter', Paul now returns to closing exhortations addressed to the church as a whole (cf. 4.1). As long ago as 3.1 he had introduced a preliminary conclusion by saying 'finally' (*to loipon*, cf. 4.8) and exhorting the Philippians to **rejoice** (*chairete*). Thus, it is only to be expected that this same concern should arise here. And just as in 3.1 he explicitly reinforced his prior exhortations to joy (1.25; 2.18, 28f.; cf. p. 180), so here he doubly underlines that previous encouragement as standing at the very heart of his message for them.

(The occasional suggestion that *chairete* here might mean 'farewell' rather than 'rejoice' (Beare, following E. Goodspeed; see above on 3.1, p. 177) is easily dismissed on the basis of the adverb *always* (**at all times**), similarly used in 1 Thess. 5.16. Cf. Bruce; Witherington 1994: 112. Similarly implausible is the REB's translation of this imperative in 3.1 and 4.4 as 'I wish you joy'. Joy is not an optional benefit of the Christian life.)

Paul's exhortation, here as elsewhere, is not a formality; nor is it glib and cloying advice to 'cheer up' or 'have a nice day'. On the meaning of joy see above, p. 59. That Christians find their joy 'in the Lord', rather than in their particular circumstances, is again hardly surprising after all that this letter has said. Such joy is the fruit, not of circumstances, but of the Spirit of the Lord (Gal. 5.22): it derives from what he has done for them in the past, from his presence with them now, and from hope in the promise of his coming (Rom. 12.12). It is this 'nearness' of the Lord (v. 5) which inspires joy along with prayer and thanksgiving (v. 6), a favourite Pauline triad of distinctive spiritual qualities which mark the Christian life (cf. 1.3–4; 1 Thess. 3.9–10; 5.16–18; Col. 1.9, 11–12).

Throughout the letter, the theme of joy is related to that of Paul's friendship with the Philippians, as he repeatedly shows himself concerned that they should know and share his own joy (e.g. 1.4, 18; 2.17f.; 4.10) and thus come to fullness of joy themselves (e.g. 1.25; 2.28f.; 3.1).

5 This joy in all circumstances is beyond mere show or feeling; indeed its most immediate outward expression here is **gentleness**. This is how *other people* are to experience the Christian's joy in the Lord (so with K. Barth, Bengel, Schenk, Fee *et al.*; *pace* O'Brien, who sees v. 5 as separate): the word **everyone** is literally 'to all people', and clearly refers to both Christians and outsiders. The internal spats among the Philippian leadership (4.2–3) and the apparent ill will surrounding Epaphroditus's assignment in Rome (see on 2.25–30) must naturally give way to the **gentleness** towards all human beings which arises from a joy that knows the Lord to be near.

The strange nominal adjective *epieikes* ('fairness, kindness') occurs only here in the undisputed letters; in the Pastoral Epistles it is the opposite of 'quarrelsome' (1 Tim. 3.3; Tit. 3.2: cf. *amachos*). Its meaning has been the subject of some discussion: Aristotle related it to equity or 'reasonableness', the opposite of an insistence on strict justice (*Nic. Eth.* 5.10). Its use in the New Testament is best understood in terms of the flavour it acquired in Jewish Hellenistic and early Christian literature. In particular, it is used of God as gentle and compassionate (Ps. 85.5 LXX [= 86.5]; *Ep. Arist.* 211; *1 Clem.* 29.1; cf. Wisd. 12.18; Bar. 2.27; *Ep. Arist.* 192, 207; Ign. *Phld.* 1.2; cf. the pagan parallel in Dio Chrysostom, *Or.* 80[30].19), and of the godly believer as manifesting tolerance and gentleness even under persecution (Wisd. 2.19; cf. Jas. 3.17; *1 Clem.* 21.7; 30.8). Above all, therefore, this is a quality of godliness that derives from the character of the Lord himself, as Paul also shows in his use of the cognate noun *epieikeia* in appealing to the Corinthians 'by the meekness and gentleness of Christ' (2 Cor. 10.1; cf. Matt. 11.29 and see Leivestad 1965–6). In a moving passage, the second-century *Epistle to Diognetus* affirms that God sent his Son not as a tyrant to inspire fear and terror, but rather 'in gentleness (*epieikeia*) and meekness (*prautés*) ... as a Saviour, using persuasion rather than force: for force is no attribute of God' (7.4).

In the present context, too, it is undoubtedly the gentleness of Christ who did not insist on his rights (2.6) which the Philippians are to adopt: both their joy and their gentleness are grounded in the fact that **the Lord is near**. At first sight, this compact phrase (*ho kurios engus*) seems perplexing and obscure. The syntax continues the asyndetic 'staccato' style of 4.4–5a, lacking any conjunction or other obvious grammatical link with what precedes or follows. What is more, the context sheds very little obvious light on the question of whether the connotations of the ambiguous term **near** (*engus*) are here primarily spatial ('close by'), or temporal ('about to appear'), or both. A related puzzle is whether this statement logically supports what precedes (joy and gentleness) or what follows (prayer and thanksgiving) or both.

These questions have no final and obvious answers, as a quick glance at the commentary literature will suffice to show. Nevertheless, it is safe to suggest that the rhetorical intention of this series of concluding statements is to sum up and bring to a point the main message of Paul's letter (cf. e.g. Witherington 1994: 110). In that sense, *all* of these brief phrases belong together and are meant to evoke in Philippi an appropriate response to Paul's exhortation as a whole.

The closely similar phrase 'the Lord is near' (*engus kurios*) is repeatedly encountered in the Psalms: e.g., 'the Lord is near to all who call upon him' (LXX Ps. 144.18 [= 145.18]; cf. 33.18 [= 34.18]; also 118.151 [= 119.151). Similarly, the eschatological dimension of this text may reflect Old Testament texts that speak of the coming 'day of the Lord' as 'near' (*engus*): these include Isa. 13.6; Ezek. 30.3; Joel 1.15; 3.14, but the phrase is also found at key points in the New Testament (e.g. Mark 13.29 par.; Rev. 1.3; 22.10; cf. Jas. 5.8). More particularly, many recent commentators point out the importance of the liturgical plea, *marana tha* ('come, our Lord': 1 Cor. 16.22; cf. Rev. 22.20). In view of Paul's description of the Christian life in 3.20f. as 'waiting for the Lord' (cf. 1 Thess. 1.10), his 'coming' is surely also implicit here (cf. K. Barth).

Whether one eventually opts for a primarily spatial or a primarily temporal interpretation, for the New Testament writers each one in any case implies the other: the Lord's nearness to believers is a nearness of the one who is coming to save; and vice versa, his imminent parousia assures believers that he is close at hand. This makes it theologically pointless to choose between these two interpretations (cf. O'Brien). For Christians, the nearness of the Lord who is the giver of joy inevitably anticipates the joy of heaven; Irenaeus writes on 1 Pet. 1.8, 'Our face shall see the face of God, and shall rejoice with joy unspeakable – that is to say, when it shall see its own Delight' (*Haer.* 5.7.2). In that sense Paul's affirmation that **the Lord is near**, both spatially and temporally, is the assurance that underpins the exhortations in 4.4–6 to joy and gentleness, to prayer and freedom from worry (cf. also Jas. 5.7–8).

6 Because 'the Lord is near', Christians are liberated from **worry**, in any and all circumstances (lit. 'stop worrying about anything'). In the Philippian church, potential causes for worry may have included such matters as external opposition, internal strife, and perhaps the future of Paul's own ministry to them. Not implausibly, many commentators see here an echo of Jesus' teaching in the Sermon on the Mount regarding undue anxiety about physical sustenance and the future (Matt. 6.25–34 par. Luke 12.22–32).

Instead, Christians are to bring their every concern before God **through prayer and petition with thanksgiving**. To do this **in every situation** (*en panti*) is the logical counterpart to ceasing from worry **about anything** (*méden*). Because the Lord is near, '*every need* can become the object of petition' (*CCC* §2633, with reference to this passage). Paul's language here echoes the charge to 'pray without ceasing' (1 Thess. 5.17) which he sent to another Macedonian church a decade earlier; it is also picked up in Polycarp's letter to Philippi half a century later (*Phil.* 4.3; cf. 7.2).

'Don't worry – just pray.' This may at first seem facile and flippant, not to say contradictory, advice. Biblical faith, however, sees prayer as a counsel not of despair but of confidence; not as a last resort but as the open-handed, yet passionate and persistent integration of human hopes and fears into the redemptive purposes of God in Christ. As the Sermon on the Mount similarly shows, prayer for one's daily bread (Matt. 6.11) goes happily hand in hand with a freedom from anxiety about sustenance (Matt. 6.25–34; cf. 1 Pet. 5.7). Worry can be the delayed symptom of a practical atheism that grows from persistent neglect of prayer and an addictive belief in self-sufficiency. Its remedy is prayer, thanksgiving and gentleness towards others (vv. 5–6).

The semantic differences between the three words **prayer** (*proseuché*), **petition** (*deésis*) and **thanksgiving** (*eucharistia*) should probably not be over-interpreted in the present context; some have argued that the first two are in fact synonymous. **Prayer** is the umbrella term, which includes all kinds of worship, petition and thanksgiving. Conversely, prayer is deficient and impoverished where Christians lack either the faith or the desire to give voice to both petition and gratitude. To express specific **requests** (*aitémata*) by way of **petition** is not of course an attempt to change God's mind, but rather to name before him the concrete areas in which one is asking for his name to be hallowed and his kingdom to come. **Petition** is an expression of hope, **thanksgiving** a generosity nourished by glad remembrance (and a safeguard against idolatry, Rom. 1.21; cf. Fee 409); together, this future and past dimension of **prayer** makes possible the Christian's freedom from anxiety in the present.

7 And so is a consecutive *kai* introducing the result of **prayer ... with thanksgiving**, namely **God's peace**. This peace of God here stands not merely for an absence of conflict but in the Hebraic, biblical sense for a healthy relationship enjoyed to the fullest. (In Jer. 16.5, for instance, God's peace is notably equated with his covenant love and mercy.) Peace is always the gift of God rather than humanly devised or achieved. It is only he who is the 'author of peace', as the Book of Common Prayer's Collect puts it (cf. Num. 6.26; Ps. 29.11; 46.9; Job 25.2; Isa. 9.6; Luke 2.14; John 14.27; 1 Cor. 14.33; 2 Cor. 13.11; Eph. 6.23); and Isa. 52.7 makes this strikingly clear in saying that the news of peace is the news that 'your God reigns'. At the same time, peace is not merely something external to God which he bestows, but also something which he both 'has' and 'is' in himself. Gideon's altar was called 'The Lord is peace' (*YHWH shalôm*, Judg. 6.24); rabbinic midrash took this passage to mean 'he called the Lord "Peace"' (e.g. *Lev.R.*

9.9; *Sifre Num.* 42 (on Num. 5.26); cf. the late fourth-century prayer in *b.Ber.* 55b: 'you are peace and your name is peace'). Peace, then, is God's very character: verse 9 refers appropriately to 'the God of peace' (cf. Rom. 15.33; 16.20; 1 Thess. 5.23; Heb. 13.20). The central relevance of this theme for Pauline theology is poignantly confirmed in the conviction that peace becomes a reality in the death and resurrection of Jesus Christ (Rom. 5.1; Col. 1.20; cf. Eph. 2.14 'he is our peace'), so that it most properly derives 'from God our Father and the Lord Jesus Christ' (as in 1.2 and other Pauline letter prescripts).

It is in the divine character of this peace that it **surpasses all understanding** (*nous*): in other words, it transcends not just rationality but 'all we can ask or imagine' (Eph. 3.20).

God's peace **will guard** (a definite future tense) the Philippians' **hearts and thoughts in Christ Jesus**, i.e. keep them safe in him who is the source of that peace. The verb *phroureô* can carry a broad sense of protection and safekeeping (cf. 1 Pet. 1.5; possibly Gal. 3.23?). Beyond that, however, Paul may also be deliberately alluding to its penal or military overtones ('keep in custody, garrison'), in order to ring bells with his readership at Philippi, where a military garrison was stationed to guard the *pax Romana* (cf. e.g. O'Brien 498, Fee 411 n.58, I.H. Marshall uses the evocative present-day image of a military 'peace-keeping force'). Such a military link may be confirmed by the fact that just as all **thoughts** (*noémata*) are here *guarded* in Christ, so in 2 Cor. 10.5 every thought is to be *taken captive* for him. In any case the significance of God's peace pertains not only to the Philippians' individual **hearts and thoughts**, but also to relations within and beyond the church, not least in view of the tensions addressed in 2.1–4 and 4.2–3. A slight variation on this theme is present in Col. 3.15, where the readers are exhorted to let the peace of Christ 'rule' or 'umpire' (*brabeuô*) in their hearts, since that is the peace 'to which you have been called in one body'.

One should not overlook the fact that the peace of God is here said to guard Philippian hearts and minds **in Christ Jesus**, i.e. as participating in the example of *his* mind, which has been a central and recurrent theme of this letter (see above all 2.5). The specific phrase *en Christô Iésou* is used eight times in this letter and occurs at several pivotal points of the argument (1.1, 26; 2.5; 3.3, 14; 4.7, 19, 21; see also above, p. 52 on the meaning of 'in Christ').

Before moving on, we should briefly note an interesting textual puzzle in parts of the Western MS tradition (F G a d; Marius Victorinus, Pelagius and the third-century papyrus p[16]), which preserve the variant *sômata* ('bodies') instead of *noémata* (**thoughts**; p[16] has both). Lohmeyer considered this reading to be

original, a fact which conveniently suited his case for the importance of martyrdom in Philippians; Silva, O'Brien and others also
give a measure of support to *sômata* on the grounds that an
alteration from 'thoughts' to 'bodies' is more difficult to explain
than vice versa. However, while Pauline parallels exist for both
the *kardia/sôma* (Rom. 1.24; cf. Heb. 10.22; Job 36.28 LXX) and
the *kardia/noéma* correlation (2 Cor. 3.14–15), neither is common
enough to suggest a deliberate scribal 'correction'; if anything, we
may suspect (e.g. with Fee 402 n.11) a possible intrusion of *sôma*
from the similar closing benediction about God's peace in 1
Thess. 5.23. What is more, it is not hard to imagine how a scribe,
copying from a worn or sloppy manuscript with tightly squeezed
letters, might read *N*OHMATA (*noémata*, 'thoughts') as ΣΩMATA
(*sômata*, 'bodies') – though probably not the reverse. On balance,
then, internal considerations reinforce the strong external MS
attestation of the conventional reading **hearts and thoughts**.

8 Many commentators regard verses 8–9 as a separate and
somewhat unrelated section of additional concluding exhortations, in fairly conventional Hellenistic mode, about 'virtue' or
'wisdom'. Paul's customary letter form would ordinarily lead us at
this point to expect him to wind up with concluding greetings,
and this does initially make the purpose of verses 8–9 seem
somewhat puzzling. Fee offers the unsupported suggestion that
these remarks are due to the genre of a 'letter of friendship'.
Supporters of fragmentary hypotheses have at times proposed
that these verses (especially the 'un-Pauline' sounding v. 8) are
the work of the redactor who spliced together the three different
Pauline letter fragments (one of which ends at 4.9; see above,
pp. 20ff.).

However, such far-fetched and fanciful arguments are really
unnecessary once we allow for the function of these verses in
their present context. Having just introduced the important but
unanticipated notion that the peace of God will guard their 'hearts
and thoughts' in Christ, it is entirely appropriate for Paul to
expand a little further as to the practical implications of this moral
and intellectual guardianship for Christian life in Roman Philippi.
This is true all the more in view of the fact that, unlike most of
Paul's epistles, Philippians does not contain an extended formal
section of 'hands-on' paraenesis. Thus, his renewed use of the
phrase **beyond that** (*to loipon*, often rendered 'finally') should be
seen not as beginning a separate final conclusion but as introducing implications loosely related to the promise of Christ's peace
and the preceding exhortations to an attitude of Christ-centred
joy, gentleness, prayer and thanksgiving (cf. p. 177 on 3.1). The

logical thrust of these two verses could be summed up as 'And otherwise, devote your thoughts to what is excellent and your actions to my example'.

If the form and function of verse 8 seem puzzling, its content is truly remarkable. Commentators generally point out that, aside from the clear address to fellow believers (lit. 'brothers'), there is little in this verse (or indeed in the next) which could not have been written as part of contemporary Stoic moral exhortation (cf. e.g. Pohlenz 1949; Sevenster 1961; Engberg-Pedersen 1994). That is to say, having repeatedly stressed the stark *antithesis* between the mind of Christ and the mind of the world (note esp. 1.27–30; 2.15, 21; 3.2–14, 18–21), Paul now offers a cross-cultural Christian exhortation *in the language of Philippi.*

It is particularly worth observing the contrast with the similarly structured 2.1: there, the mind of Christ was defined in terms of the specifically Christ-like virtues of love, heartfelt compassion and fellowship in the Spirit – qualities that would be alien and contrary to the moral and cultural heritage of a 'good pagan'. Christ and pagan culture are at odds in many respects, but here Paul shows that Christ nevertheless addresses pagan culture about the world in which it lives and in language it can understand. In these words, Paul uses the familiar concepts of ethics, aesthetics, and (v. 9) instruction by example with which his Gentile Christian readers had grown up, which they brought with them into their Christian catechesis, and which they continue to encounter daily among their pagan compatriots.

The implications of this approach are profound – for evangelism, for Christian teaching, and above all perhaps for an apologetic that is prepared to countenance Christian truth as *public* truth, relevant to a Christian ethic that can at least in part be formulated in openly accessible terms. The later church fathers, too, argued from this passage for a compatibility of the Christian and classical virtues (cf. Pelikan 1993: 129, 141). In his positive estimation of this rhythmically arranged list of Hellenistic virtues, therefore, Paul in effect asserts the moral sanity of Christian faith – professing 'the moral atmosphere of the Incarnation to be common sense', as G.K. Chesterton put it (*Orthodoxy*, ch. 9). Paul encourages his Gentile Christian friends to adopt and mature in all those qualities which are intrinsically good and benefit others (cf. O'Brien; Hawthorne; note also K. Barth).

Paul's message here, then, is that the 'mind of Christ' does not stand aloof from an accessible vision of beauty, truth and goodness. Still, he does not give a wholesale endorsement of popular Hellenistic morality; indeed in contrast to the Jewish Hellenistic Book of Wisdom (8.7; note also 7.22f.) there is here no mention of the classic four cardinal virtues of prudence, justice, courage and self-control. And while the qualities here enumerated do sound very Hellenistic, there is in fact no close parallel to Paul's list in contemporary Graeco-Roman literature. (Note, however, the second-century pagan writer Lucian of Samosata, who commends 'whatever is noble and godly', *Encomium Patriae* 1; cf. further *NW* §2f.) Fee (416, 419) may well be right to surmise that the additional phrase **if there is anything of moral excellence or praise** represents a deliberate qualification of the potentially ambivalent moral content of qualities like **pleasing** or **admirable**. In any case the list of virtues is contextualized for the Christian readership in the corroborating appeal to Paul's *example* in verse 9: this, too, would be a familiar notion for a Gentile readership accustomed to instruction by virtue *and* example (see p. 228 above on the theme of the imitation of Paul.)

In another respect, too, the Christian mind seems to be compatible with Hellenistic views of virtue: its acquisition is to a considerable extent a matter of practice. Aristotle said as much in a famous statement in his *Nicomachean Ethics* (2.1.1–3), and it was a view widely held among Stoics such as Seneca, Marcus Aurelius and Epictetus (note also Paul's quotation from Menander in 1 Cor. 15.33). The underlying thought here, however, is also in profound agreement with an important Jewish and biblical notion: we become like that which we desire, be it vile or virtuous (cf. Ps. 115.8; Hos. 9.10). And although scholars often point out that several of the terms in verse 8 are more typical of contemporary pagan than of New Testament discourse, it is also worth bearing in mind the observation (cf. Lohmeyer and others) that all except the word **admirable** (*euphéma*) are in fact used by Jews in the LXX. There is in any case, in both Greek and Jewish thought, a deeply ingrained conviction that both virtue and vice are engendered and nourished by dint of personal custom and habit.

With this in mind, we may now look briefly at the meaning of each of Paul's six adjectives introduced in 'synonymous parallelism' (O'Brien 499) and summarized by reference to **virtue** and all that is worthy of **praise**.

(1) First, the Philippians are to concentrate on **whatever is true**. Truth for Paul always has its focus in God (Rom. 1.18) and the gospel of Christ (Rom. 15.8; 2 Cor. 4.2; 11.10; Gal. 2.5, 14; Col. 1.5; note Eph. 1.13; 4.21). To deny the truth means to deny the Creator in favour of the lie of idolatry (Rom. 1.25; cf. 1 Thess. 1.9) and to reject a life of Christian integrity (1 Cor. 5.8; Gal. 5.7). Nevertheless, the frame (lit. 'whatever things are true') and the context

of the other terms suggest that Paul is interested here not merely in narrowly credal affirmations, but in God's truth in the broadest sense. This is not of course to postulate a 'natural revelation' which functions as an independent source of truth alongside the gospel; if anything, Paul's thinking here is compatible with second-century patristic assertions about the universal work of God's Logos (e.g. Justin *1 Apol.* 46; *2 Apol.* 10, 13; Irenaeus *Haer.* 3.16.6; 3.18.1). Similarly, the Old Testament wisdom tradition shows that while truth pertains firstly to God and his revelation (e.g. Ps. 119.142, 160), it is also to be found wherever there is wisdom (Prov. 23.23) and righteousness (Isa. 59.14; Jer. 4.2; Zech. 8.16; cf. Dan. 4.37). All truth is God's truth; conversely, God's truth in Christ describes the world as it truly is or is meant to be. (Cf. Vatican II, *Lumen Gentium* 1.) It is truth in this sense which is to occupy the readers' minds.

(2) Next, Paul commends what is **noble** (*semnos*), a word which in Hellenistic Greek often carries an aura of the sublime, majestic or sacred. Bruce 147 rightly cites Aristotle's definition of it as expressing 'a mild and seemly gravity' (*Rhet.* 2.17.4), and the mean between obsequiousness and stubbornness (*Eudem. Eth.* 2.34). Here, as in the Pastoral Epistles (1 Tim. 3.8, 11; Tit. 2.2) and in LXX Prov. 8.6, it probably signifies a personal moral quality of that which is dignified, upright and worthy of honour – as distinct from all that is vulgar or profane. Similar usage occurs in other ancient Jewish (e.g. *Sib.Or.* 5.262; Philo, *Sacr.* 49; *Decal.* 136; *Ep. Arist.* 31) and early Christian literature (e.g. *1 Clem.* 1.3; 47.5; Hermas *Vis.* 3.8.7; *Mand.* 12.1.1).

(3) Next, Paul urges reflection on whatever is **just** (*dikaios*). This word tends elsewhere (e.g. in Romans) to carry the theological meaning of 'righteous' before God, who alone is *dikaios* in himself and able to make people righteous by faith. But it can also mean 'just' or 'right' in the sense denoted earlier in this letter in 1.7. The meaning here should be understood broadly.

(4) The word **pure** (*hagnos*) relates in the LXX both to ritual purity and to personal integrity (e.g. Ps. 11.7 (= 12.6); Prov. 20.9); in Paul and the NT it is used in the transferred sense of moral purity and uprightness (2 Cor. 7.11; 1 Tim. 5.22; 1 John 3.3; Jas. 3.17; 1 Pet. 3.20), sometimes specifically with a view to sexual chastity (e.g. 2 Cor. 11.2; Tit. 2.5). Purity of thought and deed is similarly commended in Polycarp's letter to Philippi (Pol. *Phil.* 3.5) and Clement's to Corinth (*1 Clem.* 1.3; 21.8; 29.1; 48.1).

(5) The term *prosphilés*, here translated **pleasing**, occurs

nowhere else in the NT. Nor, for that matter, is it found in contemporary Hellenistic lists of virtues (so e.g. Wibbing 1959: 101, cited by O'Brien 505 n.28 *et al.*). Its meaning varies from 'lovely' to 'pleasing' and 'agreeable' (cf. similarly the LXX usage: Esth. 5.1[b], Sir. 4.7; 20.13; also Josephus *Ant.* 1.258). Of all the words in Paul's list, this one gives the clearest indication that the range of qualities that should shape a Gentile Christian mind includes a dimension not just of moral but of *aesthetic* truth as well. It extends to all that is beautiful in creation and in human lives.

(6) The last of Paul's six adjectives commends what is **admirable**, using a Greek word of various meanings (*euphémos*) that is found nowhere else in the NT or the LXX (see, however, Symmachus Ps. 62.6(= 63.5); Josephus *C.Ap.* 2.248). Many translations and commentators assume that its meaning is something like 'attractive', 'of good repute' or 'well spoken of' (cf. Paul's use of the corresponding noun *euphémia* in 2 Cor. 6.8). On the other hand, its meaning in classical texts (beginning with Aeschylus) and in the Jewish passages cited must be understood in the active sense of 'well-sounding', 'of fair speech', and in that sense 'winsome' and 'attractive'. In effect the meaning is not far from that of *prosphilés*, though perhaps its connotations are those of winsome speech rather than appearance.

Paul's six parallel adjectives are now reinforced with a comprehensive exhortation using the two nouns **moral excellence** and **praise**, thus recapitulating and focusing the significance of the preceding list. For all who adopt the 'mind of Christ', their thoughts are to be shaped by reflecting on whatever is intrinsically virtuous and worthy of praise. The Christian life in this respect is a pursuit of excellence. **Moral excellence** (*areté*, often rendered 'virtue' but originally meaning 'valour') had come to be used in Hellenistic philosophy to denote the highest moral quality inherent in the good person. It is a term not found elsewhere in Paul's moral instruction; the NT otherwise uses it only in 1 Pet. 2.9 (possibly influenced by Isa. 42.12; 43.21); 2 Pet. 1.3, 5 (in the Hellenistic sense). Even the LXX uses it in the sense of moral 'virtue' only in works composed in Greek (e.g. Wisd. 4.1; 5.13; 8.7; 4 Macc. 1.2, 8, 10 and *passim*; contrast e.g. Hab. 3.3; Zech 6.13). In a more developed sense that also became important for early Christianity, Philo of Alexandria regards virtue as the seed and goal of a life in keeping with the nature of God – leading him to include faith and prayer in the cardinal virtues (see the discussion in Daubercies 1995; cf. Wolfson 1947: 2.200–78). Paul's use of the word **praise** (*epainos*) usually denotes the praise given to human beings, and (despite 1.11) seems to do so here – even if in view of v. 9 it remains possible that he has in mind the sort of righteous behaviour that elicits *God's* praise.

In working out the practicalities of a Christian mind for daily life at Roman Philippi, Paul encourages the Philippians to think in terms of the highest standards of culture and morality known to their society. As the letter has shown (and will go on to show in v. 9), to be a Christian at Philippi obviously means more than that, as indeed the self-humbling of Christ counters Jewish and Graeco-Roman assumptions about status. But it is also true that the cultural face of Christianity requires *nothing less* than such excellence, if the Philippians are indeed visibly to 'shine as lights' in the midst of a crooked and perverse generation (2.15).

9 Having said all that, it is significant that Paul's exhortation does not conclude here. Instead, the 'common sense' and general virtues of verse 8 are given definition by an appeal to this letter's specifically Christian framework of imitation. There is no implied contrast of v. 8 with v. 9 (*pace* Schenk). Instead (and *pace* Fee 414 n.5), the change in Greek pronouns from the indefinite *hosa* ('which things of whatever kind') in v. 8 to the definite *ha* ('which particular things') of v. 9 indicates a more particular resumption of the former in the latter. Sentences beginning with *ha kai* often introduce a further and specific elaboration of the preceding subject at hand (cf. similarly 1 Cor. 2.13; Gal. 2.10; 1 Pet. 3.21; Acts 11.30; 26.10; 2 Macc. 4.33; 3 Macc. 3.1).

While the invitation to imitate one's teacher or rabbi was of course standard Graeco-Roman as well as Jewish didactic proce-dure, in Paul's case that invitation derives both its authority and its limitations from his own faithfulness to the prior example of Christ, who is himself the prototype and measure of all Christian discipleship (2.5ff. and *passim*). Paul's own ministry is merely the apostolic illustration and exemplification of that mind of Christ: it 'makes the truth visible' (cf. 2 Cor. 4.2). This is a motif that is central to Paul's cordial relationship with the church at Philippi, but which also frequently surfaces in other letters. See further p. 228 above on 3.17; the fact that the theme of imitation recurs as an integrating focus in every major section of Philippians would appear to cast further doubt on the need for hypotheses of partition. Verse 9 not only lends Christian substance to the exhortations of verse 8; its greater purpose, as Fee 420 n.33 rightly observes, is that it 'summarizes much of the letter'.

Whereas verse 8 contained a general commendation of pat-terns of *thought* (*tauta logizesthe*, lit. 'these things continue to consider'), Paul's concluding exhortation here in verse 9 enumerates the specific ways in which he has served the Philippians as an example of Christian *action* (*tauta prassete*, lit. 'these things continue to do').

Two pairs of related verbs describe ways in which the Philippians have had access to Paul's example: in what they **learned and received** from him, and in what they **heard and saw** in him. The former two terms (*manthanô* and *paralambanô*), although not juxtaposed in this form elsewhere, repeatedly serve Paul as technical terms for the reception and appropriation of Christian catechetical instruction (e.g. Rom. 16.17; 1 Cor. 11.23; 15.1–3; Gal. 1.9; Col. 1.7; cf. Eph. 4.20), as Bruce 147 and others rightly note. Such terminology of formal 'transmission' and 'reception' of tradition resembles a similar pattern in rabbinic practice (e.g. *m.Abot* 1.1; cf. Stemberger 1996: 4, 37–44). With Lightfoot, and others, therefore, it is best to see the first two terms as denoting the ethical substance of Paul's catechesis and the last two terms as his practical conduct embodying that teaching among the Philippians. Their (past) 'seeing' and (present) 'hearing' of Paul's ministry served to underpin a similar appeal to his apostolic example in 1.30; here as there, 'hearing' could include accounts received during his absence.

A final benediction wishes the Philippians the presence of **the God of peace**, a phrase which recurs repeatedly in Pauline letter conclusions (Rom. 15.33; 16.20; 2 Cor. 13.11; 1 Thess. 5.23; cf. Heb. 13.20). See also p. 247 above on 4.7. This promised divine peace will result (N.B. future tense; consecutive **and**) from the kind of Christian life which the Philippians have learned in the apostle's teaching and observed in his example. That the promise is one of peace is particularly à propos in view of 2.1–4 and 4.2–3. (Cf. the assurance of *T. Dan* 5.2, 'you will be at peace, since you will have with you the God of peace, and contention will have no hold over you.')

B CONTENTMENT, GENEROSITY AND PARTNERSHIP IN THE GOSPEL   (4.10–20)

This might be thought an appropriate moment to add final greetings and conclude, perhaps with 4.21–3. Like a Beethoven symphony, however, Paul's finale here has yet one more thing to say. And what is more, this seemingly routine last paragraph of the letter turns out to be singularly revealing for an understanding of Paul's friendship with the Philippians, and thus for the relational background and presuppositions of the letter as a whole. Here at long last, Paul turns to the subject that modern readers have been awaiting since the beginning of the letter: he finally offers the first explicit acknowledgement of the financial gift which the Philippians have sent to him through Epaphroditus (cf. 2.25; 4.14f. with 1.5).

A number of difficulties beset our understanding of the nature and purpose of this passage. Paul leaves his thanks till the very end of the letter, where they seem to appear at a structurally awkward and inappropriate place. And yet, paradoxically, throughout his discourse in 4.10–20 his tone is remarkably studied and restrained, rather than marked by enthusiastic gratitude; in fact he never quite seems to get round to saying 'thank you'. Both individually and together, these factors have given rise to a host of hypotheses about the rationale behind these verses. Some have found the placement of 4.10–20 so awkward as to assume that they must constitute (part of) a separate letter; others suspect that Paul may intend a measure of reproof for the Philippians' reaction to an earlier note of thanks. Then again, his restrained tone has been attributed to the long delay of their gift (v. 10), which in turn was caused by the fact that Paul's arrest had caused them to suspend their supposedly 'contractual' obligations to support his Gentile mission. Others still find in Paul's lukewarm vote of thanks a sense of embarrassment because the acceptance of a financial gift goes against all his stated principles (v. 15; cf. 1 Cor. 9.15–18; 2 Thess. 3.7–10), perhaps especially if on this occasion he had in fact requested the money (so Collange 149). Commentators of all persuasions agree that 4.10–20 are of considerable significance for Paul's relationship with the Philippians; some (e.g. Bormann 1995: 136–60; cf. Capper 1993) even argue that they provide the essential key to the Philippian correspondence as a whole, be it one letter or three.

With regard to the question of literary integrity, we need not here retrace our steps over the ground covered earlier (pp. 20ff.). For present purposes, all that is needed is a credible account of Paul's rationale in placing this paragraph where he does.

Such an account has indeed emerged from recent scholarship on Graeco-Roman social and rhetorical conventions. As several studies have shown (e.g. Bormann 1995; Witherington 1994; cf. also Peterman 1991, 1997: 73–83), an expression of effusive thanks for this benefaction would have placed Paul in the embarrassing position of having to acknowledge either a dependency on the patronage of the Philippian church, or else an obligation to reciprocate.

Paul's general concern over the issue of financial support is thus characterized by two factors: by a desire not to be a burden (2 Cor. 11.9 and *passim*) or to erect obstacles to evangelism (1 Cor. 9.13); and by his own painful awareness, in dealings with

Thessalonica and Corinth, of how easily a relationship of financial dependency might be misconstrued so as to jeopardize the authority of his ministry (cf. Bruce, O'Brien). Throughout his letters, Paul manifests a steadfast concern to refuse either payment or monetary gifts (1 Thess. 2.9; 2 Thess. 3.8; 1 Cor. 9.6ff.; 2 Cor. 12.13–16). It was only in the Philippian situation that Paul entered into a close partnership of support in which the terms were seemingly well enough understood (Phil. 4.15; 2 Cor. 11.9) – yet even here he feels a need to qualify his statement of thanks in several ways to avoid misunderstanding. *Why* Paul should nevertheless have entered such a financial partnership with Philippi in the first place, despite his principles in the matter, and why only with Philippi, is of course impossible to answer; 'that he did so, is what we learn from this passage, and nothing more' (Fee 447).

Four points may usefully be made about the nature and purpose of Paul's restrained thanks in this particular case of 4.10–20.

(1) These verses indicate Paul's desire not to compromise or complicate his warm and natural relationship with the Philippians. Interestingly, a similar unspoken subtlety of etiquette characterized some Graeco-Roman friendships: Peterman 1991 cites papyrus evidence to suggest that friends could sometimes dispense with a verbal expression of thanks on the grounds that it introduced a formality inappropriate to the cordial basis of the relationship. An expression of thanks could in certain cases be taken to formalize an obligation to reciprocity which, in a friendship, it would be odious to assert or quantify (cf. similarly Fee 446, but note Bormann's caution in 1995: 137 n.44). Certainly Aristotle, Seneca and other Hellenistic moral philosophers were at pains to distinguish friendships for noble ends from relationships that were merely 'useful' (cf. P. Marshall 1987: 24–32; Fee 427 n.14). Here, however, Paul's language is remarkable not only for its rather understated thanks (4.14), but also for elements of vacillation (4.10–13; cf. above).

(2) From the Philippian point of view, too, Paul's comments can be seen to underscore that this is not a relationship of personal convenience or mercantile 'usefulness' ('not that I speak of my own need', v. 11). Instead, here is a partnership of a kind familiar to the Philippians, which devotes resources to a public cause – in this case, the advance of the gospel. Seen in this light, the implications of this transaction are in any case no longer primarily a matter of human obligation but of what is pleasing to God (v. 18;

cf. also K. Barth). Contrary to the impression given in a number of recent treatments, the present passage is not about 'finances at Philippi' as defining the nature of Paul's relationship with the Philippians, but about a uniquely comprehensive partnership for the gospel which also expresses itself in material support (so rightly Balz 1996: 506; Hainz 1994; Peterman 1997; see on 1.5 above and 4.14, 17 below).

(3) At the same time, Paul's own perspective in these verses remains compatible with his usual principled reluctance, clearly recognizable in other letters, to establish and formalize relationships of financial dependence or reciprocal parity. The note of ambivalence in accepting the gift is thus due not to the Philippians' supposedly divided loyalty towards Paul, for which there is little evidence (*pace* Peterlin 1995: 216), but rather to his general qualms about receiving financial support. See also Best 1988: 99–104.

(4) Rhetorically, the effect of placing these verses at the end of the letter is to indicate that the gift from the Philippians is not the main purpose of Paul's writing, but secondary in importance to their own concord and adoption of the mind of Christ. At the same time, to make this matter the very last subject of his closing *peroratio* does allow Paul to leave his readers with a lingering expression of both his gratitude for their gift and his commendation of their public-spirited service of the gospel (cf. Fee 423). What is more, the note of gratitude to God (4.10) and of benediction for the Philippians (4.19–20) provides a fitting *inclusio* to bracket this section together with the opening paragraph (1.3–11) which introduced the letter's major themes.

The links of 4.10–20 with the preceding arguments provide additional evidence for the letter's integrity. These include above all Paul's reference to his 'joy in the Lord' (4.10: cf. 3.1; 4.4), his stress on the Philippians' partnership in the gospel (4.14: cf. 1.7), and his reference to 'the beginning of the gospel' (4.15: cf. 1.5). See further pp. 34ff. above on the social conventions implied in Paul's relationship with Philippi.

(10) I greatly rejoiced in the Lord that now at last your care for me has blossomed afresh; you did of course care about me, but had no opportunity to express this. (11) Not that I speak of my own need: for I have learned to be content in whatever circumstances I am. (12) I know how to live with humiliation as much as with abundance: in every circumstance I have learned both to eat my fill and to be hungry, to have more

**than enough and to go without. (13) In him who empowers me
I have the strength to do everything.**

**(14) Nevertheless, it was good of you to share in my afflic-
tion. (15) You know of course, Philippians, how in the early
days of the gospel, when I set out from Macedonia, no church
except you entered into a financial partnership with me; (16)
indeed, even to Thessalonica you sent support more than once
to supply my needs. (17) I am of course keen not so much on
your gift as on the profit that accrues to your account. (18) I
have received full payment, and am abundantly supplied.
With your gift through Epaphroditus I am fully provided for; it
is a fragrant offering, an acceptable sacrifice well-pleasing to
God.**

**(19) And my God will fully provide for all of *your* needs, too,
according to his riches in glory in Christ Jesus. (20) To our
God and Father be the glory for ever and ever, Amen.**

10   Paul begins the paragraph with an expression of joy over
their gift – but then does not indicate the true cause of that joy
until after an extensive parenthesis to guard against various
misunderstandings (vv. 10b–17). The aorist *echarén* (**I rejoiced**),
although somewhat disputed among commentators, probably
relates to the time when Epaphroditus arrived with the Philippian
gift. Paul's rejoicing over the Philippians has of course been a
repeated theme in this letter (1.4; 2.2; 4.1); and the fact that his joy
was 'in the Lord' is fully in keeping with the exhortations of 3.1
and 4.4 (cf. also p. 59 above). As Bengel rightly noted, the
Hellenistic terminology of verses 8 and 11 should not blind us to
the fact that no Stoic would have indulged in exuberant joy of this
kind; Paul, however, **greatly rejoiced**.

The occasion of Paul's joy was the Philippian gift, which he
saw as a renewed expression of their concern for him (lit., 'you
have blossomed again with regard to thinking of me'). This rich
botanical image of a newly blossoming plant is used in similarly
metaphorical contexts elsewhere, either intransitively (e.g. LXX
Ps. 27.7(=28.7); Sir. 46.12; 49.10) or transitively in the sense of
'cause to blossom' (Sir. 1.18; 11.22). Though there has been a good
deal of debate about the precise meaning of this rare verb
anathallô here, in practice the difference in meaning is fairly
slight (cf. O'Brien).

The expression *phronein huper*, here translated **care for**,
provides a powerful *inclusio* (i.e. bracket) with 1.7, where Paul
used it to speak of his own care for the Philippians; it also echoes
repeated exhortations to adopt a unity of 'mind' in Christ (2.2, 5;
3.15, 19; 4.2). Its occurrence here underlines that the Philippian

gift to Paul was in keeping both with the mutuality of their partnership and with the attitude of concord and Christ-like service which the letter extols.

More problematical is the adverbial phrase **now at last** (*édé pote*), which makes the apostle's tone sound potentially churlish and condescending, implying not gratitude but rebuke for the long delay (so e.g. Capper 1993: 207 and *passim*). However, most commentators rightly recognize that Paul himself counteracts any potential ambiguity in the second half of verse 10: he knows that the delay has been for lack of opportunity, and not for want of trying. The phrase is best understood in a neutral sense connected with the verb 'blossom afresh', i.e. to denote the revival of an activity that had lapsed or been suspended (cf. *2 Clem.* 13.1).

Verse 10b, then, opens a series of qualifying, almost apologetic remarks designed to guard against possible misinterpretation. First, Paul certainly does not wish to suggest that the extended delay in the Philippians' financial support has been due to a lapse of their **care** for him. Instead, they had lacked **opportunity** to express this (*akaireó*, unique in the NT: lit. 'you were without occasion'). This was probably due to circumstances, which might include their poverty (2 Cor. 8.1–2), the distance between them and perhaps the circumstances of Paul's detention, first in Caesarea and then in Rome. In any case the imperfect tense of both Greek verbs in this clause indicates both ongoing concern and ongoing inability to express it. (A complex discussion surrounds the relative construction *eph' hô kai*, here idiomatically translated, which picks up and confirms the predicate of the preceding clause (lit. perhaps 'for whom indeed' or 'for which indeed'). Cf. O'Brien 518 n.25, Fee, Fitzmyer 1993: 331 and see on 3.12 above.)

11 Verses 11–13 go on to dispel a second potential misunderstanding. It is not the money itself in which Paul is primarily interested; his own **need** (*husterésis*, 'lack') does not concern him. This is neither supercilious ingratitude nor indeed polite embarrassment (*pace* Beare, Bruce). Paul does not deny his lack of resources; indeed in 2.25 he was not embarrassed to admit to his readers that Epaphroditus had been 'your minister to my need (*chreia*)'. No, his joy over their gift was quite apart from the fact that it supplied his need, as verses 17–18 clearly show.

As for Paul himself, his joy in the Lord does not depend on his 'needs' being met: he has **learned** (*emathon*, a 'constative aorist' used of completed experiences) to be **content** (*autarkés*) in all his circumstances. This Greek word for contentment (cf. the noun *autarkeia*) is used to describe the classic Stoic and Cynic ideal of independent self-sufficiency and serene contentment with one's circumstances, whatever they might be (cf. Sevenster 1961: 113f. and *passim* on Seneca). At the same time, however, the term had in common parlance adopted a broader range of meaning; it frequently denoted contentment in a non-technical sense, which also accounts for its use in Jewish sources such as Philo and Josephus (see also Malherbe 1996, who connects it with friendship as based not on needs but on virtue). In the wider context of this letter it is at any rate clear that Paul intends not Stoic self-sufficiency based on one's own resources but a Christian 'God-sufficiency' supplied by Christ (v. 13, 19; 1.19; 2 Cor. 3.5; 12.9; cf. Bruce, O'Brien; also *HCNT* 482–3 with reference to Vettius Valens, *Anthologies* 5.9.2). Given the colonial Roman address on this letter, Paul's play on Stoic language and the implied view of money as an *adiaphoron* (a matter of indifference) are likely to be deliberate; nevertheless, no reader of Philippians could fail to be struck by the powerfully Christ-centred redefinition of this 'contentment'. Cf. further Jaquette 1995: 100–108.

12   To show that the preceding claim of contentment is no empty phrase, Paul substantiates it in two further clauses which elaborate the range of his experiences. The first of these is a syntactically balanced couplet, which could be literally translated, 'I know both being humbled; and I know having abundance.' This is another indication that a straightforward Stoic reading does not wholly capture Paul's sentiment: while Stoics might cope serenely with being in need, none would relish **humiliation**, which was usually regarded as a despicable state. For Paul, however, to be humbled (*tapeinousthai*) means to share in the humility of his Lord (cf. 2.8), while **abundance** is to share in the glorious riches of God in Christ (4.19). As a result, Paul has learned contentment regardless of outward circumstances (lit., 'in everything and in all things'). The verb translated **learned** (pass. *mueō*) originally meant to be inducted into the secret rites of a Hellenistic mystery cult (so also 3 Macc. 2.30); but like other mystery terminology it had come to adopt a transferred and more general meaning, not least in mystical and philosophical discourse (e.g. Philo, *Cher.* 49; *Sacr.* 62; Josephus *C. Ap.* 2.267). Initiation in the metaphorical sense may still be intended, in which case Paul's point is that Christian contentment remains unintelligible to those outside and can only be 'learned' from the God of peace (4.7, 9). Contentment is indeed a quiet secret known and cherished only by the few.

Elaborating further, Paul indicates that his contentment extends to circumstances both of hunger and of eating his fill; he has learned to cope with having either more than enough or too little. These somewhat bland-sounding expressions nevertheless echo the strikingly vivid catalogues of hardships which Paul repeatedly includes in his Corinthian correspondence (1 Cor. 4.11–13; 2 Cor. 4.8–12; 6.4–5; 11.23–9). Paul's missionary experiences did indeed include a good deal of material deprivation and misery; we know less about his times of abundance.

13 Paul closes his parenthetical remarks of verses 11–13 with a statement that has had a wide-ranging influence on later Christian history, in which it has often been cited out of context. Here is not a general affirmation that 'I can do anything'. In this context, **I have the strength to do everything** refers in the first instance to the apostle's needs, to God-given contentment in both want and plenty. The power to cope with all circumstances resides in his union with Christ (note 3.10), rather than in Paul himself. (That it is indeed *Christ* who strengthens him was made explicit in an early scribal insertion that came to form part of the Majority Text – and hence appears in translations like the KJV.) The assurance of God's power strengthening Paul and working within him is a recurrent theme of his ministry (cf. 2 Cor. 12.9f.; Col. 1.28; 1 Tim. 1.12; 2 Tim. 4.17).

14 Returning now to his earlier train of thought in verse 10, Paul counteracts yet another misunderstanding: he is by no means ungrateful or critical of the Philippians' generosity, and his remarks about contentment in verses 11–13 intend in no way to suggest that their gift was unnecessary. In this verse Paul comes closest to saying 'thank you'. Bruce 154 rightly points out that just as the aorist *kalôs epoiésate* (lit. 'you did well') means **it was good of you** in the sense of 'thank you' (cf. Acts 10.33), so the future *kalôs poiéseis* can mean 'it would be good of you' or 'please' (e.g. 3 John 6; cf. BDF §414.5). The Philippians did well to express their partnership in the gospel (*sunkoinôneô*, **share**: cf. *koinônia*, 1.5) by their active concern for Paul's hardship: making common cause for the advance of the gospel includes supporting the apostle engaged on its behalf, not least when he is suffering external **affliction** (*thlipsis*) in his imprisonment. (An exclusively eschatological meaning of the word *thlipsis* is unlikely in view of 1.7, 17 and the evident temporal reference here, *pace* Melick.) That his affliction is in fact **shared** by them as well was intimated earlier in 1.7, 29f.; it is for Paul also an appropriate expression of their common bond in the body of Christ (see Rom. 12.13; 1 Cor. 12.26; Heb. 10.33).

15 What is more, this partnership in fact goes back a very long way, as both parties know well. Paul addresses the readers by name, which elsewhere he does only in 2 Cor. 6.11 and Gal. 3.1. Here, however, he deliberately chooses (or coins? so Pilhofer 1995: 117) an artificial loan word to designate the *Roman* pedigree of the **Philippians** (*Philippésioi*, modelled on the Latin *Philippenses*).

Paul recalls how the Philippians were the only ones to support his work financially **in the early days of the gospel** (so rightly NRSV, similarly NIV; lit. 'at the beginning of the gospel', i.e., most plausibly, the arrival of Paul's mission at Philippi: cf. 1.5 and O'Brien 531f.; Lüdemann 1984: 106). Paul's assertion as a whole is reminiscent of what he said in 1.5 about their partnership 'since the first day'. Here the emphasis is on **financial partnership** (lit. 'a matter of giving and receiving', *logos doseôs kai lémpseôs*), a Hellenistic commercial term used of the accounting of payments and receipts. Even Jewish-Hellenistic writers could happily use such common financial terminology either literally (e.g. Sir. 42.7) or metaphorically of a socially reciprocal relationship (e.g. Sir. 41.21). Similar accounting terminology is found in vv. 17 and 18 (and of course previously in 3.7, 8).

It has sometimes been thought that Paul's use of such commercial language in this passage is somewhat 'tongue-in-cheek', as though to highlight the undoubted priority of theological concerns in Philippians: 'Of course you and I know very well that what *really* matters is true accounting of profit before God, whose riches exceed all that we can imagine' (note the metaphorical use of 'wealth' in v. 19, and cf. Matt. 6.19–20). This is clearly a valid point. At the same time, however, recent scholarship has also shed interesting light on this passage from the various Graeco-Roman social conventions of voluntary cultic associations, of friendship and of patronage. For all of these, the 'giving and receiving' of material benefits were a matter of considerable importance, albeit in different ways (cf. e.g. Pilhofer 1995: 147–52; Peterman 1997: 51–89 and *passim*; P. Marshall 1987: 157–64). In particular, it was generally held that full mutuality in friendships and other equal relationships was essential if an outstanding debt of obligation was not to degenerate into discord or dependency. (Cf. also Fee 443 n.21 on Hermas *Mand.* 5.2.2.)

This is not of course to suggest that Paul is particularly troubled by the precise social protocol of his relationship with the Philippians, or indeed by whether it reflected secular ideals of friendship or of patronage. As we have seen (pp. 34–8 above), this partnership reflects elements of both social forms, but without being easily identifiable under the accepted societal definitions of either. Instead, the undoubted aspects of equality and mutuality in Paul's partnership with the Philippians are underwritten by their common participation in a new identity that is constructed in Christ rather than in social or ethnic status. As the whole letter has been at pains to show, both for Paul (3.2–14) and for the Philippians (1.27; 2.15; 3.20 and *passim*) their citizenship of heaven creates new bonds in Christ and relativizes the norms and expectations of secular society.

Here, the particular point of reference is that the Philippians alone sent Paul money after his departure from Macedonia. This fact is similarly attested in 2 Cor. 11.8–9, although Paul speaks there of receiving support from a plurality of 'other churches' in Macedonia. (In view of Phil. 4.16 and 1 Thess. 2.9, however, it could be that the plural in 2 Cor. severally denotes the Christian *households* of Philippi (cf. Acts 16.15, 31), in analogy to those of Corinth (Acts 18.8; 1 Cor. 1.16; 16.15) and elsewhere (1 Cor. 16.19; Rom. 16.5; Col. 4.15). Cf. Fee 442 n.17, who suggests 'other believers'; *pace* Reumann 1993a: 439f.)

Initially more troublesome is the logic and meaning of Paul's reference to leaving Macedonia, which appears to clash with what follows.

16 Paul immediately goes on to speak of Philippian support while he was in **Thessalonica**, another Macedonian city. What might account for this strangely incongruous sequence of thoughts? Given Paul's close and long-standing association with Philippi, we can safely rule out the thought that he may be confused about the geographical facts. More likely is the suggestion that v. 15 shows Paul remembering his early Macedonian mission as 'the beginning of the gospel' – that is, perhaps, of his gospel specifically 'for the Gentiles', as agreed in Jerusalem shortly before (Gal. 2.9; cf. p. 1 above and Lüdemann 1984: 106). The meaning of the puzzling reference in v. 15b should then be as in our translation: **when I *set out* from Macedonia**, beginning of course in Philippi, Thessalonica and Beroea. (For a similar use of *exerchomai* with the preposition *apo* to mean a 'going forth' specifically inclusive of the point of origin (i.e. 'beginning in' rather than 'away from'), cf. e.g. Matt. 15.22; 24.27; 1 Cor. 14.36; and see BAGD.)

Our present verse begins with **indeed** (Gk. *hoti*, lit. 'for, since'), which here should be seen to underline the Philippian generosity: even at the very outset of Paul's Gentile mission from Macedonia, they had already become his new 'home base' and begun to contribute to his needs in Thessalonica. The phrase **more than once** (lit. 'both once and twice') is most naturally read as relating to support sent to Thessalonica, rather than further afield (cf. e.g. Fee 445 n.26, *pace* R.P. Martin, Bruce *et al.*).

17 One final qualification is now added to guard against yet another misunderstanding. Paul's point here is similar to that of verse 11, in both form and substance. Both verses begin with the emphatic negative *ouch' hoti*, 'I do not mean to say that' (lit. 'not that'); and in both Paul affirms that he is not primarily interested in money. He wants to counteract the idea that he either solicited their gift or is asking for more (*pace* Collange, Capper 1993). (The word *doma* denotes a **gift**, e.g. between friends, rather than a payment: see Fee 447 n.34.) Instead, his real desire is not his own gain but theirs, **the profit that accrues to *their* account**. This introduces a further financial metaphor, continuing those used in the preceding verses. Its meaning is straightforwardly theological, as verse 18 goes on to show: the **profit** (*karpos*, lit. 'fruit', but here used in the financial sense of 'profit' or 'interest') is not their enhanced social standing vis-à-vis Paul, but their practical praise-offering to God. The **account** is clearly held with God, as verse 19 also shows; in a similar vein are the sayings of Jesus about storing up treasure in heaven (e.g. Matt. 6.20; 19.21). The notion of bearing 'fruit' for God was earlier encountered in Paul's prayer of 1.11, thus arguably providing another instance of the numerous connections between this passage and the opening *exordium* and prayer of thanksgiving. Quite plausibly this 'fruit' should be understood in eschatological terms, too, as relating to the future reckoning on the 'day of Jesus Christ' (1.6; 2.16), when in fact the Philippian gift will not only accrue to their own account, but they themselves will be Paul's 'joy and crown' (4.1; cf. 2.16). O'Brien 539 and n.177 takes the present participle *pleonazonta* ('continuing to increase') to suggest that the profit is understood to accumulate continuously until the last day.

18 Paul's 'thank you note' introduces one further financial term. In commercial documents, the phrase **I have received ... payment** (*apechō*) typically served as a proof of receipt. Here, it means either that Paul has received the full sum that the Philippians sent, or more likely (in conjunction with the remainder of the verse) that he has received all he needed and more. By saying that he is **abundantly supplied** (*perisseuō*), Paul affirms that he now enjoys the 'plenty' of which he spoke in verses 11–12. Epaphroditus's conveyance of the Philippian gift (cf. 2.25–30) has meant that he is **fully provided for** (*peplērōmai*, lit. 'I have been filled'); the same verb is then used again in v. 19 to denote God's full provision of the Philippians' own needs.

This gift is now described as **a fragrant offering, an acceptable sacrifice well-pleasing to God**. The money of course has been given to God not directly but by being invested in the cause of the gospel. The same language of sacrifice in Paul usually refers either to the death of Christ (*thusia,* cf. Rom. 3.25f.) or to the ministry of the apostles (*osmé, euôdia,* 2 Cor. 2.14–16); in Romans 12.1 it denotes the Christian life itself as a sacrifice (*thusia*), perhaps a notion closely parallel to the present passage. The author to the Hebrews also uses related symbolism of a sacrificial Christian life in his conclusion, Heb. 13.15–16.

For Paul, the language and metaphor of sacrifice would of course have had chiefly Jewish connotations; his vocabulary here derives from the Septuagint (cf. O'Brien). It is possible that, as the human recipient of the Philippian contribution, he views his own role as that of the Israelite priest who received and benefited from the offerings of the people (cf. Rom. 15.16). Nevertheless, the subject matter was sufficiently commonplace in the Graeco-Roman world that the metaphor of a sweet-smelling sacrifice acceptable to the deity would have been widely understood by Gentiles. Thus, as we have just seen, Paul happily describes the apostolic ministry in similar terms when writing to Corinth, and in Romans he views the Christian life as a whole in terms of a 'living sacrifice'.

19 The passage closes appropriately with a promise (v. 19) and a doxology (v. 20). Just as the Philippians have 'fully provided' for Paul (v. 18), so Paul's *God* is sure to **provide** fully for **all** *their* **needs** as well. In the ancient context of reciprocal friendships, this verse is a striking departure from the expected expression of mutuality (and a good example of the 'three-way bond' high-lighted by Fee 13f. and *passim*). Here, Paul does not return the favour in kind, but assures them instead that it is 'his' **God** who will repay them. (The intensely personal phrase **my God** occurs elsewhere in Paul (e.g. Rom. 1.8; 1 Cor. 1.4; 2 Cor. 12.21) and was used earlier in this letter at 1.3; cf. 'my Lord' in 3.8. It is particularly apposite in the context of thanks for a personal benefaction.)

God's 'full provision' should be understood to cover material needs, but presumably also their need for the qualities which Paul has been encouraging in this letter: joy and steadfastness in Christ, humility and concord amongst each other. What is more, this divine provision is not according to the balanced reciprocity of a Graeco-Roman friendship, but **according to his riches in glory in Christ Jesus.** Just as the peace of God surpasses all understanding (v. 7), so the riches of God surpass every conceivable human need. God 'loves the cheerful giver' (2 Cor. 9.7) and offers lavish rewards. The implications are reminiscent of a

Lucan saying of Jesus (Luke 6.38): 'Give, and it will be given to you. A good measure, pressed down, shaken together, running over, will be put into your lap.' (The verb here is in the passive voice to indicate a divine action; the future tense, as in our passage, implies an eschatological reward.)

God's riches are said to be **in glory**, which means they derive from his heavenly presence and power. The words **in Christ Jesus** are best taken adverbially as the ultimate source and norm of God's provision (cf. Fee 453f. n.16). Together, the two phrases designate the same reality to which Paul in 3.14 aspired in terms of 'God's heavenly call in Christ Jesus'.

20 In typically Pauline vein, this passage concludes with Paul breaking out into a doxology. In some ways this is the only appropriate response to the glorious riches of God in Christ Jesus (v. 19); similar brief doxological formulas of 'glory to God' occur in 1.11 and 2.11, as well as in other Pauline letters (e.g. Rom. 11.33–6; 16.25–7; Gal. 1.5; cf. Schenk 54–6). For the purposes of this closing expression of worship, 'my God' has become the more inclusive **our God and Father** (cf. Gal. 1.4; 1 Thess. 1.3; 3.11, 13). The whole genre of such doxologies is a typically Jewish phenomenon, a fact confirmed by the eminently un-Greek eschatological affirmative **for ever and ever** (*eis tous aiônas tôn aiônôn*, lit. 'until the ages of the ages'). Paul's final **Amen** confirms that this doxology is no mere rhetorical flourish, but gives voice to his own deep conviction. It is the appropriately worshipful response to God's generous and sovereign providence in Christ Jesus.

C CLOSING GREETINGS AND BENEDICTION   (4.21–3)

After the unexpectedly extended note of thanks in 4.10–20, the letter closes on a more conventional note, in keeping with the form of many other Hellenistic letters and with the Christian substance of Paul's letter endings: greetings to the church from Paul and his companions, followed by a brief benediction. As in his other letters to familiar recipients (1 and 2 Cor., Gal., 1 and 2 Thess. (cf. Eph., if not a circular); contrast Rom., Col.), no individuals are singled out to receive greetings. Bruce suggests that these verses may well have been penned in Paul's own hand (cf. 1 Cor. 16.21; Col. 4.18; Gal. 6.11; 2 Thess. 3.17; also Phlm. 19).

The pregnant doxological conclusion of the preceding passage now renders prolonged formalities superfluous: Paul has already commended the Philippians to the glorious providence of God. After a letter marked by unusual personal warmth and spiritual

exuberance Paul is free to be brief, almost laconic in closing. All
that really matters has been said and his heart has been poured
out; an elaborate individual farewell would be needlessly irk-
some, and might be construed to show partiality in the internal
divisions at Philippi (4.3; cf. 2.1–4). With his unusual reference to
'Caesar's household', Paul adds a specific local flourish which
would carry a special significance for his Philippian readers, as
we shall see.

**(21) Greet every saint in Christ Jesus. The brothers and sisters
who are with me greet you. (22) All the saints greet you,
especially those of Caesar's household. (23) The grace of the
Lord Jesus Christ be with your spirit. Amen.**

21 The conclusion begins with another *inclusio*, which brackets
the end of the letter together with its beginning: 1.1 similarly
mentioned 'the saints in Christ Jesus' as the addressees of the
letter (see the discussion there, p. 52, on the meaning of 'saints').
The singular form (**every saint**) here may imply Paul's desire to
greet each of his friends individually, even though no names are
cited. While the theological meaning of the phrase **in Christ
Jesus** is clear from earlier uses (cf. p. 52), commentators disagree
about whether this modifies the greeting or the saints. (A similar
ambiguity was noted at 1.14 with regard to the phrase 'in the
Lord') The word order would seem to favour a reference to **every
saint in Christ Jesus**, but some scholars consider this to be
redundant and prefer to understand the greetings as being in
Christ. In practice the difference between these options is slight,
and Beare may be right to suggest that there is no need to
choose.

A number of authors suggest that the aorist imperative *aspa-
sasthe* (**greet**, a plural form) may be an instruction to the
'bishops' and 'deacons' of 1.1. Had Paul wished to convey a
general instruction to 'greet one another', he could have said
precisely that (1 Cor. 16.20; 2 Cor. 13.12; cf. Hawthorne). It may
well be that the church leaders who formally took delivery of the
letter (such as the 'loyal companion' anonymously addressed in
4.3, perhaps along with Euodia and Syntyche) would be the ones
who ensured that the letter would be publicly read and its
greetings conveyed. Quite how this would take place in Philippi,
and indeed whether 'bishops' and 'deacons' are addressed, must
remain guesswork. Beare 157 wisely notes that 'a trifle such as
this makes us realize how little we know about organization and
procedure in these early churches'.

Little more information is given about those who are *sending*
the greetings from Rome, but enough to raise some tantalizing

questions. In view of the wider reference in v. 22, **the brothers
... who are with me** must be Paul's immediate team of co-
workers in Rome; aside from Timothy and Epaphroditus they
appear to have been very few in number, as 2.20–21 suggests. Col.
4.7–14 and Phlm. 23–4 mention possible names, including one
Aristarchus of Thessalonica who may well have been known to
the Philippians (cf. Col. 4.10; Phlm. 24; Acts 19.29; 20.4). Yet those
texts may date from a different period in Paul's detention.

22 In addition to Paul and his companions, **all the saints** send
their greetings to Philippi. This is no doubt a somewhat hyper-
bolic expression for the good wishes of the church at Rome; Paul's
rival evangelists (1.15, 17) and their supporters may not have
known or wanted themselves to be included among the well-
wishers.

One group of Roman Christians, however, is being singled out
(*malista*, **especially**), as those whose greetings Paul is particularly keen to pass on – because he is especially close to them, or
they to the Philippians. This group consists of **those of Caesar's
household.** Endless debate has raged about this term, not least in
relation to whether 'Caesar's household', and with it the place of
writing, could be located anywhere but in Rome. Lightfoot, who
offered an extended excursus on this expression (pp. 171–8),
showed that it refers not to Caesar's relatives but rather to the
large number of imperial clients, friends and civil servants,
predominantly slaves and freed slaves, who were directly subject
to the Emperor (see more fully Weaver 1972). While a good many
of these civil servants would be found throughout the Empire
(and thus an Ephesian or possibly even Caesarean setting of the
letter remains a possibility, as we saw), Bruce and others are right
to suggest that the most likely location for a significant concentra-
tion of civil service converts to Christianity would have been
Rome (note p. 31 above, and see 1.13 on the *praetorium*).

The list of greetings in Romans 16 has since Lightfoot been
proposed as a starting point to discover which, if any, of those
names might correspond to **those of Caesar's household.** This
enterprise is necessarily somewhat speculative, but the list does
make for interesting reading. In particular, the 'household of
Narcissus' (Rom. 16.11) probably refers to the slaves of a wealthy
freedman named Tiberius Claudius Narcissus who became very
influential under the Emperor Claudius (AD 41–54), while 'the
household of Aristobulus' (Rom. 16.10) could be the slaves of a
grandson of Herod the Great (cf. also Herodion, Rom. 16.11) who
lived in Rome and enjoyed privileges at the court of Claudius.
(See especially Bruce 158f.)

If this link between Philippians and Romans is correct (and it does seem highly plausible), we must note that Paul evidently knew some of the members of Caesar's household before he arrived in Rome – and through them may well have met other believers (cf. Lightfoot 173–7; see also Acts 28.15). The placement of Paul's 'relative' (or fellow countryman) Herodion between the households of Narcissus and Aristobulus in Rom. 16.10–11 indicates that through his own family background among imperial freedmen (see on 3.5 above and cf. Hengel 1991: 4–17) Paul himself may have had personal connections with the civil service, and that at least one of his relatives or acquaintances in that official hierarchy had become a believer in Christ. Small wonder, then, that Paul can speak with particular confidence of greetings from Caesar's household!

What is more, this connection would of course have carried particular significance in Philippi, quite apart from the possibility that some Roman civil servants might have been known to Paul's readers (possibly as travelling couriers or perhaps as regulators of the purple dye trade in which Lydia was engaged, Acts 16.14: cf. Witherington 1994:136). Members of the imperial household were also present in Philippi: three of Augustus's freedmen erected a public inscription in Philippi in AD 36 or 37, which would presumably have been visible in Paul's day (P. Lemerle in *Bulletin de correspondance hellénique* 58 (1934) 450–52; cf. Bormann 1995: 198f.). An explicit mention of the *familia Caesaris* occurs in an inscription of AD 55 from Thracian Chersonesus (i.e. the Gallipoli peninsula, c. 180 km east of Philippi: *CIL* 3: 7380, discussed in Weaver 1972: 300).

The Philippians are a church in a Roman colony under persecution from their compatriots (1.28–30, cf. p. 100 above), while Paul similarly has suffered under Roman authorities both at Philippi and now at Rome. For both Paul and his friends, it will have been a source of hope and reassurance to know that the gospel was penetrating into the very heart of the Roman imperial apparatus. Concealed behind this innocuous greeting is a powerful symbol of the day when even in Rome, the seat of imperial power, 'every knee shall bow' to Christ (2.11).

23 Philippians closes in the same vein as every Pauline letter, with a final benediction in the form of a wish for grace. Just as Paul's letter openings are a Christian adaptation of the standard Hellenistic letter format (cf. p. 56 above), so his conclusions differ from the ordinary 'farewell' (*errōso,* cf. Acts 15.29) of contemporary Greek letters. A wish for 'grace and peace' opened the letter (see 1.2, also on the meaning of 'grace'); wishes for the 'peace of

God' (4.7, 9) and here for **the grace of the Lord Jesus Christ** stand at the end.

The simplest form of this closing Pauline benediction simply prays for this grace – which is always at least implicitly Christ's – to be 'with you' (so e.g. in Rom., 1 and 2 Cor., Col. 4.18, 1 and 2 Thess.) Here, however, Paul's prayer is for grace to be **with your spirit** (as also in Gal., Phlm.; cf. 2 Tim. 4.22). It is interesting that Paul uses the distributive singular 'spirit' even when addressing a whole congregation ('your' is of course plural, as in Gal. 6.18). The implication may be that God's grace is to be with their individual human spirits as united in the fellowship of Christ.

NA²⁷ and most modern translations end here. There is, however, excellent and widespread early textual support for a concluding **Amen** (incl. p⁴⁶ ℵ A D Ψ as well as the Majority text and ancient versions), which is also found in the King James Version. While public reading in liturgical contexts does appear to favour scribal addenda of this kind (cf. the variant readings at the end of most Pauline letters), the manuscript support in this case is exceptionally strong and much of the dissenting evidence less reliable (with the sole exception of *Codex Vaticanus*). If anything, the undisputed earlier use of *amén* in 4.20 makes a later scribal omission here more likely than an insertion. Paul himself can use **Amen** to conclude his letters (Gal. 6.18; cf. Rom. 16.27) or to lend weight to important theological assertions (e.g. Rom. 1.25; 9.5; 11.36; 15.33; Gal. 1.5; Phil. 4.20; cf. Eph. 3.21). On balance, therefore, we should follow those like O'Brien, Hawthorne and R.P. Martin who take the textual evidence in favour of retaining the word here (contrast Güting 1993 for a less sanguine view of the text-critical value of final *Amen* in the NT).

Original or not, there can be no more suitable way to end this letter. Just as **Amen** in 4.20 placed an appropriate liturgical full stop after the doxological affirmation which closed the paragraph 4.10–20, so here it aptly encapsulates the only fitting coda to Paul's epistle of joy: worship of the God who in Jesus Christ lavishes his humble and self-giving love on all humankind.

BIBLIOGRAPHY

Commentaries cited

Aquinas, St. Thomas. 1969. *Commentary on Saint Paul's First Letter to the Thessalonians and the Letter to the Philippians.* Aquinas Scripture Series, vol. 3. Trans. F.R. Larcher & M. Duffy. Albany, NY: Magi Books.

Barth, Gerhard. 1979. *Der Brief an die Philipper.* ZBKNT 9. Zurich: Theologischer Verlag.

Barth, Karl. 1962. *The Epistle to the Philippians.* Trans. J.W. Leitch. London: SCM.

Beare, Francis Wright. 1973. *The Epistle to the Philippians.* Black's NT Commentaries. 3rd edn. London: Black.

Bengel, Johann Albrecht. 1855. *Gnomon Novi Testamenti.* Ed. M.E. Bengel & J. Steudel. 3rd edn. London: Nutt, Williams & Norgate; Cambridge: Macmillan.

Bruce, F.F. 1989. *Philippians.* NIBC. 2nd edn. Peabody, MA: Hendrickson.

Caird, G.B. 1976. *Paul's Letters from Prison.* New Clarendon Bible. Oxford: Oxford University Press.

Calvin, John. 1965. *The Epistles of Paul the Apostle to the Galatians, Ephesians, Philippians and Colossians.* Trans. T.H.L. Parker. Grand Rapids: Eerdmans.

Chrysostom, St John. N.d. 'Homilies of St John Chrysostom, Archbishop of Constantinople, on the Epistle of St Paul's to the Philippians.' In *NPNF* I, 13: 181–255. [Greek text in MPG 62: 177–298.]

Collange, Jean-François. 1979. *The Epistle of Saint Paul to the Philippians.* Trans. A.W. Heathcote. London: Epworth.

Dibelius, Martin. 1937. *An die Thessalonicher I, II, an die Philipper.* HNT 11. 3rd edn. Tübingen: Mohr (Siebeck).

Fee, Gordon D. 1995. *Paul's Letter to the Philippians.* NICNT. Grand Rapids: Eerdmans.

Friedrich, Gerhard. 1990. 'Der Brief an die Philipper.' In Jürgen Becker, Hans Conzelmann & Gerhard Friedrich, *Die Briefe an die Galater, Epheser, Philipper, Kolosser, Thessalonicher und Philemon.* NTD 8. 4th edn. Göttingen: Vandenhoeck & Ruprecht.

Gnilka, Joachim. 1987. *Der Philipperbrief.* HTKNT. 4th edn. Freiburg etc.: Herder. [Cf. earlier ET: *The Epistle to the Philippians,* trans. R.A. Wilson (New York: Herder & Herder, 1971).]

Hawthorne, Gerald F. 1983. *Philippians.* WBC 43. Waco: Word.

Lightfoot, J.B. 1896. *Saint Paul's Epistle to the Philippians: A Revised Text with Introduction, Notes, and Dissertations.* 4th edn. with additions & alterations. London: Macmillan.

Loh, I-Jin & Nida, Eugene A. 1977. *A Translator's Handbook on Paul's Letter to the Philippians.* HFT 19. Stuttgart: United Bible Societies.

Lohmeyer, Ernst. 1964. *Der Brief an die Philipper, an die Kolosser und an Philemon.* KEKNT. 13th edn. Göttingen: Vandenhoeck & Ruprecht.

Marshall, I. Howard. 1991. *The Epistle to the Philippians.* Epworth Commentaries. London: Epworth.

Martin, Ralph P. 1987. *The Epistle of Paul to the Philippians: An Introduction and Commentary.* TNTC. Rev. edn. Leicester: Inter-Varsity; Grand Rapids: Eerdmans.

Melick, Richard R. 1991. *Philippians, Colossians, Philemon.* New American Commentary 32. Nashville: Broadman.

Metzger, Bruce M. 1975. *A Textual Commentary on the Greek New Testament.* 2nd edn. London/New York: United Bible Societies.

Müller, Ulrich B. 1993. *Der Brief des Paulus an die Philipper.* THKNT 11.1. Leipzig: Evangelische Verlagsanstalt.

O'Brien, Peter T. 1991. *The Epistle to the Philippians: A Commentary on the Greek Text.* NIGTC. Grand Rapids: Eerdmans.

Plummer, Alfred. 1919. *A Commentary on St Paul's Epistle to the Philippians.* London: Macmillan.

Schenk, Wolfgang. 1984. *Die Philipperbriefe des Paulus: Kommentar.* Stuttgart: Kohlhammer.

Silva, Moisés. 1988. *Philippians.* Baker Exegetical Commentary on the New Testament. Grand Rapids: Baker.

Vincent, Marvin R. 1922. *Critical and Exegetical Commentary on the Epistles to the Philippians and to Philemon.* ICC. 3rd edn. Edinburgh: T. & T. Clark. [The date of the first edition was 1897.]

Weiss, Bernhard. 1859. *Der Philipper-Brief ausgelegt und die Geschichte seiner Auslegung kritisch dargestellt.* Berlin: Hertz.

Other works cited

Abegg, Martin. 1994. 'Paul, 'Works of the Law' and MMT.' *BAR* 20.6: 52–5, 82.

Abrahamsen, Valerie A. 1987. 'Women at Philippi: The pagan and Christian evidence.' *JFSR* 3: 17–30.

1988. 'Christianity and the rock reliefs at Philippi.' *BA* 51/3: 46–56.

1995. *Women and Worship at Philippi: Diana/Artemis and other Cults in the Early Christian Era.* Portland, Maine: Astarte Shell.

Achtemeier, Paul J. 1990. '*Omne Verbum Sonat*: The New Testament and the oral development of late Western antiquity.' *JBL* 109:3–27.

Ådna, Jostein. 1996. 'Der Gottesknecht von Jesaja 53 als triumphie-render und interzessorischer Messias: Die Rezeption von Jes 52,13–53,12 im Targum Jonathan untersucht mit besonderer Berücksichtigung des Messiasbildes.' In *Der leidende Gottesknecht: Jesaja 53 und seine Wirkungsgeschichte*, 129–58. FAT 14. Ed. B. Janowski & P. Stuhlmacher. Tübingen: Mohr (Siebeck).

Aland, Kurt & Aland, Barbara. 1989. *The Text of the New Testament: An Introduction to the Critical Editions and to the Theory and Practice of Modern Textual Criticism*. Trans. E.F. Rhodes. 2nd edn. Grand Rapids: Eerdmans; Leiden: Brill.

Aland, Kurt *et al.*, eds. 1991. *Text und Textwert der griechischen Handschriften des Neuen Testaments*, vol. 3: *Galaterbrief bis Philipperbrief*. Arbeiten zur neutestamentlichen Textforschung 18. Berlin: de Gruyter.

Alexander, L.C.A. 1989. 'Hellenistic letter-forms and the structure of Philippians.' *JSNT* 37: 87–101.

Anderson, R. Dean, Jr. 1996. *Ancient Rhetorical Theory and Paul*. CBET 18. Kampen: Kok Pharos.

Antin, Paul. 1974. '*Mori Lucrum* et *Antigone* 424, 464.' *RevSR* 62:259–60.

Aspan, Paul F. 1992. *Towards a New Reading of Paul's Letter to the Philippians in the Light of a Kuhnian Analysis of New Testament Criticism*. PhD. thesis: Vanderbilt University.

Balz, Horst. 1996. 'Philipperbrief.' *TRE* 26: 504–13.

Barber, Robin. 1990. *Greece*. The Blue Guide. 5th edn. London: A. & C. Black; New York: W.W. Norton.

Barclay, John M.G. 1987. 'Mirror-reading a polemical letter: Galatians as a test case.' *JSNT* 31: 73–93.

1996. *Jews in the Mediterranean Diaspora from Alexander to Trajan (323 BCE–117 CE)*. Edinburgh: T. & T. Clark.

Barnett, Paul. 1997. *The Second Epistle to the Corinthians*. NICNT. Grand Rapids: Eerdmans.

Bartchy, S. Scott. 1992. 'Slavery: New Testament.' *ABD* 6: 65–73.

Basevi, Claudio & Chapa, Juan. 1993. 'Philippians 2.6–11: The rhetorical function of a Pauline "hymn".' In *Rhetoric and the New Testament: Essays from the 1992 Heidelberg Conference*, 338–56. JSNTSup 90. Ed. S.E. Porter & T.H. Olbricht. Sheffield: Sheffield Academic.

Bassler, Jouette M., ed. 1991. *Pauline Theology*, vol. I: *Thessalonians, Philippians, Galatians, Philemon*. Minneapolis: Fortress.

1993. 'Paul's theology: whence and whither?' In *Pauline Theology*, vol. II: *1&2 Corinthians*, 3–17. Ed. D.M. Hay. Minneapolis: Fortress.

Bauckham, Richard J. 1992. 'The worship of Jesus.' *ABD* 3:812-19.
  Ed. 1995. *The Book of Acts in Its Palestinian Setting.* Grand Rapids:
    Eerdmans; Carlisle: Paternoster.
Bauer, Johann B. 1995. *Die Polykarpbriefe.* Kommentar zu den Apos-
    tolischen Vätern 5. Göttingen: Vandenhoeck & Ruprecht.
Becker, Jürgen. 1989. *Paulus der Heidenapostel.* Tübingen: Mohr
    (Siebeck). [ET *Paul: Apostle to the Gentiles*, trans. O.C. Dean.
    Louisville: Westminster/Knox, 1993].
Beker, J. Christiaan. 1982. *Paul's Apocalyptic Gospel: The Coming
    Triumph of God.* Philadelphia: Fortress.
Berger, Klaus. 1995. 'Loyalität.' *ZTK Beiheft* 9: 120-32.
Bernheim, Pierre-Antoine. 1997. *James, Brother of Jesus.* Trans. J.
    Bowden. London: SCM.
Berry, Ken L. 1996. 'The function of friendship language in Phil-
    ippians 4:10-20.' In *Friendship, Flattery and Frankness of Speech:
    Studies on Friendship in the New Testament World*, 107-24. Ed.
    J.T. Fitzgerald. NovTSup 82. Leiden etc.: Brill.
Best, Ernest. 1988. *Paul and His Converts: The Sprunt Lectures 1985.*
    Edinburgh: T. & T. Clark.
  1996. 'The reading and writing of commentaries.' *ExpT* 107: 358-62.
Betz, Hans Dieter. 1979. *Galatians: A Commentary on Paul's Letter to
    the Churches in Galatia.* Hermeneia. Philadelphia: Fortress.
  1996. 'Heroenverehrung und Christusglaube: Religionsgeschicht-
    liche Beobachtungen zu Philostrats *Heroicus.*' In *Geschichte –
    Tradition – Reflexion: Festschrift für Martin Hengel zum 70.
    Geburtstag*, vol. 2: *Griechische und römische Religion*, 119-39. Ed.
    H. Cancik, H. Lichtenberger & P. Schäfer. Tübingen: Mohr
    (Siebeck).
Betz, Otto. 1977. 'Paulus als Pharisäer nach dem Gesetz: Phil. 3,5-6 als
    Beitrag zur Frage des frühen Pharisäismus.' In *Treue zur Thora:
    Beiträge zur Mitte des christlich-jüdischen Gesprächs. Festschrift
    für Günther Harder zum 75. Geburtstag*, 54-64. Ed. P. von der
    Osten-Sacken. Berlin: de Gruyter. [Repr. in idem, *Jesus: Der Herr
    der Kirche, Aufsätze zur biblischen Theologie* vol. 2, WUNT 52
    (Tübingen: Mohr (Siebeck), 1990), 103-13.]
  1990. 'Die Übersetzungen von Jes 53 (LXX, Targum) und die
    Theologia Crucis des Paulus.' In idem, *Jesus: Der Herr der Kirche,
    Aufsätze zur biblischen Theologie* vol. 2, 197-216. WUNT 52.
    Tübingen: Mohr (Siebeck).
Black, C.C. 1989. 'Keeping up with recent studies: 16. Rhetorical
    criticism and biblical interpretation.' *ExpT* 100: 252-8.
Black, David Alan. 1995. 'The discourse structure of Philippians: a
    study in textlinguistics.' *NovT* 37: 16-49.
Bloomquist, L. Gregory. 1993. *The Function of Suffering in Phil-
    ippians.* JSNTSup 78. Sheffield: Sheffield Academic Press.

Bockmuehl, Markus. 1988. 'A note on the text of Colossians 4:3.' *JTS* N.S. 39: 484–9.

1990. *Revelation and Mystery in Ancient Judaism and Pauline Christianity*. WUNT 2: 36. Tübingen: Mohr (Siebeck). [Repr. Grand Rapids/Cambridge: Eerdmans, 1997.]

1994–5. 'The Noachide commandments and New Testament ethics.' *RevB* 102: 72–101.

1995. 'A commentator's approach to the "effective history" of Philippians.' *JSNT* 60: 57–88.

1997. '"The form of God" (Phil. 2.6): variations on a theme of Jewish mysticism.' *JTS* N.S. 48: 1–23.

Boismard, M.-E. & Lamouille, A. 1990. *Les Actes des Deux Apôtres*. 3 vols. ÉB N.S. 12–14. Paris: Lecoffre/Gabalda.

Bormann, Lukas. 1995. *Philippi: Stadt und Christengemeinde zur Zeit des Paulus*. NovTSup 78. Leiden etc.: Brill.

Bornkamm, Günter. 1971. 'Der Philipperbrief als paulinische Briefsammlung.' In idem, *Geschichte und Glaube*, 2: 195–205. BET 53 [*Gesammelte Aufsätze*, vol. 4]. Munich: Kaiser.

Bradley, K.R. 1994. *Slavery and Society at Rome*. Cambridge: University Press.

Brandenburger, Egon. 1968. *Fleisch und Geist: Paulus und die dualistische Weisheit*. WMANT 29. Neukirchen-Vluyn: Neukirchener.

Brant, Jo-Ann A. 1993. 'The place of *mimésis* in Paul's thought.' *Studies in Religion/Sciences Religieuses* 22: 285–301.

Briggs, Sheila. 1989. 'Can an enslaved god liberate? Hermeneutical reflections on Philippians 2:6–11.' *Semeia* 47: 137–53.

Bringmann, Klaus. 1993. 'The king as benefactor: some remarks on ideal kingship in the age of Hellenism.' In *Images and Ideologies: Self-Definition in the Hellenistic World*, 7–24. Ed. A. Bulloch *et al.* Berkeley: University of California Press.

Brooke, George J. 1985. *Exegesis at Qumran: 4QFlorilegium in its Jewish Context*. JSOTSup 29. Sheffield: JSOT.

Bruce, F.F. 1981. 'St Paul in Macedonia: 3. The Philippian correspondence.' *BJRL* 63: 260–84.

Bultmann, Rudolf. 1952. *Theology of the New Testament*. Vol. 1. Trans. K. Grobel. London: SCM.

Byrskog, Samuel. 1996. 'Co-Senders, co-authors and Paul's use of the first person plural.' *ZNW* 87: 230–50.

Caird, G.B. 1994. *New Testament Theology*. Completed and edited by L.D. Hurst. Oxford: Clarendon.

Campbell, Douglas A. 1992. *The Rhetoric of Righteousness in Romans 3.21–26*. JSNTSup 65. Sheffield: JSOT.

Capper, Brian J. 1993. 'Paul's dispute with Philippi: understanding Paul's argument in Phil. 1–2 from his thanks in 4.10–20.' *TZ* 49: 193–214.

Carleton Paget, James. 1996. 'Jewish proselytism at the time of Christian origins: chimera or reality?' *JSNT* 62: 65–103.

Carls, Peter. 1995. 'Wer sind Syzygos, Euodia und Syntyche in Phil. 4,2f.?' *Protokolle zur Bibel* 4: 117–41.

Carson, D.A., Moo, Douglas J. and Morris, Leon. 1992. *An Introduction to the New Testament.* Grand Rapids: Zondervan.

Castelli, Elizabeth A. 1991. *Imitating Paul: A Discourse of Power.* Louisville: Westminster/Knox.

Cerfaux, Lucien. 1959. *Christ in the Theology of St Paul.* London: Chapman.

Chester, Andrew. 1991. 'Jewish messianic expectations and mediatorial figures and Pauline christology.' In *Paulus und das antike Judentum*, 17–89. Ed. M. Hengel & U. Heckel. WUNT 58. Tübingen: Mohr (Siebeck).

Childs, Brevard S. 1995. 'On reclaiming the Bible for Christian theology.' In *Reclaiming the Bible for the Church*, 1–17. Ed. C.E. Braaten & R.W. Jenson. Grand Rapids/Cambridge: Eerdmans.

Classen, C. Joachim. 1991. 'Paulus und die antike Rhetorik.' *ZNW* 82: 1–33.

1993. 'St Paul's epistles and Ancient Greek and Roman rhetoric.' In *Rhetoric and the New Testament: Essays from the 1992 Heidelberg Conference*, 265–91. JSNTSup 90. Ed. S.E. Porter & T.H. Olbricht. Sheffield: Sheffield Academic.

Cohen, Martin S. 1983. *The Shi'ur Qomah: Liturgy and Theurgy in Pre-Kabbalistic Jewish Mysticism.* New York/London: University Press of America.

Collart, Philippe. 1937. *Philippes, ville de Macédoine, depuis ses origines jusqu'à la fin de l'époque romaine.* 2 vols. Paris: Boccard.

Combrink, H.J. Bernard. 1989. 'Response to W. Schenk, *Die Philipperbriefe des Paulus.*' *Semeia* 48: 135–46.

Conzelmann, Hans & Lindemann, Andreas. 1995. *Arbeitsbuch zum Neuen Testament.* Uni-Taschenbücher 52. 11th edn. Tübingen: Mohr (Siebeck).

Cullmann, Oscar. 1963. *The Christology of the New Testament.* Trans. S.C. Guthrie & C.A.M. Hall. Rev. edn. Philadelphia: Westminster.

Dahl, Nils Alstrup. 1995. 'Euodia and Syntyche and Paul's letter to the Philippians.' In *The Social World of the First Christians: Essays in Honor of Wayne A. Meeks*, 3–15. Ed. L.M. White & O.L. Yarbrough. Minneapolis: Fortress.

d'Angelo, Mary Rose. 1990. 'Women partners in the New Testament.' *JFSR* 6: 65–86.

Danker, Frederick W. 1992. 'Purple.' *ABD* 5: 557–60.

Daubercies, P. 1995. 'La vertu chez Philon d'Alexandrie.' *Revue Théologique de Louvain* 26: 185–210.

de Boer, Willis Peter. 1962. *The Imitation of Paul: An Exegetical Study.* Kampen: Kok.

Dodd, C. H. 1953. 'The mind of Paul', Parts I & II. In idem, *New Testament Studies,* 67-128. Manchester: Manchester University Press.

Dorcey, Peter F. 1992. *The Cult of Silvanus: A Study in Roman Folk Religion.* Leiden etc.: Brill.

Doughty, Darrell J. 1995. 'Citizens of heaven: Philippians 3.2-21.' *NTS* 41: 102-22.

Droge, Arthur J. 1988. '*Mori Lucrum*: Paul and ancient theories of suicide.' *NovT* 30: 63-86.

Droge, Arthur J. & Tabor, James D. 1992. *A Noble Death: Suicide and Martyrdom among Jews and Christians in Antiquity.* San Francisco: Harper Collins.

Dunn, James D.G. 1980. *Christology in the Making.* London: SCM.

1990. *Jesus, Paul and the Law.* London: SCM.

1992. 'The body of Christ in Paul.' In *Worship and Ministry in the New Testament: Essays in Honour of Ralph Martin,* 146-62. Ed. M.J. Wilkins & T. Paige. Sheffield: Sheffield Academic.

1994. 'Prolegomena to a theology of Paul.' *NTS* 40: 407-32.

1997. '4QMMT and Galatians.' *NTS* 43: 147-53.

Eckman, Barbara. 1980. 'A quantitative metrical analysis of the Philippians hymn.' *NTS* 26: 258-66.

Elbogen, Ismar. 1993. *Jewish Liturgy: A Comprehensive History.* Trans. R.P. Scheindlin. New York: Jewish Publication Society.

Elliger, Winfried. 1978. *Paulus in Griechenland: Philippi, Thessaloniki, Athen, Korinth.* SBS 92/93. Stuttgart: Katholisches Bibelwerk.

Ellis, E. Earle. 1993. 'Coworkers, Paul and his.' *DPL,* 183-9.

Engberg-Pedersen, Troels. 1994. 'Stoicism in Philippians.' In idem (ed.), *Paul in his Hellenistic Context,* 256-90. SNTW. Edinburgh: T. & T. Clark.

Fee, Gordon D. 1992. 'Philippians 2:5-11: Hymn or Exalted Pauline Prose?' *Bulletin for Biblical Research* 2: 29-46.

1994. *God's Empowering Presence: The Holy Spirit in the Letters of Paul.* Peabody: Hendrickson.

Feldman, Louis H. 1993. *Jew and Gentile in the Ancient World: Attitudes and Interactions from Alexander to Justininian.* Princeton: University Press.

Field, Frederick. 1899. *Notes on the Translation of the New Testament.* Cambridge: University Press.

Fishbane, Michael. 1992. 'The "measures" of God's glory in the ancient Midrash.' In *Messiah and Christos: Studies in the Jewish Origins of Christianity Presented to David Flusser on the Occasion of His Seventy-Fifth Birthday,* 53-74. Ed. I. Gruenwald *et al.* Tübingen: Mohr.

Fitzgerald, John T. 1992. 'Philippians, Epistle to the.' *ABD* 5: 318–26.

Ed. 1996. *Friendship, Flattery and Frankness of Speech: Studies on Friendship in the New Testament World.* NovTSup 82. Leiden etc.: Brill.

Fitzmyer, Joseph A. 1981. 'The gospel in the theology of Paul.' In idem, *To Advance the Gospel: New Testament Essay,* 149–61. New York: Crossroad. [= Repr. of *Int* 33 (1979) 339–50.]

1988. 'The Aramaic Background of Philippians 2:6–11', *CBQ* 50: 470–83.

1993. 'The consecutive meaning of Εφ' Ω in Romans 5.12.' *NTS* 39: 321–39.

1995. *The Biblical Commission's Document 'The Interpretation of the Bible in the Church': Text and Commentary.* Subsidia Biblica 18. Rome: Pontifical Biblical Institute.

Flusser, David. 1988. 'Jesus' opinion about the Essenes.' In *Judaism and the Origins of Christianity,* 150–68. Jerusalem: Magnes.

1996a. 'Die Gesetzeswerke in Qumran und bei Paulus.' In *Geschichte–Tradition–Reflexion: Festschrift für Martin Hengel zum 70. Geburtstag,* vol. 1: *Judentum,* 395–403. Ed. H. Cancik, H. Lichtenberger & P. Schäfer. Tübingen: Mohr (Siebeck).

1996b. 'Paulus: II. Aus jüdischer Sicht.' *TRE* 26: 153–60.

Forbes, Christopher. 1986. 'Comparison, self-praise and irony: Paul's boasting and the conventions of Hellenistic rhetoric.' *NTS* 32: 1–30.

Fortna, Robert T. 1990. 'Philippians: Paul's most egocentric letter.' In *The Conversation Continues: Studies in Paul and John in Honor of J. Louis Martyn,* 220–34. Ed. R.T. Fortna & B. R. Gaventa. Nashville: Abingdon.

Fowl, Stephen E. 1990. *The Story of Christ in the Ethics of Paul.* JSNTSup 36. Sheffield: JSOT.

Frank, K.S. 1976. 'Gehorsam.' *RAC* 9: 390–430.

Fredrickson, David E. 1996. 'ΠΑΡΡΗΣΙΑ in the Pauline Epistles.' In *Friendship, Flattery and Frankness of Speech: Studies on Friendship in the New Testament World,* 164–83. Ed. J. T. Fitzgerald. NovTSup 82. Leiden etc.: Brill.

Fung, R.Y.K. 1993. 'Body of Christ.' *DPL,* 76–82.

Funk, Robert W. 1966. *Language, Hermeneutic and Word of God.* New York.

Furnish, Victor P. 1972. *The Love Command in the New Testament.* Nashville: Abingdon.

García Martínez, Florentino. 1996. *The Dead Sea Scrolls Translated: The Qumran Texts in English.* Trans. W.G.E. Watson. 2nd edn. Leiden etc.: Brill; Grand Rapids: Eerdmans.

Garland, David E. 1985. 'The composition and unity of Philippians: some neglected literary factors.' *NovT* 27: 141–73.

Garnsey, Peter. 1970. *Social Status and Legal Privilege in the Roman Empire*. Oxford: Clarendon.

—— 1996. *Ideas of Slavery from Aristotle to Augustine*. The WB Stanford Memorial Lectures. Cambridge etc.: Cambridge University Press.

Geoffrion, T.C. 1993. *The Rhetorical Purpose and the Political and Military Character of Philippians: A Call to Stand Firm*. Lewiston NY, etc.: Mellen Biblical.

Gill, David W.J. 1994a. 'Acts and the urban élites.' In *The Book of Acts in its Graeco-Roman Setting*, 105–18. Ed. D.W.J. Gill & C. Gempf. The Book of Acts in its First Century Setting, vol. 2. Grand Rapids: Eerdmans; Carlisle: Paternoster.

—— 1994b. 'Macedonia.' In *The Book of Acts in its Graeco-Roman Setting*, 397–417. Ed. D.W.J. Gill & C. Gempf. The Book of Acts in its First Century Setting, vol. 2. Grand Rapids: Eerdmans; Carlisle: Paternoster.

Gillman, Florence M. 1990. 'Early Christian women at Philippi.' *JGWR* 1: 59–79.

Gnilka, Joachim. 1996. *Paulus von Tarsus: Apostel und Zeuge*. HTKNTSup 6. Freiburg etc.: Herder.

Goldberg, Arnold. 1978. *Erlösung durch Leiden: Drei rabbinische Homilien über die Trauernden Zions und den leidenden Messias Efraim (PesR 34. 36. 37)*. FJS 4. Frankfurt: Gesellschaft zur Förderung Judaistischer Studien.

Goodman, Martin. 1994. *Mission and Conversion: Proselytizing in the Religious History of the Roman Empire*. Oxford: Clarendon.

Goshen Gottstein, Alon. 1995. 'Four entered Paradise revisited.' *HTR* 88: 69–133.

Gross, Walter Hatto. 1979. 'Purpur.' *Der Kleine Pauly* 4: 1243–4.

Guillet, Jean. 1981. 'Révélation: II. Nouveau Testament.' *DBSup* 56: 600–618.

Guthrie, G.H. 1995. 'Cohesion shifts and stitches in Philippians.' In *Discourse Analysis and Other Topics in Biblical Greek*. Ed. S.E. Porter & D.A. Carson. JSNTSup 113. Sheffield: Sheffield Academic Press.

Güting, Eberhard. 1993. 'Amen, Eulogie, Doxologie: Eine textkritische Untersuchung.' In *Begegnungen zwischen Christentum und Judentum in Antike und Mittelalter: Festschrift für Heinz Schreckenberg*, 133–62. Ed. D.-A. Koch & H. Lichtenberger. SIJD 1. Göttingen: Vandenhoeck & Ruprecht.

Haacker, Klaus. 1971–2. 'War Paulus Hillelit?' In *Das Institutum Iudaicum der Universität Tübingen*, 106–20. Tübingen: privately published.

1975. 'Die Berufung des Verfolgers und die Rechtfertigung des Gottlosen: Erwägungen zum Zusammenhang zwischen Biographie und Theologie des Apostels Paulus.' *Theologische Beiträge* 6: 1–19.

Haenchen, Ernst. 1968. *Die Apostelgeschichte*. KEKNT 3. 6th edn. Göttingen: Vandenhoeck & Ruprecht.

Hainz, Josef. 1982. *KOINONIA: 'Kirche' als Gemeinschaft bei Paulus*. BU 16. Regensburg: Pustet.

1994. 'KOINΩNIA bei Paulus.' In *Religious Propaganda and Missionary Competition in the New Testament World*, 375–91. Ed. L. Bormann *et al*. NovTSup 74. Leiden etc.: Brill.

Harris, Murray J. 1983. *Raised Immortal: Resurrection and Immortality in the New Testament*. London: Marshall, Morgan & Scott.

Harrison, P.N. 1936. *Polycarp's Two Epistles to the Philippians*. Cambridge: University Press.

Hawthorne, Gerald F. 1996. 'The imitation of Christ: discipleship in Philippians.' In *Patterns of Discipleship in the New Testament*, 163–79. Ed. R.N. Longenecker. Grand Rapids/Cambridge: Eerdmans.

Hays, Richard B. 1983. *The Faith of Jesus Christ: An Investigation of the Narrative Substructure of Galatians 3:1–4:11*. SBLDS 56. Chico: Scholars.

1989. *Echoes of Scripture in the Letters of Paul*. New Haven: Yale University Press.

1993. 'Christ prays the Psalms: Paul's use of an early Christian exegetical convention.' In *The Future of Christology: Essays in Honor of Leander E. Keck*, 122–36. Ed. A.J. Malherbe & W.A. Meeks. Minneapolis: Fortress.

Helewa, Giovanni. 1994. 'Carità, discernimento e cammino cristiano: Una lettura di Fil 1,9–11.' *Teresianum* 45: 363–404.

Hemer, Colin J. 1989. *The Book of Acts in the Setting of Hellenistic History*. WUNT 49. Tübingen: Mohr (Siebeck).

Hendrix, Holland L. 1992. 'Philippi (Place).' *ABD* 5: 313–17.

Hengel, Martin. 1971. 'Proseuche und Synagoge: Jüdische Gemeinde, Gotteshaus und Gottesdienst in der Diaspora und in Palästina.' In *Tradition und Glaube: Festschrift für Karl Georg Kuhn*, 157–84. Ed. G. Jeremias *et al*. Göttingen: Vandenhoeck & Ruprecht. [Repr. in idem, *Judaica et Hellenistica: Kleine Schriften I*, WUNT 90 (Tübingen: Mohr (Siebeck), 1996), 171–95.]

1977. *Crucifixion in the Ancient World and the Folly of the Message of the Cross*. Trans. J. Bowden. London: SCM.

1979. *Acts and the History of Earliest Christianity*. Trans. J. Bowden. London: SCM.

1983. *Between Jesus and Paul*. Trans. J. Bowden. London: SCM.

1989. *The Zealots*. Trans. D. Smith. Edinburgh: T. & T. Clark.

1991. *The Pre-Christian Paul.* In collaboration with R. Deines. London: SCM.

1995. 'The song about Christ in earliest worship.' In idem, *Studies in Early Christology*, 227–91. Edinburgh: T. & T. Clark.

Hengel, Martin & Schwemer, Anna Maria. 1997. *Paul Between Damascus and Antioch: The Unknown Years.* Trans. J. Bowden. London: SCM.

Hoffmann, Paul. 1978. *Die Toten in Christus: Eine religionsgeschichtliche und exegetische Untersuchung zur paulinischen Eschatologie.* NTAbh N.S. 2. 3rd edn. Münster: Aschendorff.

Hofius, Otfried. 1991. *Der Christushymnus Philipper 2,6–11: Untersuchungen zu Gestalt und Aussage eines urchristlichen Psalms.* WUNT 17. 2nd rev. edn. Tübingen: Mohr (Siebeck).

1993. 'Das vierte Gottesknechtslied in den Briefen des Neuen Testamentes.' *NTS* 39: 414–37. [Repr. in *Der leidende Gottesknecht: Jesaja 53 und seine Wirkungsgeschichte*, FAT 14, ed. B. Janowski & P. Stuhlmacher (Tübingen: Mohr (Siebeck), 1996), 107–27.]

Holmberg, Bengt. 1978. *Paul and Power: The Structure of Authority in the Primitive Church as Reflected in the Pauline Epistles.* CBNT 11. Lund: Gleerup.

Holtz, Traugott. 1985. 'Theo-logie [*sic*] und Christologie bei Paulus.' In *Glaube und Eschatologie: Festschrift für Werner Georg Kümmel zum 80. Geburtstag*, 105–21. Ed. E. Gräßer & O. Merk. Tübingen: Mohr (Siebeck). [Repr. in idem, *Geschichte und Theologie des Urchristentums: Gesammelte Aufsätze*, ed. E. Reinmuth & C. Wolff, WUNT 57 (Tübingen: Mohr (Siebeck), 1991), 189–204.]

Hooker, Morna D. 1978. 'Philippians 2:6–11.' In *Jesus und Paulus: Festschrift für Werner Georg Kümmel zum 70. Geburtstag*, 151–64. Ed. E.E. Ellis & E. Gräßer. 2nd edn. Göttingen: Vandenhoeck & Ruprecht. [Repr. in idem, *From Adam to Christ* (Cambridge: University Press, 1991).]

1989. 'ΠΙΣΤΙΣ ΧΡΙΣΤΟΥ' *NTS* 35: 321–42. [Repr. in idem, *From Adam to Christ* (Cambridge: University Press, 1991).]

Hoover, Roy W. 1971. 'The HARPAGMOS Enigma: A philosophical solution.' *HTR* 64: 95–119.

Horbury, William. 1982. '1 Thessalonians ii.3 as rebutting the charge of false prophecy.' *JTS* N.S. 33: 492–508.

1985. 'Extirpation and excommunication.' *VT* 35: 13–38.

1992. 'Jewish–Christian relations in Barnabas and Justin Martyr.' In *The Parting of the Ways: A.D. 70 to 135*, 315–45. Ed. J.D.G. Dunn. WUNT 66. Tübingen: Mohr (Siebeck).

1996. 'Land, sanctuary and worship.' In *Early Christian Thought in Its Jewish Context*, 207–24. Ed. J. Barclay & J. Sweet. Cambridge etc.: Cambridge University Press.

1997. 'Septuagintal and New Testament conceptions of the Church.' In *A Vision for the Church: Essays on Early Christian Ecclesiology in Honour of J.P.M. Sweet*, 1–17. Ed. M. Bockmuehl & M.B. Thompson. Edinburgh: T. & T. Clark.

Hübner, Hans. 1993. *Biblische Theologie des Neuen Testaments*. Vol. 2: *Die Theologie des Paulus und ihre neutestamentliche Wirkungsgeschichte*. Göttingen: Vandenhoeck & Ruprecht.

1996. 'Paulus: I. Neues Testament.' *TRE* 26: 133–53.

Hurtado, Larry W. 1984. 'Jesus as lordly example in Philippians 2:5–11.' In *From Jesus to Paul: Studies in Honour of Francis Wright Beare*, 113–26. Ed. P. Richardson & J.C. Hurd. Waterloo: Wilfrid Laurier University Press.

1988. *One God, One Lord: Early Christian Devotion and Ancient Jewish Monotheism*. Philadelphia: Fortress.

1993. 'Lord.' *DPL*, 560–69.

Hüttenmeister, Frowald G. 1993. '"Synagoge" und "Proseuche" bei Josephus und in anderen antiken Quellen.' In *Begegnungen zwischen Christentum und Judentum in Antike und Mittelalter: Festschrift für Heinz Schreckenberg*, 163–81. Ed. D.-A. Koch & H. Lichtenberger. SIJD 1. Göttingen: Vandenhoeck & Ruprecht.

Irvin, Dorothy. 1986. 'Purple.' *ISBE* 3: 1057.

Jaeger, Werner. 1939–45. *Paideia: The Ideals of Greek Culture*. 3 vols. Trans. G. Highet. Oxford: Blackwell.

Jaquette, James L. 1994. 'A not-so-noble death: figured speech, friendship and suicide in Philippians 1: 21–6.' *Neot* 28: 177–92.

1995. *Discerning What Counts: The Function of the Adiaphora Topos in Paul's Letters*. SBLDS 146. Atlanta: Scholars.

1996. 'Life and death, *Adiaphora*, and Paul's rhetorical strategies.' *NovT* 38: 30–54.

Jegher-Bucher, Verena. 1991. *Der Galaterbrief auf dem Hintergrund antiker Epistolographie und Rhetorik: Ein anderes Paulusbild*. ATANT 78. Zurich: Theologischer Verlag.

Jeremias, Joachim. 1963 'Zu Phil. ii 7: ΕΑΥΤΟΝ ΕΚΕΝΩΣΕΝ.' *NovT* 6: 182–8.

1969. 'Paulus als Hillelit.' In *Neotestamentica et Semitica: Studies in Honour of Matthew Black*, 88–94. Ed. E.E. Ellis & M. Wilcox. Edinburgh: T. & T. Clark.

Kähler, Christoph. 1994. 'Konflikt, Kompromiß und Bekenntnis: Paulus und seine Gegner im Philipperbrief.' *Kerygma und Dogma* 40: 47–64.

Karrer, Martin. 1991. *Der Gesalbte: Die Grundlagen des Christustitels*. FRLANT 151. Göttingen: Vandenhoeck & Ruprecht.

Karris, Robert J. 1996. *A Symphony of New Testament Hymns: Commentary on Philippians 2:5–11*. Collegeville: Liturgical.

Käsemann, Ernst. 1950. 'Kritische Analyse von Phil. 2,5-11.' *ZTK* 47: 313-60. [ET by A. Carse: 'A critical analysis of Philippians 2:5-11', *JTC* 5 (1968) 45-88.]

Kennedy, G.A. 1984. *New Testament Interpretation through Rhetorical Criticism.* Chapel Hill: University of North Carolina Press.

Kennel, Gunter. 1995. *Frühchristliche Hymnen? Gattungskritische Studien zur Frage nach den Liedern der frühen Christenheit.* WMANT 71. Neukirchen-Vluyn: Neukirchener.

Kilpatrick, G. D. 1968. 'ΒΛΕΠΕΤΕ: Philippians 3:2.' In *In Memoriam Paul Kahle*, 146-8. Ed. M. Black & G. Fohrer. BZAW 103. Berlin: de Gruyter.

Kim, Seyoon. 1981. *The Origin of Paul's Gospel.* WUNT 2:4. Tübingen: Mohr (Siebeck).

Kim, Y. K. 1988. 'Palaeographic dating of P^{46} to the later first century.' *Biblica* 69: 248-57.

Kirschner, R. 1986. 'Imitatio Rabbini.' *JSJ* 17: 70-79.

Klassen, W. 1992. 'Love.' *ABD* 4: 381-96.

Klein, Günter. 1989. 'Antipaulinismus in Philippi: Eine Problemskizze.' In *Jesu Rede von Gott und ihre Nachgeschichte im frühen Christentum: Beiträge zur Verkündigung Jesu und zum Kerygma der Kirche. Festschrift für Willi Marxsen zum 70. Geburtstag*, 297-313. Ed. D.-A. Koch *et al.* Gütersloh: Mohn.

Knox, Wilfred L. 1939. *St Paul and the Church of the Gentiles.* Cambridge: University Press.

1948. 'The "Divine Hero" christology in the New Testament.' *HTR* 41: 229-49.

Koester, Helmut. 1962. 'The purpose of the polemic of a Pauline fragment (Philippians iii).' *NTS* 8: 317-32.

Konstan, David. 1995. 'Patrons and friends.' *Classical Philology.* 90: 328-42.

1997. *Friendship in the Classical World.* Key Themes in Ancient History. Cambridge etc.: Cambridge University Press.

Koperski, Veronica. 1992. 'Textlinguistics and the integrity of Philippians: a critique of Wolfgang Schenk's arguments for a compilation hypothesis.' *ETL* 68: 331-67.

1993a. 'The early history of the dissection of Philippians.' *JTS* N.S. 44: 599-603.

1993b. 'The meaning of *Pistis Christou* in Philippians 3:9.' *Louvain Studies* 18: 198-216.

1996. *The Knowledge of Christ Jesus my Lord: The High Christology of Philippians 3:7-11.* CBET 16. Kampen: Kok Pharos.

Kraftchick, S.J. 1993a. 'A necessary detour: Paul's metaphorical understanding of the Philippian hymn.' *HBT* 15: 1-37.

1993b. 'Seeking a more fluid model: a response to Jouette M. Bassler.' In *Pauline Theology*, vol. 2: *1 & 2 Corinthians*, 18-34. Ed. D.M. Hay. Minneapolis: Fortress.

Krause, Jens-Uwe. 1996. *Gefängnisse im römischen Reich.* Stuttgart: Steiner.

Kreitzer, Larry Joseph. 1987. *Jesus and God in Paul's Eschatology.* JSNTSup 19. Sheffield: JSOT.

1993a. 'Eschatology.' *DPL,* 253–69.

1993b. 'Intermediate state.' *DPL,* 438–41.

Krentz, Edgar M. 1993. 'Military language and metaphors in Philippians.' In *Origins and Method: Towards a New Understanding of Judaism and Christianity: Essays in Honour of John C. Hurd,* 105–27. Ed. B.H. McLean. JSNTSup 86. Sheffield: JSOT.

Krinetzki, Leo. 1959. 'Der Einfluss von Is 52,13–53,12 Par auf Phil 2,6–11.' *TQ* 139: 157–93, 291–336.

Kron, Uta. 1996. 'Priesthoods, dedications and euergetism: what part did religion play in the political and social status of Greek women?' In *Religion and Power in the Ancient Greek World: Proceedings of the Uppsala Symposium 1993,* 139–82. Ed. P. Hellström & B. Alroth. Uppsala: Acta Universitatis Upsaliensis.

Kuhn, Peter. 1968. *Gottes Selbsterniedrigung in der Theologie der Rabbinen.* SANT 17. Munich: Kösel.

Kümmel, Werner Georg. 1975. *Introduction to the New Testament.* Trans. H.C. Kee. Rev. edn. London: SCM.

Larsson, Edvin. 1962. *Christus als Vorbild: Eine Untersuchung zu den paulinischen Tauf- und Eikontexten.* Uppsala: Gleerup.

Laub, Franz. 1982. *Die Begegnung des frühen Christentums mit der antiken Sklaverei.* SBS 107. Stuttgart: Katholisches Bibelwerk.

Légasse, Simon. 1995. 'Paul's pre-Christian career according to Acts.' In *The Book of Acts in Its Palestinian Setting,* 365–90. Ed. R.J. Bauckham. Grand Rapids: Eerdmans; Carlisle: Paternoster.

Leivestad, Ragnar. 1966. '"The Meekness and Gentleness of Christ": II Cor. X.1.' *NTS* 12: 156–64.

Lemcio, Eugene E. 1991. *The Past of Jesus in the Gospels.* SNTSMS 68. Cambridge etc.: Cambridge University Press.

Lemerle, Paul. 1945. *Philippes et la Macédoine orientale à l'époque chrétienne et byzantine: Recherches d'histoire et d'archéologie.* Bibliothèque des Écoles Françaises d'Athènes et de Rome, 158. Paris: Boccard.

Levinskaya, Irina. 1990a. 'A Jewish or Gentile prayer house? The meaning of ΠΡΟΣΕΥΧΗ.' *TynB* 41: 154–9.

1990b. 'The inscription from Aphrodisias and the problem of godfearers.' *TynB* 41: 312–18.

Lewis, C.S. 1950. *The Literary Impact of the Authorised Version.* London: Athlone.

Lim, Timothy H. 1987. '"Not in persuasive words of wisdom, but in the demonstration of the Spirit and power" (I Cor. 2.4).' *NovT* 29: 137–49.

Lincoln, Anthony T. 1981. *Paradise Now and Not Yet: Studies in the Role of the Heavenly Dimension in Paul's Thought with Special Reference to his Eschatology.* SNTSMS 43. Cambridge: Cambridge University Press.

Lindemann, Andreas. 1979. *Paulus im ältesten Christentum: Das Bild des Apostels und die Rezeption der paulinischen Theologie in der frühchristlichen Literatur bis Marcion.* BHT 58. Tübingen: Mohr (Siebeck).

Llewelyn, Stephen R. 1995. 'Sending letters in the ancient world: Paul and the Philippians.' *TynB* 46: 337–56.

Lohmeyer, Ernst. 1928. *Kyrios Jesus: Eine Untersuchung zu Phil. 2, 5–11.* Sitzungsberichte der Heidelberger Akademie der Wissenschaften, Philosophisch-historische Klasse 18.4. Heidelberg: Winter.

Longenecker, Bruce W. 1991. *Eschatology and Covenant: A Comparison of 4 Ezra and Romans 1–11.* JSNTSup 57. Sheffield: JSOT.

1995. *2 Esdras.* Sheffield: Sheffield Academic.

Louw, Johannes P. & Nida, Eugene A. 1989. *Greek-English Lexicon of the New Testament Based on Semantic Domains.* 2nd edn. New York: United Bible Societies.

Lüdemann, Gerd. 1984. *Paul, Apostle to the Gentiles: Studies in Chronology.* Trans. F.S. Jones. Philadelphia: Fortress.

1989a. *Opposition to Paul in Jewish Christianity.* Trans. M.E. Boring. Minneapolis: Fortress.

1989b. *Early Christianity According to the Traditions in Acts: A Commentary.* Trans. J. Bowden. London: SCM.

Lüderitz, Gert. 1994. 'What is the Politeuma?' In *Studies in Early Jewish Epigraphy,* 183–225. Ed. J.W. van Henten & P.W. van der Horst. Leiden etc.: Brill.

Lührmann, Dieter. 1965. *Das Offenbarungsverständnis bei Paulus und in paulinischen Gemeinden.* WMANT 16. Neukirchen-Vluyn: Neukirchener.

Luter, A. Boyd & Lee, Michelle V. 1995. 'Philippians as chiasmus: key to the structure, unity and theme questions.' *NTS* 41: 89–101.

Luz, Ulrich. 1968. *Das Geschichtsverständnis des Paulus.* BET 49. Munich: Kaiser.

Malherbe, Abraham J. 1968. 'The beasts at Ephesus.' *JBL* 87: 71–80.

1996. 'Paul's self-sufficiency (Philippians 4:11).' In *Friendship, Flattery and Frankness of Speech: Studies on Friendship in the New Testament World,* 125–39. Ed. J.T. Fitzgerald. NovTSup 82. Leiden etc.: Brill. [Also in: *Texts and Contexts: Biblical Texts in their Textual and Situational Contexts: Essays in Honor of Lars Hartman,* ed. T. Fornberg & D. Hellholm. Oslo etc.: Scandinavian University Press, 1995, 813–26.]

Malinowsky, Francis X. 1985. 'The brave women of Philippi.' *BTB* 15: 60–64.

Manzi, Franco. 1996. 'Fil 2,6–11 ed Eb 5,5–10: Due Schemi Cristologici a Confronto.' *RivBib* 44: 31–64.

Marrow, Stanley B. 1982. '*Parrhésia* and the New Testament.' *CBQ* 44: 431–46.

Marshall, I. Howard. 1993. 'The Theology of Philippians.' In K.P. Donfried & I.H. Marshall, *The Theology of the Shorter Pauline Letters*, 115–74. Cambridge: University Press.

— 1996a. 'Salvation, grace and works in the later writings in the Pauline corpus.' *NTS* 42: 339–58.

— 1996b. 'Salvation in the pastoral epistles.' In *Geschichte–Tradition–Reflexion: Festschrift für Martin Hengel zum 70. Geburtstag*, vol. 3: *Frühes Christentum*, 449–69. Ed. H. Cancik, H. Lichtenberger & P. Schäfer. Tübingen: Mohr (Siebeck).

Marshall, John W. 1993. 'Paul's ethical appeal in Philippians.' In *Rhetoric and the New Testament: Essays from the 1992 Heidelberg Conference*, 357–74. JSNTSup 90. Ed. S. E. Porter & T. H. Olbricht. Sheffield: Sheffield Academic.

Marshall, Peter. 1987. *Enmity in Corinth: Social Conventions in Paul's Relations with the Corinthians*. WUNT 2:23. Tübingen: Mohr (Siebeck).

Martin, Dale B. 1990. *Slavery as Salvation: The Metaphor of Slavery in Pauline Christianity*. New Haven: Yale University Press.

Martin, Ralph P. 1983. *Carmen Christi: Philippians 2:5–11 in Recent Interpretation and in the Setting of Early Christian Worship*. 2nd edn. Grand Rapids: Eerdmans.

— 1992. 'Hymns in the New Testament: an evolving pattern of worship responses.' *Ex Auditu* 8: 33–44.

Mason, Hugh J. 1974. *Greek Terms for Roman Institutions: A Lexicon and Analysis*. ASP 13. Toronto: Hakkert.

McKnight, Scot. 1991. *A Light Among the Gentiles: Jewish Missionary Activity in the Second Temple Period*. Minneapolis: Fortress.

Mearns, C. 1987. 'The identity of Paul's opponents at Philippi.' *NTS* 33: 194–204.

Meeks, Wayne A. 1983. *The First Urban Christians*. New Haven: Yale University.

— 1991. 'The man from heaven in Paul's letter to the Philippians.' In *The Future of Early Christianity: Essays in Honor of Helmut Koester*, 329–36. Ed. B.A. Pearson. Minneapolis: Fortress.

Mengel, Berthold. 1982. *Studien zum Philipperbrief*. WUNT 2.8. Tübingen: Mohr (Siebeck).

Merk, Otto. 1968. *Handeln aus Glauben: Die Motivierungen der paulinischen Ethik*. MTS 5. Marburg: Elwert.

Meyer, Ben F. 1989. 'Did Paul's view of the resurrection of the dead undergo development?' *Ex Auditu* 5: 57–76.

Michel, Otto. 1972. 'Freude.' *RAC* 8: 348–418.

Minear, Paul S. 1990. 'Singing and suffering in Philippi.' In *The Conversation Continues: Studies in Paul & John in Honor of J. Louis Martyn*, 202–19. Ed. R.T. Fortna & B.R. Gaventa. Nashville: Abingdon.

Mopsik, C. 1994. 'La datation du *Chi'our Qomah* d'après un texte néotestamentaire.' *RevSR* 68: 131–44.

Morray-Jones, C.R.A. 1993. 'Paradise revisited (2 Cor. 12:1–12): The Jewish mystical background of Paul's apostolate.' *HTR* 86: 177–217, 265–92.

Morrice, William G. 1985. *Joy in the New Testament.* Grand Rapids: Eerdmans.

Morris, Leon. 1981. *Testaments of Love.* Grand Rapids: Eerdmans.

Moule, C.F.D. 1959. *An Idiom Book of New Testament Greek.* 2nd edn. Cambridge, etc.: Cambridge University Press.

1970. 'Further reflections on Philippians 2:5–11.' In W.W. Gasque & R.P. Martin, *Apostolic History and the Gospel: Biblical and Historical Essays Presented to F.F. Bruce*, 264–76. Exeter: Paternoster.

Müller, Ulrich B. 1988. 'Der Christushymnus Phil 2,6–11.' *ZNW* 79: 17–44.

Murphy-O'Connor, Jerome. 1976. 'Christological anthropology in Phil. II,6–11.' *RevB* 83: 25–50.

1995. *Paul the Letter-Writer: His World, His Options, His Skills.* Good News Studies 41. Collegeville: Liturgical Press.

1996. *Paul: A Critical Biography.* Oxford: Clarendon.

Musurillo, Herbert. 1972. *The Acts of the Christian Martyrs: Introductions, Texts and Translations.* Oxford: Clarendon.

Niebuhr, Karl-Wilhelm. 1992. *Heidenapostel aus Israel: Die jüdische Identität des Paulus nach ihrer Darstellung in seinen Briefen.* WUNT 62. Tübingen: Mohr (Siebeck).

Noormann, Rolf. 1994. *Irenäus als Paulusinterpret.* WUNT 2:66. Tübingen: Mohr (Siebeck).

Nygren, Anders. 1932. *Agape and Eros.* Vol. 1: *A Study of the Christian Idea of Love.* Trans. A.G. Hebert. London: SPCK; New York: Macmillan.

Oakes, Peter Stanley. 1996. *Philippians: From People to Letter.* D. Phil. thesis: Oxford.

O'Brien, Peter T. 1977. *Introductory Thanksgivings in the Letters of Paul.* NovTSup 49. Leiden: Brill.

Oepke, Albrecht. 1950. 'Auferstehung II (des Menschen).' *RAC* 1: 930–38.

Osiek, Carolyn. 1995. 'Philippians.' In *Searching the Scriptures*, vol. 2: *A Feminist Commentary*, 237–49. Ed. E. Schüssler Fiorenza. London: SCM.

O'Toole, Robert F. 1992a. 'Philippian jailor [*sic*].' *ABD* 5: 317–18.

1992b. 'Slave girl at Philippi.' *ABD* 6: 57–8.

Otto, Randall E. 1995. ' "If possible I may attain the resurrection from the dead" (Philippians 3:11).' *CBQ* 57: 324–40.

Palmer, D.W. 1975. ' "To die is gain" (Philippians i 21).' *NovT* 17: 203–18.

Paulsen, Henning. 1985. *Die Briefe des Ignatius von Antiochia und der Brief des Polykarp von Smyrna.* HNT 18: Die Apostolischen Väter II. Tübingen: Mohr (Siebeck).

Pelikan, Jaroslav. 1993. *Christianity and Classical Culture: The Metamorphosis of Natural Theology in the Christian Encounter with Hellenism.* New Haven/London: Yale University Press.

Perkins, Pheme. 1991. 'Philippians: theology for the heavenly politeuma.' In *Pauline Theology,* 1: 89–104. Ed. J.M. Bassler. Minneapolis: Fortress.

Pesch, Rudolf. 1985. *Paulus und seine Lieblingsgemeinde: Paulus – neu gesehen: Drei Briefe an die Heiligen von Philippi.* Freiburg etc.: Herder.

Peterlin, Davorin. 1995. *Paul's Letter to the Philippians in the Light of Disunity in the Church.* NovTSup 79. Leiden/New York: Brill.

Peterman, Gerald W. 1991. ' "Thankless thanks": the epistolary social convention in Philippians 4:10–20.' *TynB* 42: 261–70.

1997. *Paul's Gift from Philippi: Conventions of Gift-exchange and Christian Giving.* SNTSMS 92. Cambridge etc.: Cambridge University Press.

Pilhofer, Peter. 1995. *Philippi.* Vol. I: *Die erste christliche Gemeinde Europas.* WUNT 87. Tübingen: Mohr (Siebeck). [Vol. II will contain a catalogue of all inscriptions.]

Pohlenz, Max. 1949. 'Paulus und die Stoa.' *ZNW* 42: 69–104.

Portefaix, Lilian. 1988. *Sisters Rejoice: Paul's Letter to the Philippians and Luke-Acts as Seen by First-Century Philippian Women.* CBNT 20. Uppsala: Gleerup.

Porter, Stanley E. 1993a. 'Word order and clause structure in New Testament Greek. An unexplored area of Greek linguistics using Philippians as a test case.' *FNT* 6: 177–206.

1993b. 'The theoretical justification for application of rhetorical categories to Pauline epistolary literature.' In Porter & Olbricht 1993: 100–22.

Porter, Stanley E. & Olbricht, Thomas H., eds. 1993. *Rhetoric and the New Testament: Essays from the 1992 Heidelberg Conference.* JSNTSup 90. Sheffield: Sheffield Academic.

Pretorius, E.A.C. 1989. 'A key to the literature on Philippians.' *Neot* 23: 125–53.

1995. 'New trends in reading Philippians: a literature review.' *Neot* 29: 273–98.

Probst, Hermann. 1991. *Paulus und der Brief: Die Rhetorik des antiken Briefes als Form der paulinischen Korintherkorrespondenz (1 Kor. 8–10).* WUNT 2: 45. Tübingen: Mohr (Siebeck).

Ramsay, W. M. 1905. *St Paul the Traveller and the Roman Citizen.* 8th edn. London: Hodder & Stoughton.

Rapske, Brian. 1994. *The Book of Acts and Paul in Roman Custody.* Grand Rapids: Eerdmans; Carlisle: Paternoster.

Reed, Jeffrey T. 1993. 'Using ancient rhetorical categories to interpret Paul's letters: a question of genre.' In *Rhetoric and the New Testament: Essays from the 1992 Heidelberg Conference,* 292–324. JSNTSup 90. Ed. S.E. Porter & T.H. Olbricht. Sheffield: Sheffield Academic.

1996. 'Philippians 3:1 and the epistolary hesitation formulas: the literary integrity of Philippians, again.' *JBL* 115: 63–90.

1997. *A Discourse Analysis of Philippians: Method and Rhetoric in the Debate over Literary Integrity.* JSNTSup 136. Sheffield: Sheffield Academic.

Reumann, John. 1984. 'Philippians 3.20–21 – a hymnic fragment?' *NTS* 30: 593–609.

1991. 'Christology in Philippians, especially chapter 3.' In *Anfänge der Christologie: Festschrift für Ferdinand Hahn zum 65. Geburtstag,* 131–40. Ed. C. Breytenbach & H. Paulsen. Göttingen: Vandenhoeck & Ruprecht.

1993a. 'Contributions of the Philippian community to Paul and to earliest Christianity.' *NTS* 39: 438–57.

1993b. 'Church office in Paul, especially in Philippians.' In *Origins and Method: Towards a New Understanding of Judaism and Christianity,* 82–91. Ed. B.H. McLean. Sheffield: JSOT.

1996. 'Philippians, especially chapter 4, as a "letter of friendship": observations on a checkered history of scholarship.' In *Friendship, Flattery, and Frankness of Speech: Studies on Friendship in the New Testament World,* 83–106. Ed. J.T. Fitzgerald. NTSup 82. Leiden etc.: Brill.

Reynolds, Joyce and Tannenbaum, Robert. 1987. *Jews and God-Fearers at Aphrodisias: Greek Inscriptions with Commentary.* Proceedings of the Cambridge Philological Society, Supplementary Volume 12. Cambridge: Cambridge Philological Society.

Richards, E. Randolph. 1991. *The Secretary in the Letters of Paul.* WUNT 2: 42. Tübingen: Mohr (Siebeck).

Richter Reimer, Ivoni. 1992. *Frauen in der Apostelgeschichte des Lukas: Eine feministisch-theologische Exegese.* Gütersloh: Mohn. [ET *Women in the Acts of the Apostles: A Feminist Liberation Perspective.* Trans. L.M. Moloney. Minneapolis: Fortress, 1995.]

Riesner, Rainer. 1994. *Die Frühzeit des Apostels Paulus: Studien zur Chronologie, Missionsstrategie und Theologie.* WUNT 71. Tübingen: Mohr (Siebeck).

Rissi, Mathias. 1987. 'Der Christushymnus in Phil 2,6–11.' *ANRW* II 25.4: 3314–26. Berlin/New York: de Gruyter.

Robinson, John A.T. 1976. *Redating the New Testament.* Philadelphia: Westminster.

Rokéah, David. 1995. 'Tacitus and ancient antisemitism.' *REJ* 154: 281–94.

——— 1996. 'Ancient Jewish proselytism in theory and in practice.' *TZ* 52: 206–24.

Rolland, Philippe. 1990. 'La structure littéraire et l'unité de l'Épître aux Philippiens.' *RevSR* 64: 213–16.

Roloff, Jürgen. 1996. 'Kirchenleitung nach dem Neuen Testament: Theorie und Realität.' *KD* 42: 136–53.

Rosenblatt, Marie E. 1995. *Paul the Accused.* Collegeville: Liturgical Press.

Rosner, Brian S. 1994. *Paul, Scripture and Ethics: A Study of 1 Corinthians 5–7.* AGJU 22. Leiden etc.: Brill.

Rowland, Christopher. 1982. *The Open Heaven: A Study of Apocalyptic in Judaism and Early Christianity.* London: SPCK.

Saldarini, Anthony J. 1992. 'Pharisees.' *ABD* 5: 289–303.

Saller, Richard P. 1982. *Personal Patronage under the Early Empire.* Cambridge: University Press.

Sampley, John Paul. 1980. *Pauline Partnership in Christ: Christian Community and Commitment in Light of Roman Law.* Philadelphia: Fortress.

Sanders, E.P. 1977. *Paul and Palestinian Judaism: A Comparison of Patterns of Religion.* London: SCM.

——— 1983. *Paul, the Law and the Jewish People.* Philadelphia: Fortress.

——— 1992. *Judaism: Practice and Belief 63 BCE–63 CE.* London: SCM.

Sanders, James A. 1975. 'Torah and Christ.' *Int* 29: 372–90.

Schäfer, Peter, ed. 1981. *Synopse zur Hekhalot-Literatur.* TSAJ 2. Tübingen: Mohr (Siebeck).

——— 1984. 'New Testament and Hekhalot literature: the journey into heaven in Paul and in Merkavah mysticism.' *JJS* 35: 19–35.

Schaller, Berndt. 1980. 'Zum Textcharakter der Hiobzitate im paulinischen Schrifttum.' *ZNW* 17: 21–6.

Schenk, Wolfgang. 1987. 'Der Philipperbrief in der neueren Forschung (1945–1985).' *ANRW* II 25.4: 3280–313.

——— 1994. 'Der Philipperbrief oder die Philipperbriefe des Paulus? Eine Antwort an V. Koperski.' *ETL* 70: 122–31.

Schlosser, J. 1995a. 'La Figure de Dieu selon l'Épître aux Philippiens.' *NTS* 41: 378–99.

1995b. 'La communauté en charge de l'Évangile: A propos de Ph 1,7.' *RHPR* 75: 67–76.

Schmithals, Walter. 1957. 'Die Irrlehrer des Philipperbriefes.' *ZTK* 54: 297–341. [Revised ET in idem, *Paul & the Gnostics*, trans. J.E. Steely (Nashville/New York: Abingdon, 1972), 65–122.]

Schneemelcher, Wilhelm, ed. 1992. *New Testament Apocrypha.* Vol. 2: *Writings Relating to the Apostles; Apocalypses and Related Subjects.* Rev. edn. of the Collection initiated by E. Hennecke. ET ed. R.McL. Wilson. Cambridge: Clarke; Louisville: Westminster/Knox.

Schnelle, Udo. 1989. *Wandlungen im paulinischen Denken.* SBS 137. Stuttgart: Katholisches Bibelwerk.

1996. *Einleitung in das Neue Testament.* 2nd edn. Göttingen: Vandenhoeck & Ruprecht.

Schnider, Franz & Stenger, Werner. 1987. *Studien zum neutestamentlichen Briefformular.* NTTS 11. Leiden: Brill.

Schoon-Janssen, Johannes. 1991. *Umstrittene 'Apologien' in den Paulusbriefen: Studien zur rhetorischen Situation des 1. Thessalonicherbriefes, des Galaterbriefes und des Philipperbriefes.* GTA 45. Göttingen: Vandenhoeck & Ruprecht.

Schottroff, Luise. 1993. 'Lydia: a new quality of power.' In idem, *Let the Oppressed Go Free: Feminist Perspectives on the New Testament*, 131–7. Trans. A.S. Kidder. Louisville: Westminster/Knox.

1996. *Lydia's Impatient Sisters: A Feminist Social History of Early Christianity.* Louisville: Westminster/Knox.

Schürer/Vermes. 1973–1987. *The History of the Jewish People in the Age of Jesus Christ (175 B.C.–A.D. 135).* New English version rev. & ed. G. Vermes *et al.* 3 vols in 4. Edinburgh: T. &T. Clark.

Schweitzer, Albert. 1953. *The Mysticism of Paul the Apostle.* Trans. W. Montgomery. 2nd edn. London: Black.

Scott, James M. 1996. 'The triumph of God in 2 Cor. 2.14: additional evidence of Merkabah mysticism in Paul.' *NTS* 42: 260–81.

Scroggs, Robin. 1991. 'Salvation history: the theological structure of Paul's thought (1 Thessalonians, Philippians, and Galatians).' In *Pauline Theology*, vol. 1: *Thessalonians, Philippians, Galatians, Philemon*, 212–26. Ed. J.M. Bassler. Minneapolis: Fortress.

Seeley, David. 1994. 'The background of the Philippians hymn (2:6–11).' *The Journal of Higher Criticism* 1: 49–72.

Segal, Alan F. 1990. *Paul the Convert: The Apostolate and Apostasy of Paul the Pharisee.* New Haven/London: Yale University.

Seifrid, Mark A. 1993. 'In Christ.' *DPL*, 433–6.

Sellew, Philip. 1994. '*Laodiceans* and the Philippians fragments hypothesis.' *HTR* 87: 17–27.

Sevenster, J.N. 1961. *Paul and Seneca.* NTSup 4. Leiden: Brill.

Sherwin-White, A.N. 1963. *Roman Society and Roman Law in the New Testament*. Grand Rapids: Baker, 1978 (= 1963).

Silva, Moisés. 1995. 'Discourse analysis and Philippians.' In *Discourse Analysis and Other Topics in Biblical Greek*, 102–106. Ed. S.E. Porter & D.A. Carson. JSNTSup 113. Sheffield: Sheffield Academic Press.

Skeat, T.C. 1995. "Bishops and deacons' in Phil. 1:1.' *NovT* 37: 12–15.

Söding, Thomas. 1995. *Das Liebesgebot bei Paulus: Die Mahnung zur Agape im Rahmen der paulinischen Ethik*. NTAbh N.S. 26. Münster: Aschendorff.

Souter, Alexander. 1927. *The Earliest Commentaries on the Epistles of Paul*. Oxford: Clarendon.

Spicq, Ceslas. 1958–9. *Agapé dans le Nouveau Testament*. 3 vols. Paris: Gabalda. [ET *Agape in the New Testament*, trans. M.A. McNamara & M.H. Richter, 3 vols. (St Louis: Herder, 1963–6).]

Staab, Karl. 1933. *Pauluskommentare aus der griechischen Kirche*. NTAbh 15. Münster: Aschendorff.

Steenburg, Dave. 1988. 'The case against the synonymity of *morphé* and *eikôn*.' *JSNT* 34: 77–86.

Stemberger, Günter. 1972. *Der Leib der Auferstehung: Studien zur Anthropologie und Eschatologie des palästinischen Judentums im neutestamentlichen Zeitalter (ca. 170 v.Cr. [sic]–100 n. Chr.)*. AnBib 56. Rome: Biblical Institute Press.

1996. *Introduction to the Talmud and Midrash*. Trans. & ed. M. Bockmuehl. 2nd edn. Edinburgh: T. &T. Clark.

Steudel, Annette. 1994. *Der Midrasch zur Eschatologie aus der Qumrangemeinde (4QMidrEschat^{a,b})*. STDJ 13. Leiden etc.: Brill.

Stowers, Stanley K. 1991. 'Friends and enemies in the politics of heaven: reading theology in Philippians.' In *Pauline Theology*, vol. 1: *Thessalonians, Philippians, Galatians, Philemon*, 105–21. Ed. J.M. Bassler. Minneapolis: Fortress.

1986. *Letter Writing in Greco-Roman Antiquity*. Philadelphia: Westminster.

Strecker, Gerhard (assisted by T. Nolting). 1995. 'Der vorchristliche Paulus: Überlegungen zum biographischen Kontext biblischer Überlieferung – zugleich eine Antwort an Martin Hengel.' In *Texts and Contexts: Biblical Texts in their Textual and Situational Contexts: Essays in Honor of Lars Hartman*, 813–26. Ed. T. Fornberg & D. Hellholm. Oslo etc.: Scandinavian University Press.

Strobel, August. 1961. *Untersuchungen zum eschatologischen Verzögerungsproblem auf Grund der spätjüdisch-urchristlichen Geschichte von Habakuk 2,2ff*. NovTSup 2. Leiden: Brill.

Stroumsa, G. G. 1983. 'Form(s) of God: some notes on Metatron and Christ.' *HTR* 76: 269–88.

Stuhlmacher, Peter. 1991. 'The Pauline Gospel.' In idem (ed.), *The Gospel and the Gospels*, 149–71. Grand Rapids: Eerdmans.

1992. *Biblische Theologie des Neuen Testaments*. Vol. 1 *Grundlegung: Von Jesus zu Paulus*. Göttingen: Vandenhoeck & Ruprecht.

1995. '"Aus Glauben zum Glauben" – zur geistlichen Schriftauslegung.' *ZTK Beiheft* 9: 133–50.

Tajra, Harry W. 1989. *The Trial of St Paul: A Juridical Exegesis of the Second Half of the Acts of the Apostles*. WUNT 2: 35. Tübingen: Mohr (Siebeck).

1994. *The Martyrdom of St Paul: Historical and Judicial Context, Traditions, and Legends*. WUNT 2: 67. Tübingen: Mohr (Siebeck).

Tannehill, Robert C. 1967. *Dying and Rising With Christ: A Study in Pauline Theology*. BZNW 32. Berlin: Töpelmann.

Taylor, Justin. 1994. *Les Actes des Deux Apôtres*. Vol. 5: *Commentaire Historique (Act. 9,1–18,22)*. EB N.S. 23. Paris: Lecoffre/Gabalda.

Tellbe, Mikael. 1994. 'The sociological factors behind Philippians 3.1–11 and the conflict at Philippi.' *JSNT* 55: 97–121.

Therrien, G. 1973. *Le discernement dans les écrits pauliniens*. EB. Paris: Lecoffre/Gabalda.

Thomas, W. Derek. 1971–2. 'The place of women in the church at Philippi.' *ExpT* 83: 117–20.

Thompson, Michael B. 1997 [forthcoming]. 'The Holy Internet: communication between churches in the first Christian generation.' In *The Gospels for all Christians*, ch. 2. Ed. R.J. Bauckham. Grand Rapids/Cambridge: Eerdmans.

Thornton, Claus-Jürgen. 1991. *Der Zeuge des Zeugen: Lukas als Historiker der Paulusreisen*. WUNT 56. Tübingen: Mohr (Siebeck).

Tomson, Peter J. 1990. *Paul and the Jewish Law: Halakha in the Letters of the Apostle to the Gentiles*. CRINT 3:1. Assen/Maastricht: Van Gorcum; Minneapolis: Fortress.

Trebilco, Paul R. 1989. 'Paul and Silas – "servants of the most high God" (Acts 16.16–18).' *JSNT* 36: 51–73.

1991. *Jewish Communities in Asia Minor*. SNTSMS 69. Cambridge etc.: Cambridge University Press.

Treiyer, E.B. 1996. 'S'en aller et être avec Christ (Philippiens 1:23).' *AUSS* 34: 47–64.

Treu, Kurt. 1972. 'Freundschaft.' *RAC* 8: 418–34.

van Unnik, W.C. 1973. 'Die Anklage gegen die Apostel in Philippi (Apostelgeschichte xvi 20f).' In idem, *Sparsa Collecta: The Collected Essays of W. C. van Unnik*, 1: 374–85. NovTSup 29. Leiden: Brill.

Vielhauer, Philipp. 1975. *Geschichte der urchristlichen Literatur: Einleitung in das Neue Testament, die Apokryphen und die Apostolischen Väter.* Berlin/New York:de Gruyter.

1979. 'Paulus und das Alte Testament.' In idem, *Oikodome: Aufsätze zum Neuen Testament,* 2: 196–228. Ed. G. Klein. Theologische Bücherei 65. Munich: Kaiser.

Volkmann, Hans. 1990. *Die Massenversklavungen der Einwohner eroberter Städte in der hellenistisch-römischen Zeit.* Forschungen zur Antiken Sklaverei 22. 2nd edn. revised by G. Horsmann. Stuttgart: Franz Steiner.

Vollenweider, Samuel. 1994. 'Die Waagschalen von Leben und Tod: Zum antiken Hintergrund von Phil 1,21–26.' *ZNW* 85: 93–115.

Wagner, G. 1986. 'Le scandale de la croix expliqué par le chant du Serviteur d'Isaïe 53. Réflections sur Philippiens 2/6–11.' *ETR* 61: 177–87.

Wallis, Ian G. 1995. *The Faith of Jesus Christ in Early Christian Tradition.* Cambridge: University Press.

Walter, Nikolaus. 1978. 'Die Philipper und das Leiden.' In *Die Kircher des Anfangs: Für Heinz Schürmann,* 417–34. Ed. R. Schnackenburg *et al.* Freiburg, etc.: Herder.

1996. 'Hellenistische Eschatologie bei Paulus? Zu 2 Kor 5,1–10.' *TQ* 176: 53–64.

Wanamaker, Charles A. 1987. 'Philippians 2.6–11: Son of God or Adamic Christology?' *NTS* 33: 179–93.

Wansink, Craig S. 1996. *Chained in Christ: The Experience and Rhetoric of Paul's Imprisonments.* JSNTSup 130. Sheffield: Sheffield Academic.

Wapnish, Paula and Hesse, Brian. 1993. 'Pampered pooches or plain pariahs? The Ashkelon dog burials.' *BA* 56.2: v55–80.

Watson, Duane F. 1988. 'A rhetorical analysis of Philippians and its implications for the unity question.' *NovT* 30: 57–88.

1995. 'Rhetorical criticism of the Pauline epistles since 1975.' *CRBS* 3: 219–48.

Watson, Francis. 1994. *Text, Church and World.* Edinburgh: T. & T. Clark.

1996a. Review of A.C. Thiselton, *New Horizons in Hermeneutics* (London: Harper Collins, 1992). In *BibInt* 4: 252–6.

1996b. 'Bible, theology and the university: a response to Philip Davies.' *JSOT* 71: 3–16.

Watson, Nigel. 1987. 'The "intentional fallacy" and Biblical exegesis.' In *The Bible and European Literature: History and Hermeneutics,* 186–96. Ed. E. Osborn & L. McIntosh. Melbourne: Academia.

Weaver, P.R.C. 1972. *Familia Caesaris: A Social Study of the Emperor's Freedmen and Slaves.* Cambridge: University Press.

Wedderburn, A.J.M. 1985. 'Some observations on Paul's use of the phrases "in Christ" and "with Christ".' *JSNT* 25: 83–97.

1987. *Baptism and Resurrection: Studies in Pauline Theology against Its Graeco-Roman Background.* WUNT 44. Tübingen: Mohr (Siebeck).

Weder, Hans. 1993. *Gegenwart und Gottesherrschaft: Überlegungen zum Zeitverständnis bei Jesus und im frühen Christentum.* Biblisch-theologische Studien 20. Neukirchen-Vluyn: Neukirchener.

Wengst, Klaus. 1986. ' "... einander durch Demut für vorzüglicher halten ...": Zum Begriff "Demut" bei Paulus und in paulinischer Tradition.' In *Studien zum Text und zur Ethik des Neuen Testaments: Festschrift zum 80. Geburtstag von Heinrich Greeven,* 428–39. Ed. W. Schrage. BZNW 47. Berlin/New York: de Gruyter.

1988. *Humility: Solidarity of the Humiliated.* Trans. J. Bowden. London: SCM.

Wenham, David. 1995. *Paul: Follower of Jesus or Founder of Christianity.* Grand Rapids: Eerdmans.

White, Carolinne. 1992. *Christian Friendship in the Fourth Century.* Cambridge: Cambridge University Press.

White, John L. 1986. *Light from Ancient Letters.* Philadelphia: Fortress.

White, L. Michael. 1990. 'Morality between two worlds: a paradigm of friendship in Philippians.' In *Greeks, Romans, and Christians: Essays in Honor of Abraham J. Malherbe,* 201–15. Ed. D. Balch *et al.* Minneapolis: Fortress.

1995. 'Visualizing the "real" world of Acts 16: toward construction of a social index.' In *The Social World of the First Christians: Essays in Honor of Wayne A. Meeks,* 234–61. Ed. L.M. White & O.L. Yarbrough. Minneapolis: Fortress.

Wibbing, Siegfried. 1959. *Die Tugend- und Lasterkataloge im Neuen Testament und ihre Traditionsgeschichte unter besonderer Berücksichtigung der Qumran-Texte.* BZNW 25. Berlin: Töpelmann.

Wick, Peter. 1994. *Der Philipperbrief: Der formale Aufbau des Briefs als Schlüssel zum Verständnis seines Inhalts.* BWANT 7.15. Stuttgart: Kohlhammer.

Wikgren, Allen P. 1981. 'The problem in Acts 16:12.' In *New Testament Textual Criticism: Its Significance for Exegesis. Essays in Honour of Bruce M. Metzger,* 171–8. Ed. E.J. Epp & G.D. Fee. Oxford: Oxford University.

Wiles, M.F. 1967. *The Divine Apostle: The Interpretation of St Paul's Epistles in the Early Church.* Cambridge: University Press.

Winter, Bruce W. 1994. *Seek the Welfare of the City: Christians as Benefactors and Citizens.* Grand Rapids: Eerdmans; Carlisle: Paternoster.

Witherington, Ben, III. 1994. *Friendship and Finances in Philippi: The Letter of Paul to the Philippians.* The New Testament in Context. Valley Forge, PA: Trinity Press International.

Wolfson, Harry Austryn. 1947. *Philo: Foundations of Religious Philosophy in Judaism, Christianity, and Islam.* 2 vols. Cambridge, MA: Harvard University Press.

Wright, N.T. 1986. 'ἁρπαγμός and the Meaning of Philippians 2:5-11.' *JTS* N.S. 37: 321-52. [Repr. with revisions in Wright 1991a: 62-90.]

1991a. *The Climax of the Covenant: Christ and the Law in Pauline Theology.* Edinburgh: T. & T. Clark.

1991b. 'Putting Paul together again: toward a synthesis of Pauline theology (1 and 2 Thessalonians, Philippians, and Philemon).' In *Pauline Theology,* vol. 1: *Thessalonians, Philippians, Galatians, Philemon,* 183-211. Ed. J.M. Bassler. Minneapolis: Fortress.

Zeller, Dieter. 1993. 'Zur Transformation des Χριστός bei Paulus.' *JBT* 8: 155-67.

Ziesler, John. 1989. *Paul's Letter to the Romans.* TPINTC. London: SCM; Philadelphia: Trinity Press International.

INDEX OF COMMENTATORS AND MODERN
AUTHORS

INDEX OF ANCIENT SOURCES

N.B. All non-biblical works are in alphabetical order.

HEBREW OLD TESTAMENT

DEUTEROCANONICAL BOOKS (APOCRYPHA)

NEW TESTAMENT

NON-BIBLICAL JEWISH WORKS

NON-BIBLICAL CHRISTIAN WORKS

OTHER ANCIENT SOURCES

SUBJECT INDEX